NEW DIRECTIONS
IN MISSION
AND EVANGELIZATION 1

New Directions in Mission and Evangelization
Edited by
James A. Scherer
Stephen B. Bevans, S.V.D.

New Directions in Mission and Evangelization is an Orbis series which offers collections of recent articles and papers, all previously published but not easily available to students and scholars of mission. Selections included in each volume represent examples of mission theology and missiological reflection which deal creatively with issues affecting the church's mission in today's postmodern world.

Volumes in the series will appear periodically and will include Roman Catholic, Orthodox, Conciliar Protestant, Evangelical, Pentecostal, and other points of view. Each volume will focus on a theme such as

- The Theological Foundations of Mission
- Contextualization of Theology
- Mission Spirituality
- Theology of Religion and Dialogue Between Persons of Living Faiths
- Ecology and Mission
- Social Justice and Mission

New Directions in Mission and Evangelization 1

Basic Statements 1974-1991

Edited by
James A. Scherer
Stephen B. Bevans, S.V.D.

ORBIS BOOKS

Maryknoll, New York 10545

The Catholic Foreign Mission Society of America (Maryknoll) recruits and trains people for overseas missionary service. Through Orbis Books, Maryknoll aims to foster the international dialogue that is essential to mission. The books published, however, reflect the opinions of their authors and are not meant to represent the official position of the society.

Library of Congress Cataloging-in-Publication Data

New directions in mission and evangelization : basic statements
    1974-1991 / edited by James A. Scherer, Stephen B. Bevans.
        p.   cm.
    Includes bibliographical references and index.
    ISBN 0-88344-792-4
    1. Missions.   2. Evangelistic work.   I. Scherer, James A.
II. Bevans, Stephen B., 1944-
BV2030.N42   1992
266'.001 – dc20   92-1273
                                                                         CIP

Contents

Part I
Conciliar Ecumenical Statements

Part II
Roman Catholic Statements

Part III
Eastern Orthodox and Oriental Church Statements

Part IV
Evangelical Protestant Statements

Acknowledgments

The editors and publishers gratefully acknowledge the permission of copyright holders to reproduce the documents contained in this volume. In particular, we acknowledge the World Council of Churches for permission to reprint documents found in Parts One and Three; the United States Catholic Conference and the Association of Member Episcopal Conferences in Eastern Africa (AMECEA) for reproducing documents in Part Two; and the Lausanne Committee on World Evangelism and the World Evangelical Fellowship for reproducing documents in Part Four. Precise references to sources will be found at the foot of the first page of each document.

Generally speaking, no attempt has been made to standardize such things as spelling, punctuation, abbreviations, and methods of scripture citations, except where the editors or the publishers found that lack of clarity caused by these variations could lead to serious misunderstandings. This has the advantage of preserving the style of the original statements and the disadvantage of inconsistencies among, for example, British, American, and Asian varieties of English usages. In certain statements and translations of statements, mistakes were, however, found and corrected.

Introduction and Overview

Statements on Mission and Evangelization, 1974-1991

JAMES A. SCHERER AND STEPHEN B. BEVANS, S.V.D.

David Bosch's magisterial work on Christian mission speaks of five historical "paradigms" according to which missionary activity has been carried out in the past, and suggests that a sixth "paradigm"—a "postmodern," "ecumenical" paradigm—is beginning to emerge in our own day. Both the church in general and Christian mission in particular are today faced with issues and invited to grow in directions which were unthinkable within the parameters of former paradigms of theology and ministry. The degree to which we are willing to respond represents the degree to which we are willing to be faithful to God's transforming call.

The emerging ecumenical paradigm underlying today's missionary praxis is determined by at least seven changes in our world: (1) we now live in a pluricentric, rather than a western-dominated world; (2) structures of oppression and exploitation are today being challenged as never before; (3) a profound feeling of ambiguity exists about the value of western technology and development, and the older idea of "progress"; (4) we inhabit a shrinking global village with finite resources, and this calls for growing mutual interdependence; (5) humans are for the first time aware of their capacity to destroy the earth and make it uninhabitable for future generations; (6) societies everywhere now seek their own local cultural identities and reject slavish imitation of western models; (7) freedom of religion and greater awareness of other faiths forces Christians to reevaluate their own earlier attitudes toward other faiths (Bosch, 188-189). Other factors might be added to this list, it is acknowledged, but the point is that "quite literally, we live in a world fundamentally different from that of the nineteenth century, let alone earlier times" (Bosch, 189). The work of mission and evangelization has begun to move in "new directions."

It is precisely this new paradigm and these new directions that this series attempts to follow. In future volumes the editors hope to offer collections of articles, all previously published but not easily available, which represent the best examples of current mission theology and missiological reflection, and which deal creatively with the emerging postmodern, ecumenical missionary paradigm.

As a preface to the entire series, this first volume concentrates on official, church-related "mission documents" of roughly the last two decades. The earliest documents included in this selection are the *Lausanne Covenant* of 1974, the 1975 World Council of Churches' Nairobi Assembly statement on "Confessing Christ Today," and Pope Paul VI's Apostolic Exhortation *Evangelii Nuntiandi* of 1975. The most recent are excerpts from Pope John Paul II's *Redemptoris Missio* (1990), a Vatican paper on *Dialogue and Proclamation* (1991), and a statement from the

World Council of Churches' Canberra Assembly (1991). While official documents are admittedly not always the most inspiring or exciting reading, they do represent a compass reading of new directions in mission and evangelism and demonstrate the various paths by which the churches have embarked on a new and exhilarating journey. Church documents included in this collection closely reflect all of the new factors that make up the emerging postmodern "ecumenical" missionary paradigm: pluricentrism, the struggle for justice, ambiguity about the future, "one world" awareness, fear of annihilation, loss of confidence in the west, and growing mutual respect among world religious communities. They seek to express ongoing missionary obligation and enduring faithfulness to the Great Commission within the parameters of a massive paradigm shift.

In order to provide our readers with a context and background for the documents included in this volume, we will sketch briefly the history and special characteristics of missiological thought in each of the four major traditions represented here: conciliar-ecumenical, Roman Catholic, Eastern Orthodox, and evangelical. Individual denominations and confessional families have also produced significant statements on mission and evangelism, but these are not included here for lack of space. Readers may be struck by the recurrence of key themes, and the manner in which all of the four traditions attempt, in their own way, to deal with the momentous challenges of modernity.

CONCILIAR ECUMENICAL MISSIOLOGY

The claim to be "ecumenical"—from *oikoumene,* "the whole inhabited earth"—can in no sense be the prerogative of any single church, denomination, or group of churches. Indeed, each of the four missionary traditions examined in this volume may rightly lay claim to ecumenicity in some sense. "Conciliar ecumenical" refers, by definition, to the movement by churches and their related mission agencies which sees membership in organized church councils—at the world, regional, national, or local level—as being the primary visible expression of Christian unity. These Christian communities and their agencies participate in the manifold activities of such councils—Faith and Order theological discussions; world service; relief and development activities; mission and evangelism coordination; advocacy of justice, peace, and human rights—as the best way to promote Christian unity and cooperation and to advance the purposes of Christ's kingdom. The World Council of Churches (WCC), founded in 1948, and various national or regional Christian councils, are primary expressions of this conciliar ecumenical movement. The WCC, with over three hundred member churches in all six continents, is "a fellowship of churches which confess the Lord Jesus Christ as God and Saviour according to the Scriptures and therefore seek to fulfill together their common calling to the glory of the one God, Father, Son, and Holy Spirit" (Van Elderen, 4). This statement, which forms the "basis" for the WCC, explains what the council is and does.

Conciliar ecumenical missiology is missiology that takes shape in the work and deliberations of the WCC's Commission on World Mission and Evangelism (CWME), created in 1961 as the successor to the former International Missionary Council (IMC, 1921-1961); in the former Division of Overseas Ministries (DOM) of the National Council of Churches of Christ in the USA and in similar national councils; and in regional councils such as the All Africa Council of Churches (AACC) or the Christian Council of Asia (CCA). In Part I we present mission and evangelism documents originating in CWME conferences and consultations, or adopted at WCC assemblies or at meetings of the WCC Central Committee or other WCC units. These provide an overview of the general contours of ecumenical missionary thinking as it formulates its own response to the postmodern missionary paradigm. No regional or national conciliar statements are included here.

Conciliar ecumenical missiology as expressed in WCC and CWME documents is in a real sense a lineal successor to the tradition of world missionary conferences going back more than a century: Liverpool (1860), London (1888), New York (1900), and culminating in Edinburgh (1910). The Edinburgh World Missionary Conference became the prototype for other worldwide missionary conferences which followed, organized under the auspices of the newly formed International Missionary Council (1921): Jerusalem (1928), Tambaram-Madras (1938), Whitby (1947), Willingen (1952), and Ghana (1958) (Hogg, 133-138). With the integration of the IMC into the World Council of Churches as its "Commission on World Mission and Evangelism" at the New Delhi Assembly (1961), it now fell to the CWME to organize succeeding ecumenical missionary conferences: Mexico City (1963), Bangkok (1973), Melbourne (1980), and San Antonio (1989) (Scherer, 93f., 126f.). Our survey includes excerpts from the Melbourne and San Antonio world missionary conferences, along with statements from the Nairobi (1975), Vancouver (1983), and Canberra (1991) WCC assemblies. Some specialized reports coming from other contexts are also included.

A few words are in order about relationships between conciliar ecumenical missiology as represented by the CWME and the other main traditions represented in this volume. The last two decades have seen a rapid increase in both informal and formal contacts and conversations among these traditions. Since 1970, as will be seen in what follows, Eastern Orthodoxy has had an official staff liaison with the CWME; and since 1974, an Orthodox Advisory Group of theologians has met regularly to prepare Orthodox responses to WCC proposals and to provide Orthodox input into CWME conferences and WCC assemblies. We have chosen, however, to present Orthodox statements on mission in a separate section, rather than subsuming them under the conciliar reports. Since the Second Vatican Council, Roman Catholic observers appointed by the Vatican Secretariat for Christian Unity have participated in CWME conferences and WCC assemblies. In 1984, the Secretariat for Unity sent a Roman Catholic staff consultant to assist in the general work of CWME. In 1980, the document *Common Witness,* produced by the Joint Working Group of the Vatican Secretariat for Christian Unity and the CWME, was approved for publication. Major excerpts appear in Part I, Chapter 3. In 1987, the CWME convened a special consultation in Stuttgart, FRG, designed to deal frankly with concerns of evangelicals within European member churches of the WCC. The report of the Stuttgart Consultation, which appears in Part I, Chapter 9, played an important role in both the CWME San Antonio conference (1989) and the Lausanne II Congress at Manila (1989). A group of evangelicals attending the San Antonio conference addressed a special letter to the Manila Congress urging that there be closer coordination with CWME in planning future world missionary conferences. Such contacts and conversations have increased trust and familiarity, and may in time also help foster greater unity and cooperation.

Finally, what can be said about the authority of conciliar ecumenical statements on missiology? It must be said at the outset that the WCC was constituted in 1948 as the *servant* of its member churches, with power to act only in matters assigned to it by those member churches. It cannot "dictate" to its member churches; no church is obliged to accept pronouncements of the WCC Central Committee or to endorse statements of WCC units. Statements issued at CWME conferences, or by WCC assemblies, are normally directed *to* WCC member churches and commended to them for study, guidance, response, and action, rather than *from* member churches to the world. Since the time of the late Anglican Archbishop William Temple, it has been said that ecumenical statements carry only as much authority as they are entitled to have by virtue of their innate wisdom. To have any effect, therefore, they must be essentially self-authenticating in terms of content. Herein lies a major difference between the authority of conciliar ecumenical statements and those issued by a Roman Pope or a Vatican curial office.

ROMAN CATHOLIC MISSIOLOGY

Before the Second Vatican Council, Roman Catholic thought on missionary activity was defined by the Sacred Congregation for the Propagation of the Faith (*Propaganda Fide*) and, in the twentieth century, by a number of mission encyclicals (Benedict XV's "Maximum Illud" [1919]), Pius XII's *Rerum Ecclesiae* (1926), *Evangelii Praecones* [1951] and *Fidei Donum* [1957], and John XXIII's *Princeps Pastorum* [1959]). These encyclicals were influenced by two prominent Catholic missiological schools. The so-called German school, based at the University of Muenster in Germany and headed by Joseph Schmidlin, emphasized mission as preaching the Gospel among non-Christians. The so-called Louvain school was headed by the Jesuit Pierre Charles and emphasized the aim of mission as the "planting of the church" (*plantatio ecclesiae*), even if the work was carried out in areas already Christian but where the institutional church was not yet firmly established (Müller, 35-38). At the Second Vatican Council (1962-1965), Catholic missiological thought was expressed primarily in the "Decree on Missionary Activity" (*Ad Gentes*, 1965), but important missiological statements were made by the council's "Dogmatic Constitution on the Church" (*Lumen Gentium*, 1964), its "Pastoral Constitution on the Church in the Modern World" (*Gaudium et Spes*, 1965), the "Declaration on the Relation of the Church to non-Christian Religions" (*Nostra Aetate*, 1965), and the "Declaration on Religious Liberty" (*Dignitatis Humanae*, 1965).

Since Vatican II, the Catholic missiological tradition has been officially articulated by papal documents (e.g., the Apostolic Exhortation *Evangelii Nuntiandi* [1975] and the encyclical *Redemptoris Missio* [1990]), by various Roman Congregations and Commissions (e.g. the Congregation for the Doctrine of the Faith's "Instruction on Christian Freedom and Liberation," and the International Theological Commission's document on "Inculturation"), and by statements and pastoral letters by various Bishops' Conferences (e.g. the "Puebla Document" of the Latin American Bishops). These documents will be found in Part II.

The tradition of a strong "teaching office" (Magisterium) in the Catholic Church has its roots in the practice of the various Ecumenical Councils (e.g., Nicea, 325) of issuing authoritative decrees, but since the late eighteenth century the power and prestige of the Magisterium, particularly that of the Pope, has grown considerably (Congar, 15-20). Especially since the Pontificate of Pius IX (1846-1878), the popes and the various Roman curial offices have published many official documents, and it has become important to note the classification of a document when it is published in order to know the level of authority that it expresses and the degree of assent that it requires. Since all of the Roman Catholic selections in Part II of this volume are magisterial documents, but of different weight, it might be helpful to provide some brief explanation of their nature.

An *encyclical* is a document of very high authority written by the pope. Originally the encyclical was written as a letter to Catholic bishops throughout the world, with the intention that its contents should be disseminated among Catholics in their respective dioceses. Since John XXIII (1958-1963), however, it has been the practice to address encyclicals to "all people of good will" as well. Encyclicals are not in themselves considered "infallible"; only decrees of ecumenical councils which are duly approved by the pope, or solemn papal teachings which pertain to "faith and morals" are said to articulate God's infallible truth. Nevertheless, they are regarded, after such infallible decrees and official documents of an ecumenical council, to possess the highest magisterial authority. Examples of encyclicals in this volume are John Paul II's *Sollicitudo Rei Socialis* (1987) and his *Redemptoris Missio* (1990).

Especially during the pontificate of Paul VI (1963-1978), another form of papal document came into prominence: the Apostolic Exhortation. This is a document that is a bit less formal than an encyclical, but also carries a great deal of weight. In Part II we have published excerpts from Paul VI's Apostolic Exhortation *Evangelii Nuntiandi* (1975) and John Paul II's *Catechesi Tradendi* (1979). A number of Vatican offices regularly publish official documents as well, and these are often given express approval by the pope. For example, the Congregation for the Doctrine of the Faith has published several mission-related documents in the last several years; here we are publishing its "Instruction on Christian Freedom and Liberation" (1986) signed by the German Cardinal Joseph Ratzinger as head of the Congregation, but also expressly approved by Pope John Paul II. As a Roman magisterial document, it calls for high respect, but its authority is considerably less than one issued by the pope himself. Finally, the Vatican has set up a number of quasi-magisterial commissions, among which is the International Theological Commission, whose document on "Inculturation" (1988) we are excerpting here.

Magisterial documents are also issued by Bishops' Conferences both on the regional and national levels, although the exact status of these teachings is still being discussed in the church (Dulles, 207-226). Statements such as that of the Latin American Bishops' Conference at Puebla (CELAM III, 1979), however, have had an enormous impact not only on the Church of Latin America, but also on the church at large; and Pastoral Letters and Statements of the U. S. Bishops, especially those on world peace (1983) and the economy (1986) have made an important impact on U. S. Catholic thinking. Although these two documents are not included in this collection, the 1986 Pastoral Statement of U. S. Bishops on World Mission has strong connections to both of them. In terms of their authority, a *Pastoral Letter* (e.g., the document *Heritage and Hope* from the U. S. Bishops) has more importance than a Pastoral *Statement.*

EASTERN ORTHODOX MISSIOLOGY

The Eastern Orthodox missionary tradition, though possessing a rich and noble legacy of missionary outreach during the first millennium of Christianity, "can be at once described as known and unknown" (Stamoolis, 1). Missionary activities from Byzantium among Goths, Huns, and pagan tribes surrounding the Eastern Roman Empire during the fourth to sixth centuries are well known, as are Orthodox missions to the Slavs during the ninth to eleventh centuries. The brothers Cyril and Methodius and their contributions to Slavonic script and culture are justly celebrated. Moreover, the millennium of the conversion of the Kievan "Rus" to Orthodoxy in 988 C.E. was observed in 1988. Thus Orthodoxy contributed extensively to the geographical spread of early Christianity, not only in Central and Eastern Europe but—through its non-Chalcedonian sister churches—to India, China, and Africa as well. With the rise of Islam in the seventh century (632 C.E.), the schism between Greek and Latin churches (1054), the tragic events of the Crusades, and finally the fall of Constantinople (1453), the earlier dynamism of Orthodox external missions appears to have been replaced by a period of missionary quiescence and inactivity. During this period Orthodoxy is seen, especially by outside observers, as withdrawing from contact with the world and focusing on the deepening of its interior spiritual life, especially through liturgy and prayer, and conserving its tradition. A perception of Orthodox indifference, or even hostility toward the missionary movement of the west, has gained some currency. If we wish to understand the reasons underlying the vigorous re-entry of Orthodox theologians into ecumenical discussions of missiology in recent years, we must be conscious not only of historical forces which gave rise to the earlier "unmissionary" image, but also of the newer historical forces which are challenging the former Orthodox missionary attitude. Orthodoxy's contribution will be seen as indispensable to an ecumenical consideration of the theology and practice of mission and evangelism.

Beginning in 1920, Eastern Orthodoxy, under the leadership of the Ecumenical Patriarch of Constantinople, embarked on a bold ecumenical initiative to promote Christian unity within a divided Christendom (Zernov, 653). This ecumenical appeal, however, was primarily concerned with "Faith and Order" issues and did not spring from positive associations with the western missionary movement which was approaching its zenith after the Edinburgh Missionary Conference (1910). Indeed, Orthodoxy used its new ecumenical contacts to complain bitterly about the proselytizing of Orthodox Christians by Protestant evangelical sects, while at the same time blaming Roman Catholic Uniate churches—in the Middle East, Asia, and the Ukraine—for causing tensions between Orthodoxy and Catholicism. "Foreign missions" acquired the generally negative image of Protestant or Roman Catholic incursions into Orthodoxy, and symbolized the invasion or penetration of Orthodox lands by hostile ecclesiastical forces. Added to this was the impact of the Marxist October Revolution in Russia (1917) and the spread of atheistic ideology into Central and Eastern Europe after 1945. The oppressive legacy of Islam, first under the Ottoman Turkish Empire but after 1945 under Islamic successor states in the Middle East, further diminished Orthodoxy's ability to engage in external missions (Bria 1980, 3-4).

Under these circumstances, the Great Commission (Matt. 28:19) tended to become, in the words of Bishop Anastasios Yannoulatos, "the forgotten commandment." Orthodox member churches in the World Council of Churches vigorously fought the integration of the International Missionary Council into the WCC at the New Delhi Assembly (1961), still believing that the western missionary movement was hostile to their own identity and interests (Lemopoulos 1989, 1). In the decade of the sixties, however, the Orthodox understanding of and involvement in mission and evangelization dramatically changed. What brought about the new Orthodox missionary orientation? In the late fifties, a group of younger Orthodox theologians, stung by the reproach of Orthodox missionary indifference, and engaged in a broadgauge movement of Orthodox renewal on several fronts, began the task of reconstructing the Orthodox missionary legacy and clarifying its understanding of mission from the standpoint of scripture and tradition. In 1958 Bishop Anastasios Yannoulatos initiated an Orthodox missionary society named *Porefthentes* ("Go Ye") out of the Pan-Orthodox Youth League, SYNDESMOS, and began editing an Orthodox journal of mission studies. Orthodox theologians began taking part in deliberations of the WCC's new Commission on World Mission and Evangelism (CWME) at its first meeting in Mexico City (1963), and played an important role in subsequent meetings (Anastasios, 76-77). Well-defined Orthodox preparatory statements now began to have considerable impact on subsequent WCC assemblies, especially Nairobi 1975, and on CWME conferences, such as Melbourne 1980 and San Antonio 1989.

The coordinated Orthodox response to the ecumenical debate on mission theology came about in part because of several organizational steps. In 1970, an Office on Orthodox Theology and Relations to the WCC was set up within the structure of the WCC-CWME; Bishop Anastasios served for three years as its staff liaison. In 1973, Professor Ion Bria assumed the duties of this office. Under his leadership, an Orthodox Advisory Commission (OAC) to the CWME was organized, and a series of annual conferences and seminars was held for the purpose of examining a wide spectrum of Orthodox missionary issues. It also sought to clarify the contribution which Orthodoxy as a whole might make to the ecumenical discussion of mission (Lemopoulos 1989, 1-2). These annual conferences were hosted by local Orthodox churches and held in Romania (1974), Armenia (1975), Czechoslovakia (1976), France (1978), Egypt (1979), Yugoslavia (1980), Syria (1982), USSR (1982), West Germany (1984), Bulgaria (1985), Neapolis, Greece (1988), Crete (1989), and Boston (1990) (Bria 1986, 101-102; Lemopoulos 1990, 3). The CWME Orthodox secretariat also undertook visits to scattered Orthodox churches in all six continents, thus promoting a closer feeling of Orthodox solidarity. During this period the Orthodox group issued invitations to representatives of Oriental (non-Chalcedonian) Eastern Churches, doctrinally estranged from Orthodoxy since 451, as a result of which these churches began moving toward reconciliation and closer unity with Orthodoxy.

Orthodox conferences also sought to clarify the various mission contexts with which Orthodoxy is currently engaged. These are seen to be: (1) Eastern Europe and the Soviet Union following the collapse of Communism. What is the meaning of Orthodox presence, and what is its missionary witness? (2) Orthodox Patriarchates in the Middle East in the continuing Palestinian crisis and the aftermath of the Gulf War. Can Orthodoxy still live and witness in the Middle East, and what should its relationships be with the two other monotheistic faiths of the region? (3) The Orthodox missionary diaspora in the west. Can Orthodoxy survive amid the pluralistic culture of the secular west, and what can it learn from its minority status? (4) The new Orthodox mission churches of Africa and Asia. How can their contributions and experiences enrich Orthodoxy? (Lemopoulos 1989, 70-71; 1990, 10-12).

The main outlines of Orthodox mission theology will be readily apparent from the selections presented in Part III. Some of its major underlying principles are: (1) a consistently trinitarian basis, fully involving each person of the Trinity in the mystery of salvation; (2) a cosmic eschatological perspective, which looks forward to the salvation of the entire creation as the goal of the kingdom; (3) the church, or Body of Christ, as the visible manifestation in the power of the Holy Spirit of the presence of Christ in human history; (4) the witness of the eucharistic community through doxology and liturgy as a primary expression of mission; (5) the contextualization of faith in the language and culture of each local community.

The Orthodox texts and reports which appear here, mostly originating in consultations of the Orthodox Advisory Group to the CWME during the seventies and eighties, are certainly *representative* of recent Orthodox thinking, but not necessarily *authoritative* in any official ecclesiastical sense. Pending the convening of a Pan-Orthodox Council, the statements should be considered *advisory* in the broadest sense of the term, both for the Orthodox family of churches and for non-Orthodox as well. In spite of the fact that Orthodoxy has since 1974 also made important direct contribution to the conciliar discussion about mission, we present these Orthodox texts here in Part III in order to provide a clear and detailed profile of Orthodox mission theology.

EVANGELICAL MISSIOLOGY

Evangelicalism is too complex a phenomenon to be dealt with in detail. Its predominant features would seem to be confidence in the power of the gospel and the authority of the scriptures, coupled with a passionate desire to reach out and share the good news with others. It has roots in nineteenth-century evangelical movements, above all the Evangelical Alliance (established 1846). But those nineteenth-century movements, in turn, stand on the shoulders of earlier post-Reformation evangelical movements, such as Pietism, Moravianism, Methodism, and similar awakening movements of the eighteenth and nineteenth centuries. Evangelicalism lays strong emphasis on mission, spiritual unity among Christians, and prayer for the advance of the kingdom. At times it has been a staunch advocate of social change, but its record in this regard is not consistent. During the last fifty years, and especially since World War II, evangelicalism has shown a "new face" and has attempted to shed some undesirable baggage from the past. During the past two decades it has carefully presented its missiological stance and goals. Like the other traditions under study here, it shows considerable vigor in responding to the new, postmodern missionary paradigm.

The evangelical movement presents a series of paradoxes. As noted above, it is in the process of renewing itself toward the end of the twentieth century, but its roots reach down toward earlier evangelical movements, and it traces its ultimate origins to the New Testament. It is characterized not only by what it wishes to *affirm* (the mandates of scripture and the power of the gospel) but certainly also by what it wishes to *reject*. It could not follow liberal Protestantism in embracing historical criticism, evolutionary theory, or the social gospel. But at the same time it sought to distance itself from fundamentalist divisiveness and polemics, and to avoid unnecessary breaches in fellowship. Evangelicalism retains many supporters and followers within mainline denominations affiliated with the conciliar ecumenical movement. At the same time, it numbers countless others related to conservative evangelical denominations and missionary associations which view the ecumenical movement with some suspicion. Some evangelicals are by temperament anti-Catholic, while others are open to reconciliation and closer relationships. Evangelicals possess a common creedal stance grounded in the essentials of Christian faith as proclaimed in the scriptures. Yet they are also likely to allow some liberty when it comes to interpreting the essentials of faith and doctrine, and are less likely than fundamentalists to break off fellowship relations over points of doctrinal interpretation.

Generally speaking, evangelicals wish to promote unity and fellowship among Christians for more effective witness to the gospel. Their preferred approach to unity is to foster interpersonal relationships of common faith, trust, and prayer, rather than relying on organizational or hierarchical structures. Evangelical diffidence toward structural expressions of Christian unity explains, in part, the cautious attitude which most evangelicals adopt toward the conciliar ecumenical movement.

For purposes of understanding evangelical missiology, we shall briefly trace the origins and contributions of two newer evangelical associations: the World Evangelical Fellowship (1951), and the Lausanne Committee for World Evangelization (1974), often simply referred to as the "Lausanne Movement." Both organizations, while primarily North American in background and support, are seeking to develop a worldwide following and a global program. The two bodies have maintained close and cooperative relationships with each other, and many evangelicals identify with both.

The World Evangelical Fellowship (WEF), organized in 1951, is an alliance of some sixty national and regional evangelical bodies, open to national fellowships of evangelical believers in any country. Since its inception, WEF has given special emphasis to evangelism, prayer life, spiritual retreats and conferences, scholarship programs for third-world students, and books for seminaries and Bible training institutes in those countries (Howard, 38-39, 156). In addition to an International Director, David M. Howard, and an international Executive Council, WEF has regional vice-presidents with responsibility for planning and programming in various regions. It operates through general conferences held roughly every three years, sometimes in conjunction with major consultations. WEF has functional commissions responsible for theology (with ethics), missions, communications, and family life (including women's concerns). Recently a commission on church renewal was added. Its important contributions to evangelical missiology have come through consultations devoted to special topics, some of them jointly convened with units of the Lausanne Committee. Among these have been consultations dealing with "The Theology of Development" and "Evangelical Commitment to Simple Lifestyle" (both 1980), "The Relation of Evangelism and Social Responsibility" (1982), "The Church in Response to Human Need" (1983), "The Work of the Holy Spirit and Evangelization" (1985), and "Conversion" (1988). Excerpts from several of these consultation reports are included in Part IV.

The Lausanne Committee for World Evangelization (LCWE), formally constituted at the International Congress on World Evangelization (ICOWE) held at Lausanne, Switzerland, in July 1974, is in reality the Continuation Committee for the Lausanne Movement (Bassham, 230-245; Scherer, 165-187). Organized under the personal initiative and leadership of Dr. Billy Graham, with major assistance from the evangelical journal *Christianity Today* and support from various evangelistic agencies and missionary associations, ICOWE carried forward the momentum of two earlier congresses held in 1966: the Wheaton Congress on the Church's Worldwide Mission, sponsored by the Interdenominational Foreign Mission Association (IFMA, 1917) and the Evangelical Foreign Missions Association (EFMA, 1945), and the Berlin World Congress on Evangelism sponsored by the journal *Christianity Today*. Employing the newer term *evangelization*, the Lausanne Congress sought to forge a bond between evangelicals concerned with world mission and those primarily interested in evangelism. LCWE, as its name suggests, is not a council of churches or religious organizations but rather a loose coalition of individual persons, mission and evangelism agencies, and institutions sharing a common theological position and with a common missionary and evangelistic purpose. It is governed by an international committee of seventy evangelical leaders. Its current International Director is Tom Houston. Identification with LCWE is made by signing the Lausanne Covenant and thereby covenanting with others "to pray, plan, and work together for the evangelization of the whole world."

In issuing invitations to the 1974 Lausanne Congress, the preparatory committee's intention was "to hasten the evangelization of all peoples of the world in obedience to the command of Jesus Christ and in anticipation of his return." This was to be done by promoting cooperative evangelistic efforts, engaging in biblical studies on evangelism, examining strategies of evangelization, and joining in united prayer (Scherer, 168). The official report of ICOWE, entitled *Let the Earth Hear His Voice,* runs to nearly 1500 closely written pages (Douglas 1975). The spirit and purpose of Lausanne were well expressed in Billy Graham's opening address, "Why Lausanne?" Graham said that the common characteristics of earlier great movements for evangelism were that they all took their stand on the basis of the scriptures, held a definite view of the need of salvation and the lostness of humans apart from Christ, strongly believed in conversion, and were convinced that evangelism was not an option but an imperative (Douglas 1975, 26f.). The conciliar ecumenical movement, Graham believed, had departed from its earlier evangelistic vision and commitment after Edinburgh 1910; evangelicals gathered at Lausanne were thus being challenged to take the lead in restoring world evangelization to its rightful place.

One of the most enduring achievements of ICOWE was the drafting and formal adoption of the fifteen-paragraph declaration known as the *Lausanne Covenant.* It was to become the ongoing basis for evangelical cooperation and a further catalyst to evangelical unity. The covenant, prepared under the leadership of Anglican evangelical John R. W. Stott, attempts to define sensitive issues of evangelical missiology: the authority of the Bible, the uniqueness of Jesus Christ, the relation between evangelism and dialogue, the relative priority of evangelization and social concern, the centrality of the church in evangelism, the necessity of partnership and cooperation, and many others. Despite the warm reception given the *Lausanne Covenant,* some issues were not settled by ICOWE, and groups such as the "radical evangelicals" and WEF commissions pressed for further clarifications and refinements. Even so, Lausanne 1974 "marks the highpoint in the development of evangelical mission theology," and the Covenant remains "the most mature and comprehensive statement produced by evangelicals" (Bassham, 243). The entire text is reproduced in Part IV.

Between 1974 and 1989, LCWE carried on its work by means of working groups on theology, mission strategy, intercession, and communication. The Theology Working Group organized consultations on "The Homogeneous Unit Principle" (1977) and on "The Gospel and Culture" (1978), in addition to holding several joint consultations with WEF units. The LCWE Strategy Working Group cooperated closely with MARC-World Vision in relation to the "Unreached Peoples" project and in designing evangelism strategies. The largest single LCWE effort in this period was expended on the planning of the 1980 Pattaya (Thailand) Consultation on World Evangelization, at which seventeen distinct "mini-consultations" were held, devoted to theological issues and strategies for reaching particular groups. Reports from these mini-consultations, most of them published as "Lausanne Occasional Papers," gave new specificity to mission frontiers identified by LCWE. Leighton Ford, LCWE president, singled out three areas for urgent ongoing attention: the world of Islam, the secular west, and the urban poor (Scherer, 190).

The most recent LCWE document in Part IV, coming from Lausanne II in Manila, the Second International Congress on World Evangelization (1989), is the *Manila Manifesto,* "An Elaboration of the Lausanne Covenant Fifteen Years Later." The full report of Lausanne II is found in *Proclaim Christ Until He Comes: Calling the Whole Church to Take the Whole Gospel to the Whole World* (Douglas 1990). The *Manila Manifesto*, again prepared under the leadership of John R. W. Stott, is in some ways an updating of the *Lausanne Covenant*, but without departing from the covenant's essential affirmations. The *Manila Manifesto* may be seen as evangelicalism's response to the postmodern missionary paradigm, with special regard for the challenges of the year A.D. 2000 and beyond. Together with the covenant, the manifesto will provide authoritative guidance and inspiration to evangelical workers and set the tone for evangelical missiology into the nineties. While possessing no official authority, these two documents embody a broad consensus of evangelical opinion and conviction about mission and evangelization. They deserve careful study by all who seek to promote mutual understanding and common witness to the gospel.

CONCLUSION

It is the hope of the editors that these documents will be useful to Christians in every one of these traditions. Our purpose will have been served if someone identified with any one of the four traditions is led to greater respect and understanding for those holding other convictions about the work of mission and evangelism. One of our aims is to further common witness to the coming of Christ's kingdom.

In regard to the use of these documents, however, we might add two small observations. In some cases, the selections included represent only brief excerpts from documents of much greater length and complexity. Readers are urged whenever possible to examine these documents in their entirety; our collection is intended merely as an introductory overview. Secondly, the documents are presented for the most part in the language in which they originally appeared. Regrettably, they may in some cases contain language which is noninclusive in character when referring to either humanity or God. An effort has been made to be sensitive to language concerns in other parts of this work.

We are certain that some important documents, particularly those issued at local levels, have been excluded from this collection. Moreover, important denominational statements have been omitted. Nevertheless, we believe that what we have provided can serve as an important tool and frame of reference for ecumenical mission study, fostering greater understanding, mutual trust, and common witness among mission partners. We hope in later volumes to include documents from every Christian tradition.

Christian mission and evangelization, at the dawn of this postmodern era and under the guidance of God's Spirit, has taken new directions. May this first volume—and this entire series—help Christians everywhere chart those directions more confidently and so help bring the Christian mission everywhere to its final destination in God.

BIBLIOGRAPHY

Anastasios of Androussa (Yannoulatos). 1989. "Orthodox Mission—Past, Present and Future." In *Your Will Be Done: Orthodoxy and Mission*, ed. G. Lemopoulos. Katerini: Tertios & Geneva: WCC, 63-92.

Bassham, Rodger C. 1979. *Mission Theology: 1948-1975*. Pasadena: William Carey Library.

Bevans, Stephen, SVD. 1991. "Reaching for Fidelity: Catholic Theology in Today's

World." In *Doing Theology in Today's World*, ed. T. McComiskey & J. Wood-bridge. Grand Rapids, Mich.: Zondervan, 1991, 321-38.

Bosch, David J. 1991. *Transforming Mission: Paradigm Shifts in Theology of Mission*. ASM Series No. 16. Maryknoll, N.Y.: Orbis Books.

Bria, Ion, ed. 1980. *Martyria/Mission: The Witness of the Orthodox Churches Today*. Geneva: WCC-CWME.

————, ed. 1986. *Go Forth in Peace: Orthodox Perspectives on Mission*. WCC Mission Series No. 7. Geneva: WCC.

Congar, Yves. 1977. "The Magisterium and Theologians – A Short History", *Theology Digest* 25: 1 (Spring 1977): 15-20.

Douglas, J. D., ed. 1975. *Let the Earth Hear His Voice: International Congress on World Evangelization*. Official Reference Volume. Minneapolis, Minn.: World Wide Publications.

————, ed. 1990. *Proclaim Christ Until He Comes: Calling the Whole Church to Take the Whole Gospel to the Whole World*. Lausanne II in Manila. International Congress on World Evangelization. Minneapolis, Minn.: World Wide Publications.

Dulles, Avery. 1988. "The Teaching Authority of Bishops' Conferences." In *The Reshaping of Catholicism: Current Challenges in the Theology of the Church*. San Francisco: Harper & Row, 207-226.

Hogg, W. Richey. 1971. "World Missionary Conferences." In *Concise Dictionary of the Christian World Mission*, ed. S. Neill, G. H. Anderson, J. Goodwin. Nashville & New York: Abingdon Press, 133-138.

Howard, David M. 1986. *The Dream That Would Not Die: Birth and Growth of the World Evangelical Fellowship, 1846-1986*. Exeter: Paternoster.

Lemopoulos, George, ed. 1989. *Your Will Be Done: Orthodoxy in Mission*. Katerini: Tertios & Geneva: WCC.

————, ed. 1990. *The Holy Spirit and Mission*. Geneva: WCC-CWME.

Müller, Karl. 1987. *Mission Theology: An Introduction*. Sankt Augustin: Steyler Verlag, 35-38.

Scherer, James A. 1987. *Gospel, Church and Kingdom: Comparative Studies in World Mission Theology*. Minneapolis, Minn.: Augsburg Press.

Stamoolis, James J. 1986. *Eastern Orthodox Mission Theology Today*. ASM Series No. 10. Maryknoll, N.Y.: Orbis Books.

Van Elderen, Martin. 1990. *Introducing the World Council of Churches*. Risk Book Series No. 46. Geneva: WCC Publications.

Zernov, Nicholas. 1954. "The Eastern Churches and the Ecumenical Movement in the Twentieth Century." In *History of the Ecumenical Movement, 1517-1948*, vol. I, ed. R. Rouse and S. C. Neill. 2d ed. 1967. Philadelphia: Westminster Press, 653f.

Part I

CONCILIAR ECUMENICAL STATEMENTS

1

Confessing Christ Today

Nairobi, 1975

WORLD COUNCIL OF CHURCHES FIFTH ASSEMBLY

The Fifth Assembly of the World Council of Churches met in Nairobi, Kenya, from November 23 to December 10, 1975, on the theme "Jesus Christ Frees and Unites." Both the time and the place were auspicious for a consideration of evangelism.

African churches were adding converts in record numbers, while at the same time the ecumenical movement was seeking to renew its evangelistic commitment. A major assembly presentation by Bishop Mortimer Arias took up the theme "That the World May Believe," while WCC Central Committee Moderator Dr. M. M. Thomas focused extensively on "The Concept of Evangelism in the Modern World" in his report.

Section I of the assembly, to which responsibility for developing the theme "Confessing Christ Today" was assigned, had before it reports from the WCC-CWME conference on "Salvation Today" (Bangkok, 1973), as well as the Lausanne Covenant from the International Congress on World Evangelization (Lausanne, 1974) and the statement from the Roman Bishops' Synod on "Evangelization in the Modern World" (Rome, 1975), which later provided the occasion for Pope Paul VI's Apostolic Exhortation Evangelii Nuntiandi *(1975). Moreover, the Orthodox Advisory Committee had also issued its preliminary report on "Confessing Christ Today" (Bucharest, 1974). The final text of Section I is a sign of growing convergence between the four major traditions surveyed in this volume.*

"Confessing Christ Today" firmly grounds the missionary witness in the confession of Jesus as "The Christ of God, the hope of the world." The report is also marked by an appeal for "wholeness" in evangelism.

SECTION I: CONFESSING CHRIST TODAY*

1. Today's world offers many political lords as well as secular and religious saviours. Nevertheless, as representatives of churches gathered together in the

---

*Reprinted from David M. Paton, ed., *Breaking Barriers: Nairobi 1975,* The Official Report of the World Council of Churches, Nairobi, 23 November-10 December, 1975 (London: SPCK and Grand Rapids, Mich.: Eerdmans, 1976), 43-57.

World Council of Churches, we boldly confess Christ alone as Saviour and Lord. We confidently trust in the power of the gospel to free and unite all children of God throughout the world.

2. Amid today's cries of anguish and shouts of oppression, we have been led by the Holy Spirit to confess Jesus Christ as Divine Confessor. Confident in the Word of God of the holy Scriptures, we confess both our human weakness and our divine strength: "Since then we have a great high priest who has passed through the heavens, Jesus, the Son of God, let us hold fast to our confession" (Heb. 4.14).

3. As our high priest, Christ mediates God's new covenant through both salvation and service. Through the power of the cross, Christ promises God's righteousness and commands true justice. As the royal priesthood, Christians are therefore called to engage in both evangelism and social action. We are commissioned to proclaim the gospel of Christ to the ends of the earth. Simultaneously, we are commanded to struggle to realize God's will for peace, justice and freedom throughout society.

4. In the same high priestly prayer which bids "that they may be one", Jesus also discloses the distinctive life-style of those who have been set apart to serve in the Churches' universal priesthood. While we are "not of" the world, even as he was not of the world, so we are also sent "into" the world, just as he was sent into the world (John 17.16, 18).

5. Christians witness in word and deed to the inbreaking reign of God. We experience the power of the Holy Spirit to confess Christ in a life marked by both suffering and joy. Christ's decisive battle has been won at Easter, and we are baptized into his death that we might walk in newness of life (Rom. 6.4). Yet we must still battle daily against those already dethroned, but not yet destroyed, "principalities and powers" of this rebellious age. The Holy Spirit leads us into all truth, engrafting persons into the Body of Christ in which all things are being restored by God.

6. Our life together is thereby committed to the costly discipleship of the Churches' Divine Confessor. His name is above every name: "that at the name of Jesus every knee should bow, in heaven and on earth, and under the earth, and every tongue confess that Jesus Christ is Lord, to the glory of God the Father" (Phil. 2.10-11).

CONFESSING CHRIST AS AN ACT OF CONVERSION

The Christ of God

7. Jesus asks: "Who do you say that I am?" At the same time he calls us into his discipleship: "If anyone would come after me, let him deny himself and take up his cross and follow me" (Matt. 16, 24). We confess Jesus as the Christ of God, the hope of the world, and commit ourselves to his will. Before we confess him, he confesses us, and in all our ways he precedes us. We therefore confess with great joy:

8. Jesus Christ is the *one witness of God,* to whom we listen and witness as the incarnate Son of God in life and death (John 14.8). "You are my witnesses. . . . I am the first and the last. There is no God except me" was said to Israel (Isa. 43.8-11). So we are the witnesses of Christ and his Kingdom to all people until the end of the world.

9. Jesus Christ is the *true witness of God* (Rev. 3.14). Into the world of lies, ambiguity and idolatry, he brings "the truth that liberates" (John 8.32). And as God has sent him, so he sends us.

10. Jesus Christ is the *faithful witness to God* (Rev. 1.5). In his self-offering on the Cross, he redeems us from sin and godless powers and reconciles creation with God. Therefore, we shall live for God and shall be saved in God. "There is no condemnation for those who are in Christ Jesus, who walk not after the flesh, but after the Spirit" (Rom. 8.1ff).

11. We believe with certainty in the *presence and guidance of the Holy Spirit,* who proceeds from the Father and bears witness to Christ (John 15.26). Our witness to Christ is made strong in the Holy Spirit and is alive in the confessing community of the Church.

Our Discipleship, His Lordship

12. In our confessing Christ today and in our continuing conversion to the way of Christ, we encourage and support one another.

13. *Confessing Christ and being converted to his discipleship belong inseparably together.* Those who confess Jesus Christ deny themselves, their selfishness and slavery to the godless "principalities and powers", take up their crosses and follow him. Without clear confession of Christ our discipleship cannot be recognized; without costly discipleship people will hesitate to believe our confession. The costs of discipleship—e.g. becoming a stranger among one's own people, being despised because of the gospel, persecuted because of resistance to oppressive powers, and imprisoned because of love for the poor and lost—are bearable in face of the costly love of God, revealed in the passion of Jesus.

14. We *deplore* cheap conversions, without consequence. We *deplore* a superficial gospel-preaching, an empty gospel without a call into personal and communal discipleship. We *confess* our own fear of suffering with Jesus. We are afraid of persecutions, fear, and death. Yet, the more we look upon the crucified Christ alone and trust the power of the Holy Spirit, the more our anxiety is overcome. "When we suffer with him, we shall also be glorified with him" (Rom. 8.17). We revere the martyrs of all ages and of our time, and look to their example for courage.

15. We *deplore* conversions without *witness* to Christ. There are millions who have never heard the good news. We *confess* that we are often ashamed of the gospel. We find it more comfortable to remain in our own Christian circles than to witness in the world. The more we look upon our risen Christ, the more our indolence is overcome and we are enabled to confess: "Woe to me if I do not preach the gospel" (I Cor. 9.16).

16. We *deplore* also that our confessing Christ today is hindered by the different denominations, which split the confessing community of the Church. We understand the confession of faith of our different traditions as guidelines, not as substitutes, for our actual confessing in the face of today's challenges. Because being converted to Christ necessarily includes membership in the confessing body of Christ, we *long and strive* for a world-wide community.

17. *In confessing Christ and in being converted to his Lordship, we experience the freedom of the Holy Spirit and express the ultimate hope for the world.* Through his true and faithful witness Jesus Christ has set us free from the slavery of sin to the glorious freedom of the Spirit. Within the vicious circle of sin, death and the devil are the vicious circles of hunger, oppression and violence. Likewise, liberation to justice, better community, and human dignity on earth is within the great freedom of the Spirit, who is nothing less than the power of the new creation.

18. We regret all divisions in thinking and practise between the personal and the corporate dimensions. "The whole gospel for the whole person and the whole

world" means that we cannot leave any area of human life and suffering without the witness of hope.

19. We regret that some reduce liberation from sin and evil to social and political dimensions, just as we regret that others limit liberation to the private and eternal dimensions.

20. In the witness of our whole life and our confessing community we *work* with passionate love for the total liberation of the people and *anticipate* God's Kingdom to come. We *pray* in the freedom of the Spirit and *groan* with our suffering fellow human beings and the whole groaning creation until the glory of the Triune God is revealed and will be all in all. Come, Lord Jesus, come to us, come to the world!

MANY CULTURES, ONE CHRIST

Search for Cultural Identity

21. In all societies today there is a search for cultural identity; Christians around the world find themselves caught up in this quest. The Bangkok Conference on Salvation Today (1973) asked: "Culture shapes the human voice that answers the voice of Christ. . . . How can we responsibly answer the voice of Christ instead of copying foreign models of conversion . . . imposed, not truly accepted?"

22. In our sharing with one another we have discovered that the Christ who meets us in our own cultural contexts is revealed to us in a new way as we confess him. Further, since Christ shares in a special way with all who are exploited and oppressed, we find when we meet with them that our understanding of him is enlarged and enriched.

23. We affirm the necessity of confessing Christ as specifically as possible with regard to our own cultural settings. We have heard him confessed in that way at this Assembly by Christians from all parts of the world. In partial answer to the question raised by the Bangkok Conference, we can say that Jesus Christ does not make copies; he makes originals. We have found this confession of Christ out of our various cultural contexts to be not only mutually inspiring, but also a mutually corrective exchange. Without this sharing our individual affirmations would gradually become poorer and narrower. We need each other to regain the lost dimensions of confessing Christ and even to discover dimensions unknown to us before. Sharing in this way we are all changed and our cultures are transformed.

24. There is great diversity in our confessions of Christ. Nevertheless, through the illumination of the Holy Spirit, we have been able to recognize him in the proclamation of Christians in cultural situations different from our own. This is possible because we confess Christ as God and Saviour *according to the Scriptures.* And although our reading and interpretation of the Scriptures is to a certain extent itself culturally conditioned, we believe that it is part of the mystery of Christ that even as we confess him in different ways it is he who draws us together.

25. We believe that in addition to listening to one another, we need to know what people of other faiths and no faith are saying about Jesus Christ and his followers. While we cannot agree on whether or how Christ is present in other religions, we do believe that God has not left himself without witness in any generation or any society. Nor do we exclude the possibility that God speaks to Christians from outside the Church. While we oppose any form of syncretism, we affirm the necessity for dialogue with men and women of other faiths and ideologies as a means of mutual understanding and practical cooperation.

THE CONFESSING COMMUNITY

Community in the Spirit

32. Confessing Christ is not only intensely personal; it is also essentially communal.

33. Those who take part in the life of Christ and confess him as Lord and Saviour, Liberator and Unifier, are gathered in a community of which the author and sustainer is the Holy Spirit. This communion of the Spirit finds its primary aim and ultimate purpose in the eucharistic celebration and the glorification of the Triune God. The doxology is the supreme confession which transcends all our divisions.

34. Through word, sacrament and mutual care he transforms us, makes us grow, and leads us to the integration of worship and action. This power fills our weakness.

35. Confessing Christ *today* means that the Spirit makes us struggle with all the issues the Assembly has talked about: sin and forgiveness, power and powerlessness, exploitation and misery, the universal search for identity, the widespread loss of Christian motivation, and the spiritual longings of those who have not heard Christ's name.

36. It means that we are in communion with the prophets who announced God's will and purpose for humankind and society, with the martyrs who sealed their confession with suffering and death, and also with the doubtful who can only whisper their confession of the Name. The confession of Christ holds in one communion our divided churches and the many communities, new and old, within and around them.

37. When the Holy Spirit empowers us to confess Christ today, we are called to speak and act with concern and solidarity for the whole of God's creation. Concretely: when the powerful confess Christ, the suffering must be enabled to concur; when the exploited confess Christ, the rich should be enabled to hear in such confession their own freedom announced.

38. Within the communion of the Church, we witness in our time the emergence of many new communities: missionary orders, ecumenical experiments, communes and action groups, which are trying out age-old or spontaneous and new forms of worship and action. All these groups represent attempts to find answers to the fragmentation of our societies and to the loneliness which results from the disintegration of traditional community life. They also express the lasting strength of the call of the gospel to communion and mutual care, which the Spirit instills in everybody who is touched. Despite the problems these groups often give to the institutional churches, we recognize a creative challenge in them. We urge the churches to be sensitive to such groups, to respect the search for authenticity which they represent, and not to reject them, lest such groups turn away from the larger communion and lose the opportunity to share their discoveries and spiritual fruits with all the others.

39. Again: all Christian community life is a creation of the Spirit of Christ, nourished by his work and sacraments, held together by love, and pushed forward by hope. Worship is its anchor and the source of its energy. So, through informed intercessions, naming people far away and close by, they live in solidarity with the whole community of grace and also, irresistibly, with all those who suffer and yearn for dignity. Through these prayers and through old and new forms of direct *diakonia,* they forge links which embrace the earth, breaking through man-made divisions of race and class, power and exploitation.

Prayer and Suffering

40. Worship, especially the Eucharist, is the instrument through which all these communities open themselves up to God and his creation; thus it breaks down walls of divisions and stimulates creative forms of solidarity. In worship we are constantly reminded of the age to come and made to live in anticipation of the messianic kingdom; thus confidence and urgency are wedded in one common life. It is our lasting shame and pain that we have not overcome our divisions at the Lord's table, where we experience God's salvation for and on behalf of all humanity. . . .

41. Confessing Christ in communion means confessing the suffering and risen Lord. We should not refuse his Cross. He will not refuse us his life.

42. We know that acceptance of the suffering Christ is the only way to overcome our feelings of powerlessness over against evil. We also know that this acceptance would make us once again credible in the eyes of the world. We therefore pray that our churches will again and again return to the reality and the promise of the Cross, so that together we may find ourselves the stewards of the new life in Christ.

CONFESSING CHRIST IN WORSHIP AND LIFE

Facing Reality

43. "Confessing Christ" or "Christian Witness" describes, above all, that continuous act by which a Christian or Christian community proclaims God's acts in history and seeks to manifest Christ as "the Word that was made flesh and dwelt among us" (John 1.14). Our confessing Christ today would deny God's incarnation if it were limited to only some areas of life. It concerns the wholeness of human life: our words and acts, our personal and communal existence, our worship and responsible service; our particular and ecumenical context.

44. All this is done under the guidance of the Holy Spirit in order that all may be reconciled and be gathered into Christ's one and only Body (Col. 1.18; Eph. 1.22-23) and attain life everlasting — to know and love the true God and him whom he has sent (John 17.3).

45. Confessing Christ is an act of gratitude for God's faithfulness and his liberating presence in our life. His is the power and the glory. At the same time, Christian witness has to do with Christians struggling against the power of evil within themselves, within the churches, and in society. This power expresses itself in many ways — in temptations of various kinds, in prejudices nurtured in us by birth, sex, class, race, religion, or nationality; in dehumanizing political and socioeconomic forces; in hostility which disrupts human relationships; in selfish ambition which thrives on the misery and sufferings of others; in sicknesses which have no cure. In the midst of such reality each of us is called in our baptism to confess Christ according to the special gift (*charisma*) which one has received from God.

46. Liturgical worship, an action of the Church centered around the Eucharist, in itself thankfully proclaims the death and resurrection of the Lord "until he comes again" and incorporates people into mystical union with God, because in the act of baptism they have been identified with that death and resurrection. Confessions of faith and creeds are expressions of the communion of the Christian life both of yesterday and today. Our witness is rooted and nourished in that communion. Yesterday flows into today, the present engages the past, in continual dialogue. We approach our biblical and confessional heritage with questions that arise from contemporary involvement. At the same time, we gratefully receive from that heritage both criticism and encouragement for concrete service and fellowship.

Christian Authenticity

47. Though it seems flat and even naive on paper, we insist on repeating that the key to authentic confession is the Christian who indeed is a Christian within the community of faith. Authentic Christians live the death and resurrection of Christ by living the forgiven life in selfless service to others, and believe in the Spirit by whose power alone we are able to live our life of discipleship (I Cor. 12.3). Especially in a secularized environment or in situations where religious commitments are scorned or even attacked, the primary confessors are precisely those non-publicized, unsensational people who gather together in small, caring communities. They remain free to proclaim Christ out of their self-acknowledged condition of weakness and sin. Their individual and communal life-style provokes the question: "What is the meaning of your life, and why do you live as you do?" One must name the Name. Yet shared experiences reveal how often today Christ is confessed not in loud and frequent words or in massive programmes of varied activities, but in the very silence of a prison cell or of a restricted but still serving, waiting, praying Church. Today, as always in the Church, we are blessed by confessors, martyrs, "even unto death".

48. Indeed, in those milieux which seem so hardened to any religious confession or in areas which for centuries have seen so little "success", confessing Christ may rest in the very hope that flows from our incorporation through the Spirit into the mission, death, and life of Jesus Christ. Only that hope holds us, only that hope never abandons us.

49. The call to confess Christ is a vocation also to that *common* witness in each place which the churches, even while separated, bear together. By sharing resources and experiences in mission, they witness to whatever divine gift of truth and life they already share in common. Such witness should proclaim together the content of Christian faith, as fully as possible. Furthermore, such ecumenical faithfulness of the churches in each place includes fidelity to the needs of the local churches which elsewhere are also striving to give common witness.

50. For many Christians in very diverse situations, confessing Christ amounts almost to the same thing as involvement in struggles for justice and freedom. In many instances Christian faith has become a dynamic force, awakening the conscience of the people and bringing new hope to hopeless situations. In this way, confessing Christ is liberated from mere verbalism which renders the life and ministry of the Church stagnant, introverted and contentious.

51. What are our hesitations about explicitly confessing our faith before others?

(a) A loss of confidence in the God we proclaim and in the power of the gospel so that we lack confidence in our mission as Christians?

(b) By not experiencing deeply enough the joyful, healing love of God so that we are unable *honestly* to give an account of the hope within us?

(c) An unreadiness to be different before those to whom the good news is heard as bad news?

(d) By misunderstanding our belief in the uniqueness and finality of Jesus Christ as "arrogant doctrinal superiority", and not understanding it as the humble and obedient stewardship of the Church which knows it has been "put in trust with the gospel?"

52. We confess Christ in the perspective of the coming Kingdom. His Spirit is the Spirit of the New Age. This vision makes us both sober and hopeful. None of

the achievements as individuals, churches, societies will in themselves inaugurate the messianic era. Never can women and men be justified by works. Yet the promise of the Kingdom is valid and encourages Christians to respond in prayer and action. Confessing Christ shall not be in vain.

A CALL TO CONFESS AND PROCLAIM

53. We do not have the option of keeping the good news to ourselves. The uncommunicated gospel is a patent contradiction.

54. We are called to preach Christ crucified, the power of God and the wisdom of God (I Cor. 1.23, 24).

55. Evangelism, therefore, is rooted in gratitude for God's self-sacrificing love, in obedience to the risen Lord.

56. Evangelism is like a beggar telling another beggar where they both can find bread.

The Whole Gospel

57. The gospel is good news from God, our Creator and Redeemer. On its way from Jerusalem to Galilee and to the ends of the earth, the Spirit discloses ever new aspects and dimensions of God's decisive revelation in Jesus Christ. The gospel always includes: the announcement of God's Kingdom and love through Jesus Christ, the offer of grace and forgiveness of sins, the invitation to repentance and faith in him, the summons to fellowship in God's Church, the command to witness to God's saving words and deeds, the responsibility to participate in the struggle for justice and human dignity, the obligation to denounce all that hinders human wholeness, and a commitment to risk life itself. In our time, to the oppressed the gospel may be new as a message of courage to persevere in the struggle for liberation in this world as a sign of hope for God's inbreaking Kingdom. To women the gospel may bring news of Christ who empowered women to be bold in the midst of cultural expectations of submissiveness. To children the gospel may be a call of love for the "little ones" and to the rich and powerful it may reveal the responsibility to share the poverty of the poor.

58. While we rejoice hearing the gospel speak to our particular situations and while we must try to communicate the gospel to particular contexts, we must remain faithful to the historical apostolic witness as we find it in the holy Scriptures and tradition as it is centered in Jesus Christ—lest we accommodate them to our own personal desires and interests.

The Whole Person

59. The gospel, through the power of the Holy Spirit, speaks to all human needs, transforms our lives. In bringing forgiveness, it reconciles us to our Creator, speaks within us the true joy of knowing God, and promises eternal life. In uniting us as God's people, it answers our need for community and fellowship. In revealing God's love for all persons, it makes us responsible, critical, creative members of the societies in which we live. The good news of Christ's resurrection assures us that God's righteous purpose in history will be fulfilled and frees us to work for that fulfilment with hope and courage.

The Whole World

60. The world is not only God's creation; it is also the arena of God's mission. Because God loved the whole world, the Church cannot neglect any part of it—

neither those who have heard the saving Name nor the vast majority who have not yet heard it. Our obedience to God and our solidarity with the human family demand that we obey Christ's command to proclaim and demonstrate God's love to every person, of every class and race, on every continent, in every culture, in every setting and historical context.

The Whole Church

61. Evangelism cannot be delegated to either gifted individuals or specialized agencies. It is entrusted to the "whole Church", the body of Christ, in which the particular gifts and functions of all members are but expressions of the life of the whole body.

62. This wholeness must take expression in every particular cultural, social and political context. Therefore, the evangelization of the world starts at the level of the congregation, in the local and ecumenical dimensions of its life: worship, sacrament, preaching, teaching and healing, fellowship and service, witnessing in life and in death.

63. Too often we as churches and congregations stand in the way of the gospel — because of our lack of missionary zeal and missionary structures, because of our divisions, our self-complacency, our lack of catholicity and ecumenical spirit.

64. The call to evangelism, therefore, implies a call to repentance, renewal and commitment for visible unity. We also deplore proselytism of any sort which further divides the Church.

65. Yet, even imperfect and broken, we are called to put ourselves humbly and gladly at the service of the unfinished mission. We are commissioned to carry the gospel to the whole world and to allow it to permeate all realms of human life.

70. Confessing Christ must be done *today*. "Behold, now is the acceptable time; behold, now is the day of salvation" (II Cor. 6.2). It cannot wait for a time that is comfortable for us. We must be prepared to proclaim the gospel when human beings need to hear it. But in our zeal to spread the good news, we must guard against fanaticism which disrupts the hearing of the gospel and breaks the community of God. The world requires, and God demands, that we recognize the urgency to proclaim the saving word of God — today. God's acceptable time requires that we respond in all haste. "And how terrible it would be for me if I did not preach the gospel!" (I Cor. 9.16).

2

Guidelines on Dialogue

Kingston, 1979

WORLD COUNCIL OF CHURCHES

Although some view of the meaning and practice of dialogue is found in several earlier WCC assembly and CWME conference statements, the WCC took no official stance on this controversial issue until the 1979 Central Committee meeting. In response to numerous requests from WCC member churches, the WCC in 1971 first adopted an "interim" policy statement with guidelines on dialogue at the 1971 meeting of the Central Committee. At the same time, it authorized the holding of several bilateral and multilateral meetings with persons of other faiths to explore the issues involved.

A statement prepared by a WCC consultation held in Chiang Mai, Thailand, in 1977 on the theme "Dialogue in Community" was received by the Central Committee at its 1977 meeting. The Chiang Mai statement, revised and amplified, was formally adopted by the WCC Central Committee at its 1979 meeting.

The statement is noteworthy for its emphasis on the sharing of their faith by Christians with neighbors of other faiths and ideologies, with whom they share a common human community, rather than on scholarly exchanges between religious specialists. "As Christians enter dialogue with their commitment to Jesus Christ, time and again the relation of dialogue gives opportunity for authentic witness." Dialogue is commended as one way in which Jesus Christ can be confessed in the world today. At the same time, Christians engaged in dialogue with neighbors of other faiths will be compelled to rethink their own faith in the light of issues and experiences raised by the dialogue. Part II of the Chiang Mai statement deals with reasons for the dialogue and with the theological significance of other faiths. Part III contains guidelines recommended to the churches for study and action.

ON DIALOGUE*

C. REASONS FOR DIALOGUE

16. The term "dialogue in community" is useful in that it gives concreteness to Christian reflection on dialogue. Moreover it focuses attention on the reasons for

---

*Reprinted from *Guidelines on Dialogue with People of Living Faiths and Ideologies* (Geneva: WCC, 1979).

being in dialogue, which can be identified in two related categories.

Most Christians today live out their lives in actual community with people who may be committed to faiths and ideologies other than their own. They live in families sometimes of mixed faiths and ideologies; they live as neighbours in the same towns and villages; they need to build up their relationships expressing mutual human care and searching for mutual understanding. This sort of dialogue is very practical, concerned with the problems of modern life – the social, political, ecological, and, above all, the ordinary and familiar.

But there are concerns beyond the local which require Christians to engage in dialogue towards the realization of a wider community in which peace and justice may be more fully realized. This leads in turn to a dialogue between communities, in which issues of national and international concern are tackled.

17. No more than "community" can "dialogue" be precisely defined. Rather it has to be described, experienced and developed as a life-style. As human beings we have learned to speak; we talk, chatter, give and receive information, have discussions – all this is not yet dialogue. Now and then it happens that out of our talking and our relationships arises a deeper encounter, an opening up, in more than intellectual terms, of each to the concerns of the other. This is experienced by families and friends, and by those who share the same faiths, or ideology; but we are particularly concerned with the dialogue which reaches across differences of faith, ideology and culture, even where the partners in dialogue do not agree on important central aspects of human life. Dialogue can be recognized as a welcome way of obedience to the commandment of the Decalogue: "You shall not bear false witness against your neighbour". Dialogue helps us not to disfigure the image of our neighbours of different faiths and ideologies. It has been the experience of many Christians that this dialogue is indeed possible on the basis of a mutual trust and a respect for the integrity of each participant's identity.

18. Dialogue, therefore, is a fundamental part of Christian service within community. In dialogue Christians actively respond to the command to "love God and your neighbour as yourself". As an expression of love engagement in dialogue testifies to the love experienced in Christ. It is a joyful affirmation of life against chaos, and a participation with all who are allies of life seeking the provisional goals of a better human community. Thus "dialogue in community" is not a secret weapon in the armoury of an aggressive Christian militancy. Rather it is a means of living our faith in Christ in service of community with one's neighbours.

19. In this sense dialogue has a distinctive and rightful place within Christian life, in a manner directly comparable to other forms of service. But "distinctive" does not mean totally different or separate. In dialogue Christians seek "to speak the truth in a spirit of love", not naively "to be tossed to and fro, and be carried about with every wind of doctrine" (Eph. 4:14-15). In giving their witness they recognize that in most circumstances today the spirit of dialogue is necessary. For this reason we do not see dialogue and the giving of witness as standing in any contradiction to one another. Indeed, as Christians enter dialogue with their commitment to Jesus Christ, time and time again the relationship of dialogue gives opportunity for authentic witness. Thus, to the member churches of the WCC we feel able with integrity to commend the way of dialogue as one in which Jesus Christ can be confessed in the world today; at the same time we feel able with integrity to assure our partners in dialogue that we come not as manipulators but as genuine fellow pilgrims, to speak with them of what we believe God to have done in Jesus Christ who has gone before us, but whom we seek to meet anew in dialogue.

D. THE THEOLOGICAL SIGNIFICANCE OF PEOPLE OF OTHER FAITHS AND IDEOLOGIES

20. Christians engaged in faithful "dialogue in community" with people of other faiths and ideologies cannot avoid asking themselves penetrating questions about the place of these people in the activity of God in history. They ask these questions not in theory, but in terms of what God may be doing in the lives of hundreds of millions of men and women who live in and seek community together with Christians, but along different ways. So dialogue should proceed in terms of people of other faiths and ideologies rather than of theoretical, impersonal systems. This is not to deny the importance of religious traditions and their inter-relationships but it is vital to examine how faiths and ideologies have given direction to the daily living of individuals and groups and actually affect dialogue on both sides.

21. Approaching the theological questions in this spirit Christians should proceed . . .

with repentance, because they know how easily they misconstrue God's revelation in Jesus Christ, betraying it in their actions and posturing as the owners of God's truth rather than, as in fact they are, the undeserving recipients of grace;

with humility, because they so often perceive in people of other faiths and ideologies a spirituality, dedication, compassion and a wisdom which should forbid them making judgements about others as though from a position of superiority; in particular they should avoid using ideas such as "anonymous Christians", "the Christian presence", "the unknown Christ", in ways not intended by those who proposed them for theological purposes or in ways prejudicial to the self-understanding of Christians and others;

with joy, because it is not themselves they preach; it is Jesus Christ, perceived by many people of living faiths and ideologies as prophet, holy one, teacher, example; but confessed by Christians as Lord and Saviour, Himself the faithful witness and the coming one (Rev. 1.5-7);

with integrity, because they do not enter into dialogue with others except in this penitent and humble joyfulness in the Lord Jesus Christ, making clear to others their own experience and witness, even as they seek to hear from others their expressions of deepest conviction and insight. All these would mean an openness and exposure, the capacity to be wounded which we see in the example of our Lord Jesus Christ and which we sum up in the word vulnerability.

22. Only in this spirit can Christians hope to address themselves creatively to the theological questions posed by other faiths and by ideologies. Christians from different backgrounds are growing in understanding in the following areas in particular:

that renewed attention must be given to the doctrine of creation, particularly as they may see it illuminated by the Christian understanding of God as one Holy Trinity and by the resurrection and glorification of Christ;

that fundamental questions about the nature and activity of God and the doctrine of the Spirit arise in dialogue, and the christological discussion must take place with this comprehensive reference;

that the Bible, with all the aids to its understanding and appropriation from the churches' tradition and scholarship, is to be used creatively as the basis for Christian reflection on the issues that arise, giving both encouragement and warning, though it cannot be assumed as a reference point for partners in dialogue;

that the theological problems of church unity also need to be viewed in relation to the concern for dialogue;

that the aim of dialogue is not reduction of living faiths and ideologies to the lowest common denominator, not only a comparison and discussion of symbols and concepts, but the enabling of a true encounter between those spiritual insights and experiences which are only found at the deepest levels of human life.

23. We look forward to further fruitful discussions of these issues (among many others) within our Christian circles and also in situations of dialogue. There are other questions, where agreement is more difficult and sometimes impossible, but these also we commend for further theological attention:

What is the relation between the universal creative/redemptive activity of God towards all humankind and the particular creative/redemptive activity of God in the history of Israel and in the person and work of Jesus Christ?

Are Christians to speak of God's work in the lives of all men and women only in tentative terms of hope that they may experience something of Him, or more positively in terms of God's self-disclosure to people of living faiths and ideologies and in the struggle of human life?

How are Christians to find from the Bible criteria in their approach to people of other faiths and ideologies, recognizing, as they must, the authority accorded to the Bible by Christians of all centuries, particular questions concerning the authority of the Old Testament for the Christian Church, and the fact that the partners in dialogue have other starting points and resources, both in holy books and traditions of teaching?

What is the biblical view and Christian experience of the operation of the Holy Spirit, and is it right and helpful to understand the work of God outside the Church in terms of the doctrine of the Holy Spirit?

E. SYNCRETISM

24. In dialogue Christians are called to be adventurous, and they must be ready to take risks, but also to be watchful and wide awake for God. Is syncretism a danger for which Christians must be alert?

25. There is a positive need for a genuine "translation" of the Christian message in every time and place. This need is recognized as soon as the Bible translators begin their work in a particular language and have to weigh the cultural and philosophical overtones and undertones of its words. But there is also a wider "translation" of the message by expressing it in artistic, dramatic, liturgical and above all in relational terms which are appropriate to convey the authenticity of the message in ways authentically indigenous, often through the theologically tested use of the symbols and concepts of a particular community.

26. Despite attempts to rescue the word "syncretism" it now conveys, after its previous uses in Christian debate, a negative evaluation. This is clearly the case if it means, as the Nairobi Assembly used the word, "conscious or unconscious human attempts to create a new religion composed of elements taken from different religions". In this sense syncretism is also rejected by the dialogue partners, although there may be some who in their alienation are seeking help from many sources and do not regard syncretism negatively.

27. The word "syncretism" is, however, more widely used than at Nairobi and particularly to warn against two other dangers.

The first danger is that in attempting to "translate" the Christian message for a cultural setting or in approach to faiths and ideologies with which Christians are in dialogue partnership, they may go too far and compromise the authenticity of

Christian faith and life. They have the Bible to guide them but there is always risk in seeking to express the Gospel in a new setting: for instance, the early Christian struggle against heresy in the debate with Gnosticism; or the compromising of the Gospel in the so-called "civil religions" of the West. It is salutary to examine such examples lest it be supposed that syncretism is a risk endemic only in certain continents.

A second danger is that of interpreting a living faith not in its own terms but in terms of another faith or ideology. This is illegitimate on the principles of both scholarship and dialogue. In this way Christianity may be "syncretized" by seeing it as only a variant of some other approach to God, or another faith may be wrongly "syncretized" by seeing it only as partial understanding of what Christians believe that they know in full. There is a particular need for further study of the way in which this kind of syncretism can take place between a faith and an ideology.

28. Both these are real dangers and there will be differences of judgement among Christians and between churches as to when these dangers are threatening, or have actually overtaken particular Christian enterprises. Despite the recognized dangers Christians should welcome and gladly engage in the venture of exploratory faith. The particular risks of syncretism in the modern world should not lead Christians to refrain from dialogue, but are an additional reason for engaging in dialogue so that the issues may be clarified.

29. Within the ecumenical movement the practice of dialogue and the giving of witness have sometimes evoked mutual suspicion. God is very patient with the Church, giving it space and time for discovery of His way and its riches (cf. II Pet. 3.9). There is need within the ecumenical fellowship to give one another space and time – space and time, for instance, in India or Ghana to explore the richness of the Gospel in a setting very different from that of "Hellenized" Europe; space and time, for instance, in Korea to develop the present striking evangelistic work of the churches; space and time, for instance, in Europe to adjust to a new situation in which secularity is now being changed by new religious interest not expressed in traditional terms. The diversity of dialogue itself must be recognized in its particular content and in its relation to specific context.

GUIDELINES RECOMMENDED TO THE CHURCHES FOR STUDY AND ACTION

From the experiences of Christians in dialogue with people of living faiths and ideologies and from the statement of the Central Committee on "Dialogue in Community" it is evident that dialogue has become urgent for many Christians today. The *Guidelines* which follow are built upon the Christian convictions expressed in the first two parts of this statement; the statement and the guidelines should be read together.

It is Christian faith in the Triune God – Creator of all humankind, Redeemer in Jesus Christ, revealing and renewing Spirit – which calls us Christians to human relationship with our many neighbours. Such relationship includes dialogue: witnessing to our deepest convictions and listening to those of our neighbours. It is Christian faith which sets us free to be open to the faiths of others, to risk, to trust and to be vulnerable. In dialogue, conviction and openness are held in balance.

In a world in which Christians have many neighbours, dialogue is not only an activity of meetings and conferences, it is also a way of living out Christian faith in relationship and commitment to those neighbours with whom Christians share towns, cities, nations, and the earth as a whole. Dialogue is a style of living in relationship with neighbours. This in no way replaces or limits our Christian obligation to witness, as partners enter into dialogue with their respective commitments.

These guidelines are offered to member churches of the WCC and to individual congregations in awareness of the great diversity of situations in which they find themselves. The neighbours with whom Christians enter into relationship in dialogue may be partners in common social, economic and political crises and quests; companions in scholarly work or intellectual and spiritual exploration; or, literally, the people next door. In some places, Christians and the church as an institution are in positions of power and influence, and their neighbours are without power. In other places it is the Christians who are the powerless. There are also situations of tension and conflict where dialogue may not be possible or opportunities very limited. In many places people of different faiths interact not only with each other, but also with people of various ideologies, though sometimes it is difficult to make a clearcut distinction between religions and ideologies, for there are religious dimensions of ideologies and ideological dimensions of religions, Christianity included. The emergence of new religious groups in many countries has brought new dimensions and tensions to inter-religious relationships. With all this diversity in mind, the following guidelines are commended to member churches for their consideration and discussion, testing and evaluation, and for their elaboration in each specific situation.

3

Christian Witness — Common Witness

1980

JOINT WORKING GROUP

Following the Second Vatican Council, a Joint Working Group was established by the Vatican Secretariat for Christian Unity and the WCC Commission on World Mission and Evangelism. In 1970 the group presented an ecumenical appeal for common witness between local Roman Catholic churches and WCC member churches in a document entitled "Common Witness and Proselytism."

In 1980, taking into account similar appeals in the report of Section I of the Nairobi Assembly, "Confessing Christ Today," in the 1974 Roman Bishops' Synod, the Apostolic Exhortation Evangelii Nuntiandi *(1975), as well as the* Lausanne Covenant *(1974), the JWG issued this enlarged and updated version of the earlier document.*

"Common Witness" is presented as an existing reality, as a theologically grounded imperative, but also as an opportunity that is not without its problems and tensions. The document is further testimony to the ecumenical rapprochement between conciliar ecumenism and Roman Catholicism in the post-Vatican II period.

II. CHRISTIAN WITNESS — COMMON WITNESS*

A) THE COMMON GROUND

15. The command of Jesus Christ and the power of his grace lead the Church to proclaim the Good News he has brought us; finally this Good News is Christ himself. This gospel message gives Christian communities the common ground for their proclamation. They accept the content of the biblical witness and the Creeds of the early Church. Today they desire to reach beyond what separates them by stressing the essential and returning to the foundation of their faith, Jesus Christ (I Cor. 3:11), (cf. *Common Witness and Proselytism*, 2). They recognize that baptism, as the effective sign of their unity, brings them into communion with Christ's fol-

---

*Reprinted from *Common Witness:* A Study Document of the Joint Working Group of the Roman Catholic Church and the World Council of Churches, CWME Series No. 1 (Geneva: WCC-CWME, 1980), 12-20.

lowers and empowers them to confess him as Lord and Saviour. Therefore the Lord's gift of unity already exists among Christians and, although it is not yet realized perfectly, it is real and operative. This unmerited gift requires that witness be borne in common as an act of gratitude and the witness in turn is a means of expressing and deepening unity.

B) THE SOURCE OF WITNESS

i) The Father

16. Christian witness has its source in the Father who testified to Christ his beloved Son, sent visibly into the world. He bore witness to him on the cross and by raising him from the dead through the Holy Spirit. So Christ received the fulness of the Holy Spirit to be in the world, himself the divine fulness for the human family (Col. 2:9-10).

"When God raised up his servant, he sent him to bless you" (Acts 3:26; 26:23). Jesus could say: "I am going away and I shall come back to you" (John 14:28). He who "has become for us wisdom and justification, sanctification and liberation" (I Cor. 1:30) has been sent into the world that those who receive him in faith may find in him that sanctification and liberation. God now sends him into the world in the Church which he has made his body in spite of the sin of its members. The disciple can say: "Christ lives in me" (Gal. 2:20; cf. II Cor. 4:10-12) and "Christ speaks in me" (II Cor. 13:3). Christian witness is an epiphany of Christ who took the form of a servant, and became obedient unto death (Phil. 2:6).

ii) Jesus Christ

17. Jesus Christ is the one witness of God, true and faithful (Rev. 3:14; 1:5; vid. *Confessing Christ Today:* 8, 9, 10). The witness he gave to the Father through his life was sealed by the martyrdom of the cross. His death evidenced total dedication to the witness he bore; it was the testimony he gave to himself as "the truth that liberates" (John 8:32). The cause of the Father had consumed his life to the point of martyrdom. In his death and resurrection his entire existence disclosed the meaning of the message. Through those events he breathed forth his Spirit to animate his followers, drawing them together in the community of witness, his mystical body which is the Church. It would pay a similar price for the witness which he would give through it (I Pet. 5:9). From the beginning the followers of Jesus as confessors and martyrs became the vehicle of the Spirit in their suffering unto death, inseparably linked with the inspired words they uttered in the power of the same Spirit.

iii) The Holy Spirit

18. The Spirit plays such an important role in Christian witness that he too can be said to be the witness of Christ in the world: "The Spirit of truth himself who comes from the Father will bear witness to me" (John 15:26). For it is in the Spirit that God raises Christ (Rom. 8:11); it is in the Spirit that he glorifies him (John 16:14-15); it is the Spirit who convicts the world in the trial which brings it into contradiction with Jesus (John 16:8). The Spirit bears this witness by means of the Church. He makes the Church the body (I Cor. 12:13) and thus the manifestation of Christ in the world. The Spirit is communion (II Cor. 13:13) so he unites us to Christ; and in the same movement, brings about communion among men and women.

19. The Spirit comes upon the faithful and makes them also witnesses of Christ

(Acts 1:8). In him the word and action of Christians become a "demonstration of spirit and power" (I Cor. 2:4). We must encounter Christ to be his witnesses, to be able to say what we know about him (cf. I John 1:3-4; 4:14). It is the Holy Spirit who enables the faithful to meet Christ, to experience him. Believers are led to witness to their faith before humankind, because the Spirit witnesses to Jesus in their hearts (John 15:16-17; Rom. 8:16; Gal. 4:6). In the debate between Jesus and the world, he takes the part of Jesus in strengthening believers in their faith (John 16:8; cf. I John 5: 6), but he also deepens the faith of believers by leading them to the whole truth (John 16:13). He is thus the master of Christian witness enabling us to say "Jesus is Lord" (I Cor. 12:3), he is the inspiration and teacher of the Church (John 16:13).

C) THE CHURCH

20. The Church received its commission from the Lord Jesus Christ himself, "You shall be my witnesses" (Acts 1:8). It takes upon itself the witness which the Father bore to his Son (cf. John 5:32) when, in front of those who put him to death, he raised him and made him Christ and Lord for the salvation of all (Acts 2:23, 24, 36). The Christian witness receives its incarnation and force out of the calling of the People of God to be a pilgrim people giving witness to Christ our Lord in communion with the cloud of witnesses (Heb. 12:1).

21. Following the apostles (Acts 2:32) the Church today testifies to these saving acts of God in front of the world and proclaims that Jesus Christ is Saviour and Lord of all mankind and of all creation. Through proclamation and bearing witness, Christians are making known the saving Lordship of Christ, so that the one in whom God wills to achieve this salvation may be "believed in the world" (I Tim. 3:16), so that people may confess "that Jesus Christ is Lord to the glory of God the Father" (Phil. 2:11).

The Church as a whole is the primary subject of Christian witness. As the Church is one body of many members, Christian witness is by its nature communitarian. When one of the faithful acts in individual witness this is related to the witness of the whole Christian community. Even when the witness is given by Christians in separated churches it should be witness to the same Christ and necessarily has a communitarian aspect.

D) CHARACTERISTICS OF CHRISTIAN WITNESS

22. Witness was a distinctive mark of the Church in the time of the apostles. In giving its witness today the Church continues to be faithful to this apostolic commission. Through the same Holy Spirit it shares their motivation and power. As the body of Christ the Church manifests him in the world. Its nature is to give witness.

23. Witness is what we are before God. It consists in the first place in being. It ought to be rooted in contemplation. The Church is already giving witness then when it deepens its spiritual life and when it devises new styles of life which commend the Gospel in today's world. In many parts of the world Christians are discovering this afresh by their experiences in small communities, but the need of renewal extends to all manifestations of the life of the Body.

Aware of the failings of those who belong to it, the Church seeks in its worship to be transformed into the likeness of Christ. He must be shown to the world in its members. For this the Church needs the nourishment it draws from prayer, the

Word and the Sacraments. It depends on the continual renewal they provide for the authenticity and effectiveness of its witness.

24. Authentic witness is a channel of the divine love to all people. That love expresses itself in discerning the ways in which witness can be given most tellingly in each circumstance of contact. In some sense readiness for martyrdom is the norm of witness since it testifies to the orientation of a life which is itself a sign of a person's conviction and devotion to a cause, even to the point of dying for one's belief. It is conviction incarnated in life which must make proclamation credible. The authenticity of witness is finally to be judged not by the listener's response, but before God. From this point of view there is a gratuitousness about witness that is to be associated with the gratuitousness of God's grace in his dealings with humankind. It is in the life of the witness that the message of the Gospel has to be made present. The life of the witness is the valid exposition of the message. It is from this point that the necessary effort to make the Christian message speak to people and situations has to begin and no ready-made formula can be a substitute. There must always be a dialogue established between situations and people and the Church, for there is a necessary listening process in discovering effective means of witness. Since the medium through which the sign comes to others and communicates its meaning to them is important, the sign has to be given expression in terms of each society and culture.

25. Witness seeks a response, but there is always an element of mystery and miracle about the way in which the witness the Spirit gives to Jesus comes home to the heart of a person. It is always something fresh, often totally surprising and unexpected.

26. The witness of Christ has to be given and shaped by the community which lives in Christ and is animated by a spirit of love and freedom, confidence and joy. Words alone cannot stress sufficiently that the love of God has come to us through Christ, that it has overcome sin and death, and that it lives on among us. It demands a comprehensive witness, credible and full of love, given both by the Christian and the Church in every part of life. Without love such witness is only "a sounding gong or clanging cymbal" (I Cor. 13:1). The liberating action of Christ must mean that witness is given in freedom and with respect for the freedom of those to whom it is addressed.

27. Christian witness also must be given in humility. Its source is in the Father who, by the Spirit, raised Christ from the dead and sends him visibly to humankind by means of those who are his witnesses. It is therefore a commission from God, not something one takes upon oneself. It requires the witness to listen before proclaiming the Good News and to cooperate with the unpredictable leading of the Spirit. It does not provide a blueprint that will guarantee success in all situations. Rather it is the task of a co-worker with God in the service of all peoples.

E) EFFECTS OF WITNESS

28. Witness moves from one unity to another—from that of the members of the Body of Christ in the one Spirit to the greater unity in which all things in heaven and earth will come together under the one Head who is Christ (Eph. 1:10). Essentially it is a work of reconciliation, of people with God, and with one another. To take part in Christian witness also deepens the unity that already exists among Christians. Witness tends always to extend the fellowship of the Spirit, creating new community. At the same time it is an essential help for Christians themselves. It

promotes among them the conversion and renewal which they always need. It can strengthen their faith and open up new aspects of the truth of Christ. As such it is a fundamental part of the life of the community that is fully committed to Christ.

29. When witness is being given in a context of unbelief it often calls forth opposition. The Church has to be ready to pay the price of misunderstanding, frustration and suffering, even, on occasion, of martyrdom. From the beginning the reality of the Cross has been the inevitable context of Christian witness (II Cor. 4:8-12). That witness has to be made also before the principalities and powers of this age (Eph. 6:12; cf. Rom. 8:38-39). The experience of Christians in exile, prison and the arena in other times is often repeated today. The Church has to bring its message of love and reconciliation to even the most difficult situations so it is not surprised when its witness has to be given even at the cost of life itself.

F) COMMON WITNESS

30. When he prayed that all be one so the world might believe (John 17:21), Jesus made a clear connection between the unity of the Church and the acceptance of the Gospel. Unhappily Christians are still divided in their churches and the testimony they give to the Gospel is thus weakened. There are, however, even now many signs of the initial unity that already exists among all followers of Christ and indications that it is developing in important ways. What we have in common, and the hope that is in us, enable us to be bold in proclaiming the Gospel and trustful that the world will receive it. Common witness is the essential calling of the Church and in an especial way it responds to the spirit of this ecumenical age in the Church's life. It expresses our actual unity and increases our service to God's Word, strengthening the churches both in proclaiming the Gospel and in seeking for the fulness of unity.

31. Yet the tragedy of our divisions remains with us at the focal point of our testimony to Jesus: the Holy Eucharist. It is urgent that all Christians intensify their prayer for the full realization of this unity and witness.

"This fellowship in prayer, nevertheless, sharpens the pain of the churches' division at the point of eucharistic fellowship which should be the most manifest witness of the one sacrifice of Christ for the whole world" (*Common Witness and Proselytism*, 16).

G) SITUATIONS OF COMMON WITNESS

32. Common witness is called for in a great many different situations. The variety of groups and individuals taking part in some act of common witness should make it possible to have a more realistic awareness of the situation, to adapt to it in solidarity and to orient the witness concretely to it.

33. This does not at all mean diluting the truth of the Gospel to fit every situation. Rather those who hand it on and those who receive it must undergo change. Thus common witness should bring about the creative transformation of a given situation.

34. Witness does not mean debating possibilities but brings people to face reality. It calls forth reflection, discussion, decision. In every thing those who witness should show they have Good News to proclaim. The Kingdom of God whose coming they have to proclaim in word and deed consists in "justice, peace and joy in the Holy Spirit" (Rom. 14:17).

H) IN THE WORLD

35. In bearing this witness Christians are committing themselves to the service of others, for it is the Good News of God they are bringing (Acts 13:32, 33). Through proclaiming the cross and resurrection of Christ they affirm that God wills the salvation of his people in all dimensions of their being, both eternal and earthly.

36. The whole of creation groans and is in travail as it seeks adoption and redemption (Rom. 8:22). Salvation in Jesus Christ has cosmic dimensions. Christian witness is given not only to fulfill a missionary vocation but also to respond to the aspirations of the universe. Human needs and the challenge of a broken and unbelieving world compel the churches to cooperate with God in using his gifts for the reconciliation of all peoples and things in Christ.

The contemporary thirst for meaning, for a spiritual base, for God, is also an occasion for common witness by the full manifestation of Jesus Christ in prayer, worship and in daily life.

37. The search for Gospel values such as human dignity, justice, peace and fraternity invites participation by a common witness, which always points to Jesus Christ as Lord and Saviour of all. This means Christian involvement in matters of social justice in the name of the poor and the oppressed. We must relearn the patristic lesson that the Church is the mouth and the voice of the oppressed in the presence of the powers that be. Thus Christian witness will mean participation in the struggle for human rights, at all levels, in economic sharing and in liberation from social and political oppression. All are parts of the task required by obedience to the truth of God and its consequences.

38. In fact in the last decade there has been a most positive advance in a variety of common witness at all these levels of Christian life. A growing sensitivity to the manipulative attitudes and behaviour often fostered by contemporary cultures is forcing Christian churches and communities to a drastic reappraisal of their relation to the world in mission, and is bringing them together to witness to the gifts of truth and life bestowed in Christ, which are the source of their life and which provide access to salvation (cf. *Common Witness and Proselytism*, 11).

III. REALIZATIONS OF COMMON WITNESS

A) OCCASIONS AND POSSIBILITIES

39. Christ's commission to his Church (Matt. 28:18-20) and the gift of the Spirit to enable this task to be fulfilled impose a missionary obligation upon Christians in every circumstance. It causes them to cross social and geographical boundaries: yet it is present also in their everyday surroundings. It demands obedience even in situations where explicit preaching is impossible and witness has usually to be silent.

40. The inspired phrase from the Faith and Order meeting in Lund 1952 invited the churches to do all things together except where fidelity to conscience would forbid. Yet so many years later we are not yet putting this into practice. It is a principle which if applied would multiply enormously the occasions of common witness, putting it in the daily agenda of each church. Its intent was expressed in *Common Witness and Proselytism*, 13: "Christians cannot remain divided in their witness. Any situation where contact and cooperation between churches are refused must be regarded as abnormal."

41. By coming together in witness it becomes possible to know and recognize

the manifold gifts that God has granted to his Church. The peculiar history, tradition and experience which each brings enriches the quality of the common witness. Instead of each losing identity, it is seen in the wider context of the one Church willed by Christ in which all are to grow to the fulness of Christ in whom is their final destiny. Specific gifts are not eliminated but rather increase their potential for witness, and the value of other traditions is discovered and enhanced.

42. Thus common witness influences the whole of our witness to Jesus Christ. It does not eliminate distinctive witness but enriches it and it centres the emphasis in the common treasure of the Gospel—Jesus Christ is Lord and Saviour. The invitation to join the family of the Church will always be made with due respect to the integrity of the Gospel message, to the catholicity of the Church and the fulness of unity which is sought. The respective witness of various confessions could often respond to geographical, linguistic and cultural situations. As Christians and churches grow together in unity, the witness given in separation will become progressively a dimension and complementary part of the total witness given by all Christians to Jesus Christ.

43. Common initiatives defending and promoting human dignity are by their nature a privileged field of common witness. The groups engaged in them often have a deep experience of Christian community, especially when they draw their strength from common prayer and Bible work and to the extent that the members are rooted in their own liturgies. Such communities of service are a sign of the kingdom.

44. Evangelization by direct proclamation which is organized together, retreats, Bible courses, study and action groups, religious education undertaken jointly or in collaboration are an expression of growing acceptance of the primacy of the saving truth and essential kerygma which announces Jesus as Lord and Saviour, present and acting now in his Spirit. Therefore, joint or coordinated pastoral and missionary actions are instances of common witness or at least prepare the ground and the preliminary structures to enable it.

45. Intrinsic clarity of meaning is a test which must be applied to witness. Do people really experience it as a good gift coming from above? Is it transparent to those of good will?

46. Common witness is also given through reciprocal support. The hope is to see Christians of all confessions side by side as they share by word and deed in testifying to the saving will of God. For various reasons of language, history, ideology, this is not always possible. In such a case the witness given by one church or group of Christians can however be supported by the prayers, gifts, visits and sympathy of others. Thus the witness given by Orthodox, Catholics, Anglicans or Protestants becomes in a sense the vicarious means of presenting the witness of other Christians too. So the faithful witness given by one church in a particular place can be part of the rich and diverse witness of the whole Church. The Church cannot shut its eyes to the sufferings, injustices and violence taking place within a large proportion of humankind but, when she is not able to express openly the cries and appeals of all those who suffer, she should seek to make possible a silent witness of solidarity and intercession.

B) PROBLEMS AND TENSIONS

47. We recognize that for "conscience sake" our churches sometimes feel obliged not only to a separate witness, but even to a contradictory one. While we pray and

work for the fulness of church unity we recognize the existence of divisions as a reality to be taken into account. The honesty of our common witness is demonstrated by the open and public nature of our disagreement. We believe that the expression of different solutions for ethical issues will highlight the importance and credibility of our common witness. A divided witness can become a counter witness. The reality of our divisions will therefore always be a call to common prayer, study and research, in the hope that we will grow in unity and love.

48. In its witness the Church addresses the Gospel to a specific situation or context. Common witness also in order to be effective must be concrete. The challenge and condition for common witness may be very different from one situation to another. Cultural, historical, and socio-political factors will contribute to the shaping of it.

This can however lead to tensions and even new divisions within one church or between churches. What is a powerful common witness in one place may be perceived as a source of division in another. The more honestly this problem is being recognized the more creative the tension may become.

49. The activities entailed in giving witness can bring tensions. Some of these are healthy; others create or exacerbate tension between or within churches. It may be for example that some Christians who are active in local communities feel the pace of ecumenical advance should be more rapid. In their own informal experiences of living, working, and praying together they may have discovered a communion which they claim is so developed as to call for expressions that go beyond what official teaching or discipline permits. In such cases it can be very difficult to work out a solution that respects the values at stake and the integrity of those concerned. Hence the need to keep alive dialogue and communication. The occurrence and difficulty of such situations seems to indicate there should be some study of them as an ecumenical problem that calls for attention.

50. Christians of all churches agree that membership in the Church is an essential part of the Christian message. The Gospel invitation to accept Christ as Lord and Saviour is an invitation also to be a member of His Body, a member of a local church in communion with all the churches, which together live the word of God in faith, sacrament and witness.

51. When churches are still divided and not yet at one in understanding the Gospel of Christ, this necessary connection of witness and community, of proclamation and church membership raises the question of those kinds of witness which are distorted by certain motives, attitudes, behaviour and methods. These are called proselytism and must be evaluated as an unworthy kind of witness. The problem has been stated and treated in the 1970 study *Common Witness and Proselytism*, 25-28. Much of the material is still useful for situations where the problem is actual.

52. In the first place proselytism includes whatever violates the right of the human person, Christian or non-Christian, to be free from every type of physical coercion, moral restraint or psychological pressure which could deprive a person or a community of freedom of judgement and responsible choice. The truth and love of God must always be offered and accepted in freedom.

53. Proselytism also means anything in the proclamation of the Gospel which replaces selfless love by personal or group egoism, substitutes the primary trust in the surprises of the Spirit with an over-confidence in one's own predetermined methods and programmes, fears the truth by misrepresenting the beliefs and practices of other religious communities in the hope of winning adherents.

IV. STRUGGLE AND HOPE

63. Common witness is deeply rooted in our faith and is a demand of the very Gospel we proclaim. Its urgency is underlined when we realize the seriousness of the human predicament and the tremendous task waiting for the churches at present. Common witness is not an abstract theological concept. It is very much more than friendly ecumenical relations. It is a responsible way of relating to the human problems of today: the growing traffic in human life through prostitution or in drugs, the corruption in international economic practice, the armaments race, the growing power of the mass media in shaping people's minds. We discover that those challenges touch each and all of the churches when we look beyond our own and see the millions of people who do not know the Gospel of Jesus Christ. There is a pressing need to join forces to proclaim the Gospel of the kingdom to all peoples. A common effort is required that will multiply our capacity to give a clear and powerful witness. Faced with the challenge of the world, the churches in joining forces to witness to Jesus Christ will find new spiritual strength, new relevance for the human predicament.

64. Often it is socially and politically more difficult to witness together since the powers of this world promote division. In such situations common witness is particularly precious and Christ-like. Witness that dares to be common is a powerful sign of unity coming directly and visibly from Christ and a glimpse of his kingdom.

65. In a world where there is confusion, where many people seem uncertain, the search for unity and a common witness is an act and sign of hope. Unity is required to face the challenge, and as the churches respond they will in turn be led into the fuller unity which the Lord wills and by the means he wills. It is an integral part of the hope that all humankind will be confronted with the full presence of God in judgement and grace. Waiting for the eschatological test of their witness, already rejoicing in the risen life of Christ through the gifts of the Holy Spirit, Christians are required to give courageous account of the hope that is in them.

4

Your Kingdom Come

Melbourne, 1980

WORLD CONFERENCE ON MISSION AND EVANGELISM

The 1980 CWME World Conference on Mission and Evangelism, held in Melbourne, Australia, from May 12-25, 1980, was the third in the series of WCC-sponsored global conferences on mission (following Mexico City, 1963, and Bangkok, 1973). It ranks as one of the most important and influential ecumenical missionary conferences for this period.

The theme chosen for the conference, "Your Kingdom Come," implies both a call to pray for the coming of God's kingdom and also to work actively for its coming. The theme is developed under four sectional issues: I. "Good News to the Poor"; II. "The Kingdom of God and Human Struggles"; III. "The Church Witnesses to the Kingdom"; and IV. "Christ—Crucified and Risen—Challenges Human Power."

While the kingdom was the main theme, focus on the poor and the church's response to the poor became the defining feature of the Melbourne meeting. Following Melbourne it was said that the church's relation to the poor had become the new yardstick for judging its missionary faithfulness. This CWME meeting followed closely on the heels of the Third Latin American Conference of Catholic Bishops (Puebla, 1979), at which the church's "preferential option" for the poor was reaffirmed.

SECTION I: GOOD NEWS TO THE POOR*

THE POOR AND THE RICH AND THE COMING OF THE KINGDOM

1. The kingdom of God which was inaugurated in Jesus Christ brings justice, love, peace and joy, and freedom from the grasp of principalities and powers, those demonic forces which place human lives and institutions in bondage and infiltrate their very textures. God's judgment is revealed as an overturning of the values and

---

* Reprinted from *Your Kingdom Come: Mission Perspectives,* Report on the World Conference on Mission and Evangelism, Melbourne, Australia, 12-25 May, 1980 (Geneva: WCC-CWME, 1980), 171-178, 193-207.

structures of this world. In the perspective of the kingdom, God has a preference for the poor.

Jesus announced at the beginning of his ministry, drawing upon the Word given to the prophet Isaiah, "The Spirit of the Lord is upon me, because he has anointed me to preach the good news to the poor . . . " (Luke 4.18). This announcement was not new; God had shown his preference for the poor throughout the history of Israel. When Israel was a slave in Egypt, God sent Moses to lead the people out to the land which he had promised, where they established a society according to God's revelation given through Moses, a society in which all were to share equally. After they had come into the land, God required them to remember that they had once been slaves. Therefore, they should care for the widow, the fatherless, the sojourner within their gates, their debtors, their children, their servants and even their animals (Deut. 5.13-15, 15.1-18). Time and again the prophets had to remind Israel of the need to stand for the poor and oppressed and to work for God's justice.

God identified with the poor and oppressed by sending his Son Jesus to live and serve as a Galilean speaking directly to the common people; promising to bless those who met the needs of the hungry, the thirsty, the stranger, the naked, the sick and the prisoner; and finally meeting death on a cross as a political offender. The good news handed on to the Church is that God's grace was in Jesus Christ, who "though he was rich, yet for your sake he became poor, so that by his poverty you might become rich" (II Cor. 8.9).

2. Poverty in the Scriptures is affliction, deprivation and oppression. But it can also include abundant joy and overflow in liberality (II Cor. 8.1f). The Gospel which has been given to the Christian Church must express this continuing concern of God for the poor to whom Jesus has granted the blessing of the kingdom.

Jesus' blessing for the poor challenges everyone and shows how the kingdom of God is to be received. The poor are "blessed" because of their longing for justice and their hope for liberation. They accept the promise that God has come to their rescue, and so discover in his promise their hopes for liberation and a life of human dignity.

3. The Good News to the rich affirms what Jesus proclaims as the Gospel for the poor, that is, a calling to trust in God and his abundant mercy. This is a call to repentance:

—to renounce the security of wealth and material possessions which is, in fact, idolatry;

—to give up the exploiting power which is the demonic feature of wealth; and

—to turn away from indifference and enmity toward the poor and toward solidarity with the oppressed.

4. The coming of the kingdom as hope for the poor is thus a time of judgement for the rich. In the light of this judgement and this hope, all human beings are shown to be less than human. The very identification of people as either rich or poor is now seen to be a symptom of this dehumanization. The poor who are sinned against are rendered less human by being deprived. The rich are rendered less human by the sinful act of depriving others.

The judgement of God thus comes as a verdict in favour of the poor. This verdict enables the poor to struggle to overthrow the powers that bind them, which then releases the rich from the necessity to dominate. Once this has happened, it is possible for both the humbled rich and the poor to become human, capable of response to the challenge of the kingdom.

To the poor this challenge means the profound assurance that God is with them and for them. To the rich it means a profound repentance and renunciation. To all who yearn for justice and forgiveness Jesus Christ offers discipleship and the demand of service. But he offers this in the assurance of victory and in sharing the power of his risen life. As the kingdom in its fulness is solely the gift of God himself, any human achievement in history can only be approximate and relative to the ultimate goal—that promised new heaven and new earth in which justice abides. Yet that kingdom is the inspiration and constant challenge in all our struggles.

THE CHURCHES AND THE POOR

16. The Church of Jesus Christ is called to preach Good News to the poor, even as its Lord has in his ministry announced the kingdom of God to them. The churches cannot neglect this evangelistic task. Most of the world's people are poor and they wait for a witness to the Gospel that will really be "Good News". The Church of Jesus Christ is commissioned to disciple the nations, so that others may know that the kingdom of God has already drawn near and that its signs and first fruits can be seen in the world around the churches, as well as in their own life. Mission that is conscious of the kingdom will be concerned for liberation, not oppression; justice, not exploitation; fulness, not deprivation; freedom, not slavery; health, not disease; life, not death. No matter how the poor may be identified, this mission is for them.

17. As we look at the churches in the world today, we find some places where a new era of evangelization is dawning, where the poor are proclaiming the Good News. We find other places where the churches understand the situation of the poor and have begun to witness in ways that are Good News. . . . The base communities in Latin America are churches of the poor that have been willing to share in their poverty and oppression, so that they can struggle to reach a just society and the end of exploitation. Some local churches and church organizations have been willing to redistribute their wealth for the benefit of the self-development of the poor. Some church leaders and denominational groups have been working to challenge the transnational corporations at their business meetings and in their board rooms. Through ecumenical bodies, churches have joined in the search for a new social, political and economic order, and committed themselves to support those organizations, churches and national leaders that share this vision.

18. We have heard of more places where the churches are indifferent to the situation of the poor or—far worse—actively allied with those forces which have made them poor, while enjoying the fruits of riches that have been accumulated at the expense of the poor. All over the world in many countries with a capitalist system, the churches are part of the establishment, assisting in the maintenance of a status quo that exploits not only nations and nature but the poor of their own country. The churches are alienated from the poor by their middle-class values. Whereas Jesus identified with the poor in his life and ministry, the churches today are full of satisfied, complacent people who are not willing to look at the Lazarus on their doorstep. In some socialist countries, although a measure of economic equality has been achieved, the churches have yet to recognize their responsibility toward the kinds of poverty that still exist among the people. And in developing countries, where poverty is the inescapable lot of the overwhelming majority of the population, some churches have been content to make ways for a limited number of the poor to join the elite without working to overcome injustice. We have also heard many stories of ways in which the missionary enterprise of the churches, both

overseas and in their own countries, has been financed with the fruits of exploitation, conducted in league with oppressive forces, and has failed to join the struggle of the poor and oppressed against injustice. We need to become more aware of these shortcomings and sins, to repent genuinely and find ways to act that will be Good News to the world's poor.

19. The message which the churches proclaim is not only what they preach and write and teach. If they are to preach the Good News, their own lifestyle and what they do—or fail to do—will also carry a message. In his earthly ministry, Jesus Christ was consistent in proclaiming Good News by what he said, what he did and what he was. If the churches are to be faithful disciples and living members of the Body of Christ, they too must be consistent in what they say, what they do and what they are.

20. We wish to *recommend* the following to the churches:

a) Become churches in solidarity with the struggles of the poor

The poor are already in mission to change their own situation. What is required from the churches is a missionary movement that supports what they have already begun, and that focuses on building evangelizing and witnessing communities of the poor that will discover and live out expressions of faith among the masses of the poor and oppressed.

The churches will have to surrender their attitudes of benevolence and charity by which they have condescended to the poor; in many cases this will mean a radical change in the institutional life of the missionary movement. The churches must be ready to listen to the poor, to learn about the ways in which they have helped to make them poor.

Ways of expressing this solidarity are several, but each must be fitted to the situation of the poor and respect their leadership in the work of evangelization and mission. There is the call to act in support of the struggles of the poor against oppression. This means support across national boundaries and between continents, without neglecting the struggles within their own societies. There is the call to participate in the struggle themselves. To free others of poverty and oppression is also to release the bonds that entangle the churches in the web of international exploitation. There is the call to become churches of the poor. Although not all will accept the call to strip themselves of riches, the voluntary joining in the community of the poor of the earth could be the most telling witness to the Good News.

b) Join the struggle against the powers of exploitation and impoverishment

Poverty, injustice and oppression do not voluntarily release their grip on the lives of the poor. Therefore, the struggle against the powers that create and maintain the present situation must be actively entered. These powers include the transnational corporations, governments and the churches themselves and their missionary organizations where they have joined in exploitation and impoverishment. In increasing numbers, those who will claim the rewards that Jesus promised to those who are persecuted or the martyr's crown of victory in today's world are those who join the struggle against these powers at the side of the poor.

c) Establish a new relationship with the poor inside the churches

Many of the poor belong to the churches, but only the voices of a few are heard or their influence felt. The New Testament churches were taught not to be respecters of persons but many churches today have built the structures of status, class, sexual and racial division into their fellowship and organization. The churches should be open to the presence and voice of the poor in their own life. The structures of mission and church life still must be changed to patterns of partnership and servanthood. This will require a more unified mission outreach that does not perpetuate the wastefulness and confusion of denominational divisions. The life-styles of both clergy and lay leaders need to be changed to come closer to the poor. The churches, which now exploit women and youth, will need to create opportunities for them to participate in leadership and decision-making.

d) Pray and work for the kingdom of God

When the churches emphasize their own life, their eyes are diverted from the kingdom of God, the heart of our Lord's message and the hope of the poor. To pray for the kingdom is to concentrate the church's attention on that which God is trying to give to his whole creation. To pray for the kingdom will enable the churches to work more earnestly for its development, to look more eagerly for its signs in human history and to await more patiently its final consummation.

SECTION III: CHURCH WITNESSES TO THE KINGDOM

1. . . . The whole church of God, in every place and time, is a sacrament of the kingdom which came in the person of Jesus Christ and will come in its fulness when he returns in glory.

2. The life and witness of our present churches is very diverse, and it is not our calling to be judges of their value to God. We can only look at some aspects of that life and witness to see how the church can more effectively carry the marks of Christ himself and be a sign of the kingdom.

The proclamation of the word of God is one such witness, distinct and indispensable. The story of God in Christ is the heart of all evangelism, and this story has to be told, for the life of the present church never fully reveals the love and holiness and power of God in Christ. The telling of this story is an inescapable mandate for the whole church; word accompanies deed as the kingdom throws its light ahead of its arrival and men and women seek to live in that light.

The church is called to be a community, a living, sharing fellowship. This sign of the kingdom is evident where our churches are truly open to the poor, the despised, the handicapped. for whom our modern societies have little care. Then a church becomes a witness to the Lord who rejoiced in the company of outcasts.

3. There is a healing ministry which many of us have too readily neglected and which the Spirit is teaching us anew. It is intimately connected with evangelism, as the commissioning of the disciples by Jesus makes plain (Luke 9.1-6). It has to do with the whole person, body, mind and spirit, and it must be related to the healing gift of modern medical science and the traditional skills found in many parts of the world.

As the whole church is set in a world of cultures and nations, we have to witness to the kingdom by reflecting both the universality of the Gospel and its local expression. As Christians work together to serve the needs of struggling people, so they reveal the unifying power of Christ. As they honour the inheritance of each person (culture, language and ideals) so they witness to the personal care of God.

At the centre of the church's life is the Eucharist, the public declaration of thanksgiving for God's gift in Christ, and the participation of the disciples in the very life of Christ. It is a foretaste of the kingdom which proclaims the Lord's death until he comes. We celebrate the Eucharist during the "in-between", recalling God's act in history (anamnesis), experiencing the presence of the risen Lord, and anticipating the great feast at the end when God is all in all.

I. PROCLAMATION OF THE WORD OF GOD

4. The proclamation of the Good News is the announcement that the kingdom of God is at hand, a challenge to repent and an invitation to believe. So Jesus, in proclaiming that the kingdom of God is close at hand, calls for repentance and faith in the Gospel (Mark 1.15). The time has come when the ancient hope as expressed by the prophet Isaiah for that kingdom will be fulfilled. Jesus is sent to proclaim Good News to the poor, release to the captives and sight to the blind, to set at liberty those who are oppressed, to proclaim the acceptable year of the Lord (Luke 4.18-19), as Isaiah had seen in his vision. By Jesus, and in his name, the powers of that kingdom bring liberation and wholeness, dignity and life both to those who hunger after justice and to those who struggle with consumerism, greed, selfishness and death.

The kingdom of God is made plain as the Holy Spirit reveals Jesus Christ to us. The Word has become flesh in him, and his followers proclaim in ever new ways and words the glories of their Saviour. Paul says it with singular fulness and intensity: therefore if anyone is in Christ—new creation! The old has passed away; behold, the new has come. All this is from God who, through Christ, has reconciled us to himself and given us the ministry of reconciliation. It is the kingdom that we proclaim until it comes, by telling the story of Jesus Christ, teacher and healer, crucified and risen, truly human and truly divine, Saviour and Lord.

5. There are false proclamations and false gospels, which use the language of the Bible to draw people not toward God as revealed in Jesus but a God made by human imagination. One part of the church's teaching is to help people discern for themselves this distinction.

6. Proclamation is the responsibility of the whole church and of every member, although the Spirit endows some members with special gifts to be evangelists, and a great diversity of witness is found. Both the church and those within it who are gifted as evangelists are themselves part of the message they proclaim. The credibility of the proclamation of the Word of God rests upon the authenticity of the total witness of the church.

Authentic proclamation will be the spontaneous offering of a church (a) which is a truly worshipping community, (b) which is able to welcome outsiders, (c) whose members offer their service in both church and society, and (d) which is ready to move like a pilgrim. Such a church will not defend the privileges of a select group, but rather will affirm the God-given rights of all. It is the Lord who chooses his witnesses, however, particularly those who proclaim the Good News from inside a situation—the poor, the suffering and the oppressed—and strengthens them through the Holy Spirit with the power of the incarnated Word.

7. The proclamation of the Good News is a continual necessity and all people, believers and unbelievers, are challenged to hear and respond since conversion is never finished. We acknowledge and gladly accept our special obligation to those who have never heard the Good News of the kingdom. New frontiers are continually being discovered. Jesus our Lord is always ahead of us and draws us to follow him, often in unexpected ways. The Christian community is a community on the way,

making its proclamation, both to itself and to those beyond its fellowship, even as it shows forth its other marks "on the way". On this pilgrimage, proclamation is always linked to a specific situation and a specific moment in history. It is God's Good News contrasted with the bad news of that specific situation. We therefore affirm present efforts within the church to contextualize the Gospel in every culture.

8. One area of concern is the widespread oppression of women in both church and society, and we look with gratitude and expectation to the work of those women who are seeking to proclaim a Gospel of Liberation for both women and men.

10. Preaching expects conversion. Conversion resulting from the action of the Holy Spirit may be individual, spiritual or emotional—and these three elements are of vital importance—but much more is entailed. It involves a turning *from* and a turning *to*. It always implies a transfer of loyalty and means becoming a citizen of God's kingdom through faith in Jesus Christ. Conversion involves leaving our old security behind (Matt. 16.24) and putting ourselves at risk in a life of faith. This leads to a degree of earthly homelessness (Matt. 8.20), for even the church is only an emergency residence (paroikia).

Conversion implies a new relationship both with God and with others and involves becoming part of a community of believers. It is individual and societal, vertical and horizontal, faith and works (James 2.19-20). It has to do with things which may not be bad in themselves, but which stand in the way of our relationship with God and our fellows (Gen. 22; Phil, 3.2-8; Luke 18.22; Luke 3.13). It is an ongoing process.

No one can know the kingdom of God present in Jesus and accept that authority except by the Spirit. This is so far-reaching and decisive an experience that Jesus referred to it as "being born all over again" (John 3.3-8) and Paul as "putting on the new self which is created in God's likeness" (Eph. 4.24).

II. IN SEARCH OF A LIVING COMMUNITY AT THE LOCAL LEVEL, OR LIVING THE FUTURE NOW

11. The church should be searching for an authentic community in Christ at the local level. This will encompass but be larger than the local church community because the kingdom is wider than the church. The kingdom is seen as an inclusive and open reality, stretching to include people irrespective of their sex, race, age and colour, and it is found in caring and fulfilling relationships and environments where people are reconciled and liberated to become what God wants them to be. It is not self-preserving but self-denying. The kingdom is found in the willingness to accept suffering and sacrifices for others. Also in willingness to reflect on and respond to needs and ideas beyond our own community, thus entering into dialogue and service. The concerns, convictions, aspirations and needs of individuals and groups are received with understanding. . . .

12. As Christians, we recognize the discrepancy between the reality of the kingdom of God and the actual conditions of our empirical local congregations. Some of us have therefore sought different ways for bringing the fellowship of the church toward a clearer likeness of the fellowship of the kingdom that Christ proclaimed. The institutional church is not to be rejected as it is one of the forms in which renewal can occur. Under the influence of liturgical and sacramental renewal, charismatic movements and parish weekend retreats, local congregations are attempting to realize the fulness of Christian fellowship. House churches and other small prayer and study groups are providing greater opportunities for more honest and caring

personal relationships than can be achieved in larger groups. Such small groups very often become ecumenical.

A particularly vital form of congregational life is known as Base Christian Communities. These communities, arising among the poor and disenfranchised and committed to the struggle for their liberation, express common concerns for identity and a new dignity. They are a gift of God; offering renewal to the church and calling it to a new presence among the poor and disenfranchised.

There are other experiments that arise as alternatives to parish life and that focus on particular aspects of the demands of the kingdom, e.g. seeking a simpler lifestyle, a concern for conservation, or as a political protest. Monastic communities, after a traumatic period of reassessment, are emerging with new confidence in their vocation in the modern world.

III. THE HEALING COMMUNITY . . .

IV. COMMON WITNESS TO GOD'S KINGDOM

Common Witness and Cultural Identity

21. In its mission in any culture, the Church is called to witness to the Incarnated Christ, in family life, in common celebrations, in art and in its struggles.

We affirm the need and the possibility for common witness to populations and groups not sufficiently acquainted with the Gospel, both in cultural groupings where the Gospel has never been proclaimed and in societies where many people no longer believe the Gospel. We must cooperate in realizing where such populations and grouping exist and how they can be reached. What preparations and initiatives to proclaim the kingdom to them can be undertaken together? We must explore how to coordinate the efforts to witness to these various cultural groupings and how to avoid competition and proselytizing. We encourage all those who are working to enable the Gospel to take genuine root within different cultures.

22. We affirm the need and possibility for common witness to people of other religions and ideologies, especially in societies where these religions and ideologies constitute a majority or have the power of the state at their disposition. Within this framework, we reflect on the role of martyrdom and the special meaning of common witness in situations of active persecution, whether of one church or of all Christian churches. Even churches that are not in full unity must struggle together to join efforts in securing more freedom of witness for all. No religious community, including Christian churches, must ask for privileges which it is not ready to grant to others. Common witness may be a crucial antidote for the attempt to set various Christian communities and denominations against one another in order to isolate them and prevent them from constituting a presence in public life. Dialogue with people of living faiths can show us how they and we may serve the common needs of humanity. We may also discover that God has fresh inspiration for us in the experience of other religions.

Common Witness and Confessional Diversity

26. a) We all share in a common basic faith commitment, the core and foundation of common witness to the kingdom.

b) Common witness is obscured, hampered or prevented, for example, where:

(i) interchurch aid in human, financial and other forms leads to cultural insensitivity, church dependency and inappropriate lifestyle, which deform the Gospel, deny a culture and bribe a people;

(ii) interchurch aid fosters church divisions, when partner churches, agencies and groups work separately and even competitively in mission and development;

(iii) interchurch aid disregards existing local churches, their identity and mission within their own contexts.

c) Efforts can be made, are being made and should be made to overcome disruptive efforts on common witness. Such efforts are:

(i) putting together shared resources to be allocated locally in an ecumenical style;

(ii) recognizing national and local councils of churches as places and opportunities to share the strength as well as the weaknesses of all members, not seeking to retain the best assets for each church's purposes;

(iii) promoting corporate Bible translations and distribution;

(iv) developing theological training of laity and clergy ecumenically, whenever, wherever and to whatever extent possible;

(v) strengthening cooperation in pastoral and diaconal ministries, as a means of practical recognition of common ministry and witness. . . .

(vi) fostering common pastoral care for mixed marriages, cooperation in the use of the mass media, the press and publication, common initiatives in the realm of spiritual life;

(vii) forming lifestyles of churches and Christians in accordance with the local context. . . .

(viii) respecting the ministry and the worship of other churches, and discouraging a competitive attitude towards one another or proselytizing among other churches.

CONCLUSION

32. Having examined these ways of the Church's witness to the kingdom, we are compelled to ask, what does this mean for the congregation where I shall worship next Sunday, bearing in mind the global context of our local Christian obedience? . . .

a) Do we know Jesus Christ in such a way that we can speak convincingly of him?

b) Is our congregation reaching out and truly welcoming all those in need and all those who seek?

c) Are we expressing the Spirit's ministry of healing for those with broken hearts, disturbed minds and bodies?

d) Are we sharing with all Christians the deep concern in our neighborhood and nation for better ways of living?

e) As we receive the Eucharist, God's all for us, are we giving our all to him and his needy children?

No congregation can ever give entirely adequate answers to these questions. They are always a spur to self-examination, to repentance and to growth. All Christians live in hope, expecting the powers of the Spirit to transform life, and trusting in God's mercy when the Lord comes in judgement and kingly rule.

5

Ecumenical Affirmation: Mission and Evangelism

1982

WCC CENTRAL COMMITTEE

The Ecumenical Affirmation *which follows may be the single most important ecumenical statement on mission in this period.*

In 1976, following the Fifth Assembly of the World Council of Churches at Nairobi (1975), the WCC Central Committee asked the CWME to prepare a document containing the basic convictions of the ecumenical movement on mission and evangelism. In response to this mandate, the CWME drew up an interim document which became the subject of fruitful conversation with Orthodox, Protestant, and Catholic groups, and underwent review at the CWME Melbourne Conference (1980).

In July 1982 the Central Committee gave its approval to the document, which was then sent to member churches for their study, inspiration, and guidance. The document has been warmly acclaimed in both conciliar and non-conciliar circles as a statement of convergence. The key to the document's favorable reception lies in its simple, nontechnical, biblical language and in its selection of seven "basic convictions" on mission and evangelism.

An opening exhortation and call to mission and witness (paras. 1-9) leads to seven convictions which are seen as normative for ecumenical missionary practice: conversion (10-13); the Gospel to all realms of life (14-19); the church and its unity in God's mission (20-27); mission in Christ's way (28-30); Good News to the poor (31-36); mission in and to six continents (37-40); and witness among people of living faiths (41-45). The "convictions" can easily be traced to earlier ecumenical documents, especially Nairobi (1975) and Melbourne (1980), and they foreshadow San Antonio (1989). This document remains a benchmark ecumenical statement.

PREFACE*

The biblical promise of a new earth and a new heaven where love, peace and justice will prevail (Ps. 85:7-13; Isa. 32:17-18, 65:17-25 and Rev. 21:1-2) invites our

---

*Reprinted from *International Review of Mission* 71:284 (October 1982), 427-447.

actions as Christians in history. The contrast of that vision with the reality of today reveals the monstrosity of human sin, the evil unleashed by the rejection of God's liberating will for humankind. Sin, alienating persons from God, neighbour and nature, is found both in individual and corporate forms, both in slavery of the human will and in social, political and economic structures of domination and dependence.

The Church is sent into the world to call people and nations to repentance, to announce forgiveness of sin and a new beginning in relations with God and with neighbours through Jesus Christ. This evangelistic calling has a new urgency today. In a world where the number of people who have no opportunity to know the story of Jesus is growing steadily, *how necessary it is to multiply the witnessing vocation of the church!*

In a world where the majority of those who do not know Jesus are the poor of the earth, those to whom he promised the kingdom of God, *how essential it is to share with them the Good News of that kingdom!*

In a world where people are struggling for justice, freedom and liberation, often without the realization of their hopes, *how important it is to announce that God's kingdom is promised to them!*

In a world where the marginalized and the drop-outs of affluent society search desperately for comfort and identity in drugs or esoteric cults, *how imperative it is to announce that he has come so that all may have life and may have it in all its fullness (John 10:10)!*

In a world where so many find little meaning, except in the relative security of their affluence, *how necessary it is to hear once again Jesus' invitation to discipleship, service and risk!*

In a world where so many Christians are nominal in their commitment to Jesus Christ, *how necessary it is to call them again to the fervour of their first love!*

In a world where wars and rumours of war jeopardize the present and future of mankind, where an enormous part of natural resources and people are consumed in the arms race, *how crucial it is to call the peace-makers blessed, convinced that God in Christ has broken all barriers and has reconciled the world to himself (Eph. 2:14; II Cor. 5:19)!*

This ecumenical affirmation is a challenge which the churches extend to each other to announce that God reigns, and that there is hope for a future when God will "unite all things in him, things in heaven and things on earth" (Eph. 1:10). Jesus is "the first and last, and the Living One" (Rev. 1:17-18), who "is coming soon" (Rev. 22:12), who "makes all things new" (Rev. 21:5).

THE CALL TO MISSION

1. The present ecumenical movement came into being out of the conviction of the churches that the division of Christians is a scandal and an impediment to the witness of the Church. There is a growing awareness among the churches today of the inextricable relationship between Christian unity and missionary calling, between ecumenism and evangelization. "Evangelization is the test of our ecumenical vocation."[1]

As "a fellowship of churches which confess the Lord Jesus Christ as God and Saviour, according to the Scriptures, and therefore seek to fulfil together their common calling to the glory of the one God, Father, Son and Holy Spirit",[2] the rallying point of the World Council of Churches is the common confession of Jesus Christ. The saving ministry of the Son is understood within the action of the Holy

Trinity; it was the Father who in the power of the Spirit sent Jesus Christ the Son of God incarnate, the Saviour of the whole world. The churches of the WCC are on a pilgrimage towards unity under the missionary vision of John 17:21, "that they may all be one; even as thou, Father, art in me, and I in thee, that they also may be in us, so that the world may believe that thou hast sent me".[3]

2. Already in the Old Testament the people of Israel were looking forward to the day of peace where God's justice will prevail (Isa. 11:1-9). Jesus came into that tradition announcing that the kingdom of God was at hand (Mark 1:15), that in him the reality of the kingdom was present (Luke 4:15-21). God was offering this new justice to the children, to the poor, to all who labour and are heavy laden, to all those who will repent and will follow Jesus. The early Church confessed Jesus as Lord, as the highest authority at whose name every knee shall bow, who in the cross and in the resurrection has liberated in this world the power of sacrificial love.

3. Christ sent the disciples with the words: "As the Father has sent me, even so I send you" (John 20:21). The disciples of Jesus were personal witnesses of the risen Christ (I John 1:2-3). As such they were sent—commissioned apostles to the world. Based on their testimony which is preserved in the New Testament and in the life of the Church, the Church has as one constitutive mark its being apostolic, its being sent into the world. God in Christ has equipped the Church with all gifts of the Spirit necessary for its witness. "You shall receive power when the Holy Spirit has come upon you; and you shall be my witnesses in Jerusalem, and in all Judaea and Samaria, and to the end of the earth" (Acts 1:8).

4. The book of Acts tells the story of the expansion of the early Church as it fulfils its missionary vocation. The Holy Spirit came upon that small Jerusalem community on the day of Pentecost (Acts 2:1-39), in order that through them and through others who were to believe in Christ through their word (John 17:20), the world may be healed and redeemed.

The early Church witnessed to its Risen Lord in a variety of ways, most specially in the style of life of its members. "And day by day, attending the temple together and breaking bread in their homes, they partook of food with glad and generous hearts, praising God and having favour with all the people. And the Lord added to their number day by day those who were being saved" (Acts 2:46-47). Through the persecutions suffered by the early Christians, the word spread spontaneously: "Now those who were scattered went about preaching the word" (Acts 8:4). The apostles then came to confirm the faith of those who had accepted the Word of God (Acts 8:14-17). At other times, the word spread through more explicit and purposeful ministries. The church in Antioch organized the first missionary trip. Barnabas and Paul were sent by the church in response to the Holy Spirit (Acts 13:1-4). Time and time again, the church was surprised by God's calling to face entirely new missionary situations (Acts 8:26; 10:17; 16:9-10).

5. Jesus Christ was in himself the complete revelation of God's love, manifested in justice and forgiveness through all aspects of his earthly life. He completed the work of the Father. "My food is to do the will of him who sent me, and to accomplish his work" (John 4:34). In his obedience to the Father's will, in his love for humanity, he used many ways to reveal God's love to the world: forgiving, healing, casting out demons, teaching, proclaiming, denouncing, testifying in courts, finally surrendering his life. The Church today has the same freedom to develop its mission, to respond to changing situations and circumstances. It is sent into the world, participating in that flow of love from God the Father. In that mission of love (Matt. 22:37) through

all aspects of its life, the Church endeavours to witness to the full realization of God's kingdom in Jesus Christ. The Church is called, like John the Baptist, to point towards the "lamb of God who takes away the sin of the world" (John 1:29).

THE CALL TO PROCLAMATION AND WITNESS

6. The mission of the Church ensues from the nature of the Church as the Body of Christ, sharing in the ministry of Christ as Mediator between God and His Creation. This mission of mediation in Christ involves two integrally related movements—one from God to Creation, and the other from Creation to God. The Church manifests God's love for the world in Christ—through word and deed, in identification with all humanity, in loving service and joyful proclamation; the Church, in that same identification with all humanity, lifts up to God its pain and suffering, hope and aspiration, joy and thanksgiving in intercessory prayer and eucharistic worship. Any imbalance between these two directions of the mediatory movement adversely affects our ministry and mission in the world.

Only a Church fully aware of how people in the world live and feel and think can adequately fulfil either aspect of this mediatory mission. It is at this point that the Church recognizes the validity and significance of the ministry of others to the Church, in order that the Church may better understand and be in closer solidarity with the world, knowing and sharing its pains and yearnings. Only by responding attentively to others can we remove our ignorance and misunderstanding of others, and be better able to minister to them.

At the very heart of the Church's vocation in the world is the proclamation of the kingdom of God inaugurated in Jesus the Lord, crucified and risen. Through its internal life of eucharistic worship, thanksgiving, intercessory prayer, through planning for mission and evangelism, through a daily lifestyle of solidarity with the poor, through advocacy even to confrontation with the powers that oppress human beings, the churches are trying to fulfil this evangelistic vocation.

7. The starting point of our proclamation is Christ and Christ crucified. "We preach Christ crucified, a stumbling block to Jews and folly to Gentiles" (I Cor. 1:23). The Good News handed on to the Church is that God's grace was in Jesus Christ, who "though he was rich, yet for your sake he became poor, so that by his poverty you might become rich" (II Cor. 8:9).

Following human wisdom, the wise men from the Orient who were looking for the child went to the palace of King Herod. They did not know that "there was no place for him in the inn" and that he was born in a manger, poor among the poor. He even went so far in his identification with the poverty of humankind that his family was obliged to take the route of political refugee to Egypt. He was raised as a worker, came proclaiming God's caring for the poor, announced blessedness for them, sided with the underprivileged, confronted the powerful and went to the cross to open up a new life for humankind. As his disciples, we announce his solidarity with all the downtrodden and marginalized. Those who are considered to be nothing are precious in God's eyes (I Cor. 1:26-31). To believe in Jesus the King is to accept his undeserved grace and enter with him into the Kingdom, taking sides with the poor struggling to overcome poverty. Both those who announce Jesus as the servant king and those who accept this announcement and respond to it are invited to enter with him daily in identification and participation with the poor of the earth. With the Apostle Paul and all Christian churches, we confess Christ Jesus, "who, though he was in the form of God, did not count equality with God a thing to be grasped, but emptied himself, taking on the form of a servant, being born in the likeness of men. And being found in human form he humbled himself and became obedient unto death, even death on a cross. Therefore God has highly exalted him and bestowed on him the name which is above every name, that at the name of Jesus every knee should bow, in heaven and on earth and under the earth, and every tongue confess that Jesus Christ is Lord, to the glory of God the Father" (Phil. 2:6-11).

8. But Christ's identification with humanity went even more deeply, and while nailed on the cross accused as a political criminal, he took upon himself the guilt even of those who crucified him. "Father, forgive them; for they know not what they do" (Luke 23:34). The Christian confession reads, "For our sake he made him to be sin who knew no sin, so that in him we might become the righteousness of God" (II Cor. 5:21). The cross is the place of the decisive battle between the powers of evil and the love of God. It uncovers the lostness of the world, the magnitude of human sinfulness, the tragedy of human alienation. The total self-surrendering of Christ reveals the immeasurable depth of God's love for the world (John 3:16).

On this same cross, Jesus was glorified. Here God the Father glorified the Son of man, and in so doing confirmed Jesus as the Son of God (John 13:31). "The early Christians used many analogies to describe what they had experienced and what they believed had happened. The most striking picture is that of a sacrificed lamb, slaughtered but yet living, sharing the throne, which symbolized the heart of all power and sovereignty, with the living God himself."[4]

It is this Jesus that the Church proclaims as the very life of the world because on the cross he gave his own life for all that all may live. In him misery, sin and death are defeated once forever. They cannot be accepted as having final power over human life. In him there is abundant life, life eternal. The Church proclaims Jesus, risen from the dead. Through the resurrection, God vindicates Jesus, and opens up a new period of missionary obedience until he comes again (Acts 1:11). The power of the risen and crucified Christ is now released. It is the new birth to a new life, because as he took our predicament on the cross, he also took us into a new life in his resurrection. "When anyone is united to Christ, there is a new creation; the old has passed away, behold, the new has come" (II Cor. 5:17).

Evangelism calls people to look towards that Jesus and commit their life to him, to enter into the kingdom whose king has come in the powerless child of Bethlehem, in the murdered one on the cross.

ECUMENICAL CONVICTIONS

9. In the ecumenical discussions and experience, churches with their diverse confessions and traditions and in their various expressions as parishes, monastic communities, religious orders, etc., have learned to recognize each other as participants in the one worldwide missionary movement. *Thus, together, they can affirm an ecumenical perception of Christian mission expressed in the following convictions under which they covenant to work for the kingdom of God.*

1. CONVERSION

10. The proclamation of the Gospel includes an invitation to recognize and accept in a personal decision the saving lordship of Christ. It is the announcement of a personal encounter, mediated by the Holy Spirit, with the living Christ, receiv-

ing his forgiveness and making a personal acceptance of the call to discipleship and a life of service. God addresses himself specifically to each of his children, as well as to the whole human race. Each person is entitled to hear the Good News. Many social forces today press for conformity and passivity. Masses of poor people have been deprived of their right to decide about their lives and the life of their society. While anonymity and marginalization seem to reduce the possibilities for personal decisions to a minimum, God as Father knows each one of his children and calls each of them to make a fundamental personal act of allegiance to him and his kingdom in the fellowship of his people.

11. While the basic experience of conversion is the same, the awareness of an encounter with God revealed in Christ, the concrete occasion of this experience and the actual shape of the same differs in terms of our personal situation. The calling is to specific changes, to renounce evidences of the domination of sin in our lives and to accept responsibilities in terms of God's love for our neighbour. John the Baptist said very specifically to the soldiers what they should do; Jesus did not hesitate to indicate to the young ruler that his wealth was the obstacle to his discipleship.

Conversion happens in the midst of our historical reality and incorporates the totality of our life, because God's love is concerned with that totality. Jesus' call is an invitation to follow him joyfully, to participate in his servant body, to share with him in the struggle to overcome sin, poverty and death.

12. The importance of this decision is highlighted by the fact that God himself through his Holy Spirit helps the acceptance of his offering of fellowship. The New Testament calls this a new birth (John 3:3). It is also called conversion, metanoia, total transformation of our attitudes and styles of life. Conversion as a dynamic and ongoing process "involves a turning *from* and a turning *to*. It always demands reconciliation, a new relationship both with God and with others. It involves leaving our old security behind (Matt. 16:24) and putting ourselves at risk in a life of faith."[5] It is "conversion *from* a life characterized by sin, separation from God, submission to evil and the unfulfilled potential of God's image, *to* a new life characterized by the forgiveness of sins, obedience to the commands of God, renewed fellowship with God in trinity, growth in the restoration of the divine image and the realization . . . of the love of Christ . . ."[6]

The call to conversion, as a call to repentance and obedience, should also be addressed to nations, groups and families. To proclaim the need to change from war to peace, from injustice to justice, from racism to solidarity, from hate to love is a witness rendered to Jesus Christ and to his kingdom. The prophets of the Old Testament addressed themselves constantly to the collective conscience of the people of Israel calling the rulers and the people to repentance and to renewal of the covenant.

13. Many of those who are attracted to Christ are put off by what they see in the life of the churches as well as in individual Christians. How many of the millions of people in the world who are not confessing Jesus Christ have rejected him because of what they saw in the lives of Christians! Thus the call to conversion should begin with the repentance of those who do the calling, who issue the invitation. Baptism in itself is a unique act, the covenant that Christians no longer belong to themselves but have been bought forever with the blood of Christ and belong to God. But the experience of baptism should be constantly re-enacted by daily dying with Christ to sin, to themselves and to the world and rising again with him into the servant body of Christ to become a blessing for the surrounding community.

The experience of conversion gives meaning to people in all stages of life, endurance to resist oppression, and assurance that even death has no final power over human life because God in Christ has already taken our life with him, a life that is "hidden with Christ in God" (Col. 3:3).

2. THE GOSPEL TO ALL REALMS OF LIFE

14. In the Bible, religious life was never limited to the temple or isolated from daily life (Hos. 6:4-6; Isa. 58:6-7). The teaching of Jesus on the kingdom of God is a clear reference to God's loving lordship over all human history. We cannot limit our witness to a supposedly private area of life. The lordship of Christ is to be proclaimed to all realms of life. In the Great Commission, Jesus said to his disciples: "All authority in heaven and on earth has been given to me. Go, therefore, and make disciples of all nations, baptizing them in the name of the Father and of the Son and of the Holy Spirit, teaching them to obey all that I have commanded you. And lo, I am with you always, to the close of the age" (Matt. 28:19-20). The Good News of the kingdom is a challenge to the structures of society (Eph. 3:9-10; 6:12) as well as a call to individuals to repent. "If salvation from sin through divine forgiveness is to be truly and fully personal, it must express itself in the renewal of these relations and structures. Such renewal is not merely a consequence but an essential element of the conversion of whole human beings."[7]

15. "The Evangelistic Witness is directed towards all of the *ktisis* (creation) which groans and travails in search of adoption and redemption ... The transfiguring power of the Holy Trinity is meant to reach into every nook and cranny of our national life ... The Evangelistic Witness will also speak to the structures of this world; its economic, political, and societal institutions ... We must re-learn the patristic lesson that the Church is the mouth and voice of the poor and the oppressed in the presence of the powers that be. In our own way we must learn once again 'how to speak to the ear of the King', on the people's behalf ... Christ was sent for no lesser purpose than bringing the world into the life of God."[8]

16. In the fulfilment of its vocation, the Church is called *to announce* Good News in Jesus Christ, forgiveness, hope, a new heaven and a new earth; *to denounce* powers and principalities, sin and injustice; *to console* the widows and orphans, healing, restoring the brokenhearted; and *to celebrate* life in the midst of death. In carrying out these tasks, churches may meet limitations, constraints, even persecution from prevailing powers which pretend to have final authority over the life and destiny of people.

17. In some countries there is pressure to limit religion to the private life of the believer—to assert that freedom to believe should be enough. The Christian faith challenges that assumption. The Church claims the right and the duty to exist publicly—visibly—and to address itself openly to issues of human concern. "Confessing Christ *today* means that the Spirit makes us struggle with ... sin and forgiveness, power and powerlessness, exploitation and misery, the universal search for identity, the widespread loss of Christian motivation, and the spiritual longings of those who have not heard Christ's name. It means that we are in communion with the prophets who announced God's will and promise for humankind and society, with the martyrs who sealed their confession with suffering and death, and also with the doubtful who can only whisper their confession of the Name."[9]

18. The realm of science and technology deserves particular attention today. The everyday life of most children, women and men, whether rich or poor, is affected

by the avalanche of scientific discoveries. Pharmaceutical science has revolutionized sexual behaviour. Increasingly sophisticated computers solve problems in seconds for which formerly a whole lifetime was needed; at the same time they become a means of invading the privacy of millions of people. Nuclear power threatens the survival of life on this planet, while at the same time it provides a new source of energy. Biological research stands at the awesome frontier of interference with the genetic code which could—for better or for worse—change the whole human species. Scientists are, therefore, seeking ethical guidance. Behind the questions as to right or wrong decisions and attitudes, however, there are ultimate theological questions: what is the meaning of human existence? the goal of history? the true reality within and beyond what can be tested and quantified empirically? The ethical questions arise out of a quest for a new world view, a faith.

19. The biblical stories and ancient creeds do furnish precious insights for witnessing to the Gospel in the scientific world. Can theologians, however, with these insights, help scientists achieve responsible action in genetic engineering or nuclear physics? It would hardly seem possible so long as the great communication gap between these two groups persists. Those directly involved in and affected by scientific research can best discern and explicate the insights of Christian faith in terms of specific ethical positions.

Christian witness will point towards Jesus Christ in whom real humanity is revealed and who is in God's wisdom the centre of all creation, the "head over all things" (Eph. 1:10; 22f.). This witness will show the glory and the humility of human stewardship on this earth.

3. THE CHURCH AND ITS UNITY IN GOD'S MISSION

20. To receive the message of the kingdom of God is to be incorporated into the body of Christ, the Church, the author and sustainer of which is the Holy Spirit. The churches are to be a sign for the world. They are to intercede as he did, to serve as he did. Thus Christian mission is the action of the body of Christ in the history of humankind—a continuation of Pentecost. Those who through conversion and baptism accept the Gospel of Jesus partake in the life of the body of Christ and participate in an historical tradition. Sadly there are many betrayals of this high calling in the history of the churches. Many who are attracted to the vision of the kingdom find it difficult to be attracted to the concrete reality of the Church. They are invited to join in a continual process of renewal of the churches. "The challenge facing the churches is not that the modern world is unconcerned about their evangelistic message, but rather whether they are so renewed in their life and thought that they become a living witness to the integrity of the Gospel. The evangelizing churches need themselves to receive the Good News and to let the Holy Spirit remake their life when and how he wills."[10]

21. The celebration of the eucharist is the place for the renewal of the missionary conviction at the heart of every congregation. According to the Apostle Paul, the celebration of the eucharist is in itself a "proclamation of the death of the Lord until he comes" (I Cor. 11:26). "In such ways God feeds his people as they celebrate the mystery of the Eucharist so that they may confess in word and deed that Jesus Christ is Lord, to the glory of God the Father."[11]

The eucharist is bread for a missionary people. We acknowledge with deep sorrow the fact that Christians do not join together at the Lord's table. This contradicts God's will and impoverishes the body of Christ. The credibility of our Christian witness is at stake.

22. Christians are called to work for the renewal and transformation of the churches. Today there are many signs of the work of the Holy Spirit in such a renewal. *The house gatherings of the Church in China or the Basic Ecclesial Communities in Latin America, the liturgical renewal, biblical renewal, the revival of the monastic vocation, the charismatic movement, are indications of the renewal possibilities of the Church of Jesus Christ.*

23. In the announcement to the world of the reconciliation in Jesus Christ, churches are called to unite. Faced with the challenge and threat of the world, the churches often unite to defend common positions. But common witness should be the natural consequence of their unity with Christ in his mission. The ecumenical experience has discovered the reality of a deep spiritual unity. The common recognition of the authority of the bible and of the creeds of the ancient Church and a growing convergence in doctrinal affirmations should allow the churches not only to affirm together the fundamentals of the Christian faith, but also to proclaim together the Good News of Jesus Christ to the world. In solidarity, churches are helping each other in their respective witness before the world. In the same solidarity, they should share their spiritual and material resources to announce together and clearly their common hope and common calling.

24. "Often it is socially and politically more difficult to witness together since the powers of this world promote division. In such situations common witness is particularly precious and Christ-like. Witness that dares to be common is a powerful sign of unity coming directly and visibly from Christ and a glimpse of his kingdom."[12]

The impulse for common witness comes from the depth of our faith. "Its urgency is underlined when we realize the seriousness of the human predicament and the tremendous task waiting for the churches at present."[13]

25. It is at the heart of Christian mission to foster the multiplication of local congregations in every human community. The planting of the seed of the Gospel will bring forward a people gathered around the Word and sacraments and called to announce God's revealed purpose. Thanks to the faithful witness of disciples through the ages, churches have sprung up in practically every country. This task of sowing the seed needs to be continued until there is, in every human community, a cell of the kingdom, a church confessing Jesus Christ and in his name serving his people. The building up of the Church in every place is essential to the Gospel. The vicarious work of Christ demands the presence of a vicarious people. A vital instrument for the fulfilment of the missionary vocation of the Church is the local congregation.

26. The planting of the Church in different cultures demands a positive attitude towards inculturation of the Gospel. Ancient churches, through centuries of intimate relations with the cultures and aspirations of their people, have proved the powerful witnessing character of this rooting of the churches in the national soil. "Inculturation has its source and inspiration in the mystery of the Incarnation. The Word was made flesh. Here flesh means the fully concrete, human and created reality that Jesus was. Inculturation, therefore, becomes another way of describing Christian mission. If proclamation sees mission in the perspective of the Word to be proclaimed, inculturation sees mission in the perspective of the flesh, or concrete embodiment, which the Word assumes in a particular individual, community, institution or culture."[14]

Inculturation should not be understood merely as intellectual research; it occurs when Christians express their faith in the symbols and images of their respective culture. *The best way to stimulate the process of inculturation is to participate in the struggle of the less privileged for their liberation. Solidarity is the best teacher of common cultural values.*

27. This growing cultural diversity could create some difficulties. In our attempt to express the catholicity of the Church we may lose the sense of its unity. But the unity we look for is not uniformity but the multiple expression of a common faith and a common mission. "We have found this confession of Christ out of our various cultural contexts to be not only a mutually inspiring, but also a mutually corrective exchange. Without this sharing our individual affirmations would gradually become poorer and narrower. We need each other to regain the lost dimensions of confessing Christ and to discover dimensions unknown to us before. Sharing in this way, we are all changed and our cultures are transformed."[15]

The vision of nations coming from the East, the West, the North and the South to sit at the final banquet of the kingdom should always be before us in our missionary endeavour.

4. MISSION IN CHRIST'S WAY

28. "As the Father has sent me, even so I send you" (John 20:21). The self-emptying of the servant who lived among the people, sharing in their hopes and sufferings, giving his life on the cross for all humanity—this was Christ's way of proclaiming the Good News, and as disciples we are summoned to follow the same way. "A servant is not greater than his master; nor is he who is sent greater than he who sent him" (John 13:16).

Our obedience in mission should be patterned on the ministry and teaching of Jesus. He gave his love and his time to all people. He praised the widow who gave her last coin to the temple; he received Nicodemus during the night; he called Matthew to the apostolate; he visited Zacchaeus in his home; he gave himself in a special way to the poor, consoling, affirming and challenging them. He spent long hours in prayer and lived in dependence on and willing obedience to God's will.

An imperialistic crusader's spirit was foreign to him. Churches are free to choose the ways they consider best to announce the Gospel to different people in different circumstances. But these options are never neutral. Every methodology illustrates or betrays the Gospel we announce. In all communications of the Gospel, power must be subordinate to love.

29. Our societies are undergoing a significant and rapid change under the impact of new communication technologies and their applications. We are entering the age of the information society, characterized by an ever increasing media presence in all relationships, both interpersonal and intersocial. Christians need to re-think critically their responsibility for all communication processes and re-define the values of Christian communications. In the use of all new media options, the communicating church must ensure that these instruments of communication are not masters, but servants in the proclaiming of the kingdom of God and its values. As servants, the new media options, kept within their own limits, will help to liberate societies from communication bondage and will place tools in the hands of communities for witnessing to Jesus Christ.

30. Evangelism happens in terms of interpersonal relations when the Holy Spirit quickens to faith. Through sharing the pains and joys of life, identifying with people, the Gospel is understood and communicated.

Often, the primary confessors are precisely the nonpublicized, unsensational people who gather together steadfastly in small caring communities, whose life prompts the question: "What is the source of the meaning of your life? What is the power of your powerlessness?", giving the occasion to name THE NAME. Shared experiences reveal how often Christ is confessed in the very silence of the prison cell or of a restricted but serving, waiting, praying church.

Mission calls for a serving church in every land, a church which is willing to be marked with the stigmata (nail marks) of the crucified and risen Lord. In this way the church will show that it belongs to that movement of God's love shown in Christ who went to the periphery of life. Dying outside the gates of the city (Heb. 13:12) he is the high priest offering himself for the salvation of the world. Outside the city gates the message of a self-giving, sharing love is truly proclaimed, here the Church renews its vocation to be the body of Christ in joyful fellowship with its risen Lord (I John 3:16).

5. GOOD NEWS TO THE POOR

31. There is a new awareness of the growing gap between wealth and poverty among the nations and inside each nation. It is a cruel reality that the number of people who do not reach the material level for a normal human life is growing steadily. An increasing number of people find themselves marginalized, second-class citizens unable to control their own destiny and unable to understand what is happening around them. Racism, powerlessness, solitude, breaking of family and community ties are new evidences of the marginalization that comes under the category of poverty.

32. There is also a tragic coincidence that most of the world's poor have not heard the Good News of the Gospel of Jesus Christ; or they could not receive it, because it was not recognized as Good News in the way in which it was brought. This is a double injustice: they are victims of the oppression of an unjust economic order or an unjust political distribution of power, and at the same time they are deprived of the knowledge of God's special care for them. To announce the Good News to the poor is to begin to render the justice due to them. The Church of Jesus Christ is called to preach the Good News to the poor following the example of its Lord who was incarnated as poor, who lived as one among them and gave to them the promise of the kingdom of God. Jesus looked at the multitudes with compassion. He recognized the poor as those who were sinned against, victims of both personal and structural sin.

Out of this deep awareness came both his solidarity and his calling to them (Matt. 11:28). His calling was a personalized one. He invited them to come to him, to receive forgiveness of sins and to assume a task. He called them to follow him, because his love incorporated his respect for them as people created by God with freedom to respond. He called them to exercise this responsibility towards God, neighbours and their own lives. The proclamation of the Gospel among the poor is a sign of the messianic kingdom and a priority criterion by which to judge the validity of our missionary engagement today.

33. This new awareness is an invitation to re-think priorities and lifestyles both in the local church and in the worldwide missionary endeavour. Of course, churches and Christians find themselves in very different contexts: some in very wealthy settings where the experience of poverty as it is known to millions in the world today is practically unknown, or in egalitarian societies where the basic needs of life seem to be assured for almost everybody, to situations of extreme poverty. But the consciousness of the global nature of poverty and exploitation in the world

today, the knowledge of the interdependence between nations and the understanding of the international missionary responsibility of the Church—all invite, in fact oblige, every church and every Christian to think of ways and means to share the Good News with the poor of today. An objective look at the life of every society, even the most affluent and those which are, theoretically, more just, will show the reality of the poor today in the marginalized, the drop-outs who cannot cope with modern society, the prisoners of conscience, the dissidents. All of them are waiting for a cup of cold water or for a visit in the name of Christ. Churches are learning afresh through the poor of the earth to overcome the old dichotomies between evangelism and social action. The "spiritual Gospel" and "material Gospel" were in Jesus one Gospel.

34. There is no evangelism without solidarity; there is no Christian solidarity that does not involve sharing the knowledge of the kingdom which is God's promise to the poor of the earth. There is here a double credibility test: A proclamation that does not hold forth the promises of the justice of the kingdom to the poor of the earth is a caricature of the Gospel; but Christian participation in the struggles for justice which does not point towards the promises of the kingdom also makes a caricature of a Christian understanding of justice.

A growing consensus among Christians today speaks of God's preferential option for the poor.[16] We have there a valid yardstick to apply to our lives as individual Christians, local congregations and as missionary people of God in the world.

35. This concentration point, God's preferential option for the poor, raises the question of the Gospel for all those who objectively are not poor or do not consider themselves as such. *It is a clear Christian conviction that God wants all human beings to be saved and to come to the knowledge of truth, but we know that, while God's purpose is for the salvation of all, he has worked historically through the people of Israel and through the incarnation of his own son Jesus Christ. While his purpose is universal, his action is always particular.* What we are learning anew today is that God works through the downtrodden, the persecuted, the poor of the earth. And from there, he is calling all humanity to follow them. "If any one would come after me, let him deny himself and take up his cross and follow me" (Matt. 16:24).

For all of us, the invitation is clear: to follow Jesus in identification and sharing with the weak, marginalized and poor of the world, because in them we encounter him. Knowing from the Gospel and from historical experience that to be rich is to risk forfeiting the kingdom, and knowing how close the links are, in today's world, between the abundance of some and the needs of others, Christians are challenged to follow him, surrendering all they are and have to the kingdom, to a struggle that commits us against all injustice, against all want. The preferential option for the poor, instead of discriminating against all other human beings, is, on the contrary, a guideline for the priorities and behaviour of all Christians everywhere, pointing to the values around which we should organize our lives and the struggle in which we should put our energy.

36. There is a long experience in the Church of voluntary poverty, people who in obedience to their Christian calling cast aside all their belongings, make their own the fate of the poor of the earth, becoming one of them and living among them. Voluntary poverty has always been recognized as a source of spiritual inspiration, of insight into the heart of the Gospel.

Today we are gratefully surprised, as churches are growing among the poor of the earth, by the insight and perspective of the Gospel coming from the communities of the poor. They are discovering dimensions of the Gospel which have long been forgotten by the Church. The poor of the earth are reading reality from the other side, from the side of those who do not get the attention of the history books written by the conquerors, but who surely get God's attention in the book of life. Living with the poor and understanding the bible from their perspective helps to discover the particular caring with which God both in the Old and in the New Testament thinks of the marginalized, the downtrodden and the deprived. We realize that the poor to whom Jesus promised the kingdom of God are blessed in their longing for justice and in their hope for liberation. They are both subjects and bearers of the Good News; they have the right and the duty to announce the Gospel not only among themselves, but also to all other sectors of the human family.

Churches of the poor are spreading the liberating Gospel of Jesus Christ in almost every corner of the earth. The richness and freshness of their experience is an inspiration and blessing to churches with a centuries-old history. The centres of the missionary expansion of the Church are moving from the North to the South. God is working through the poor of the earth to awaken the consciousness of humanity to his call for repentance, for justice and for love.

6. MISSION IN AND TO SIX CONTINENTS

37. Everywhere the churches are in missionary situations. Even in countries where the churches have been active for centuries we see life organized today without reference to Christian values, a growth of secularism understood as the absence of any final meaning. The churches have lost vital contact with the workers and the youth and many others. This situation is so urgent that it commands priority attention of the ecumenical movement. The movement of migrants and political refugees brings the missionary frontier to the doorstep of every parish. The Christian affirmations on the worldwide missionary responsibility of the Church will be credible if they are authenticated by a serious missionary engagement at home. As the world becomes smaller, it is possible even for Christians living far away to be aware of and inspired by faithful missionary engagement in a local situation. Of special importance today is the expression of solidarity among the churches crossing political frontiers and the symbolic actions of obedience of one part of the body of Christ that enhance the missionary work of other sectors of the Church. So, for example, while programmes related to the elimination of racism may be seen as problems for some churches, such programmes have become, for other churches, a sign of solidarity, an opportunity for witness and a test of Christian authenticity.

Every local congregation needs the awareness of its catholicity which comes from its participation in the mission of the Church of Jesus Christ in other parts of the world. Through its witnessing stance in its own situation, its prayers of intercession for churches in other parts of the world, and its sharing of persons and resources, it participates fully in the world mission of the Christian Church.

38. This concern for mission everywhere has been tested with the call for a moratorium, a halt—at least for a time—to sending and receiving missionaries and resources across national boundaries, in order to encourage the recovery and affirmation of the identity of every church, the concentration on mission in its own place and the freedom to reconsider traditional relations. The Lausanne Covenant noted that "the reduction of foreign missionaries and money in an evangelized country may sometimes be necessary to facilitate the national church's growth and self-reliance and to release resources for unevangelized areas".[17] Moratorium does not mean the end of the missionary vocation nor of the duty to provide resources for

missionary work, but it does mean freedom to reconsider present engagements and to see whether a continuation of what we have been doing for so long is the right style of mission in our day.

Moratorium has to be understood *inside* a concern for world mission. It is faithfulness of commitment to Christ in each national situation which makes missionary concern in other parts of the world authentic. There can never be a moratorium of mission, but it will always be possible, and sometimes necessary, to have a moratorium for the sake of better mission.

39. The story of the churches from their earliest years is the story of faithfulness in their respective localities, but also the story of the carrying of the Gospel across national and continental boundaries; first from Jerusalem to Judaea and Samaria, then to Asia Minor, Africa and Europe, now to the ends of the earth. Christians today are heirs of a long history of those who left their home countries and churches, apostles, monastics, pilgrims, missionaries, emigrants, to work in the name of Jesus Christ, serving and preaching where the Gospel had not yet been heard or received. With the European colonization of most of the world and later on with the expansion of the colonial and neo-colonial presence of the western powers, the churches which had their bases mainly in the West have expanded their missionary service to all corners of the earth.

Surely, many ambiguities have accompanied this development and are present even today, not the least the sin of proselytism among other Christian confessions. Churches and missionary organizations are analysing the experience of these past centuries in order to correct their ways, precisely with the help of the new churches which have come into being in those countries. The history of the Church, the missionary people of God, needs to continue. Each local parish, each Christian, must be challenged to assume responsibility in the total mission of the Church. There will always be need for those who have the calling and the gift to cross frontiers, to share the Gospel of Jesus Christ and to serve in his name.

40. Out of this sense of being the whole Church in mission, we recognize the specific calling to individuals or communities to commit themselves full time to the service of the church, crossing cultural and national frontiers. The churches should not allow this specialized calling of the few to be an alibi for the whole Church, but rather it should be a symbolic concentration of the missionary vocation of the whole Church. Looking at the question of people in mission today, "We perceive a change in the direction of mission, arising from our understanding of the Christ who is the centre and who is always in movement towards the periphery. While not in any way denying the continuing significance and necessity of a mutuality between the churches in the northern and southern hemispheres, we believe that we can discern a development whereby mission in the eighties may increasingly take place within these zones. We feel there will increasing traffic between the churches of Asia, Africa and Latin America among whose numbers both rich and poor are counted. This development, we expect, will take the form of ever stronger initiatives from the churches of the poor and oppressed at the peripheries. Similarly among the industrialized countries, a new reciprocity, particularly one stemming from the marginalized groups, may lead to sharing at the peripheries of the richer societies. While resources may still flow from financially richer to poorer churches, and while it is not our intention to encourage isolationism, we feel that a benefit of this new reality could well be the loosening of the bond of domination and dependence that still so scandalously characterizes the relationship between many churches of the northern and southern hemispheres respectively."[18]

7. WITNESS AMONG PEOPLE OF LIVING FAITHS

41. Christians owe the message of God's salvation in Jesus Christ to every person and to every people. Christians make their witness in the context of neighbours who live by other religious convictions and ideological persuasions. True witness follows Jesus Christ in respecting and affirming the uniqueness and freedom of others. We confess as Christians that we have often looked for the worst in others and have passed negative judgement upon other religions. We hope as Christians to be learning to witness to our neighbours in a humble, repentant and joyful spirit.

42. The Word is at work in every human life. In Jesus of Nazareth the Word became a human being. The wonder of his ministry of love persuades Christians to testify to people of every religious and non-religious persuasion of this decisive presence of God in Christ. In him is our salvation. Among Christians there are still differences of understanding as to how this salvation in Christ is available to people of diverse religious persuasions. But all agree that witness should be rendered to all.

43. Such an attitude springs from the assurance that God is the creator of the whole universe and that he has not left himself without witness at any time or any place. The Spirit of God is constantly at work in ways that pass human understanding and in places that to us are least expected. In entering into a relationship of dialogue with others, therefore, Christians seek to discern the unsearchable riches of God and the way he deals with humanity. For Christians who come from cultures shaped by another faith, an even more intimate interior dialogue takes place as they seek to establish the connection in their lives between their cultural heritage and the deep convictions of their Christian faith.

44. Christians should use every opportunity to join hands with their neighbours, to work together to be communities of freedom, peace and mutual respect. In some places, state legislation hinders the freedom of conscience and the real exercise of religious freedom. Christian churches as well as communities of other faiths cannot be faithful to their vocation without the freedom and right to maintain their institutional form and confessional identity in a society and to transmit their faith from one generation to another. In those difficult situations, Christians should find a way, along with others, to enter into dialogue with the civil authorities in order to reach a common definition of religious freedom. With that freedom comes the responsibility to defend through common actions all human rights in those societies.

45. Life with people of other faiths and ideologies is an encounter of commitments. Witness cannot be a one-way process, but of necessity is two-way; in it Christians become aware of some of the deepest convictions of their neighbours. It is also the time in which, within a spirit of openness and trust, Christians are able to bear authentic witness, giving an account of their commitment to the Christ, who calls all persons to himself.

LOOKING TOWARD THE FUTURE

46. Whether among the *secularized masses of industrial societies,* the *emerging new ideologies* around which societies are organized, *the resurging religions* which people embrace, the *movements of workers and political refugees,* the *people's search for liberation and justice,* the *uncertain pilgrimage of the younger generation* into a future both full of promise and overshadowed by nuclear confrontation — the Church is called to be present and to articulate the meaning of God's love in Jesus Christ for every person and for every situation.

47. The missionary vocation of the Church and its evangelistic calling will not resist the confrontation with the hard realities of daily life if it is not sustained by faith, *a faith supported by prayer, contemplation and adoration.* "Gathering and dispersing, receiving and giving, praise and work, prayer and struggle — this is the true rhythm of Christian engagement in the world."[19] Christians must bring their hearts, minds and wills to the altar of God, knowing that from worship comes wisdom, from prayer comes strength, and from fellowship comes endurance. "To be incorporated into Christ through the work of the Holy Spirit is the greatest blessing of the kingdom, and the only abiding ground of our missionary activity in the world."[20] The same Lord who sends his people to cross all frontiers and to enter into the most unknown territories in his name, is the one who assures: "I am with you always, to the close of the age."

NOTES

1. Philip Potter's speech to the Roman Catholic Synod of Bishops, Rome, 1974.
2. Constitution of the World Council of Churches.
3. Constitution of the Conference on World Mission and Evangelism.
4. *Your Kingdom Come,* p. 210.
5. Ibid., p. 196.
6. *Confessing Christ Today,* Reports of Groups at a Consultation of Orthodox Theologians, p. 8.
7. *Breaking Barriers,* p. 233.
8. *Confessing Christ Today,* pp. 10 and 3.
9. *Breaking Barriers,* p. 48.
10. Philip Potter, op. cit.
11. *Your Kingdom Come,* p. 206.
12. *Common Witness,* p. 28.
13. Ibid.
14. SEDOS Bulletin 81/No. 7.
15. *Breaking Barriers,* p. 46.
16. Catholic Bishops' Conference, Puebla, 1979, para. 1134.
17. Lausanne Covenant, No. 9.
18. *Your Kingdom Come,* pp. 220-221.
19. Ibid., p. 205.
20. Ibid., p. 204.

6

Baptism, Eucharist and Ministry

Lima, 1982

WORLD COUNCIL OF CHURCHES

This widely acclaimed statement of ecumenical convergence, the result of a fifty-year process of ecumenical study and consultation, is included here because of its missiological implications. Baptism, Eucharist and Ministry *was adopted at Lima in 1982 and transmitted to the churches for study, official response, and reception. The texts of the statements on baptism and eucharist, from which brief extracts are given here, not only develop the theological meaning of the two sacraments but also express their implications for Christian witness and service.*

BAPTISM*

6. Administered in obedience to our Lord, baptism is a sign and seal of our common discipleship. Through baptism, Christians are brought into union with Christ, with each other and with the Church of every time and place. Our common baptism, which unites us to Christ in faith, is thus a basic bond of unity. We are one people and are called to confess and serve one Lord in each place and in all the world. The union with Christ which we share through baptism has important implications for Christian unity. "There is . . . one baptism, one God and Father of us all . . . " (Eph. 4.4-6). When baptismal unity is realized in one holy catholic, apostolic Church, a genuine Christian witness can be made to the healing and reconciling love of God. Therefore, our one baptism into Christ constitutes a call to the churches to overcome their divisions and visibly manifest their fellowship.

7. Baptism initiates the reality of the new life given in the midst of the present world. It gives participation in the community of the Holy Spirit. It is a sign of the Kingdom of God and of the life of the world to come. Through the gifts of faith, hope and love, baptism has a dynamic which embraces the whole of life, extends to all nations, and anticipates the day when every tongue will confess that Jesus Christ is Lord to the glory of the Father.

10. As they grow in the Christian life of faith, baptized believers demonstrate that humanity can be regenerated and liberated. They have a common responsi-

---

* Reprinted from *Baptism, Eucharist and Ministry*, Faith and Order Paper No. 111 (Geneva: WCC, 1982), 3, 14-15.

bility, here and now, to bear witness together to the Gospel of Christ, the Liberator of all human beings. The context of this common witness is the Church and the world. Within a fellowship of witness and service, Christians discover the full significance of the one baptism as the gift of God to all God's people. Likewise, they acknowledge that baptism, as a baptism into Christ's death, has ethical implications which not only call for personal sanctification, but also motivate Christians to serve for the realization of the will of God in all realms of life (Rom. 6.9ff; Gal. 3.27-28; I Pet. 2.21-4.6).

EUCHARIST

22. The eucharist opens up the vision of the divine rule which has been promised as the final renewal of creation, and is a foretaste of it. Signs of this renewal are present in the world wherever the grace of God is manifest and human beings work for justice, love and peace. The eucharist is the feast at which the Church gives thanks for these signs and joyfully celebrates and anticipates the coming of the Kingdom in Christ (I Cor. 11.26; Matt. 26.29).

24. Reconciled in the eucharist, the members of the body of Christ are called to be servants of reconciliation among men and women and witnesses of the joy of resurrection. As Jesus went out to publicans and sinners and had table-fellowship with them during his earthly ministry, so Christians are called in the eucharist to be in solidarity with the outcast and to become signs of the love of Christ who lived and sacrificed himself for all and now gives himself in the eucharist.

25. The very celebration of the eucharist is an instance of the Church's participation in God's mission to the world. This participation takes everyday form in the proclamation of the Gospel, service of the neighbour, and faithful presence in the world.

26. As it is entirely the gift of God, the eucharist brings into the present age a new reality which transforms Christians into the image of Christ and therefore makes them his effective witnesses. The eucharist is precious food for missionaries, bread and wine for pilgrims on their apostolic journey. The eucharistic community is nourished and strengthened for confession by word and action of the Lord Jesus who gave his life for the salvation of the world . . .

7

Witnessing in a Divided World

Vancouver, 1983

WORLD COUNCIL OF CHURCHES SIXTH ASSEMBLY

The Sixth Assembly of the WCC met in Vancouver July 24–August 10, 1983, under the theme, "Jesus Christ — the Life of the World." The assembly message called on the churches in "life together" to renew their commitment to unity, mission and evangelism, justice and peace. Mission and evangelism were the subjects of issue group 3.1, "Witnessing in a Divided World," which took up five subtopics: the cultural context, worship, witness among children, witness among the poor, and witness among people of other living faiths. Extracts from two subgroup reports are included here.

CULTURE: THE CONTEXT FOR OUR WITNESSING (ISSUE 3.1)*

. . . the issue of culture has arisen in a fresh way because we are coming (a) to a deeper understanding of the meaning and function of culture and of its plurality, (b) to a better understanding of the ways in which the Gospel has interacted with cultures, and (c) to a clearer realization of the problems that have been caused by ignoring or denigrating the receptor cultures during the Western missionary era that often went hand in hand with western colonial expansion.

5. Culture is what holds a community together, giving a common framework of meaning. It is preserved in language, thought patterns, ways of life, attitudes, symbols and presuppositions, and is celebrated in art, music, drama, literature and the like. It constitutes the collective memory of the people and the collective heritage which will be handed down to generations still to come.

6. While we affirm and celebrate cultures as expressing the plural wonder of God's creation, we recognize that not all aspects of every culture are necessarily good. There are aspects within each culture which deny life and oppress people. Also emerging in our time are certain forms of religious culture and sub-cultures which are demonic because they manipulate people and project a world-view and values which are life-denying rather than life-affirming.

---

*Reprinted from David Gill, ed., *Gathered for Life,* Official Report, VI Assembly World Council of Churches, Vancouver, Canada, 24 July-10 August, 1983 (Geneva: WCC and Grand Rapids, Mich.: Eerdmans, 1983), 32-34, 39-41.

7. Given on the one hand the richness and variety of cultures, and on the other the conflict between life-affirming and life-denying aspects within each culture, we need to look again at the whole issue of Christ and culture in the present historical situation.

11. ... we now have indigenous or local expressions of the Christian faith in many parts of the world, which present more manifestations of diverse forms of Christianity. The Gospel message becomes a transforming power within the life of a community when it is expressed in the cultural forms in which the community understands itself.

12. Therefore, in the search for a theological understanding of culture we are working towards a new ecumenical agenda in which various cultural expressions of the Christian faith may be in conversation with each other. In this encounter the theology, missionary perspectives and historical experiences of many churches, from the most diverse traditions ... offer fresh possibilities.

13. With this background in mind we need to take specific steps: a) In the search for a theological understanding of culture, we can do the following: share a rich diversity of manifestations of the Christian faith; discover the unity that binds these together; and affirm together the Christological centre and Trinitarian source of our faith in all of its varied expressions.

b) We need to be aware of the possibility of our witness to the Gospel becoming captive to any culture, recognizing the fact that all cultures are judged by the Gospel.

c) In contemporary societies there is an evolution of a new culture due in part to modernization and technology. There is a search for a culture that will preserve human values and build community. We need to reassess the role played by, in particular, the relationship between this process and the demands of the Gospel and our witness to it.

d) While we recognize the emergence of Christian communities within minority groups that affirm their cultural identity, we should pay special attention to the fact that many of these are in danger of being destroyed because they are seen as a threat to the dominant culture.

e) We need to look again at the whole matter of witnessing to the Gospel across cultural boundaries, realizing that listening to and learning from the receptor culture is an essential part of the proclamation of the Christian message.

WITNESSING AMONG PEOPLE OF LIVING FAITHS

40. We live as people and as Christians in a religiously and ideologically pluralistic world. Christians from all parts of the oikoumene raise questions about living alongside of, and witnessing to, neighbours of other faiths and diverse ideological commitments who have their own specific testimonies to offer. In such situations witness is not a one-way process: "from us to them". There is also a witness from "them to us" ... Of all the things we do as Christians, witnessing among peoples of living faiths and ideologies causes the most difficulty and confusion. In this task we are hesitant learners and need to acquire sensitivity not only to peoples of other faiths and ideologies, but also to Christians caught up in situations of witness and dialogue in different parts of the world.

42. We see ... the need to distinguish between witness and dialogue, whilst at the same time affirming their interrelatedness.

43. Witness may be described as those acts and words by which a Christian or

community gives testimony to Christ and invites others to make their response to him. In witness we expect to share the good news of Jesus and be challenged in relation to our understanding of and our obedience to that good news.

44. Dialogue may be described as that encounter where people holding different claims about ultimate reality can meet and explore these claims in a context of mutual respect. From dialogue we expect to discern more about how God is active in our world, and to appreciate for their own sake the insights and experiences people of other faiths have of ultimate reality.

45. Dialogue is not a device for nor a denial of Christian witness. It is rather a mutual venture to bear witness to each other and the world, in relation to different perceptions of ultimate reality.

46. While distinctions can be made between dialogue, cooperation and mutual witness in the real experience of living in a religiously and ideologically pluralistic situation they in practice intermingle and are closely inter-related.

8

Urban Rural Mission

1986

WCC-CWME URBAN RURAL MISSION

At the WCC Third Assembly at New Delhi (1961) special attention was given to the concerns of mission in an urban and industrial society, and in 1964 a desk was established in the CWME for urban industrial evangelism. Pilot programs sought to demonstrate the church's identification with the marginal and oppressed, to promote local action, and to empower people who are victims of oppression. In 1978 the CWME merged Urban Industrial Mission and Rural Agricultural Mission into "Urban Rural Mission."

On the twenty-fifth anniversary of the New Delhi Assembly, in 1986, URM asked a small group of persons from five regions to reflect together on the history and philosophy of urban rural mission. The present document sets forth the the-ological assumptions and strategic goals of URM.

B. BASIC AFFIRMATIONS*

1. THE MISSION OF GOD IS A PROCLAMATION OF LIFE

"I have come in order that they may have life—life in all its fullness" (John 10:10). This was the mission of Jesus, that God's kingdom may come and his will be done on earth. This is still his mission; this is what Christ, through the Holy Spirit, is doing, and we are called to take part in this work of God—bringing life, restoring life.

In order to perform this task and show the way, and enable humanity to partic-ipate in it, "the Word became flesh and dwelt among us" (John 1:14). Here in essence is a way of describing the content and method of mission. But the question must be asked: what does this mean?

What does it mean, now, for example, for the enslaved women workers in the sweatshops of Asian cities, for the migrant workers living in barbaric conditions in South Africa, for the exploited sugarcane workers of Brazil, for marginalized Sur-

---

*Reprinted from *Mission from Three Perspectives* [Originally published as *Urban Rural Mission Reflections*, WCC-CWME, 1986] (Geneva: WCC-CWME, 1989), 7-18.

inamese immigrants in Holland, for the fishworkers of Goa, for the indigenous peoples of Canada?

This is the prime challenge. It is not enough to *talk* in the traditional language of mission—to simply proclaim salvation in Christ through the power of the Holy Spirit. We must "give flesh" to these statements in terms of what it means to bring that fullness of life to actual people in specific and concrete situations.

What sort of life do they struggle for, and how is it found, received and shared? The answer can never be discovered in the abstract. We must be *there* first. We cannot say what it means until we go to people, stay with them, listen and learn what it means to talk about that life which Jesus wants for them.

Our perspective therefore comes from our practice and is constantly revised by our practice.

2. THE MISSION OF GOD STARTS WITH PEOPLE

The fact that God's mission starts with people needs emphasizing because it reflects (and affects) our whole attitude to people and the way in which the gospel is communicated and shared. The Pharisees failed to start with people; instead they began with a set of theological certitudes and "forced" them into the human situation, with tragic results. Jesus started with the human condition and asks what will bring, restore life. People come first.

a) Mission Starts with an Awareness of Who People Are

Mission starts with an awareness of who people are in relation to the Creator and to each other, in terms of both the limitations and the potentialities of existence.

This involves certain assumptions concerning the nature of humanity. It is crucial that these assumptions be deliberately and consciously articulated.

i) People are made in God's image.

This fundamental biblical assertion is of enormous importance to the dignity of all human beings, to their personhood and relationship with the Creator, and to any understanding of ecumenism. The destiny of people made in the image of God is to be fully human—"subjects" (active participants in the history of their lives) and not "objects" (passive recipients of the dictates and impositions of others).

The growth and freedom of human beings is always *in relation* to other members of the human community. An exaggerated individualism is totally alien to the biblical understanding of the social and political nature of people. People's existence is possible only in the context of some ordering of the structures of society—the human community.

ii) People exist in a cultural and religious history/heritage.

Mission that starts with people (who they *are*) will be deeply sensitive to the cultural reality, which is the very soil in which each person's existence is rooted. Given the social nature of people, the failure to respect their cultural reality is a failure to respect their personhood. The cultural reality of people includes their religious heritage.

This way of approaching people in their cultural reality does not imply a static or even uncritical acceptance of all cultural expression. Nevertheless, the key to the Christ-like way of mission, which starts with people in their cultural reality, is *respect*. God is there already—his Spirit has been at work from the beginning.

iii)People are stewards of creation—participators in God's work.

The conviction that people are stewards of God's creation is central to the

Christian understanding of "who people are." It flows from the truth that human beings are made in God's image, and as such, are given responsibility (dominion) for the created order. People are therefore co-stewards with God of creation. The assertion that people are to be subjects, not objects, is again confirmed. Any form of human life (structures of society) that maintains people as objects and denies them their right to be "subjects of their history" is a violation of their personhood and destiny as stewards of God's creation.

iv) People are stewards of God's power.

Stewardship of God's work involves the stewardship of his power. This arises theologically from people being co-participators in God's work. How are God's stewards to deal with the problems posed by the use and abuse of power?

Throughout the ages, people's experience of power has been dominated by its abuse. It is therefore not surprising that power has come to be regarded almost as an evil in itself—something that "good people" shun and forego. Such a response, however, constitutes a refusal to fulfil the task of stewardship.

Power is God's gift of the enabling capacities and potentialities of existence. To have power is of the essence of our humanity. Power is "the condition of the possibility of freedom."[1] Since the exercise of power is fundamental to the exercise of human freedom, human beings must wield power.

Since power comes from God, it is meant to be used for his creative and redemptive purposes. Insofar as it is abused and used for evil purposes, human beings, as stewards of creation, have a duty to prevent and correct the misuse of power.

b) Mission Starts with "People in Pain"[2]

While the mission of Jesus is a universal one, that all may "be saved and come to the knowledge of the truth" (1 Tim. 2:4), it is also true that Jesus shows a special concern for "people in pain." In his great Nazareth sermon at the beginning of his ministry (Luke 4:18-19), Jesus takes upon himself the words of the prophet Isaiah:

> The Spirit of the Lord is upon me,
> because he has anointed me to preach good news to the
>   poor.
> He has sent me to proclaim release to the captives
> and recovering of sight to the blind,
> to set at liberty those who are oppressed,
> to proclaim the acceptable year of the Lord.

This is how Jesus understood his mission.

The present-day proclamation of God's deliberate choice to side with the oppressed is true to this biblical revelation. Karl Barth asserted this biblical teaching long before (1961) it was taken up as the central theme of "liberation" theology.

> The human righteousness required by God ... has necessarily the character of a vindication of right in favour of the threatened innocent, the oppressed poor, widows, orphans and aliens. ... God always takes his stand unconditionally and passionately on this side and on this side alone ... against those who already enjoy right and privilege and on behalf of those who are denied it and deprived of it.[3]

3. THE MISSION OF GOD TAKES POLITICS SERIOUSLY

The experiences of poor communities have led URM to understand "politics" as those dimensions of human existence which relate to the ordering and functioning of the human community.

The command to love has decisive political dimensions. Christians who care about their neighbours will care about the nature of the political kingdom, which radically affects them.

The command to love is the key to the relationship between seeking the kingdom of God and working for a more just society—for a better political kingdom. It is widely accepted that the political kingdom is not synonymous with the kingdom of God. In this context Jürgen Moltmann warns that there can be "no equations . . . only parables."[4]

In his parable concerning active care for the hungry, the naked and those in prison (Matt. 25:31-46), Jesus makes an essential connection between entry into the kingdom of God, and meaningful concern for the quality of the political kingdom.

In seeking to love one's neighbour, the Christian "begins to resist and to change the scheme of this world and the systems of the present."[5] This will mean being thoroughly concrete about involvement in the political kingdom. It has been the distinctive contribution of theologians from Latin America (arising out of the oppressive poverty around them) to take up this vital point and develop it. Míguez Bonino puts this question: "Are we really for the poor and oppressed if we fail . . . to say *how* we are 'for them' in their concrete historical situation?"[6] It is in the striving for a more human community (political kingdom) that we faithfully give ourselves to working with God for his kingdom within history and beyond history.

Mission therefore demands a serious commitment to the political task of working for a world that more faithfully reflects gospel values. Responsible political involvement requires careful analysis of society. People are in pain—why? What are the causes? Efficacious and responsible love for one's neighbour always involves more than simply responding to symptoms. If one really cares for the liberation of people, one will analyse and seek to understand the complex nature and dynamic of society that prevents their liberation. This will involve a consideration of all models of society that prove most fruitful in revealing and explaining the causes and nature of oppression, exploitation and human alienation.

Authentic mission takes seriously the task of analysing society as a vital prerequisite for finding concrete ways and expressions of the total liberation which Christ came to bring to humanity.

4. THE MISSION OF GOD IS ACTION

The scriptures witness very clearly to Jesus' teaching that mission is not so much something we say, but something we do. "You will know them by their fruits" (Matt. 7:16). "Not everyone who says to me, 'Lord, Lord,' shall enter the kingdom of heaven, but [the one] who does the will of my Father who is in heaven" (Matt. 7:21). The apostolic church emphasized this fundamental characteristic of the Christian life: "Be doers of the word" (James 1:22). Anything less is pseudo-gospel, the tragic delusion of a "pharisaical faith."

Mission is the action of Christ, and the action of Christ is the action of love. Love is the heart of mission. "If I have prophetic powers, and understand all mysteries and all knowledge, and if I have all faith, so as to remove mountains, but have not love, I am nothing" (I Cor. 13:2).

It is in the context of the *practice* of this truth that the New Testament command to proclaim the gospel must be understood. When Paul speaks about being sent "to preach the gospel" (I Cor. 1:17), he is speaking from an experience and practice of bearing the cross, of walking with Jesus.

The Bangkok World Mission Conference of 1973 acknowledged that there can be different "entry points" into the process of total liberation.[7] But if mission is to be authentic it cannot remain at the "entry point" of traditional "evangelism." Emilio Castro writes:

Even as concern for peace in Vietnam is not the whole of salvation, so also telling the story of Jesus is not the whole of salvation, unless in both cases we point with our words and our deeds beyond those particular emphases, to the total dynamics of the kingdom of God.[8]

While it is true that, according to the gospel story, Jesus began by proclaiming a message about his kingdom, the heart of the message does not ultimately lie in what he said, but in who he was and what he did. *The* proclamation is his cross and resurrection. It is his love poured out in his life and death that validates and gives life and power to his spoken word. This is the ultimate evangelizing act. "As the kernel and centre of his Good News, Christ proclaims salvation, this great gift of God which is liberation from everything that oppresses men."[9]

Mission is action directed at this task and purpose of God; involving oneself in this struggle is the essence of Christian response. Failure to be involved with Christ where people are in pain inevitably leads to a lopsided gnostic theology—as if people are saved by right knowledge (orthoteaching) rather than by right action—Godly action (orthopraxis).

The fact remains that weak involvement leads to weak theology. It leads to that dangerous dualism which would separate one's religious being from one's secular reality, and so perpetuate a false consciousness about the nature of sin and oppression that Christ came to destroy.

Real involvement, on the other hand, leads to a truly incarnational biblical theology and to an authentic understanding and practice of mission.

Mission is essentially living the Christian life with Jesus, in solidarity with humanity. Mission is the task of leavening the lump of God's creation, the human community. The *content* of this action is the life of the kingdom—making actual the reality of Christ's Lordship in the life of the world.

5. THE MISSION OF GOD IS ACTION FOR TRANSFORMATION IN THE PERSPECTIVE OF THE KINGDOM

In asserting that "mission is action" it is obvious that the action referred to is whatever expresses and presses forward the realization of the kingdom of God.

Christians should become the ferment within history which could save that history. The transfiguration of the world is the goal towards which our Christian mission should work.[10]

a) Liberation of the Oppressed for Justice

This transformation of the world calls for liberation of human beings at every level of existence where people are bound and oppressed in any way that denies their humanity. Ultimately "liberation" and "salvation" are synonyms, and it is helpful to express a comprehensive understanding of the work of salvation in the following dimensions:

> Salvation works in the struggle for *economic justice* against the exploitation of people by people.
> Salvation works in the struggle for *human dignity* against political oppression of human beings by their fellow men.
> Salvation works in the struggle for *solidarity* against the alienation of person from person.
> Salvation works in the struggle of *hope against despair* in personal life.[11]

The Christian understanding of liberation is informed by the biblical understanding of justice. Liberation is no mere overturning of one particular set of power roles only to be replaced by another. Its goal is nothing less than the peace (shalom) of God in a qualitatively new community in which the role of oppressor and oppressed is completely done away with. The values of God's kingdom become the touchstone for a comprehensive and authentic liberation. Mission as action in the struggle for liberation is always "in the perspective of the kingdom" – the Lordship of Christ. This is our goal; it is for this that we offer our lives.

b) Organizing for Justice/Organizing for Power

Many powerful interests are at work against liberation. Clearly there will be no freedom without a struggle. If people are going to be successful in this struggle, then organizing for power – i.e., enabling people to discover their worth as human beings in the image of God, their dignity, their confidence and their collective wisdom, which lead to effective community action – is absolutely essential. Given the realities of the "principalities and powers" as they are manifest in the structures of society, the struggle for people's comprehensive liberation necessitates organizing for power.

The failure to recognize this need reveals a culpable ignorance of the forces of evil, and a refusal to recognize a vital dimension in the process by which they are contained and defeated.

c) The Imperative of Participation

People must be involved in the process of their own liberation. Freedom is a function of being human. Participation is the practice of freedom. Unless people are encouraged and enabled to participate fully in the process of liberation, there can be no true liberation at all. Such is the fundamental importance of participation as a quality of being human, and of the human community. Any "liberation project" that undervalues and discounts participation as a fundamental feature of the way (and goal) of liberation, should be regarded with profound suspicion. Christians believe they have a particular insight into the depth of evil and its various manifestations, subtle and otherwise. The best protection against all forms of fascism and totalitarianism is full and meaningful participation of people in the process of liberation.

Organizing for power in a way that fulfils the goals of Christian mission will always be characterized by the reality of people's participation.

d) The Imperative of Resistance

Those who hope in Christ can no longer put up with reality as it is, but begin to suffer under it and to contradict it. . . . Peace with God means conflict with the world. Hope makes the Christian Church a constant disturbance in society.[12]

Christians belong to Christ, not to Caesar. They cannot "serve two masters." They are committed to establishing the values of the kingdom. They have no choice but to resist the forces of evil. Their vocation is characterized by this imperative of resistance.

Resistance is an attitude of vigilance in the defence of the fullness of life. It is every attitude and action, individual and corporate, which goes against powers which threaten people and God's creative work in the world (such specific threats include economic exploitation, and the marginalization and victimization of people).[13]

That Christians are called to resistance, therefore, should not even be regarded as a matter of debate in the Christian community. Wherever the laws of a society consistently and grossly violate the laws of God, there should be no doubt where the Christian duty lies. There are many situations in life where obedience to God requires disobedience to Caesar.

Civil disobedience will become a necessary quality of Christian mission wherever the laws of a society do gross damage to human beings. Such laws are "lawless laws"—the laws of criminal oppressors. Human beings have a moral obligation to resist them. "We must obey God rather than people" was a discovery of the very first Christians as they set out to live the new life of Christ.

6. MISSION IN CHRIST'S WAY

Christians are those joined to Christ and empowered by the Holy Spirit to participate in God's work of freeing his creation to be all that he intends it to be. To be joined to Christ is to be joined into a community with a special role within, and on behalf of, humanity. The church of Christ—his body—exists for the world. It is an instrument of God's saving purposes for the whole creation, God's "plan for the fullness of time, to unite all things in him, things in heaven and things on earth" (Eph. 1:10).

Through lives given for the healing of the human community, Christians witness to the reality of God, who empowers them. They witness to the fullness of life and liberation, which is found in being sons and daughters of the creator in a community sustained by the one who is the bread of life. Living this life for the world is what it means to be "doing mission" in Christ's way.

This community encounters God in worship and prayer and in the breaking of the bread, as it encounters God incarnate very specially in those in pain. "Where I am, there shall my servant be" (John 12:26). God is in the hungry, cold and naked; God is in the poor and in those in prison.

True evangelization, therefore, is to encounter God in the midst of history where he is at work, "placing the totality of life under the Lordship of Jesus Christ."[14] Mission in Christ's way involves "making concrete the liberation that he won on the cross."[15]

It is this commitment that motivates those involved in Urban Rural Mission—together with many others—and leads to "active involvement in solidarity with the struggle of people to transform the structures of power to build a just and human society."[16]

Throughout the world an increasing number of Christians are discovering here the heart of mission in Christ's way.

God is our hope and strength;
he is the rock of our liberation.

This is our story and we tell it by living it.

NOTES

1. Karl Rahner, *Theological Investigations*: 4 (London: Darton Longman & Todd, 1966), p. 399.

2. This term is taken from an interview with a black migrant worker in Cape Town, South Africa, 1985.

3. Karl Barth, *Church Dogmatics,* vol. 2:1 (Edinburgh: T. & T. Clark, 1961), p. 386.

4. Jürgen Moltmann, *The Crucified God* (London: SCM Press, 1974), p. 320.

5. Jürgen Moltmann, *The Future of Creation* (London: SCM Press, 1979), p. 17.

6. José Míguez Bonino, *Doing Theology in a Revolutionary Age* (Philadelphia: Fortress Press, 1975), p. 148.

7. *Bangkok Assembly, 1973* (Geneva: WCC/CWME, 1973), p. 90.

8. Emilio Castro, *Sent Free* (Geneva: WCC, 1985), p. 24.

9. Pope Paul VI, *Evangelization in the Modern World* (Pretoria, Southern Africa Catholic Bishops' Conference), p. 8.

10. Castro, p. 27.

11. *Bangkok Assembly, 1973,* p. 89.

12. Jürgen Moltmann, *The Theology of Hope* (London: SCM Press, 1967), pp. 21-22.

13. *Resistance as a Form of Christian Witness* (Geneva: WCC/CWME-URM, 1986), p. 4.

14. C. R. Padilla, ed., *The New Face of Evangelism* (London: Hodder & Stoughton, 1976), p. 14.

15. J. Eagleson and P. Sharper, eds., *Puebla and Beyond* (Maryknoll, N.Y.: Orbis Books, 1979), p. 191.

16. "The Role of UIM with 'People's Groups' and 'People's Movements'," in report of Expanded Advisory Group on Urban Industrial Mission (Tokyo: WCC-CWME-UIM, 1975), p. 3.

9

Stuttgart Consultation

Stuttgart, 1987

WORLD COUNCIL OF CHURCHES CWME

In March 1987 the WCC Commission on World Mission and Evangelism invited representatives of WCC European member churches and agencies for mission and evangelism to a consultation in Stuttgart to consider the place of evangelism in programs of the WCC and its member churches. Attending the meeting were evangelicals belonging to WCC member churches and others not related to the WCC. The consultation statement, using the WCC's Ecumenical Affirmation *as one point of departure, covered a broad range of issues and served as a bridge between conciliar Christians and evangelicals in the period before San Antonio and Lausanne II. The statement is noteworthy for its emphasis on "wholistic" or "integral" evangelism.*

STUTTGART CONSULTATION OF EVANGELISM*

We have gathered here at Stuttgart from different parts of the world to consider the place of evangelism in the program of the World Council of Churches and of our respective churches and organizations. Of the many who are evangelicals here, some belong to churches that are members of the WCC, while others belong to churches that are not. Some of us are particularly involved in the work of promoting evangelism in our own denomination, local church or area. We have come with varying degrees of ecumenical experience.

Coming from very different theological and ecclesial backgrounds, we have become deeply conscious of our fellowship in the gospel and of our common desire to carry out mission in Christ's way so that God's will may be done. We acknowledge humbly that mission is God's mission and that the evangel is God's good news for humankind. We are unworthy servants, earthenware vessels, who have been entrusted with a priceless treasure (II Cor. 4:7). This treasure we seek to share with all, grateful that this sharing brings a blessing to us as well as to those with whom we share (I Cor. 9:23).

We have heard different emphases on how the gospel is to be shared. Some emphasized the sharing of the gospel through resisting oppression and exploitation

---

*Reprinted from *Mission from Three Perspectives* (Geneva: WCC-CWME, 1989), 20-31.

of the poor and identifying with the marginalized. Others, while not denying the necessity for such an attitude on the part of the churches, have, nevertheless, emphasized the necessity for an explicit invitation to faith in Jesus Christ. While recognizing these different emphases, we have come to a common mind on certain matters, which are set out below. We offer this statement to the CWME in the hope that it will stimulate reflection on the place of evangelism in the conciliar movement, especially in the planning of the 1989 Conference on World Mission and Evangelism.

THE NATURE OF EVANGELISM

1. In our reflections we were reminded of the following statements in *Mission and Evangelism: An Ecumenical Affirmation:*
"The Church is sent into the world to call people and nations to repentance, to announce forgiveness of sin and a new beginning in relations with God and with neighbours through Jesus Christ. This evangelistic calling has a new urgency today" (Preface).
"The proclamation of the Gospel includes an invitation to recognize and accept in a personal decision the saving lordship of Christ. It is the announcement of a personal encounter, mediated by the Holy Spirit, with the living Christ, receiving his forgiveness and making a personal acceptance of the call to discipleship and a new life of service" (para. 10).
We did not spend much time in trying to identify evangelism. Even so, there is broad agreement among us that evangelism always means that—in one way or another—people are to be called to faith in Christ. We therefore endorse the *Ecumenical Affirmation* when it states: "Each person is entitled to hear the Good News" (para. 10). The essence of this good news is that God was in Christ reconciling the world unto himself and has now called us to a ministry of reconciliation. This ministry pertains both to reconciliation between God and humans, as well as to reconciliation between individuals and groups alienated from each other. The gospel is the good news of the possibility of a new beginning.

2. This ministry of reconciliation, however, has to be exercised within the specific context of every person or group. There are different entry points for the love of God into the lives of people, both as individuals and as communities. It is only in dependence upon God's Spirit that we can develop a sensitivity toward these and thus become able to minister authentically to people's deepest needs.

3. In view of the above, it has to be emphasized that we can only communicate the gospel to people if we open ourselves to them and enable them to open themselves to us. This means that listening to them is crucial in the sharing of the gospel with them; we cannot share the gospel without sharing ourselves. We live by the gospel of an incarnate Lord; this implies that the gospel has to become incarnated in ourselves, the "evangelists." This is not to suggest that, in our evangelism, we proclaim ourselves, but that those whom we wish to invite to faith in Christ will invariably look for signs of that faith in us. And what will happen if they do not find these? Does not the credibility of our evangelism, to some extent at least, depend on the authenticity of our own lives? Can we evangelize others without becoming vulnerable ourselves?

4. Radio and television have contributed greatly to the spread of the gospel. They penetrate areas where they are the only means of putting people in touch with the gospel and extend information about the witness of the church well beyond

its membership. We have grave reservations, however, about uses of the media in evangelism that are not related to or point to local Christian communities. When evangelists and audience cannot experience mutual sharing together or engage in processes of reconciliation with others we have to ask whether such evangelism does full justice to the ministry of reconciliation with which the church is entrusted. We should do all we can to encourage uses of the media that are responsible and consonant with the nature of the gospel itself.

5. We are agreed that evangelism always includes the explication of the gospel. We recognize, however, that we cannot generalize about the way this should be done. We realize that there are places and situations where the public, verbal witness to the gospel is virtually impossible. A "silent" Christian lifestyle, however, is not in itself sufficiently explicit. We should always be prepared—under the guidance of the Holy Spirit—"to give an account of the hope that is within us" (I Peter 3:15).

6. The church's evangelistic ministry can never be detached from its other ministries. If the church chooses to remain silent in the face of injustice and oppression, both in society at large and in the church itself, it jeopardises its entire evangelistic ministry. These concerns—which scripture consistently summarizes as the plight of the widow, the orphan, the alien and the poor—are inseparably related to evangelism, and every effort to drive a wedge between these is to be rejected as the proclamation of spurious gospel.

We were told of situations where Christians are involved in such integral evangelism, by challenging unjust structures and mobilizing themselves and their neighbours in the struggle for justice and peace. Their actions are motivated by their joint study of the scriptures and as such often lead to a profound conversion of those who join hands against oppression. This experience of incarnational evangelism, in which *kerygma* and *diakonia* are integrated, usually transcends denominational and confessional barriers. We see here a new form of contextual evangelism.

7. We have been reminded of the fact that "the blood of the martyrs is the seed of the church" and that, in God's mysterious ways, it is often a persecuted church that grows, both in number and in maturity. We have also, however, been reminded that the issue is not martyrdom as such but faithfulness, and that it is precisely our faithful witness (*martyria*) to the gospel that may lead the church into situations where it is ostracized, marginalized or even persecuted. But we also know that martyrdom has always been one of the lesser threats to the life and survival of the church; lesser, certainly, than complacency and pride in whom we are and what we have achieved. Since no authentic evangelism can issue from a complacent church we solemnly pledge, constantly and prayerfully, to challenge ourselves, and examine our own lives and the lives of our churches in the light of our high calling. We recognize that such an attitude of humble self-examination will also imply that we judge ourselves before we judge others.

8. We were told of countries and situations where whole communities of Christians boldly and courageously witness to Christ, with the result that people in their thousands turn to faith in him. We rejoice with our brothers and sisters in those situations. We are challenged to ascertain whether such evangelistic efforts might not be appropriate also in other contexts. At the same time, we sadly ask whether the absence of these bold, widespread evangelism activities might be attributable, in some cases, to timidity and failure of nerve, or to lack of confidence in the power of Christ through the gospel, or even to not affirming the necessity of inviting others to faith in Christ.

9. We recognize, however, that there may be situations where people have lost confidence in the church and have become impervious to the gospel and its claims. We do not believe that such situations spell the end of all evangelism, but simply that they may call for another evangelistic style and approach. We have been reminded of the profound impact and influence music has, particularly on the youth, and been given examples of how music, drama and other forms of the arts may be used to present the gospel to people. Christians, who are sensitive to the promptings of the Spirit, will be inventive and will always discover new ways of presenting the Word of Life to those who have not yet made a commitment to Christ. The dissemination of scripture and of other appropriate literature also remains a powerful means of reaching such people.

10. In our evangelism we are challenged to be sensitive to people's cultures. This means, *inter alia,* that we cannot simply export models of evangelism from one culture to another. Some of us are particularly concerned about the highly individualistic approach in evangelism in the west that is often conducted in exactly the same way in other parts of the world, with the result that converts are often isolated and even alienated from their families and communities. We were reminded of the fact that, in some cultures, important decisions—and is not the decision to become a disciple of Jesus Christ an eminently important one?—are never taken individually but always corporately. We must respect such values in these cultures, not least because they help us become more sensitive to the biblical understanding of our humanity, and also challenge the excessive individualism in some cultures.

11. We acknowledge that we can never wholly determine in advance the road our evangelistic ministry will take, nor the way the gospel will come alive in the life and culture of a community. The outcome of our evangelistic ministry may often surprise and sometimes even perplex us, but it belongs to the authenticity of our evangelism and the trust we have in both the gospel and the people to whom we go, that we shall desist from any attempt at manipulation. The outcome of Peter's first evangelistic encounter with somebody outside the Jewish nation was a surprise to him (Acts 10:14, 34) and precipitated a fundamental crisis in the Jerusalem church (Acts 11:2, 3). This has happened before and the same may happen today.

12. The Christian faith is by its very nature a missionary faith. It is therefore intrinsic to the Christian church to always wish to cross frontiers and share the gospel with others. Even so, it is not the church or the individual Christian who converts people, but God. It is not we who bring people to faith but the grace of God, which works through us. Evangelism is therefore, ultimately, not dependent on our technology, resources or expertise but on the mysterious and unfathomable workings of the Holy Spirit in the human heart. There is, therefore, a strange and wonderful paradox here: On the one hand we are to give our all to the evangelization of God's world and yet, on the other hand, we are given the assurance that it is God's work and that God will do it. The awareness of this paradox makes us bold and committed to the task of evangelism, yet, at the same time, relaxed in the knowledge that God's Spirit is the supreme evangelist.

LOCAL CHRISTIAN COMMUNITIES AND EVANGELISM

13. Jesus Christ, our Lord, gave the missionary mandate "Go therefore, and make disciples of all nations" not to a believer in isolation but to believers in community. The disciples to whom he addressed this command constituted the nucleus of the early Christian church. Scripturally and ideally, therefore, evangelism

should be centred in a local church—enhancing its life, strengthening its vision and extending its influence.

Though there is validity in discussing the theologies, strategies and program of evangelism at national and international consultations, we believe that the experiences and concerns of local churches and groups should not only be reported in these meetings, but should feature prominently in the agenda of such meetings.

14. In God's rich and gracious provision, believers are endowed with different gifts (Rom. 12:3-8; I Cor. 12). These gifts are ennobling and enabling means of presenting a winsome, saving and reconciling God in Jesus Christ. Thus evangelism, insofar as the diversity of gifts is concerned, cannot be limited to one or even a series of activities. As believers become faithful in expressing their particular gifts, the Holy Spirit defines for them their avenues of service.

God calls all believers to participate in the evangelistic task. Men and women, clergy and laity, young and old—all are one in Christ, one in the Spirit (Gal. 3:28; I Cor. 12:13), all are proclaimers, in word and act, of the good news they share together.

We are aware that there are still structures that inhibit the full participation of all believers in evangelism, particularly women and youth.

15. The local churches are highly diverse in location, history, culture, sociopolitical situation and religious ethos. Therefore, there cannot be the same evangelism agenda for all churches everywhere.

Local churches should take seriously the need to develop incarnational models as part of their evangelistic obedience to God. They should be given ample creative space to evolve these models, based on much prayer and reflection on God's word and their personal and communal experiences with God.

EVANGELISM AND THE RENEWAL OF THE CHURCH

16. Authentic evangelism renews the church; a renewed church evangelizes. Believers appropriate in their own lives—individually and corporately—the transforming grace and power of the good news as they proclaim it to others. Such manifestations of growing Christ-likeness before the world, commend the evangelistic message, which in turn is used by the Holy Spirit to draw others. The early churches in the Book of Acts showed this life-giving, life-changing dynamism. So do many local churches today.

As we have already seen, the Holy Spirit is the Great Evangelist. The Spirit's role in evangelism is often ignored, though lip-service may be paid to it. Churches are in danger of centering their evangelistic efforts only on personnel, denominations, programs and money.

The local church must learn to be still, to wait upon the wind of the Spirit's stirring, which often comes in quietness, worship and prayer; to listen carefully to the Spirit's voice in humble obedience. A reflective local church will be effective in its evangelism.

17. Commitment to other brothers and sisters in Christ is an aspect of church renewal that in itself has evangelistic dimensions. People everywhere are searching for meaningful human relationships that will help them weather many of the storms of life. Such relationships do not exploit or discriminate; they help people define their identity; they help them to share in the struggles of others; and to rejoice with them. Sadly, however, relationships in many church circles can be superficial and artificial. Authentic relationships are nurtured when we submit to each other in obedience to the Lord (Phil. 2:1-8; Eph. 5:21).

18. A corporate commitment to worship, prayer, fellowship and celebration of the good news is another aspect of church renewal and evangelism. Such a commitment characterized the churches mentioned in the Book of Acts. These churches grew (Acts 2:47, 5:14). In times of persecution and danger their solidarity in Christ and with each other helped them stand, even to the point of death.

EVANGELISM AND THE UNITY OF THE CHURCH

19. "God was in Christ reconciling the world to himself" (II Cor. 5:19). We are called to be ambassadors of and for our reconciling God, ambassadors who bear, individually and corporately, the signs of reconciliation—at one with each other as Christ is at one with the Father.

The nature of evangelism will rise out of our understanding of the good news that is being proclaimed and will colour the nature of the good news that is received.

Salvation brings spiritual and total wholeness to the individual at one with God in Jesus Christ. Such wholeness gives people a new identity, not by affirming them in their self-centredness but by calling them to give themselves to others in Christ's way. The New Testament communities of faith were rebuked when they divided to suit the taste, preference or personal loyalties of individuals (I Cor. 1:10-13).

20. Our Lord Jesus Christ (in John 17) prayed for the unity of his followers. Forms of evangelism that cater primarily to denominational aggrandizement fail to affirm the indivisibility of the one body of Christ. Authentic evangelism calls people into a community with all Christian people, a community that—in spite of denominational and other barriers—lives under the sign of at-one-ment under the cross.

21. We have discerned two related circumstances that jeopardize the unity and the evangelistic effectiveness of the church.

a) In some places, churches that have been present for a long time consider that the unity of Christ's people is not helped by the activities of groups undertaking direct evangelism towards persons who have a traditional relationship to those churches.

b) In the opinion of others, some of these churches appear defensive about "their" nominal members but are unable or perhaps are not even interested in active evangelism towards them. They believe there is an imperative to evangelize in such circumstances.

We need to address these issues with care and creative sensitivity.

22. Any evangelism that does not build up good relationships with other Christians in the community must inevitably come under question. Local churches therefore should be encouraged to pray and work together in a cooperative and loving spirit as a sign of witness and of the attractiveness of the face of Jesus Christ: "See how they love one another."

23. We affirm that Christian unity, important as it is, must never be a unity for its own sake. It is a unity so that all may believe, and in harmony with a mission in Christ's way on behalf of, and in identification with, the poor, the lost and the least in God's creation.

THE ROLE OF PARA-CHURCH ORGANIZATIONS IN EVANGELISM

24. We give thanks for the dedicated individuals and the stewardship of resources in organizations and agencies that work to support the churches and serve the world in the name of Christ. We greatly value the work done by these bodies when they

act after consultation, and in conjunction with the churches and communities of Christ's people in local areas, in such a way as to build up the sign of Christ's unifying love, and to empower the actions of Christ's people there.

25. We hear the cries of pain of churches and communities of Christ's people in local areas when some outside agencies, driven by the ardour of their convictions, have acted—in the opinion of some local churches—without consultation, to the detriment of the work and vision of these churches. Such action does not strengthen, but weakens the credibility and witness of the church.

EVANGELISM IN THE CONTEXT OF OTHER FAITHS

26. We acknowledge and affirm that authentic witness to Jesus Christ should be carried out in a spirit of respect for the beliefs and devotion of others. It can never be simply a "telling" but must also be a sensitive "listening." Furthermore, it must always respect the freedom of others and should not be coercive or seductive in any way. We acknowledge that God has not left himself without witness anywhere (Acts 16:17), and we joyfully recognize a knowledge of God, a sense of the transcendent, among many human communities, including many faith communities. At the same time, it needs to be pointed out that humankind's knowledge of God is vitiated by sin and God's gracious revelation in Christ is needed to call us all back to an authentic vision of God. We agree with the *Ecumenical Affirmation* (para. 43) that the Spirit of God is at work in the world convincing humankind of God's righteousness and convicting them of their own sin (John 16:8). As we enter into dialogue with those of other faiths we should keep in mind both the knowledge of God, which is available to all, and the work of the Spirit ahead of our own witness. We recognize also the figure of Christ in the poor, the needy, the ill and the oppressed (Matt. 25:31-46).

27. Christians, nevertheless, owe the message of God's salvation in Jesus Christ to every person and to every people (*Ecumenical Affirmation,* para. 41). As we have already said, the proclamation of the gospel includes an invitation to each person to recognize and accept in a personal decision the saving Lordship of Christ (para. 10). This might be seen as a fulfilment of the aspirations of humankind expressed sometimes in religious traditions but at other times in non-religious movements, and even at times in counter-religious movements. Such proclamation may also be understood as a making explicit of an implicit knowledge; or as bringing assurance and certainty of salvation to all those who, without prior explicit knowledge of Jesus Christ, the only Saviour and Lord, have nevertheless realized their own inadequacy and sin and have thrown themselves on the mercy of God. While the proclamation of the gospel will affirm and confirm certain aspects of a person's or a people's previous religious experience, it will also challenge and judge other aspects of such an experience. It is always, therefore, a call to repentance and new life. We recognize that dialogue is not to be used for cheap proselytism but we believe that it can be a medium of authentic witness, though we are aware that there are other reasons for the necessity of dialogue with those of other faiths. Such reasons would include the building up of community, common witness about the dignity and rights of human beings, and addressing human need.

28. As Christians we welcome the fact that many societies are moving towards greater openness and pluralism. In some cases the emergence of a plural society makes the existence of Christian churches, in a predominantly non-Christian culture, possible. In others, societies, which have hitherto been largely "Christian,"

become increasingly plural with many different old and new faiths represented in them. We recognize both phenomena as within God's providence and as giving Christians fresh opportunities to love, serve and witness to their neighbours. We are concerned that some societies remain closed and continue to deny freedom of belief, of conscience and of free expression to their members. As Christians we are committed to the promotion of these freedoms in our respective societies.

Mission in Christ's Way:
Your Will Be Done

San Antonio, 1989

WORLD CONFERENCE ON MISSION AND EVANGELISM

The fourth WCC-sponsored World Conference on Mission and Evangelism met in San Antonio, Texas, May 22-June 2, 1989, on the theme "Your Will Be Done: Mission in Christ's Way." The CWME meeting preceded LCWE's Lausanne II at Manila congress by only six weeks, the two events being linked by a significant group of "concerned evangelicals" who attended both.

San Antonio dealt with the mission agenda under four sectional themes: I. "Turning to the Living God"; II. "Participating in Suffering and Struggle"; III. "The Earth is the Lord's"; and IV. "Towards Renewed Communities in Mission." Each section report ended with a series of "Acts of Faithfulness" embodying some important conviction or ongoing challenge.

Stewardship of creation was for the first time given major attention at a missionary conference. In Section I, "Turning to the Living God," the main emphases of the 1982 Ecumenical Affirmation *are again taken up in a fresh way. Reference is also made to the work of the Melbourne Conference (1980), the Stuttgart Consultation (1987), and the report of the Orthodox Advisory Group (1988). According to the conference message, the two most significant trends were "the spirit of universality (catholicity) of the gathering, and its concern for the fulness of the gospel." Mission in Christ's Way was understood as a "creative tension" between spiritual and material needs, prayer and action, evangelism and social responsibility, dialogue and witness, power and vulnerability, the local and the universal.*

SECTION I. TURNING TO THE LIVING GOD*

I. MISSION IN THE NAME OF THE LIVING GOD

1. At the very heart of the church's vocation in the world is the proclamation of the kingdom of God inaugurated in Jesus the Lord, crucified and risen (ME 6)[1] and made present among us by the Holy Spirit.

---

*Reprinted from Frederick R. Wilson, ed., *The San Antonio Report:* Your Will Be Done — Mission in Christ's Way (Geneva: WCC, 1990), 25-35.

The Triune God, Father, Son and Holy Spirit, is a God in mission, the source and sustainer of the church's mission (John 20:21; Acts 2). The church's mission cannot but flow from God's care for the whole creation, unconditional love for all people and concern for unity and fellowship with and among all human beings.

2. As we reflected on the section theme within the context of the overall conference theme we were made conscious of the fact that we are enabled to turn to the living God and become involved in God's mission only because the living God has created us for life in communion, has first turned to us in grace and love, and has done so supremely in Jesus Christ, our Lord and Saviour. Our ministry of witness therefore primarily flows from gratitude, not just from an obligation laid upon us.

3. God's people know God's will because the holy and Triune God in diverse ways has revealed himself. The prophets of the old covenant proclaim the will of God in new ways in ever-changing circumstances. Finally and uniquely, God's will is made known in Jesus Christ (Heb. 1:1-4). Testimony to this is given throughout the New Testament. We have to confess that, as sinful people, we recognize the will of God for ourselves only partially and provisionally. At the same time we are confident that the Holy Spirit enlightens us, teaches us to understand the will of God for ourselves and our time, and also enables us to do the will of God. The unity of the divine and human will in the person of Jesus Christ is the source of and model for our mission according to God's will.

4. "The mission of the church has cosmic dimensions" (Orthodox, p. 33). "The biblical promise of a new earth and a new heaven where love, peace and justice will prevail . . . invites our action as Christians in history" (ME preface). Since our mission serves the coming of the reign of God, it is concerned with bringing the future into the present, serving the cause of God's reign: the new creation.

5. These tremendous affirmations have, however, to be viewed in light of the present moment in history. In some parts of the world people face a total system of death, of monstrous false gods, of exploitative economic systems, of violence, of the disintegration of the fundamental bonds of society, of the destruction of human life, of helplessness of persons in the face of impersonal forces. We are called to exercise our mission in this context of human struggle, and challenged to keep the earth alive and to promote human dignity, since the living God is both creator of heaven and earth and protector of the cause of the widow, the orphan, the poor and the stranger. To respond to all this is a part of our mission, just as inviting people to put their trust in God is part of that mission. The "material gospel" and the "spiritual gospel" have to be *one,* as was true of the ministry of Jesus (ME 33). Frequently the world's poor are also those who have not yet heard the good news of the gospel; to withhold from them justice as well as the good news of life in Christ is to commit a "double injustice" (ME 32). There is no evangelism without solidarity; there is no Christian solidarity that does not involve sharing the message of God's coming reign (ME 33).

6. Mission in the name of the living God of necessity leads to repentance on the part of those who are involved in this mission. Any call to conversion and to service for the reign of God "should begin with the repentance of those who do the calling, who issue the invitation" (ME 13). " 'Your Will Be Done': this prayer of Christ to the Father is a continuous reminder of the need for repentance and forgiveness of sins. It is a call to reexamine our lives in the light of Christ's life. It is a call addressed personally to each of us for metanoia and conversion, a call to literally 'turn around' our lives and recommit ourselves to Christ" (Orthodox, p. 42).[2] We have to repent

of our arrogance and insensitivity, but also of our failure of nerve and inertia. "The crucified and risen Christ is a judge of shallow life-styles and invites the churches to repentance and new life. In many situations today, renewed life-styles will be the most authentic and unambiguous way to proclaim and live out the Gospel" (Melbourne, p. 190).[3] A call to repentance is, however, not a call to drop important work, but to do it differently. In repentance, the fountains of life are cleansed. True repentance does not paralyze: it invigorates; after repentance one gets up and walks — in a new way.

7. We have been made aware of a new and widespread interest in evangelism in communities linked with the ecumenical movement in the north as well as the south. The love of God for the world is the source of our missionary motivation. This love creates an urgency to share the gospel invitingly in our time (even if we recognize with deep regret that some of our missionary endeavours may be attributed to impure motivations — concerns about declining church membership, subtle political agendas, and the like). Christians desire to "confess the life and work of Jesus Christ as unique, decisive, and universally significant" (Tambaram II);[4] we therefore invite our churches to subscribe to the CWME aim, as endorsed by the Nairobi assembly of the WCC (1975), that the Christian community should be assisted to proclaim "the gospel of Jesus Christ, by word and deed, to the whole world to the end that all may believe in him and be saved".

II. THE LIVING GOD CALLS US TO UNITY IN MISSION

8. The present ecumenical movement came into being out of the conviction that the division of Christians is a scandal and an impediment to the witness of the church. There is a growing awareness among the churches today of the inextricable relationship between Christian unity and missionary calling, between ecumenism and evangelization (ME 1).

"The impulse for common witness comes from the depth of our faith. Its urgency is underlined when we realize the seriousness of the human predicament." (ME 24).

9. In a special way the theme "Mission in Christ's Way" sets unity and mission in an inseparable relation. The risen Christ who sends us is our peace, who breaks down the dividing wall of hostility, reconciling us in one body through the cross (Eph. 2:14-15). The churches are called to give a common witness to this reconciling ministry in the power of the Spirit.

10. Christian mission is the humble involvement of the one body of Christ in liberating and suffering love, the witness of God's saving acts in Christ, and the practice of God's incarnational love for all humankind. This mission is expressed through the communion of love and justice which embodies the church's self-giving solidarity with the human family.

11. When churches and missions really go *the way of Christ* instead of their own ways, they will necessarily join their actions whenever possible. Our divisions weaken our efforts at living in solidarity with the poor, the hungry and the oppressed. To be called to unity in mission involves becoming a community that transcends in its life the barriers and brokenness in the world, and living as a sign of at-one-ment under the cross. The search for visible unity "in one faith and in one eucharistic fellowship" (Vancouver, pp. 43ff.)[5] and the struggle to overcome injustice and alienation in the human family are one single response to the gospel. Unity-in-mission and advocacy of justice are therefore not differing phases of the

ecumenical movement, as though we could separate between the church's being and doing, between faith and action, between theology and involvement. Consequently, unity is vital to the missional health of the church and the future of humankind. The church is called again and again to be a prophetic sign and foretaste of the unity and renewal of the human family as envisioned in God's promised reign.

12. In spite of our many failures in the area of unity in mission, we also have reason to celebrate the manifestations of such unity which have come to our attention. We were told stories of joint projects in mission in many places, and we rejoice in these. In fact, our very coming together as an ecumenical fellowship here in San Antonio is a manifestation and celebration of unity in mission and we affirm joyfully that "the churches of the WCC are on a pilgrimage towards unity under the missionary vision of John 17:21" (ME 1). We have noted with gratitude the coming into existence of united churches in many parts of the world as well as church union negotiations still in process, and we pray that the churches renewed in unity may also be renewed in mission. Yet even apart from these few scattered examples of unity-in-practice, we confess that we are already one in mission because of what the living God has done to and for us. Our unity is a reality we cannot undo, even if we wished: we are given to one another as sisters and brothers in the one household of God.

13. Mission in unity requires Christians to work for the authenticity of the apostolic faith. Doctrinal divisions, especially those that prevent the sharing of the eucharist and the full participation of women in the church, keep Christians from making a common witness. The eucharist, which is the most central sacrament of our faith, also is the place where our divisions become most painfully apparent. The one faith we share and the one cup and one bread we are given should be vital actions for mission, particularly if "the eucharist is bread for a missionary people" (ME 21). At the same time, in light of the fact that many people around us do not even know the name of the Triune God except in blasphemy, we call into question the endless debates and time-consuming preoccupations demanding an "open" eucharist.

14. One of the most sensitive areas in our discussions on unity in mission concerned the issue of *proselytism*. The aim of our evangelism should be the building up of the body of Christ, service in the world, and the glory of God. Instead, evangelism sometimes turns into programmes for denominational aggrandizement. We believe that any evangelism that does not promote good relationships with other Christians in the community must inevitably be called into question (Stuttgart, p. 27).[6] Our witness may deteriorate into counterwitness, thereby in effect denying the authenticity of the faith experience of other Christians. All unhealthy competition in mission work should be avoided as constituting a distorted form of mission (Orthodox, p. 39). At the same time we realize that faith communities may become ingrown and stagnant, lose their vision, and become unable or perhaps not even interested in getting involved in evangelism and pastoral renewal in their environment (Stuttgart, p. 27). In such situations other Christians, rather than ignoring the presence and integrity of the traditional faith communities, may perhaps be privileged to play a catalytic role in renewal for mission. They will, however, only be able to do so if they identify with the local faith community and treat it with sensitivity, respect and integrity.

III. WITNESS IN A SECULAR SOCIETY

15. Everywhere the churches are in missionary situations. Even in countries where the churches have been active for centuries we see life organized today

without reference to Christian values, a growth of secularism understood as the absence of any final meaning. The churches have lost vital contact with the workers and the youth and many others. The situation is so urgent that it demands priority attention of the ecumenical movement (ME 37).

16. Many would see "secularization" partly as a fruit of the gospel, releasing humankind from ancient powers and emancipating people to make mature choices and take responsibility for their destiny. "Secularism," on the other hand, refers to a closed system, a context in which people live and act without reference to God. Today, many who have experienced secularization in recent decades have however given up faith in its value: a post-secular era announces itself.

17. There may be a variety of manifestations of secularism; the situation in North Atlantic countries differs from that in the socialist world, or in Latin America, or in Asia and the South Pacific. Each context calls for an appropriate response.

18. Secularism has not diminished people's desire to relate to some "ultimate reality". The shrine does not remain empty. "Secular" religion may find expression in the worship of the modern idols of consumerism, or of economic, political and military power, in which individual and collective selfishness reigns supreme. The religious quest of humankind may also find expression in the search for meaning and coherence articulated in the ideologies of our time; at other times it expresses itself in a bewildering plurality of religious sects, some of an exotic nature.

19. Our church communities are part of society and exposed to the same seemingly irresistible advance of the forces of secularism in the world. Secularism is not just something "out there": it has infiltrated and profoundly influenced our churches. Not only have some churches often adopted the same secularist ideologies that operate in society at large (pragmatism, functionalism, etc.), they have also themselves contributed to the spread of secularism. Some results of this have been the compartmentalization of life into "public" and "private" spheres and the relegation of "religion" to the latter, as well as the rise of individualism leading to breakdown in community. Specifically in our witness we have often absorbed the dichotomy between spiritual and social, and word and action, resulting in a distortion of the biblical concern for witness to persons in the totality of their need.

20. The advance of secularism and the collapse of traditional religious frames of reference also have a positive influence on our churches' practice. Stripped of their power base, they are called—in a new and challenging way—to become servants in society. In some parts of the world this means that our churches, for the first time in many centuries, have the opportunity to become what they always should have been: powerless and vulnerable witnesses to the faith they proclaim and by which they live.

21. Our churches should at all times resist the temptation both to succumb to the spirit of the age and to withdraw into a ghetto existence. One way of articulating this resistance is to reclaim for ourselves cardinal elements of the spirit and practice of the ascetic tradition: a simple life in which sharing and solidarity have priority over possession and individualism, the boldness to refuse to conform to the pattern of this world (cf. Rom. 12:2), and the resilience to persist on the road of faith and service.

22. The fountainhead of our practice of resistance to the dominant ethos and of our witness to secular society ought to be the local worshipping community: believers gathered—sometimes in small house groups—around the word and the sacraments, empowered by the continual renewal of their faith, emboldened to become relevant to what is happening in secular society. From this base, believers

go forth to meet people and witness to them, realizing that their witness depends more on who they are than on what they do or say; no matter how eloquent our verbal testimony, people will always believe their eyes first. Nevertheless, what Christians say matters and should be relevant to people's actual ways of speaking about their fears and hopes. The whole people of God—clergy and laity, women and men, mothers and fathers, single people, children and youth—are involved in this witness of life. We were greatly encouraged by stories of such witness to faith in Christ, even by small children acting as partners with the local church, often in contexts saturated with secularism and atheism.

23. For the sake of their survival—no, for the sake of the gospel itself and of the cause of Christ—the Christian churches will have to conduct ongoing and penetrating studies of the issues of secularization and secularism and of ways of responding to this challenge faithfully, sensitively, and with integrity.

IV. WITNESS AMONG PEOPLE OF OTHER LIVING FAITHS

24. True witness follows Jesus Christ in respecting and affirming the uniqueness and freedom of others. . . . Such an attitude springs from the assurance that God is the creator of the whole universe and that he has not left himself without a witness at any time or any place. The Spirit of God is constantly at work in ways that pass human understanding. In entering into a relationship of dialogue with others, Christians seek to discern the unsearchable riches of God and the way he deals with humanity (ME 41, 43).

The proclamation of the gospel includes an invitation to recognize and accept in a personal decision the saving lordship of Christ. It is the announcement of a personal encounter, mediated by the Holy Spirit, with the living Christ, receiving his forgiveness and making a personal acceptance of the call to discipleship and a life of service (ME 10).

Christians owe the message of God's salvation in Jesus Christ to every person and to every people. . . . The wonder of [Jesus'] ministry of love persuades Christians to testify to people of every religious and non-religious persuasion of this decisive presence of God in Christ. In him is our salvation (ME 41, 42).

25. In reaffirming the "evangelistic mandate" of the ecumenical movement, we would like to emphasize that we may never claim to have a full understanding of God's truth: we are only the recipients of God's grace. Our ministry of witness among people of other faiths presupposes our *presence* with them, *sensitivity* to their deepest faith commitments and experiences, *willingness* to be their servants for Christ's sake, *affirmation* of what God has done and is doing among them, and *love for them. Since God's mystery in Christ surpasses our understanding and since our knowledge of God's saving power is imperfect, we Christians are called to be witnesses* to others, not judges of them. We also affirm that it is possible to be non-aggressive and missionary at the same time—that it is, in fact, the only way of being truly missionary.

26. We cannot point to any other way of salvation than Jesus Christ; at the same time we cannot set limits to the saving power of God. At times the debate about salvation focuses itself only on the fate of the individual's soul in the hereafter, whereas the will of God is life in its fullness even here and now. We therefore state: (a) that our witness to others concerning salvation in Christ springs from the fact that we have encountered him as our Lord and Saviour and are hence urged to share this with others; and (b) that in calling people to faith in Christ, we are not

only offering personal salvation but also calling them to follow Jesus in the service of God's reign.

27. We have paid attention to the complex debate about the relationship between *witness* and *dialogue*. We recognize that both witness and dialogue presuppose two-way relationships. We affirm that witness does not preclude dialogue but invites it, and that dialogue does not preclude witness but expands and deepens it.

28. Dialogue has its own place and integrity and is neither opposed to nor incompatible with witness or proclamation. We do not water down our own commitment if we engage in dialogue; as a matter of fact, dialogue between people of different faiths is spurious unless it proceeds from the acceptance and expression of faith commitment. Indeed, life with people of other faiths and ideologies is by its very nature an encounter of commitments (ME 45). In dialogue we are invited to listen in openness to the possibility that the God we know in Jesus Christ may encounter us also in the lives of our neighbours of other faiths. On the other hand, we also see that the mutual sharing with people of other faiths in the efforts for justice, peace and service to the environment engages us in dialogue – the dialogue of life. We wish to commend that, in recognition that all humankind is responsible before God and the human family.

29. In affirming the dialogical nature of our witness, we are constrained by grace to affirm that "salvation is offered to the whole creation through Jesus Christ" (Tambaram II). "Our mission to witness to Jesus Christ can never be given up" (Melbourne, p. 188). We are well aware that these convictions and the ministry of witness stand in tension with what we have affirmed about God being present in and at work in people of other faiths; we appreciate this tension, and do not attempt to resolve it.

30. We affirm our unequivocal endorsement of the principle and practice of religious freedom. We are aware that many people are discriminated against, harassed and even persecuted for their faith, often when they have converted from one faith to another; we deplore this and every manifestation of religious or ideological fanaticism. We commend to our Christian communities all those who suffer for their faith, whatever their religious persuasion may be.

V. COMMUNICATING THE GOSPEL TODAY

31. To receive the message of the kingdom of God is to be incorporated into the body of Christ, the church, the author and sustainer of which is the Holy Spirit. The churches are to be a sign for the world. They are to intercede as he did, to serve as he did. Thus Christian mission is the action of the body of Christ in the history of mankind – a continuation of Pentecost (ME 20).

Churches are free to choose the ways they consider best to announce the gospel to different people in different circumstances. But these options are never neutral. Every methodology illustrates or betrays the gospel we announce. In all communications of the gospel, power must be subordinated to love (ME 28).

32. The Vancouver assembly of the WCC (1983) recommended that "the church must relate to the media in a manner which is pastoral, evangelical and prophetic" (Vancouver, p. 107). In communicating the gospel to people, we acknowledge the ambivalence of the media at our disposal. We recognize that the media not only *reflect* reality, but also shape, distort, and hide it. In its use of the media the church must be critical of these characteristics of the modern media and at the same time guard against becoming guilty of similar abuses. The way we use the media should

be in harmony with the gospel we seek to proclaim. In communicating the gospel, both message and response are shaped by the authenticity of the communicator. The gospel proclaims a personal, interactive relationship among and between God and human persons; therefore, our means of communication must not only reflect but demonstrate the image we wish to transmit.

33. The faith evoked through the communication of the gospel needs nurture within the body of Christ. This nurture includes prayer and the study of God's word in a language and cultural form which communicates without alienation and which facilitates the discernment of the contours of God's reign in all realms of life. We can and may never determine in advance the way the gospel will come alive in the life, context and culture of a community. We affirm true Christian communication to be an act of worship, a praise of God through the shared word and action of persons-in-community, reflecting the life of the Holy Trinity. Christ's mission to the world manifests the outpouring of God's love through the Son and the Spirit. The ground of unity of the church, the body of Christ, is the love and unity eternally manifested in the life of the Triune God. The church as God's chosen instrument for proclaiming the good news of the reign of God is meant to embody and communicate values of oneness, reconciliation, equality, justice, freedom, harmony, peace and love. In the image of the Trinity, we must hold together this witness of the worshipping and serving community united in love, with that of its evangelistic task of sending forth persons to proclaim the word to those who have not yet heard or realized its fulfilling and saving grace.

34. As we seek to communicate God's image to others, we realize that our own lives and stories, as well as non-discursive ways of communicating through hymn or song, icon or symbol, movement or silence, may be more effective personal and experiential ways of sharing the faith than some forms of mass media. The church is also challenged to proclaim the gospel today in new languages, in both written and oral forms, and in the idioms and symbols of the cultures in which it is carried. Many millions have not heard the story of Jesus, even in cultures where historically the gospel was common knowledge.

35. Christian communication does not end with the proclamation of the message, but continues in an unending process directed to the education and formation of persons in the Christian life, helping them to grasp more deeply and to enter more fully into the Christian story. The development of one's spirituality involves the capacity to communicate with God through prayers, and to apprehend how Christ enters into and claims all of life, guiding one's priorities and actions in every aspect of life.

36. "The vicarious work of Christ demands the presence of a vicarious people" (ME 25). We stand in awe in the awareness of the belief that God has committed to our faltering faith communities the message of God's love and reign. We witness to the humble power and servant lordship of the Crucified and Risen, seeking to be faithful to him who called us into discipleship and into the ministry of witnessing to the living God.

NOTES

1. ME: *Mission and Evangelism — an Ecumenical Affirmation*. Geneva: WCC, 1982.
2. Orthodox: "Consultation of Eastern and Orthodox Churches, Neapolis, Greece, 1988," in *Mission from Three Perspectives*. Geneva: WCC-CWME, 1989.

3. Melbourne: *Your Kingdom Come — Mission Perspectives, Report on the World Conference on Mission and Evangelism, Melbourne, 1980.* Geneva: WCC, 1981.

4. Tambaram II: "Dialogue and Mission: Issues for Further Study," questions approved at Tambaram consultation, January 1988, in *International Review of Mission,* Vol. LXXVIII, No. 307, July 1988, p. 449.

5. Vancouver: *Gathered for Life: Official Report of the Sixth Assembly of the World Council of Churches, Vancouver, 1983.* Geneva: WCC, 1983.

6. Stuttgart: "Consultation on Evangelism, Stuttgart, 1987," in *Mission from Three Perspectives.*

11

Justice, Peace and the Integrity of Creation

Seoul, 1990

WORLD COUNCIL OF CHURCHES

The Seoul Convocation (March 5-12, 1990) was an important milestone in the conciliar process of committing WCC member churches to a mutual covenant for "Justice, Peace and the Integrity of Creation" (JPIC). Though the Seoul convocation was planned by another WCC unit than the one responsible for mission and evangelism, JPIC — along with mission and church unity — is quickly becoming an integral expression of ecumenical solidarity, inseparable from the conciliar understanding of world mission. "Now is the time to commit ourselves anew to God's justice. . . . Now is the time when the ecumenical movement needs a greater sense of binding, mutual commitment and solidarity in word and action. It is the promise of God's covenant for our time and our world to which we respond. . . . Now is the time for the ecumenical movement to articulate its vision of all people living on earth and caring for creation as a family where each member has the same right to wholeness of life" (Convocation Message).

Cited here are the ten affirmations on justice, peace, and the integrity of creation, and four "concretizations" of the act of covenanting among the churches. They express a concrete program of action which parallels the spiritual vision of the kingdom as the goal of God's mission.

TEN AFFIRMATIONS ON JUSTICE, PEACE AND THE INTEGRITY OF CREATION*

I.   *We affirm that all exercise of power is accountable to God.*

II. *We affirm God's option for the poor.*

III. *We affirm the equal value of all races and peoples.*

IV. *We affirm that male and female are created in the image of God.*

V.   *We affirm that truth is at the foundation of a community of free people.*

*Reprinted from *Now Is The Time:* Final Document and Other Texts, World Convocation on Justice, Peace and the Integrity of Creation, Seoul, Republic of Korea, 5-12 March 1990 (Geneva: WCC-JPIC Office, 1990), 12-21, 22-33.

VI. *We affirm the peace of Jesus Christ.*
VII *We affirm the creation as beloved of God.*
VIII. *We affirm that the earth is the Lord's.*
IX. *We affirm the dignity and commitment of the younger generation.*
X. *We affirm that human rights are given by God.*

FOUR COMMITMENTS FROM THE ACT OF COVENANT

1. For a just economic order on local, national, regional and international levels for all people; for liberation from the foreign debt bondage that affects the lives of hundreds of millions of people. We commit ourselves to work and to engage our churches to work . . .

2. For the true security of all nations and peoples; for the demilitarization of international relations; against militarism and national security doctrines and systems; for a culture of non-violence as a force for change and liberation. We commit ourselves to work and to engage our churches to work . . .

3. For building a culture that can live in harmony with creation's integrity; for preserving the gift of the earth's atmosphere to nurture and sustain the world's life; for combating the causes of destructive changes to the atmosphere which threaten to disrupt the earth's climate and create widespread suffering. We commit ourselves to work and to engage our churches to work . . .

4. For the eradication of racism and discrimination on national and international levels for all people; for the breaking down of walls which divide people because of their ethnic origin; for the dismantling of the economic, political and social patterns of behaviour that perpetuate and allow individuals to consciously and unconsciously perpetuate the sin of racism. We commit ourselves to work and to engage our churches to work . . .

12

Come, Holy Spirit

Canberra, 1991

WORLD COUNCIL OF CHURCHES SEVENTH ASSEMBLY

The Seventh Assembly of the World Council of Churches was held in Canberra, Australia, February 7-20, 1991, on the theme, "Come, Holy Spirit — Renew the Whole Creation." For the first time an entire WCC assembly was devoted to the theology and work of the Holy Spirit — in creation, in the social order, and in the church's calling to mission and unity.

"Through our acceptance of the ministry of reconciliation, we become a missionary people, not in that sense of dominating over peoples and nations which has all too often characterized missionary work, but in the sense of sharing God's own mission of bringing all humanity into communion with God through Christ in the power of the Spirit, sharing our faith and our resources with all people" (Assembly Message). The Report of Section III reflects on the Christian community as a koinonia *in the Spirit called to mission.*

SECTION III: SPIRIT OF UNITY — RECONCILE YOUR PEOPLE!*

"Through Christ God reconciled us to himself and gave us the ministry of reconciliation" (2 Cor. 5:18).

58. Christians see truth in different ways and yet at the same time are united in the power of the Holy Spirit. Our rich diversity of insights and practices is a gift of the Holy Spirit. Sadly all too often diversity is a cause of division even in the life of the church. Yet as members of the body of Christ we are already united by our common baptism; guided by the Holy Spirit, we are drawn into a koinonia (communion) rooted in the giving and receiving life of the Holy Trinity. What we work towards is unity of faith, life and witness. In this process it will be especially important to face up to the divisions which prevent us from sharing the eucharist together, and make it possible for churches to recognize each other's ministries.

59. Christians are even more deeply divided from people of other faiths and ideologies, even though we share a common humanity and face common challenges and tasks. There are also deep divisions within and between other living faiths and ideologies.

---

*Reprinted from *Ecumenical Review* 43:2 (April 1991), 270-273.

60. From the depth and pain of our divisions we cry "Spirit of unity—reconcile your people". Reconciliation happens when there is honest recognition of the actual sin committed against our neighbour and when practical restitution has been made for it. When costly repentance meets costly forgiveness the Holy Spirit can lead us into community (koinonia).

CHRISTIAN COMMUNITY AS KOINONIA IN THE SPIRIT

61. In developing perspectives on ecclesiology, in discussing the nature and mission of the church, the idea of koinonia can be most helpful. This is so particularly as we reflect upon the identity of our own church in relation to ecumenical developments such as the text *Baptism, Eucharist and Ministry (BEM)*, which has received encouraging responses from so many churches. Koinonia in the Holy Spirit is based on sharing in the life of the Trinitarian God and is expressed by sharing life within the community. It becomes possible through reconciliation with God and with one another in the power of the Holy Spirit.

62. Unity and diversity are twin elements in Christian koinonia, but that diversity must have its limits. For example, amidst all diversity the confession must be maintained of Jesus Christ as God and Saviour, the same yesterday, today and forever. And a diversity that divides and excludes, thus destroying the life of the body of Christ, is unacceptable.

63. The gospel finds its historical expression in many cultures, which are transformed, renewed and corrected by it. Though national and ethnic identities are legitimate they should not be allowed to impair the unity of the church, or to become masks which shelter un-Christian elements.

64. In reflecting on the relationship between unity and koinonia we find a new vision in the statement entitled "The Unity of the Church as Koinonia: Gift and Calling", which was prepared by the Faith and Order Commission at the invitation in 1987 of the WCC central committee and has been adopted by this assembly.

65. The statement affirms that the purpose of God according to holy scripture is to gather, by the power of the Holy Spirit, the whole of creation under the Lordship of Jesus Christ. The church is the foretaste of this communion with God and with one another; its purpose is to manifest this communion in prayer and action and thus point to the fullness of communion with God, humanity, and the whole creation in the glory of the kingdom. It is called to be a sign of God's reign and a servant of that reconciliation with God which is promised for the whole creation. It is called to proclaim reconciliation and to provide healing, to overcome divisions based on race, gender, age, culture or colour and to bring all people into communion with God. It is a sad fact that churches have failed to draw the consequences for their own life from the degree of communion which they have already experienced, and from the agreements already achieved through the ecumenical movement.

66. The unity of the church is envisioned as a koinonia (communion) given and expressed in the common confession of the apostolic faith; a common sacramental life entered by the one baptism and celebrated together in one eucharistic fellowship; a common life in which members and ministries are mutually recognized and reconciled; and a common mission witnessing to the gospel of God's grace to all people and serving the whole of creation. The goal of the search for full communion is realized when all the churches are able to recognize in one another the one, holy, catholic and apostolic church in its fullness. This urges action, for in taking specific

steps together the churches express and encourage the enrichment and renewal of Christian life.

67. A true community of women and men is God's gift and promise for humanity, which is created "in God's image" — male and female (Gen. 1:27); and the church, as sign of that which God desires for women and men, is called to embody that community in its own life. Today Christians from many traditions look together for a more complete and authentic community of women and men. We affirm that the domination of women by men does not belong to human community as intended in God's creation (Gen. 1, 2) but to the consequences of sin, which distort the community of women and men as well as the relationship between human beings and nature (Gen. 3:16-19). The God who created us as women and men calls us into community. The Christ who identifies with our suffering calls us to become his body. The Spirit who empowers us to witness and serve sends us forth as God's agents, co-workers for a new heaven and a new earth.

TOWARDS A WIDER ECUMENICAL COMMUNITY

68. Particularly in this century the world has witnessed the rise and growth of movements which emphasize the Holy Spirit and the gifts of the Holy Spirit (charisms) or, as they themselves like to put it, "baptism in the Spirit" or "filling with the Spirit". They are not all of the same type but are called charismatic or pentecostal movements and, in Africa, are sometimes identified with African instituted churches.

69. In their emphases on the charisms of the Spirit described in the New Testament and their rediscovery of the ministry of healing, these movements are valid expressions of Christian faith. If seen as based on a reappropriation of the gifts received in baptism they can be integrated into the life of the churches, bringing them many gifts. They may also represent stronger faith and fellowship, increased spontaneity, openness and freedom among worshippers, all of these leading to greater participation in the life of the churches. There are, however, negative implications for the ecumenical movement if "filling with the Spirit" as a "second experience" after baptism is seen as normative for all Christians. Such teaching may be divisive, as may be an overemphasis on the Holy Spirit as working independently of the Father and the Son.

70. There is often misunderstanding between Pentecostals and Christians of other traditions. Some Pentecostals have rejected the traditional churches in a desire to enliven their own worship; some have rejected the ecumenical movement as a "human" attempt to produce Christian unity, or because of genuine theological differences about the nature of the Christian faith and its expression in the modern world. But others have sought fellowship with Christians outside their boundaries, particularly with evangelicals. They have begun to take an interest in questions of visible church unity; traditional churches have in turn become more open to the spiritual and theological insights that Pentecostals bring. In Latin America, for example, Pentecostals (now the numerically dominant form of Protestantism in the region) take part in the Latin American Council of Churches. Similar dialogue has been taking place in other areas as well. These hopeful signs bode well for future efforts to bring the churches closer together.

THE CHRISTIAN COMMUNITY IN MISSION

71. A reconciled and renewed creation is the goal of the church's mission. The vision of God uniting all things in Christ (Eph. 1:10) is the driving force of the

church's life of sharing, motivating all efforts to overcome economic inequality and social divisions.

72. Whatever our approach to mission at home or abroad, our mission needs to be "in Christ's way". Wholeness of mission demands a will to break down barriers at every level, and involves the whole people of God in sharing, serving and renewal in a spirit of love and respect. Each church acting in mission is acting on behalf of the whole body of Christ. At the same time we affirm local ecumenical endeavours in mission. Always we need to remember our original understanding of mission, which is preaching, teaching and healing. It is best done together, and should never divide, alienate or oppress. Our conviction is not hesitant or partial that Jesus Christ through the action of the Holy Spirit is God's saving presence for *all*.

73. Since the church's mission is to reconcile all with God and with one another, sharing can be recognized as part of mission in Christ's way. It includes sharing faith, sharing power, sharing material resources. Such sharing encourages reconciliation. We affirm that what we call "ours" is given by God in love, and is given to be shared. At times sharing offers up and receives emptiness and suffering as well as fullness and joy. There can and must be no barriers to sharing, whether giving or receiving. In this spirit we affirm the WCC "Guidelines for Sharing" as an important means towards common mission and service.

74. The gospel of Jesus Christ must become incarnate in every culture. When Christianity enters any culture there is a mutual encounter, involving both the critique of culture by the gospel and the possibility of the culture questioning our understanding of the gospel. Some of the ways in which the gospel has been imposed on particular cultures call for repentance and healing. In each case we need to ask: Is the church creating tension or promoting reconciliation?

THE CHRISTIAN COMMUNITY IN RELATION TO OTHERS

75. The Holy Spirit works in ways that surpass human understanding. The Bible testifies to God as sovereign of all nations and peoples. God's love and compassion include everyone. We witness to the truth that salvation is in Christ, but we seek also to remain open to other people's expression of truth as they have experienced it.

76. Today in many parts of the world religion is used as a divisive force, with religious language and symbols being used to exacerbate conflicts. Ignorance and intolerance make reconciliation difficult. We seek to live in respect and understanding with people of other living faiths, and to this end we need to build mutual trust and a "culture of dialogue". This begins at the local level as we relate to people of other faiths, and take common action especially in promoting justice and peace. The first step is to come to know and to trust each other, telling our stories of faith and sharing mutual concerns. Both the telling and the hearing of faith are crucial in discerning God's will. Dialogue is an authentic form of Christian witness and ministry. As Christians we affirm the Holy Spirit counselling us to hold fast to the revealed Christ, to keep faith, and to encounter the other's faith.

77. Ideologies may be constructive or destructive; but both types tend to demand absolute loyalty and to ignore the essential ingredient of accountability, thus causing conflict. In recent years this has most strongly affected churches in Marxist-influenced societies. Now we have experienced the collapse of this system; but this is no reason for triumphalism about the free market system, as we are increasingly confronted with its negative effects throughout the world. We all, as Christians,

need to analyze and understand the ideologies under which we live. Some are "hidden"—not openly acknowledged and discussed—yet deeply rooted and influential in society. Among these are wealth and achievement-oriented value systems which ignore human and personal factors. The task of the community of faith is to apply prophetic, biblical values to all ideologies.

78. Ideological trends can be found in fundamentalism and nationalism. We must learn to distinguish between fundamentalism as an approach to biblical hermeneutics and fundamentalism (whether Christian or non-Christian) which is an intolerant ideological imperialism, closed to other approaches and realities. Nationalism is positive when it unites people in the struggle for cultural, religious and political self-determination, but it is negative when used to dominate some and to exclude others. It may be even more oppressive when it contains elements that equate faith with a particular nationality.

Part II

ROMAN CATHOLIC STATEMENTS

1

Evangelii Nuntiandi

Rome, December 8, 1975

POPE PAUL VI

On December 8, 1975, exactly ten years and one day after the promulgation of Vatican II's decree on missionary activity (Ad Gentes), *Pope Paul VI issued his Apostolic Exhortation "On Evangelization in the Modern World,"* Evangelii Nuntiandi (EN). *A year before, the Third Synod of Bishops had been devoted to the topic of evangelization, but only a brief closing statement had been issued, together with a request that the pope issue a fuller statement at some future date. EN is the result.*

The document begins with a Christology and ecclesiology, both of which emphasize the centrality of the Reign of God and the essential nature of Jesus' and the church's evangelizing activity (#1-16). This is followed by a second chapter (#17-24) which lays out the complex character of evangelization as a process which necessarily includes witness of life, explicit preaching, incorporation into the ecclesial community, and the sending out of new evangelizers. Chapter III (#25-39) deals with the content *of evangelization; Chapter IV (#40-48) sketches out the various* methods *of evangelization; and Chapters V and VI (#49-58; 59-73) speak respectively of the recipients of and workers for evangelization. Chapter VIII (#74-80) outlines some elements toward a spirituality of evangelization.*

Although part of the document's concern was to counter some developments perceived by the pope as dangerous to the evangelization enterprise — the burgeoning theologies of liberation and inculturation and an emerging consciousness of autonomy in various local churches, especially in Africa, Asia, and Latin America — EN was hailed at its publication as a landmark magisterial document, and even today continues to be widely read and studied by Christians of all churches. The document contains important developments in the church's official teaching about its relation to the Reign of God (#6,8) and its essential missionary nature (#14-15); it also contains pioneering statements on the need to evangelize culture (#20), the liberating nature of evangelization (#30), popular piety (#48), and basic ecclesial communities (#58). The following sections from the document represent passages which express some of these ground-breaking missiological ideas.

EVANGELII NUNTIANDI*

(From Chapter I: "From Christ the Evangelizer to the Evangelizing Church")

WITNESS AND MISSION OF JESUS

6. The witness that the Lord gives of himself and that Saint Luke gathers together in his Gospel — "I must proclaim the Good News of the kingdom of God"[1] — without doubt has enormous consequences, for it sums up the whole mission of Jesus: "That is what I was sent to do."[2] These words take on their full significance if one links them with the previous verses, in which Christ has just applied to himself the words of the Prophet Isaiah: "The Spirit of the Lord has been given to me, for he has anointed me. He has sent me to bring the good news to the poor."[3]

Going from town to town, preaching to the poorest — and frequently the most receptive — the joyful news of the fulfillment of the promises and of the Covenant offered by God is the mission for which Jesus declares that he is sent by the Father. And all the aspects of his mystery — the Incarnation itself, his miracles, his teaching, the gathering together of the disciples, the sending out of the Twelve, the Cross and Resurrection, the permanence of his presence in the midst of his own — were components of his evangelizing activity.

PROCLAMATION OF THE KINGDOM OF GOD

8. As an evangelizer, Christ first of all proclaims a kingdom, the Kingdom of God; and this is so important that, by comparison, everything else becomes "the rest," which is "given in addition."[4] Only the Kingdom therefore is absolute, and it makes everything else relative. The Lord will delight in describing in many ways the happiness of belonging to this Kingdom (a paradoxical happiness which is made up of things that the world rejects),[5] the demands of the Kingdom and its Magna Charta,[6] the heralds of the Kingdom,[7] its mysteries,[8] its children,[9] the vigilance and fidelity demanded of whoever awaits its definitive coming.[10]

FOR AN EVANGELIZED AND EVANGELIZING COMMUNITY

13. Those who sincerely accept the Good News, through the power of this acceptance and of shared faith, therefore gather together in Jesus' name in order to seek together for the Kingdom, build it up and live it. They make up a community which is in its turn evangelizing. The command to the Twelve to go out and proclaim the Good News is also valid for all Christians, though in a different way. It is precisely for this reason that Peter calls Christians "a people set apart to sing the praises of God,"[11] those marvelous things that each one was able to hear in his own language.[12] Moreover, the Good News of the Kingdom which is coming and which has begun is meant for all people of all times. Those who have received the Good News and who have been gathered by it into the community of salvation can and must communicate and spread it.

---

*Reprinted from Paul VI, *On Evangelization in the Modern World: Apostolic Exhortation "Evangelii Nuntiandi,"* (Washington, D.C.: United States Catholic Conference, 1976).

EVANGELIZATION: VOCATION PROPER TO THE CHURCH

14. The Church knows this. She has a vivid awareness of the fact that the Saviour's words, "I must proclaim the Good News of the kingdom of God,"[13] apply in all truth to herself. She willingly adds with Saint Paul: "Not that I boast of preaching the gospel, since it is a duty that has been laid on me; I should be punished if I did not preach it!"[14] It is with joy and consolation that at the end of the great Assembly of 1974 we heard these illuminating words: "We wish to confirm once more that the task of evangelizing all people constitutes the essential mission of the Church."[15] It is a task and mission which the vast and profound changes of present-day society make all the more urgent. Evangelizing is in fact the grace and vocation proper to the Church, her deepest identity. She exists in order to evangelize, that is to say in order to preach and to teach, to be the channel of the gift of grace, to reconcile sinners with God, and to perpetuate Christ's sacrifice in the Mass, which is the memorial of his death and glorious Resurrection.

RECIPROCAL LINKS BETWEEN THE CHURCH AND EVANGELIZATION

15. Anyone who re-reads in the New Testament the origins of the Church, follows her history step by step and watches her live and act, sees that she is linked to evangelization in her most intimate being:

— The Church is born of the evangelizing activity of Jesus and the Twelve. She is the normal, desired, most immediate and most visible fruit of this activity: "Go, therefore, make disciples of all the nations."[16] Now, "they accepted what he said and were baptized. That very day about three thousand were added to their number. . . . Day by day the Lord added to their community those destined to be saved."[17]

— Having been born consequently out of being sent, the Church in her turn is sent by Jesus. The Church remains in the world when the Lord of glory returns to the Father. She remains as a sign — simultaneously obscure and luminous — of a new presence of Jesus, of his departure and of his permanent presence. She prolongs and continues him. And it is above all his mission and his condition of being an evangelizer that she is called upon to continue.[18] For the Christian community is never closed in upon itself. The intimate life of this community — the life of listening to the Word and the Apostles' teaching, charity lived in a fraternal way, the sharing of bread[19] — this intimate life only acquires its full meaning when it becomes a witness, when it evokes admiration and conversion, and when it becomes the preaching and proclamation of the Good News. Thus it is the whole Church that receives the mission to evangelize, and the work of each individual member is important for the whole.

— The Church is an evangelizer, but she begins by being evangelized herself. She is the community of believers, the community of hope lived and communicated, the community of brotherly love; and she needs to listen unceasingly to what she must believe, to her reasons for hoping, to the new commandment of love. She is the People of God immersed in the world, and often tempted by idols, and she always needs to hear the proclamation of the "mighty works of God"[20] which converted her to the Lord; she always needs to be called together afresh by him and reunited. In brief, this means that she has a constant need of being evangelized, if she wishes to retain freshness, vigor and strength in order to proclaim the Gospel. The Second Vatican Council recalled[21] and the 1974 Synod vigorously took up again this theme of the Church which is evangelized by constant conversion and renewal, in order to evangelize the world with credibility.

— The Church is the depositary of the Good News to be proclaimed. The promises of the New Alliance in Jesus Christ, the teaching of the Lord and the Apostles, the Word of life, the sources of grace and of God's loving kindness, the path of salvation — all these things have been entrusted to her. It is the content of the Gospel, and therefore of evangelization, that she preserves as a precious living heritage, not in order to keep it hidden but to communicate it.

— Having been sent and evangelized, the Church herself sends out evangelizers. She puts on their lips the saving Word, she explains to them the message of which she herself is the depositary, she gives them the mandate which she herself has received and she sends them out to preach. To preach not their own selves or their personal ideas,[22] but a Gospel of which neither she nor they are the absolute masters and owners, to dispose of it as they wish, but a Gospel of which they are the ministers, in order to pass it on with complete fidelity.

(From Chapter II: "What Is Evangelization?")

EVANGELIZATION OF CULTURES

20. All this could be expressed in the following words: what matters is to evangelize man's culture and cultures (not in a purely decorative way as it were by applying a thin veneer, but in a vital way, in depth and right to their very roots), in the wide and rich sense which these terms have in *Gaudium et Spes*,[23] always taking the person as one's starting-point and always coming back to the relationships of people among themselves and with God.

The Gospel, and therefore evangelization, are certainly not identical with culture, and they are independent in regard to all cultures. Nevertheless, the Kingdom which the Gospel proclaims is lived by men who are profoundly linked to a culture, and the building up of the Kingdom cannot avoid borrowing the elements of human culture or cultures. Though independent of cultures, the Gospel and evangelization are not necessarily incompatible with them; rather they are capable of permeating them all without becoming subject to any one of them.

The split between the Gospel and culture is without a doubt the drama of our time, just as it was of other times. Therefore every effort must be made to ensure a full evangelization of culture, or more correctly of cultures. They have to be regenerated by an encounter with the Gospel. But this encounter will not take place if the Gospel is not proclaimed.

(From Chapter III: "The Content of Evangelization")

MESSAGE TOUCHING LIFE AS A WHOLE

29. But evangelization would not be complete if it did not take account of the unceasing interplay of the Gospel and of man's concrete life, both personal and social. This is why evangelization involves an explicit message, adapted to the different situations constantly being realized, about the rights and duties of every human being, about family life without which personal growth and development is hardly possible,[24] about life in society, about international life, peace, justice and development — a message especially energetic today about liberation.

A MESSAGE OF LIBERATION

30. It is well known in what terms numerous Bishops from all the continents spoke of this at the last Synod, especially the Bishops from the Third World, with a pastoral accent resonant with the voice of the millions of sons and daughters of the Church who make up those peoples. Peoples, as we know, engaged with all their energy in the effort to struggle to overcome everything which condemns them to remain on the margin of life: famine, chronic disease, illiteracy, poverty, injustices in international relations and especially in commercial exchanges, situations of economic and cultural neo-colonialism sometimes as cruel as the old political colonialism. The Church, as the Bishops repeated, has the duty to proclaim the liberation of millions of human beings, many of whom are her own children—the duty of assisting the birth of this liberation, of giving witness to it, of ensuring that it is complete. This is not foreign to evangelization.

NOTES

Numbers in parentheses refer to the number of the note in the original text. The note number is the number according to how it appears in the present text.

1. (12) Lk. 4:43.
2. (13) *Ibid.*
3. (14) Lk. 4:18; cf. Is. 61:1.
4. (16) Cf. Mt. 6:33.
5. (17) Cf. Mt. 5:3-12.
6. (18) Cf. Mt. 5-7.
7. (19) Cf. Mt. 10.
8. (20) Cf. Mt. 13.
9. (21) Cf. Mt. 18.
10. (22) Cf. Mt. 24-25.
11. (32) 1 Pt. 2:9.
12. (33) Cf. Acts 2:11.
13. (34) Lk. 4:43.
14. (35) 1 Cor. 9:16.
15. (36) "Declaration of the Synod Fathers," 4: *L'Osservatore Romano* (October 27, 1974), p. 6.
16. (37) Mt. 28:19.
17. (38) Acts 2:41, 47.
18. (39) Cf. Second Vatican Ecumenical Council, Dogmatic Constitution on the Church *Lumen Gentium*, 8: *AAS* 57 (1965), p. 11; Decree on the Church's Missionary Activity *Ad Gentes*, 5: *AAS* 58 (1966), pp. 951-952.
19. (40) Cf. Acts 2:42-46; 4:32-35; 5:12-16.
20. (41) Cf. Acts 2:11; 1 Pt. 2:9.
21. (42) Cf. Decree on the Church's Missionary Activity *Ad Gentes*, 5, 11-12: *AAS* 58 (1966), pp. 951-952, 959-961.
22. (43) Cf. 2 Cor. 4:5; Saint Augustine, *Sermo XLVI, De Pastoribus, CCL XLI*, pp. 529-530.
23. (50) Cf. 53: *AAS* 58 (1966), p. 1075.
24. (60) Cf. Second Vatican Ecumenical Council, Pastoral Constitution on the Church in the Modern World *Gaudium et Spes* 47-52: *AAS* 58 (1966), pp. 1067-74; Paul VI, Encyclical Letter *Humanae Vitae: AAS* 60 (1968), pp. 481-503.

2

Catechesi Tradendae

Rome, October 16, 1979

POPE JOHN PAUL II

In October 1977, the Fourth Synod of Bishops devoted itself to the theme "Catechesis in Our Time, Particularly that of Children and Youth." At the Synod's end the bishops presented Pope Paul VI with a large amount of documentation on the topic, and the pope set to work composing a message to the Church on the model of his 1975 Evangelii Nuntiandi. *Paul VI died on August 6, 1978, and his successor, John Paul I, attempted to continue work on the document, only to die himself in September of the same year. John Paul II accordingly took up the task and issued this Apostolic Exhortation,* Catechesi Tradendae, *on October 16, 1979.*

Catechesis, says the pope, has its roots in Jesus' ministry (#5-9) and in the earliest tradition of the church (#10-17). It is an essential part of the church's mission (#18-25), and has the task of handing on the entire "content" of evangelization (#26-34). Although the present document focuses particularly on the catechizing of youth, the pope makes it clear that every Christian needs constantly to be catechized (#35-45). The ministry of catechizing, finally, is one shared by all members of the church (#62-71). The selection reprinted here is from Chapter VII, "How to Impart Catechesis." In #53 the term inculturation *appears for the first time in a major papal document.*

CATECHESI: TRADENDAE:*

(From Chapter VII: "How to Impart Catechesis")

AT THE SERVICE OF REVELATION AND CONVERSION

52. The first question of a general kind that presents itself here concerns the danger and the temptation to mix catechetical teaching unduly with overt or masked ideological views, especially political and social ones, or with personal political options. When such views get the better of the central message to be transmitted,

---

*Reprinted from John Paul II, *On Catechesis in Our Time: Apostolic Exhortation "Catechesi Tradendae,"* (Washington, D.C.: U.S. Catholic Conference, 1979).

to the point of obscuring it and putting it in second place or even using it to further their own ends, catechesis then becomes radically distorted. The Synod rightly insisted on the need for catechesis to remain above one-sided divergent trends — to avoid "dichotomies" — even in the field of theological interpretation of such questions. It is on the basis of Revelation that catechesis will try to set its course, Revelation as transmitted by the universal Magisterium of the Church, in its solemn or ordinary form. This Revelation tells of a creating and redeeming God, whose Son has come among us in our flesh and enters not only into each individual's personal history but into human history itself, becoming its center. Accordingly, this Revelation tells of the radical change of man and the universe, of all that makes up the web of human life under the influence of the Good News of Jesus Christ. If conceived in this way, catechesis goes beyond every form of formalistic moralism, although it will include true Christian moral teaching. Chiefly, it goes beyond any kind of temporary, social or political "messianism." It seeks to arrive at man's innermost being.

THE MESSAGE EMBODIED IN CULTURES

53. Now a second question. As I said recently to the members of the Biblical Commission: "The term 'acculturation' or 'inculturation' may be a neologism, but it expresses very well one factor of the great mystery of the Incarnation."[1] We can say of catechesis, as well as of evangelization in general, that it is called to bring the power of the Gospel into the very heart of culture and cultures. For this purpose, catechesis will seek to know these cultures and their essential components; it will learn their most significant expressions; it will respect their particular values and riches. In this manner it will be able to offer these cultures the knowledge of the hidden mystery[2] and help them to bring forth from their own living tradition original expressions of Christian life, celebration and thought. Two things must however be kept in mind.

On the one hand the Gospel message cannot be purely and simply isolated from the culture in which it was first inserted (the Biblical world or, more concretely, the cultural milieu in which Jesus of Nazareth lived), nor, without serious loss, from the cultures in which it has already been expressed down the centuries; it does not spring spontaneously from any cultural soil; it has always been transmitted by means of an apostolic dialogue which inevitably becomes part of a certain dialogue of cultures.

On the other hand, the power of the Gospel everywhere transforms and regenerates. When that power enters into a culture, it is no surprise that it rectifies many of its elements. There would be no catechesis if it were the Gospel that had to change when it came into contact with the cultures.

To forget this would simply amount to what Saint Paul very forcefully calls "emptying the cross of Christ of its power."[3] It is a different matter to take, with wise discernment, certain elements, religious or otherwise, that form part of the cultural heritage of a human group and use them to help its members to understand better the whole of the Christian mystery. Genuine catechists know that catechesis "takes flesh" in the various cultures and milieux: one has only to think of the peoples with their great differences, of modern youth, of the great variety of circumstances in which people find themselves today. But they refuse to accept an impoverishment of catechesis through a renunciation or obscuring of its message by adaptations, even in language, that would endanger the "precious deposit" of the faith,[4] or by concessions in matters of faith or morals. They are convinced that true catechesis eventually enriches these cultures by helping them to go beyond the defective or even inhuman features in them, and by communicating to their legitimate values the fullness of Christ.[5]

THE CONTRIBUTION OF POPULAR DEVOTION

54. Another question of method concerns the utilization in catechetical instruction of valid elements in popular piety. I have in mind devotions practised by the faithful in certain regions with moving fervour and purity of intention, even if the faith underlying them needs to be purified or rectified in many aspects. I have in mind certain easily understood prayers that many simple people are fond of repeating. I have in mind certain acts of piety practised with a sincere desire to do penance or to please the Lord. Underlying most of these prayers and practises, besides elements that should be discarded, there are other elements which, if they were properly used, could serve very well to help people advance towards knowledge of the mystery of Christ and of his message: the love and mercy of God, the Incarnation of Christ, his redeeming Cross and Resurrection, the activity of the Spirit in each Christian and in the Church, the mystery of the hereafter, the evangelical virtues to be practised, the presence of the Christian in the world, etc. And why should we appeal to non-Christian elements, refusing to build on elements which, even if they need to be revised and improved, have something Christian at their root?

NOTES

Numbers in parentheses refer to numbers of notes in the original text. The note numbers below refer to the text in this volume.

1. (94) Cf. *AAS* 71 (1979), p. 607.
2. (95) Cf. Rom. 16:25; Eph. 3:5.
3. (96) 1 Cor. 1:17.
4. (97) 2 Tim. 1:14.
5. (98) Cf. Jn. 1:16; Eph. 1:10.

3

Third General Congress

Puebla de los Angeles, Mexico, 1979

CONFERENCE OF LATIN AMERICAN BISHOPS

In late January and early February of 1979 the Third General Congress of the Latin American Episcopate was held in Puebla de los Angeles, Mexico. Although a first General Congress had been held in Rio de Janeiro, Brazil, in 1955, it was the second General Congress, held in Medellín, Colombia, in 1968 and inspired by the Spirit of Vatican II's Pastoral Constitution on the Church in the Modern World (Gaudium et Spes) *that represented a real breakthrough for the church's life in Latin America. Of the sixteen documents issued at Medellín, several focused on themes which were inspired by the then-emerging theology of liberation: the social and structural nature of sin, the imperative of siding with the poor, political involvement as an essential component of Christian existence, and the importance of what were developing as "basic ecclesial communities"* (comunidades eclesiales de base).

As this theology of liberation began to find more and more resonance in the Latin American church, some more "conservative" bishops became so alarmed that they attempted to make the Puebla Conference the occasion to articulate a theological stance quite different from that worked out in 1968, one that would stress "development" and "communion and participation" over "liberation" and solidarity with Latin America's oppressed poor. While some of this more conservative theology is in evidence in Puebla's stress on "communion and participation," the unmistakable emphasis on the "preferential option for the poor," given papal approval as well in many of the talks of John Paul II during his visit to Mexico at the time of the Congress, marks Puebla as a conference which sanctioned liberation theology's deepest concerns.

The long final document—240 pages in the original Spanish—is divided into five major parts. Part I (#3-161) presents a sociological analysis of the Latin American situation, very much in the spirit of the first part of Gaudium et Spes *and the theological method operative at Medellín. Part II gives a summary of the general content of evangelization (#165-339), and then focuses on the evangelizing task within Latin America itself (#340-562). Part III deals with one of the central themes in the document, that of "communion and participation," and reflects on it from a variety of angles (#567-1133). In Part IV the document focuses on the missionary dimension of the church in Latin America, with special emphasis on the church's preferential option for the poor and for young people*

(#1134-1293); and in the very short Part V (1306-1310), the document briefly lays out a few "pastoral options."

Despite what might be called a "coldness of tone" in the document and the compromises resulting in the tension between "development" and "liberation" positions, the Puebla Document is a significant one, and stands as a charter for efforts of evangelization in Latin America in our day. Reprinted here are selections from the second chapter of Part II, selections which deal with issues of evangelization over against culture, popular religiosity, and sociopolitical reality.

(From Part II: "God's Saving Plan for Latin America," Chapter II: "What Does Evangelization Entail?")*

2. "THE EVANGELIZATION OF CULTURE"

2.1 CULTURE AND CULTURES

385. The new and important pastoral contribution of *Evangelii Nuntiandi* lies in Paul VI's summons to face up to the task of evangelizing culture and cultures (EN:20).

386. The term "culture" means the specific way in which human beings belonging to a given people cultivate their relationship with nature, with each other, and with God in order to arrive at "an authentic and full humanity." It is the shared lifestyle that characterizes different peoples around the earth, and so we can speak about "a plurality of cultures" (GS:53; EN:20).

387. So conceived, culture embraces the whole life of a people. It is the whole web of values that inspire them and of disvalues that debilitate them; insofar as they are shared in common by all the members, they bring them together on the basis of a "collective consciousness" (EN:18). Culture also embraces the forms in which these values or disvalues find configuration and expression—i.e., customs, languages, societal institutions and structures—insofar as they are not impeded or suppressed by the intervention of other, dominant cultures.

388. In the context of this totality, evangelization seeks to get to the very core of a culture, the realm of its basic values, and to bring about a conversion that will serve as the basis and guarantee of a transformation in structures and the social milieu (EN:18).

389. The essential core of a culture lies in the way in which a people affirms or rejects a religious tie with God, that is, in its religious values or disvalues. These values or disvalues have to do with the ultimate meaning of life. Their roots lie in the deeper zone where human beings formulate answers to the basic, ultimate questions that vex them. The answer may be a positively religious orientation on the one hand, or an atheistic orientation on the other hand. Thus religion or irreligion is a source of inspiration for all the other areas of a culture—family life, economics, politics, art, etc. They are either freed to seek out some transcendent meaning, or else they are locked up in their own immanent meaning.

390. Evangelization takes the whole human being into account, and so it seeks to reach the total human being through that being's religious dimension.

---

*Reprinted from John Eagleson and Philip Scharper, eds., *Puebla and Beyond*, (Maryknoll, N.Y.: Orbis Books, 1979).

391. Culture is a creative activity of human beings. Thus it is in line with the vocation given to them by God to perfect all creation (Genesis), and hence their own spiritual and corporeal qualities and capabilities (GS:53; 57).

392. Culture is continually shaped and reshaped by the ongoing life and historical experience of peoples; and it is transmitted by tradition from generation to generation. Thus human beings are born and raised in the bosom of a given society, conditioned and enriched by a given culture. They receive a culture, creatively modify it, and then continue to pass it on. Culture is a historical and social reality (GS:53).

393. Cultures are continually subjected to new developments and to mutual encounter and interpenetration. In the course of their history they go through periods in which they are challenged by new values or disvalues, and by the need to effect new syntheses of their way of life. The Church feels particularly summoned to make its presence felt, to be there with the Gospel, when old ways of social life and value-organization are decaying or dying in order to make room for new syntheses (GS:5). It is better to evangelize new cultural forms when they are being born than when they are already full-grown and established. This is the global challenge that confronts the Church today because we truly can "speak of a new age in human history" (GS:54). Hence the Latin American Church seeks to give new impetus to the evangelization of our continent.

2.4 EVANGELIZATION OF CULTURE IN LATIN AMERICA

408. Our Church, for its part, carries out this work in the particular human area known as Latin America, whose historical and cultural process has already been described (see Part One).

So let us briefly review some of the principal items already established in Part One of this document so that we may be able to single out the challenges and problems posed to evangelization by the present moment of history.

409. *Types of culture and stages in the cultural process.* The origin of present-day Latin America lies in the encounter of the Spanish and Portuguese peoples with the pre-Columbian and African cultures. Racial and cultural intermingling has profoundly marked this process, and there is every indication that it will continue to do so now and in the future.

410. This fact should not prompt us to disregard the persistence of indigenous cultures or Afro-American cultures in a pure state, nor the existence of groups who are integrated into the nation in varying degrees.

411. Subsequently, during the last two centuries, new waves of immigrants have flowed into Latin America, and particularly into the southern cone of our continent. These immigrants brought their own characteristics with them, which basically were integrated with the underlying cultural stratum.

412. In the first epoch, from the sixteenth to the eighteenth centuries, were laid the bases of Latin American culture and its solid Catholic substrate. In that period evangelization was deep enough for the faith to become a constitutive part of Latin America's life and identity. It provided Latin America with a spiritual unity that still persists, despite later splintering into separate nations and divisions on the economic, social, and political planes.

413. So our culture is impregnated with the faith, even though it frequently has lacked the support of a suitable catechesis. This is evident in the distinctive religious attitudes of our people, which are imbued with a deep sense of transcendence and

the nearness of God. It finds expression in a wisdom of the common people that has contemplative features and that gives a distinctive direction to the way our people live out their relationship with nature and their fellow human beings. It is embodied in their sense of work and festiveness, of solidarity, friendship, and kinship; and in their feel for their own dignity, which they do not see diminished by their own lives as simple, poor people.

414. Preserved more vividly as an articulation of life as a whole among the poor, this culture bears in particular the seal of the heart and its intuitions. Rather than finding expression in scientific categories and ways of thinking, it is more likely to find expression in artistic forms, in piety as a lived reality, and in solidary forms of social life.

415. From the eighteenth century on, this culture began to feel the impact of the dawning urban-industrial civilization, with its physico-mathematical brand of knowledge and its stress on efficiency. The impact was first felt by the *mestizo* culture, and then gradually by various enclaves of indigenous peoples and Afro-Americans.

416. The new urban-industrial civilization is accompanied by strong tendencies toward personalization and socialization. It produces a sharpened acceleration of history, demanding great efforts at assimilation and creativity from all peoples if they do not want to see their cultures left behind or even eliminated.

417. Urban-industrial culture, which has as a consequence the intense proletarianization of various social strata and even peoples, is controlled by the great powers in possession of science and technology. It is a historical process that tends to make the problem of dependence and poverty more and more acute.

418. The advent of urban-industrial civilization also entails problems on the ideological level, threatening the very roots of our culture. For in terms of real-life history and its workings, this civilization comes to us imbued with rationalism and inspired by two dominant ideologies: liberalism and Marxist-collectivism. In both we find a tendency, not just to a legitimate and desirable secularization, but also to "secularism."

419. Within this basic historical process we see arising on our continent certain particular but important phenomena and problems: increased migration and displacement of the population from rural to urban areas; the rise of various religious phenomena, such as the invasion of sects, which should not be disregarded by evangelizers simply because they may seem to be marginal; the enormous influence of the media of social communications as vehicles of new cultural guidelines and models; the yearning of women to better their situation, in line with their dignity and distinctiveness, within the overall framework of society; and the emergence of a laborer's world that will be decisive in the new configuration of our culture.

420. *Evangelizing activity: challenges and problems.* The data given above also point to the challenges that must be faced by the Church. The problems are manifestations of the signs of the times, pointing toward the future where culture is now heading. The Church must be able to discern these signs if it is to consolidate the values and overthrow the idols that are feeding this historical process.

421. *The coming world culture.* This urban-industrial culture, which is inspired by the scientific-technological outlook, driven by the great powers, and characterized by the aforementioned ideologies, proposes to be a universal one. Various peoples, local cultures, and human groups are invited or even constrained to become an integral part of it.

422. In Latin America this tendency again brings to the fore the whole problem

of integrating indigenous ethnic groups and realities into the political and cultural fabric of our nations. For our nations find themselves challenged to move toward greater development, to win new hands and lands for more efficient production, so that they can become a more integral and dynamic part of the accelerating thrust of world civilization.

423. This new universality has different levels. First there is the level of scientific and technical elements, which are the instruments of development. Second, there is the level of certain values that are given new emphasis: e.g., labor and the increased possession of consumer goods. And then there is the whole matter of "lifestyle" as a whole, which entails a particular hierarchy of values and preferences.

424. Finding themselves at this critical juncture in history, some ethnic and social groups draw back into themselves, defending their own distinctive culture in and through a fruitless sort of isolationism. Other groups, on the other hand, allow themselves to be readily absorbed by lifestyles introduced by the new world culture.

425. In its work of evangelization, the Church itself moves ahead by a process of delicate and difficult discernment. By virtue of its own evangelical principles, the Church looks with satisfaction on the impulses of humanity leading toward integration and universal communion. By virtue of its specific mission it feels that it has been sent, not to destroy cultures, but to help them consolidate their being and identity. And it does this by summoning human beings of all races and peoples to unite in faith under Christ as one single People of the universal God.

426. The Church itself promotes and fosters things that go beyond this catholic union in the same faith, things that find embodiment in forms of communion between cultures and of just integration on the economic, social, and political levels.

427. But the Church, as one would expect, calls into question any "universality" that is synonymous with uniformity or levelling, that fails to respect different cultures by weakening them, absorbing them, or annihilating them. With even greater reason the Church refuses to accept universality when it is used as a tool to unify humanity by inculcating the unjust, offensive supremacy and domination of some peoples or social strata over other peoples and social strata.

428. The Church of Latin America has resolved to put fresh vigor into its work of evangelizing the culture of our peoples and the various ethnic groups. It wants to see the faith of the Gospel blossom or be restored to fresh life. And with this as the basis of communion, it wants to see it burgeon into forms of just integration on all levels—national, continental Latin American, and universal. This will enable our peoples to develop their own culture in such a way that they can assimilate the findings of science and technology in their own proper way.

429. *The city.* In the transition from an agrarian culture to an urban-industrialized one, the city becomes the moving force behind the new world civilization. This fact calls for a new type of discernment on the part of the Church. In general, it should find its inspiration in the vision of the Bible. On the one hand the Bible has a positive view of the human tendency to create cities, where human beings can live together in a more corporate and humane way; on the other hand it is highly critical of the inhumanness and sinfulness that has its origin in urban life.

430. In the present situation, therefore, the Church does not favor as an ideal the creation of huge metropolises, which become inhuman beyond all repair. Nor does it favor an excessively accelerated pace of industrialization that will cost today's generations their own happiness and require inhuman sacrifices.

431. The Church also recognizes that urban life and industrial change pose unprecedented problems. They undermine traditional patterns of behavior and

institutions: the family, the neighborhood, and work life. And hence they also undermine the living situation of the religious human being, the faithful, and the Christian Community (OA:10).

These characteristics are aspects of what is called "the process of secularization," which is evidently bound up with the emergence of science and technology and the increase in urbanization.

432. There is no reason to assume that the elemental forms of religious awareness are exclusively bound up with agrarian culture. The transition to an urban-industrial civilization need not entail the abolition of religion. But it obviously poses a challenge because it entails new forms and structures of living that condition religious awareness and the Christian life.

433. So the Church is faced with a challenge. It must revitalize its work of evangelization so that it will be able to help the faithful live as Christians amid the new conditioning factors created by the urban-industrial society. And it must realize that these new factors do have an influence on the practice of holiness, on prayer and contemplation, on interhuman relationships (that have now become more functional and anonymous), on people's work life, production, and consumption.

434. *Secularism*. The Church accepts the process of secularization insofar as it means the legitmate autonomy of the secular realm. Taking it in this sense (GS:36; EN:55), it regards it as just and desirable. But the fact is that the shift to an urban-industrial society, viewed in terms of the real-life process of western history rather than in the abstract, has been inspired by the ideology that we call "secularism."

435. Secularism essentially separates human beings from God and sets up an opposition between them. It views the construction of history as purely and exclusively the responsibility of human beings, and it views them in merely immanent terms. The world "is explained solely on its own terms, without any necessary reference to God. God, then, is superfluous, if not a downright obstacle. So in order to recognize the power of human beings, this brand of secularism ends up bypassing God, or even denying God altogether. The result seems to be new forms of atheism—an anthropocentric atheism that is practical and militant rather than abstract and metaphysical. And bound up with this atheistic secularism we find a consumer civilization, a hedonism exalted as the supreme value, a will to power and domination, and discrimination of all sorts. These are some of the other inhuman tendencies of this 'humanism' " (EN:55).

436. Committed to its task to evangelize people and to arouse faith in God, the provident Father, and in Jesus Christ, who is actively present in history, the Church finds itself in a radical confrontation with this secularistic movement. It sees it as a threat to the faith and the very culture of our Latin American peoples. Our aim is that they themselves will be able to incorporate the values of the new urban-industrial civilization into a new vital synthesis, which will continue to be grounded on faith in God rather than on the atheism that is the logical consequence of the movement toward secularism.

Conversion and structures. We have alluded to the inconsistency that exists between the culture of our people, whose values are imbued with the Christian faith, and the impoverished condition in which they are often forced to live by injustice.

437. Undoubtedly situations of injustice and acute poverty are an indictment in themselves, indicating that the faith was not strong enough to affect the criteria and the decisions of those responsible for ideological leadership and the organization of our people's socio-economic life together. Our peoples, rooted in the

Christian faith, have been subjected to structures that have proved to be wellsprings of injustice. These structures are linked with the expansion of liberal capitalism, though in some areas they have been transformed under the inspiration of Marxist collectivism; but they arise out of the ideologies of the dominant cultures, and they are inconsistent with the faith that is part of our people's culture.

438. The Church thus calls for a new conversion on the level of cultural values, so that the structures of societal life may then be imbued with the spirit of the Gospel. And while it calls for a revitalization of evangelical values, it simultaneously urges a rapid and thoroughgoing transformation of structures. For by their very nature these structures are supposed to exert a restraining influence on the evil that arises in the human heart and manifests itself socially; and they are also meant to serve as conditioning pedagogical factors for an interior conversion on the plane of values (Med-P:16).

439. *Other problems.* Within this general situation and its overall challenges are inscribed certain specific problems of major importance that the Church must heed in its new effort at evangelization. They include the following:

440. —There must be a critical yet constructive examination of the educational system established in Latin America.

441. —Using past experience and imagination, the Church must draw up criteria and approaches for a pastoral effort directed at city life, where the new cultural styles are arising. At the same time the Church must also work to evangelize and promote indigenous groups and Afro-Americans.

442. —The Church must establish a new evangelizing presence among workers as well as intellectual and artistic elites.

443. —Humanistically and evangelically the Church must contribute to the betterment of women, in line with their specific identity and femininity.

3. "EVANGELIZATION AND THE PEOPLE'S RELIGIOSITY"

3.1 BASIC STATEMENTS ABOUT THIS NOTION

444. By the religion of the people, popular religiosity, or popular piety (EN:48), we mean the whole complex of underlying beliefs rooted in God, the basic attitudes that flow from these beliefs, and the expressions that manifest them. It is the form of cultural life that religion takes on among a given people. In its most characteristic cultural form, the religion of the Latin American people is an expression of the Catholic faith. It is a people's Catholicism.

445. Despite the defects and the sins that are always present, the faith of the Church has set its seal on the soul of Latin America (HZ:2). It has left its mark on Latin America's essential identity, becoming the continent's cultural matrix out of which new peoples have arisen.

446. It is the Gospel, fleshed out in our peoples, that has brought them together to form the original cultural and historical entity known as Latin America. And this identity is glowingly reflected on the *mestizo* countenance of Mary of Guadalupe, who appeared at the start of the evangelization process.

447. This people's religion is lived out in a preferential way by the "poor and simple" (EN:48). But it takes in all social sectors; and sometimes it is one of the few bonds that really brings together the people living in our nations, which are so divided politically. But of course we must acknowledge that there is much diversity amid this unity, a diversity of social, ethnic, and even generation groups.

448. At its core the religiosity of the people is a storehouse of values that offers the answers of Christian wisdom to the great questions of life. The Catholic wisdom of the common people is capable of fashioning a vital synthesis. It creatively combines the divine and the human, Christ and Mary, spirit and body, communion and institution, person and community, faith and homeland, intelligence and emotion. This wisdom is a Christian humanism that radically affirms the dignity of every person as a child of God, establishes a basic fraternity, teaches people how to encounter nature and understand work, and provides reasons for joy and humor even in the midst of a very hard life. For the common people this wisdom is also a principle of discernment and an evangelical instinct through which they spontaneously sense when the Gospel is served in the Church and when it is emptied of its content and stifled by other interests (OAP:III,6).

449. Because this cultural reality takes in a very broad range of social strata, the common people's religion is capable of bringing together multitudes. Thus it is in the realm of popular piety that the Church fulfills its imperative of universality. Knowing that the message "is not reserved for a small group of initiates or a chosen privileged few, but is meant for all" (EN:57), the Church accomplishes its task of convening the masses in its sanctuaries and religious feasts. There the gospel message has a chance, not always pastorally utilized, of reaching "the heart of the masses" (EN:57).

450. The people's religious life is not just an object of evangelization. Insofar as it is a concrete embodiment of the Word of God, it itself is an active way in which the people continually evangelize themselves.

451. In Latin America this Catholic piety of the common people has not adequately impregnated certain autochthonous cultural groups and ones of African origin. Indeed in some cases they have not even been evangelized at all. Yet these groups do possess a rich store of values and "seeds of the Word" as they await the living Word.

452. Though the popular religiosity has set its seal on Latin American culture, it has not been sufficiently expressed in the organization of our societies and states. It has left standing what John Paul II has once again called "sinful structures" (HZ:3). The gap between rich and poor, the menacing situation faced by the weakest, the injustices, and the humiliating disregard and subjection endured by them radically contradict the values of personal dignity and solidary brotherhood. Yet the people of Latin America carry these values in their hearts as imperatives received from the Gospel. That is why the religiosity of the Latin American people often is turned into a cry for true liberation. It is an exigency that is still unmet. Motivated by their religiosity, however, the people create or utilize space for the practice of brotherhood in the more intimate areas of their lives together: e.g., the neighborhood, the village, their labor unions, and their recreational activities. Rather than giving way to despair, they confidently and shrewdly wait for the right opportunities to move forward toward the liberation they so ardently desire.

453. Due to lack of attention on the part of pastoral agents and to other complicated factors, the religion of the people shows signs of erosion and distortion. Aberrant substitutes and regressive forms of syncretism have already surfaced. In some areas we can discern serious and strange threats to the religion of the people, framed in terms that lay excessive stress on apocalyptic fantasies.

3.4. TASKS AND CHALLENGES

460. We face an urgent situation. The shift from an agrarian to an urbanized industrial society is subjecting the people's religion to a decisive crisis. As this

millennium draws to a close in Latin America, the great challenges posed by the people's piety entail the following pastoral tasks:

461. a. We must offer adequate catechesis and evangelization to the vast majority of the people who have been baptized but whose popular Catholicism is in a weakened state.

462. b. We must mobilize apostolic movements, parishes, base-level ecclesial communities, and church militants in general so that they may be a "leaven in the dough" in a more generous way. We must re-examine the spiritual practices, attitudes, and tactics of church elites vis-à-vis the common people's religiosity. As the Medellín Conference pointed out: "Given this type of religious sense among the masses, the Church is faced with the dilemma of either continuing to be a universal Church or, if it fails to attract and vitally incorporate such groups, of becoming a sect" (Med-PM:3). We must develop in our militants a mystique of service designed to evangelize the religion of their people. That task is even more to the point today, and it is up to elites to accept the spirit of their people, purify it, scrutinize it, and flesh it out in a prominent way. To this end elites must participate in the assemblies and public manifestations of the people so that they may offer their contribution.

463. c. We must proceed to put more planned effort into transforming our sanctuaries so that they might be "privileged locales" of evangelization (HZ:5). This would entail purifying them of all forms of manipulation and commercialism. A special effort in this direction is demanded of our national sanctuaries, which stand as symbols of the interaction between the faith and the history of our peoples.

464. d. We must pay pastoral attention to the popular piety of the peasants and the indigenous peoples, so that they might enjoy growth and renewal in line with their own proper identity and development and in accordance with the emphases spelled out by Vatican II. This will ensure better preparation for more generalized cultural change.

465. e. We must see to it that the liturgy and the common people's piety cross-fertilize each other, giving lucid and prudent direction to the impulses of prayer and charismatic vitality that are evident today in our countries. In addition, the religion of the people, with its symbolic and expressive richness, can provide the liturgy with creative dynamism. When examined with proper discernment, this dynamism can help to incarnate the universal prayer of the Church in our culture in a greater and better way.

466. f. We must try to provide the religiosity of the common people with the necessary reformulations and shifts of emphasis that are required in an urban-industrial civilization. The process is already evident in the big cities of the continent, where the Catholicism of the people is spontaneously finding new forms of expression and enriching itself with new values that have matured within its own depths. In this respect we must see to it that the faith develops a growing personalization and liberative solidarity. The faith must nurture a spirituality that is capable of ensuring the contemplative dimension, i.e., gratitude to God and a poetic, sapiential encounter with creation. The faith must be a wellspring of joy for the common people and a reason for festivity even in the midst of suffering. In this way we can fashion cultural forms that will rescue urban industrialization from oppressive tedium and cold, suffocating economicism.

467. g. We must support the religious expressions of the common people *en masse* for the evangelizing force that they possess.

468. h. We must assume the religious unrest and excitement that is arising as a form of historical anxiety over the coming end of the millennium. This unrest and

excitement must be framed in terms of the lordship of Christ and the providence of the Father, so that the children of God may enjoy the peace they need while they struggle and labor in time.

469. If the Church does not reinterpret the religion of the Latin American people, the resultant vacuum will be occupied by sects, secularized political forms of messianism, consumptionism and its consequences of nausea and indifference, or pagan pansexualism. Once again the Church is faced with stark alternatives: what it does not assume in Christ is not redeemed, and it becomes a new idol replete with all the old malicious cunning.

4. "EVANGELIZATION, LIBERATION, AND HUMAN PROMOTION"

In this section we shall discuss evangelization in terms of its connection with human promotion, liberation, and the social doctrine of the Church.

4.1. A WORD OF ENCOURAGEMENT

470. We fully recognize the efforts undertaken by many Latin American Christians to explore the particularly conflict-ridden situations of our peoples in terms of the faith and to shed the light of God's Word on them. We encourage all Christians to continue to provide this evangelizing service and to consider the criteria for reflection and investigation; and we urge them to put special care into preserving and promoting ecclesial communion on both the local and the universal levels.

471. We are also aware of the fact that since the Medellín Conference pastoral agents have made significant advances and encountered quite a few difficulties. Rather than discouraging us, this should inspire us to seek out new paths and better forms of accomplishment.

4.3. DISCERNING THE NATURE OF LIBERATION IN CHRIST

480. At the Medellín Conference we saw the elucidation of a dynamic process of integral liberation. Its positive echoes were taken up by *Evangelii Nuntiandi* and by John Paul II in his message to this conference. This proclamation imposes an urgent task on the Church, and it belongs to the very core of an evangelization that seeks the authentic realization of the human being.

481. But there are different conceptions and applications of liberation. Though they share common traits, they contain points of view that can hardly be brought together satisfactorily. The best thing to do, therefore, is to offer criteria that derive from the magisterium and that provide us with the necessary discernment regarding the original conception of Christian liberation.

482. There are two complementary and inseparable elements. The first is liberation from all sorts of bondage, from personal and social sin, and from everything that tears apart the human individual and society; all this finds its source to be in egotism, in the mystery of iniquity. The second element is liberation for progressive growth in being through communion with God and other human beings; this reaches its culmination in the perfect communion of heaven, where God is all in all and weeping forever ceases.

483. This liberation is gradually being realized in history, in our personal history and that of our peoples. It takes in all the different dimensions of life: the social,

the political, the economic, the cultural, and all their interrelationships. Through all these dimensions must flow the transforming treasure of the Gospel. It has its own specific and distinctive contribution to make, which must be safeguarded. Otherwise we would be faced with the situation described by Paul VI in *Evangelii Nuntiandi*: "The Church would lose its innermost significance. Its message of liberation would have no originality of its own. It would be prone to takeover or manipulation by ideological systems and political parties" (EN:32).

484. It should be made clear that this liberation is erected on the three great pillars that John Paul II offered us as defining guidelines: i.e. the truth about Jesus Christ, the truth about the Church, and the truth about human beings.

485. Thus we mutilate liberation in an unpardonable way if we do not achieve liberation from sin and all its seductions and idolatry, and if we do not help to make concrete the liberation that Christ won on the cross. We do the very same thing if we forget the crux of liberative evangelization, which is to transform human beings into active subjects of their own individual and communitarian development. And we also do the very same thing if we overlook dependence and the forms of bondage that violate basic rights that come from God, the Creator and Father, rather than being bestowed by governments or institutions, however powerful they may be.

486. The sort of liberation we are talking about knows how to use evangelical means, which have their own distinctive efficacy. It does not resort to violence of any sort, or to the dialectics of class struggle. Instead it relies on the vigorous energy and activity of Christians, who are moved by the Spirit to respond to the cries of countless millions of their brothers and sisters.

487. We pastors in Latin America have the most serious reasons for pressing for liberative evangelization. It is not just that we feel obliged to remind people of individual and social sinfulness. The further reason lies in the fact that since the Medellín Conference the situation has grown worse and more acute for the vast majority of our population.

488. We are pleased to note many examples of efforts to live out liberative evangelization in all its fullness. One of the chief tasks involved in continuing to encourage Christian liberation is the creative search for approaches free of ambiguity and reductionism (EN:32) and fully faithful to the Word of God. Given to us in the Church, that Word stirs us to offer joyful proclamation to the poor as one of the messianic signs of Christ's Kingdom.

489. John Paul II has made this point well: "There are many signs that help us to distinguish when the liberation in question is Christian and when, on the other hand, it is based on ideologies that make it inconsistent with an evangelical view of humanity, of things, and of events (EN:35). These signs derive from the content that the evangelizers proclaim or from the concrete attitudes that they adopt. At the level of content one must consider how faithful they are to the Word of God, to the Church's living tradition, and to its magisterium. As for attitudes, one must consider what sense of communion they feel, with the bishops first of all, and then with the other sectors of God's People. Here one must also consider what contribution they make to the real building up of the community; how they channel their love into caring for the poor, the sick, the dispossessed, the neglected, and the oppressed; and how, discovering in these people the image of the poor and suffering Jesus, they strive to alleviate their needs and to serve Christ in them (LG:8). Let us make no mistake about it: as if by some evangelical instinct, the humble and simple faithful spontaneously sense when the Gospel is being served in the Church

and when it is being eviscerated and asphyxiated by other interests" (OAP:III,6).

490. Those who hold to the vision of humanity offered by Christianity also take on the commitment not to measure the sacrifice it costs to ensure that all will enjoy the status of authentic children of God and brothers and sisters in Jesus Christ. Thus liberative evangelization finds its full realization in the communion of all in Christ, as the Father of all people wills.

5. "EVANGELIZATION, IDEOLOGIES, AND POLITICS"

5.2. EVANGELIZATION AND POLITICS

513. The political dimension is a constitutive dimension of human beings and a relevant area of human societal life. It has an all-embracing aspect because its aim is the common welfare of society. But that does not mean that it exhausts the gamut of social relationships.

514. Far from despising political activity, the Christian faith values it and holds it in high esteem.

515. Speaking in general, and without distinguishing between the roles that may be proper to its various members, the Church feels it has a duty and a right to be present in this area of reality. For Christianity is supposed to evangelize the whole of human life, including the political dimension. So the Church criticizes those who would restrict the scope of faith to personal or family life; who would exclude the professional, economic, social, and political orders as if sin, love, prayer, and pardon had no relevance in them.

5.4. REFLECTIONS ON POLITICAL VIOLENCE

531. Faced with the deplorable reality of violence in Latin America, we wish to express our view clearly. Condemnation is always the proper judgement on physical and psychological torture, kidnapping, the persecution of political dissidents or suspect persons, and the exclusion of people from public life because of their ideas. If these crimes are committed by the authorities entrusted with the task of safeguarding the common good, then they defile those who practice them, notwithstanding any reasons offered.

534. "We are obliged to state and reaffirm that violence is neither Christian nor evangelical, and that brusque, violent structural changes will be false, ineffective in themselves, and certainly inconsistent with the dignity of the people" (Paul VI, Address in Bogotá, 23 August 1968). The fact is that "the Church realizes that even the best structures and the most idealized systems quickly become inhuman if human inclinations are not improved, if there is no conversion of heart and mind on the part of those who are living in those structures or controlling them" (EN:36).

5.7. CONCLUSION

562. The mission of the Church is immense and more necessary than ever before, when we consider the situation at hand: conflicts that threaten the human race and the Latin American continent; violations of justice and freedom; institutionalized injustice embodied in governments adhering to opposing ideologies; and terrorist violence. Fulfillment of its mission will require activity from the Church as a whole: pastors, consecrated ministers, religious, and lay people. All must carry out their

own specific tasks. Joined with Christ in prayer and abnegation, they will commit themselves to work for a better society without employing hate and violence; and they will see that decision through to the end, whatever the consequences. For the attainment of a society that is more just, more free, and more at peace is an ardent longing of the peoples of Latin America and an indispensable fruit of any liberative evangelization.

KEY TO ABBREVIATIONS IN THE TEXT

EN–Pope Paul VI, *Evangelii Nuntiandi* (On Evangelization in the Modern World), December 8, 1975.

GS–Second Vatican Council, Pastoral Constitution on the Church in the Modern World, *Gaudium et Spes*, December 7, 1965.

HZ–Pope John Paul II, Homily in Zopapán, México, January 30, 1979.

LG–Second Vatican Council, Dogmatic Constitution on the Church, *Lumen Gentium*, November 21, 1964.

Med-P–Second General Conference of Latin American Bishops at Medellín, Colombia, 1968. Document on Peace.

Med-PM–Second General Conference of Latin American Bishops at Medellín, Colombia, 1968. Document on the Pastoral Care of the Masses.

OA–Pope Paul VI, Letter to Cardinal Maurice Roy, *Octogesima Adveniens*, May 14, 1971.

OAP–Pope John Paul II, Opening Address at Puebla, January, 1979.

4

Apostles of the Slavs

Rome, June 2, 1985

POPE JOHN PAUL II

In 1985, on the occasion of the eleventh centenary of the death of St. Methodius, Pope John Paul II issued an encyclical letter to commemorate the missionary work of the saint, together with that of his brother St. Cyril (sometimes called "Constantine" but not to be confused with the fourth-century emperor), who died in 869. The evangelizing work of these saints among the Slavic peoples, says the pope, is extremely significant today, especially in the light of contemporary efforts to balance a sense of the catholicity of the faith with the necessity of expressing faith in the context of local cultures: their work might very well be considered a model of missionary and theological inculturation. One might say, as does Aylward Shorter, that the two brothers' emphasis on catholicity rather outweighs their acceptance of the value of the local culture (cf. Towards a Theology of Inculturation, *[Maryknoll, N.Y.: Orbis Books, 1988], pp. 231-32). Nevertheless their work, along with that of Ricci and di Nobili hundreds of years later, forms one of the classic efforts of inculturation.*

The document is written in a style that is very different from most papal encyclical letters. Rather than a systematic and doctrinal development, the pope's style is narrative and anecdotal. In another departure from the typical "encyclical style," the pope quotes liberally from the lives of the two saints, and quotes less frequently from conciliar or magisterial sources. The pope's personal affection and regard for these patrons of his own Slavic culture is evident throughout.

In the selection from the encyclical reprinted here, the pope discusses the various contributions that Cyril and Methodius made toward the development of Slavic culture, and stresses that such commitment to culture worked also to preserve the church from any narrow particularism (cf.#11).

APOSTLES OF THE SLAVS*

III. HERALDS OF THE GOSPEL

8. Byzantine in culture, the brothers Cyril and Methodius succeeded in becoming apostles of the Slavs in the full sense of the word. Separation from one's homeland,

---

*Reprinted from John Paul II, *Slavorum Apostolorum* ("Apostles of the Slavs"), Encyclical

which God sometimes requires of those He has chosen, when accepted with faith in His promise, is always a mysterious and fertile precondition for the development and growth of the people of God on earth. The Lord said to Abraham: "Go from your country and your kindred and your father's house to the land that I will show you. And I will make of you a great nation, and I will bless you, and make your name great, so that you will be a blessing."[1]

In the dream which St. Paul had at Troas in Asia Minor, a Macedonian, therefore an inhabitant of the European continent, came before him and implored him to come to his country to proclaim there the word of God: "Come over to Macedonia and help us."[2]

Divine providence, which for the two holy brothers expressed itself through the voice and authority of the emperor of Byzantium and of the patriarch of the Church of Constantinople, addressed to them a similar exhortation when it asked them to go as missionaries among the Slavs. For them, this task meant giving up not only a position of honor but also the contemplative life. It meant leaving the area of the Byzantine Empire and undertaking a long pilgrimage in the service of the Gospel among peoples that in many aspects were still very alien to the system of civil society based on the advanced organization of the state and the refined culture of Byzantium, embued with Christian principles. A similar request was addressed three times to Methodius by the Roman Pontiff when he sent him as bishop among the Slavs of Greater Moravia, in the ecclesiastical regions of the ancient Diocese of Pannonia.

9. The Slavonic *Life* of Methodius reports in the following words the request made by the Prince Rastislav to the Emperor Michael III through his envoys: "Many Christian teachers have reached us from Italy, from Greece and from Germany, who instruct us in different ways. But we Slavs . . . have no one to direct us toward the truth and instruct us in an understandable way."[3] It was then that Constantine and Methodius were invited to go there. Their profoundly Christian response to the invitation in this circumstance and on all similar occasions is admirably expressed by the words of Constantine to the emperor: "However tired and physically worn out I am, I will go with joy to that land";[4] "with joy I depart for the sake of the Christian faith."[5]

MYSTERY OF REDEMPTION

The truth and the power of their missionary mandate came from the depths of the mystery of the redemption, and their evangelizing work among the Slav peoples was to constitute an important link in the mission entrusted by the Savior to the Church until the end of time. It was a fulfillment—in time and in concrete circumstances—of the words of Christ, who in the power of His cross and resurrection told the apostles: "Preach the Gospel to the whole creation";[6] "go therefore and make disciples of all nations."[7] In so doing, the preachers and teachers of the Slav peoples let themselves be guided by the apostolic ideal of St. Paul: "For in Christ Jesus you are all children of God, through faith. For as many of you as were baptized into Christ have put on Christ. There is neither Jew nor Greek, there is neither slave nor free, there is neither male nor female; for you are all one in Christ Jesus."[8]

Together with a great respect for persons and a disinterested concern for their

Letter to the Universal Church for the Eleventh Centenary of the apostolic work of Saints Cyril and Methodius, co-patrons of Europe, June 2, 1985 (Washington, D.C: United States Catholic Conference, 1985).

true good, the two holy brothers had the resources of energy, prudence, zeal and charity needed for bringing the light to the future believers and at the same time for showing them what is good and offering concrete help for attaining it. For this purpose they desired to become similar in every aspect to those to whom they were bringing the Gospel; they wished to become part of those peoples and to share their lot in everything.

10. Precisely for this reason they found it natural to take a clear position in all the conflicts which were disturbing the societies as they became organized. They took as their own the difficulties and problems inevitable for peoples who were defending their own identity against the military and cultural pressure of the new Romano-Germanic Empire and who were attempting to resist forms of life which they felt to be foreign. It was also the beginning of wider divergencies, which were unfortunately destined to increase, between Eastern and Western Christianity, and the two holy missionaries found themselves personally involved in this, but they always succeeded in maintaining perfect orthodoxy and consistent attention both to the deposit of tradition and to the new elements in the lives of the peoples being evangelized. Situations of opposition often weighed upon them in all their uncertain and painful complexity. But this did not cause Constantine and Methodius to try to withdraw from the trial. Misunderstanding, overt bad faith and even, for St. Methodius, imprisonment accepted for love of Christ, did not deflect either of them from their tenacious resolve to help and to serve the good of the Slav peoples and the unity of the universal Church. This was the price which they had to pay for the spreading of the Gospel, the missionary enterprise, the courageous search for new forms of living and effective ways of bringing the good news to the Slav nations which were then forming.

For the purposes of evangelization the two holy brothers—as their biographies indicate—undertook the difficult task of translating the texts of the Sacred Scriptures, which they knew in Greek, into the language of the Slav population which had settled along the borders of their own region and native city. Making use of their own Greek language and culture for this arduous and unusual enterprise, they set themselves to understanding and penetrating the language, customs and traditions of the Slav peoples, faithfully interpreting the aspirations and human values which were present and expressed therein.

CREATING AN ALPHABET

11. In order to translate the truths of the Gospel into a new language, they had to make an effort to gain a good grasp of the interior world of those to whom they intended to proclaim the word of God in images and concepts that would sound familiar to them. They realized that an essential condition of the success of their missionary activity was to transpose correctly biblical notions and Greek theological concepts into a very different context of thought and historical experience. It was a question of a new method of catechesis. To defend its legitimacy and prove its value, St. Methodius, at first together with his brother and then alone, did not hesitate to answer with docility the invitations to come to Rome, invitations received first from Pope Nicholas I in 867 and then from Pope John VIII in 879. Both Popes wished to compare the doctrine being taught by the brothers in Greater Moravia with that which the holy apostles Peter and Paul had passed down, together with the glorious trophy of their holy relics, to the Church's chief Episcopal See.

Previously, Constantine and his fellow workers had been engaged in creating a new alphabet so that the truths to be proclaimed and explained could be written in old Slavonic and would thus be fully comprehended and grasped by their hearers. The effort to learn the language and to understand the mentality of the new peoples to whom they wished to bring the faith was truly worthy of the missionary spirit. Exemplary, too, was their determination to assimilate and identify themselves with all the needs and expectations of the Slav peoples. Their generous decision to identify themselves with those peoples' life and traditions, once having purified and enlightened them by revelation, make Cyril and Methodius true models for all the missionaries who in every period have accepted St. Paul's invitation to become all things to all people in order to redeem all. And in particular for the missionaries, who from ancient times until the present day, from Europe to Asia and today in every continent, have labored to translate the Bible and the texts of the liturgy into the living languages of the various peoples so as to bring them the one word of God, thus made accessible in each civilization's own forms of expression.

Preserving the Church from Particularism

Perfect communion in love preserves the church from all forms of particularism, ethnic exclusivism or racial prejudice, and from any nationalistic arrogance. This communion must elevate and sublimate every purely natural legitimate sentiment of the human heart.

V. CATHOLIC SENSE OF THE CHURCH

16. It is not only the evangelical content of the doctrine proclaimed by Sts. Cyril and Methodius that merits particular emphasis. Also very expressive and instructive for the Church today is the catechetical and pastoral method that they applied in their apostolic activity among the peoples who had not yet heard the sacred mysteries celebrated in their native language, nor heard the word of God proclaimed in a way that completely fitted their own mentality and respected the actual conditions of their own life.

We all know that the Second Vatican Council, 20 years ago, had as one of its principal tasks that of re-awakening the self-awareness of the Church and, through its interior renewal, of impressing upon it a fresh missionary impulse for the proclamation of the eternal message of salvation, peace and mutual concord among peoples and nations, beyond all the frontiers that yet divide our planet, which is intended by the will of God the Creator and Redeemer to be the common dwelling for all humanity. The dangers that in our times are accumulating over our world cannot make us forget the prophetic insight of Pope John XXIII, who convoked the council with the intent and the conviction that it would be capable of preparing and initiating a period of springtime and rebirth in the life of the Church.

And, among its statements on the subject of universality, the same council included the following: "All men are called to belong to the new People of God. Wherefore this people, while remaining one and unique, is to be spread throughout the whole world and must exist in all ages, so that the purpose of God's will may be fulfilled. In the beginning God made human nature one. After His children were scattered, He decreed that they should at length be unified again (cf. Jn. 11:52). . . . The Church or People of God takes nothing away from the temporal welfare of any people by establishing that kingdom. Rather does it foster and take to itself, insofar as they are good, the abilities, resources and customs of each people. Taking them to itself it purifies, strengthens, and ennobles them. . . . This characteristic of universality which adorns the People of God is a gift from the Lord himself. . . . In virtue of this catholicity, each individual part of the Church contributes through its special gifts to the good of the other parts and of the whole Church. Thus through the common sharing of gifts and through the common effort to attain fullness in unity, the whole and each of its parts receive increase."[9]

17. We can say without fear of contradiction that such a traditional and at the same time extremely up-to-date vision of the catholicity of the Church—like a symphony of the various liturgies in all the world's languages united in one single liturgy, or a melodious chorus sustained by the voices of unnumbered multitudes, rising in countless modulations, tones and harmonies for the praise of God from every part of the globe, at every moment of history—this vision corresponds in a particular way to the theological and pastoral vision which inspired the apostolic and missionary work of Constantine the Philosopher and Methodius, and which sustained their mission among the Slav nations.

DEFENSE OF THE VISION

In Venice, before the representatives of the ecclesiastical world, who held a rather narrow idea of the Church and were opposed to this vision, St. Cyril defended it with courage. He showed that many peoples had already in the past introduced and now possessed a liturgy written and celebrated in their own language, such as "the Armenians, the Persians, the Abasgians, the Georgians, the Sogdians, the Goths, the Avars, the Tirsians, the Khazars, the Arabs, the Copts, the Syrians and many others."[10]

Reminding them that God causes the sun to rise and the rain to fall on all people without exception,[11] he said: "Do not all breathe the air in the same way? And you are not ashamed to decree only three languages (Hebrew, Greek and Latin), deciding that all other peoples and races should remain blind and deaf! Tell me: do you hold this because you consider God is so weak that He cannot grant it, or so envious that He does not wish it?"[12] To the historical and logical arguments which they brought against him, Cyril replied by referring to the inspired basis of Sacred Scripture: "Let every tongue confess that Jesus Christ is Lord, to the glory of God the Father";[13] "All the Earth worships You; they sing praises to your name";[14] "Praise the Lord, all nations! Extol Him, all peoples!"[15]

18. The Church is catholic also because it is able to present in every human context the revealed truth, preserved by it intact in its divine content, in such a way as to bring it into contact with the lofty thoughts and just expectations of every individual and every people. Moreover, the entire patrimony of good which every generation transmits to posterity, together with the priceless gift of life, forms as it were an immense and many-colored collection of tesserae that together make up the living mosaic of the *Pantocrator*, who will manifest himself in His total splendor only at the moment of the Parousia.

The Gospel does not lead to the impoverishment or extinction of those things which every individual, people and nation and every culture throughout history recognize and bring into being as goodness, truth and beauty. On the contrary, it arrives to assimilate and to develop all these values: to live them with magnanimity and joy and to perfect them by the mysterious and ennobling light of revelation.

The concrete dimension of catholicity, inscribed by Christ the Lord in the very makeup of the Church, is not something static, outside history and flatly uniform. In a certain sense it wells up and develops every day as something new from the unanimous faith of all those who believe in God, one and three, revealed by Jesus Christ and preached by the Church through the power of the Holy Spirit. This dimension issues quite spontaneously from mutual respect—proper to fraternal love—for every person and every nation, great or small, and from the honest acknowledgement of the qualities and rights of brethren in the faith.

"THINGS OLD AND NEW"

19. The catholicity of the Church is manifested in the active joint responsibility and generous cooperation of all for the sake of the common good. The Church everywhere effects its universality by accepting, uniting and exalting in the way that is properly its own, with motherly care, every real human value. At the same time, it strives in every clime and every historical situation to win for God each and every human person, in order to unite them with one another and with Him in His truth and His love.

All individuals, all nations, cultures and civilizations have their own part to play and their own place in God's mysterious plan and in the universal history of salvation. This was the thought of the two holy brothers: God, "merciful and kind,"[16] "waiting for all people to repent, so that all may be saved and come to the knowledge of the truth[17] . . . does not allow the human race to succumb to weakness and perish and to fall into the temptation of the enemy. But year by year and at every time he does not cease to lavish on us a manifold grace, from the beginning until today in the same way: first, through the patriarchs and fathers, and after them through the prophets; and again through the apostles and martyrs, the just men and the doctors whom he chooses in the midst of this stormy life."[18]

20. The message of the Gospel which Sts. Cyril and Methodius translated for the Slav peoples, drawing with wisdom from the treasury of the Church "things old and new,"[19] was transmitted through preaching and instruction in accordance with the eternal truths, at the same time being adapted to the concrete historical situation. Thanks to the missionary efforts of both saints, the Slav peoples were able for the first time to realize their own vocation to share in the eternal design of the most Holy Trinity, in the universal plan for the salvation of the world. At the same time, they also recognized their role at the service of the whole history of the humanity created by God the Father, redeemed by the Son our Savior and enlightened by the Holy Spirit. Thanks to their preaching, duly approved by the authorities of the Church—the bishops of Rome and the patriarchs of Constantinople—the Slavs were able to feel that they too, together with the other nations of the Earth, were descendants and heirs of the promise made by God to Abraham.[20] In this way, thanks to the ecclesiastical organization created by St. Methodius and thanks to their awareness of their own Christian identity, the Slavs took their destined place in the Church which had now arisen also in that part of Europe. For this reason, their modern descendants keep in grateful and everlasting remembrance the one who becomes the link that binds them to the chain of the great heralds of the divine revelation of the Old and New Testaments: "After all of these, the merciful God, in our own time, raised up for the good work, for the sake of our own people, for whom nobody had ever cared, our teacher, the holy Methodius, whose virtues and struggles we unblushingly compare, one by one, to those of these men pleasing to God."[21]

NOTES

Numbers in parentheses refer to the number of the note in the original text. The note numbers below refer to the text in this volume.

1. (13) Gen. 12:1-2.
2. (14) Acts 16:9.
3. (15) *Vita Methodii,* V, 2: ed. cit., p. 223 [the Pope is referring to: *Constantinus et Methodius Thessalonicenses, Fontes,* edited and illustrated by Fr. Grivec and Fr. Tomsic (Radovi Staroslavenskog Instituta, Knjiga 4, Zagreb, 1960 – eds.].
4. (16) *Vita Constantini,* ed. cit., p. 200.
5. (17) *Vita Constantini,* ed. cit., p. 179.
6. (18) Mk. 16:15.
7. (19) Mt. 28:19.
8. (20) Gal. 3:26-28.
9. (28) Second Vatican Council, Dogmatic Constitution on the Church *Lumen Gentium,* 13.
10. (29) *Vita Constantini,* ed. cit., p. 205.
11. Cf. Mt. 5:45.
12. (31) *Vita Constantini,* ed. cit., p. 205.
13. (32) *Vita Constantini,* ed. cit., p. 208; Phil. 2:11.
14. (33) *Vita Constantini,* ed. cit., p. 206; Ps. 66 (65):4.
15. (34) *Vita Constantini,* ed. cit., p. 206; Ps. 117 (116):1.i.
16. (35) Cf. Ps. 112 (113):4, Jn. 2-13 [This second reference is unclear – eds.].
17. (36) Cf. 1 Tim. 2:4.
18. (37) *Vita Constantini,* 1: ed. cit., p. 169.
19. (38) Cf. Mt. 13:52.
20. (39) Cf. Gen. 15:1-21.
21. (40) *Vita Methodii,* II, 1: ed. cit., pp. 220f.

5

Final Report

Rome, December 8, 1985

EXTRAORDINARY SYNOD OF BISHOPS

In 1984 Pope John Paul II announced that in late 1985 there would take place an extraordinary session of the Synod of Bishops to commemorate the twentieth anniversary of the completion of the Second Vatican Council. There was speculation from some quarters that the synod would revise some of Vatican II's more open attitudes toward church reform, and it was therefore anticipated with not a little anxiety. Despite such fears, however, the synod actually reaffirmed the general direction of the council, even though it acknowledged that some interpretations and applications had been contrary to the council's true spirit. In the excerpt from the synod's final statement which is published here, it is clear that the synod sees as very much included in the church's mission the ideas of inculturation, dialogue, solidarity with the poor, and commitment to justice. The 1985 Extraordinary Synod, therefore, far from compromising the ecclesiology of Vatican II, actually went somewhat beyond it by dealing positively with several movements which had emerged in the council's wake.

(From "D": "The Church's Mission in the World")*

1. IMPORTANCE OF THE CONSTITUTION "GAUDIUM ET SPES"

The Church as communion is a sacrament for the salvation of the world. Therefore, the authorities in the Church have been placed there by Christ for the salvation of the world. In this context, we affirm the great importance and timeliness of the pastoral constitution *Gaudium et Spes*. At the same time, however, we perceive that the signs of our time are, in part, different from those of the time of the council, with greater problems and anguish. Today, in fact, everywhere in the world we witness an increase in hunger, oppression, injustice and war, sufferings, terrorism, and other forms of violence of every sort. This requires a new and more profound theological reflection in order to interpret these signs in the light of the Gospel.

*Reprinted from: "The Final Report," Extraordinary Synod of Bishops, November 24-December 8, 1985. Published in *A Message to the People of God and The Final Report* (Washington, D.C.: United States Catholic Conference, 1986), pp. 21-24.

2. THEOLOGY OF THE CROSS

It seems to us that in the present-day difficulties God wishes to teach us more deeply the value, the importance, and the centrality of the cross of Jesus Christ. Therefore, the relationship between human history and salvation history is to be explained in the light of the paschal mystery. Certainly, the theology of the cross does not at all exclude the theology of the Creation and Incarnation but, as is clear, it presupposes it. When we Christians speak of the cross, we do not deserve to be labeled pessimists, but we rather base ourselves upon the realism of Christian hope.

3. "AGGIORNAMENTO"

From this paschal perspective, which affirms the unity of the cross and the resurrection, the true and false meaning of so-called *aggiornamento* is discovered. An easy accommodation that could lead to the secularization of the Church is to be excluded. Also excluded is an immobile closing in upon itself of the community of the faithful. Affirmed instead is a missionary openness for the integral salvation of the world. Through this, all truly human values not only are accepted but energetically defended: the dignity of the human person, fundamental human rights, peace, freedom from oppression, poverty, and injustice. But integral salvation is obtained only if these human realities are purified and further elevated, through grace, to human familiarity with God, through Jesus Christ in the Holy Spirit.

4. INCULTURATION

From this perspective, we also find the theological principle for the problem of inculturation. Because the Church is communion, which joins diversity and unity in being present throughout the world, it takes from every culture all that it encounters of positive value. Yet, inculturation is different from a simple external adaptation because it means the intimate transformation of authentic cultural values through their integration in Christianity in the various human cultures.

The separation of Gospel and culture was defined by Paul VI as

the drama of our age, as it was for other ages. It is therefore necessary to make every effort toward a generous evangelization of culture, more precisely of cultures. They must be regenerated through the encounter with the Good News. But this encounter will not be brought about if the Good News is not proclaimed (*Evangelii Nuntiandi*, 20).

5. DIALOGUE WITH NON-CHRISTIAN RELIGIONS AND UNBELIEVERS

The Second Vatican Council affirmed that the Catholic Church refuses nothing of what is true and holy in non-Christian religions. Indeed, it exhorted Catholics to recognize, preserve, and promote all the good spiritual and moral — as well as sociocultural — values that they find in their midst: all of this with prudence and charity, through dialogue and collaboration with the faithful of other religions, giving testimony to the Christian faith and life (*Nostra Aetate*, 2). The council also affirmed that God does not deny the possibility of salvation to anyone of good will (*Lumen Gentium*, 16). The concrete possibilities of dialogue in the various regions depend on many concrete circumstances. All of this is also true for dialogue with nonbelievers. Dialogue must not be opposed to mission. Authentic dialogue tends to bring the human person to open up and communicate his interiority to the one with whom he is speaking. Moreover, all Christians have received from Christ the mission to make all people disciples of Christ (Mt. 28:18). In this sense, God can use the dialogue between Christians and non-Christians and between Christians and unbelievers as a pathway for communicating the fullness of grace.

6. PREFERENTIAL OPTION FOR THE POOR AND HUMAN PROMOTION

Following the Second Vatican Council, the Church became more aware of her mission in the service of the poor, the oppressed, and the outcast. In this preferential option, which must not be understood as exclusive, the true spirit of the Gospel shines forth. Jesus Christ declared the poor blessed (Mt. 5:3; Lk. 6:20), and he himself wished to be poor for us (2 Cor. 8:9).

Besides material poverty, there is the lack of liberty and of spiritual goods which in some way may be considered forms of poverty, and it is particularly grave when religious liberty is suppressed by force.

The Church must prophetically denounce every form of poverty and oppression and everywhere defend and promote the fundamental and inalienable rights of the human person. This is, above all, the case where it is a question of defending human life from the time of its very beginning, of protecting it from aggressors in every circumstance, and of effectively promoting it in every respect.

The Synod expresses its communion with those brothers and sisters who suffer persecution because of their faith and who suffer for the promotion of justice. The Synod lifts up prayers to God for them.

The salvific mission of the Church in relation to the world must be understood as an integral whole. Though it is spiritual, the mission of the Church involves human promotion, even in its temporal aspects. For this reason, the mission of the Church cannot be reduced to monism, no matter how the latter is understood. In this mission, there is certainly a clear distinction—but not a separation—between the natural and the supernatural aspects. This duality is not a dualism. It is thus necessary to put aside the false and useless oppositions between, for example, the Church's spiritual mission and *diaconia* for the world.

6

Instruction on Christian Freedom and Liberation

Rome, March 22, 1986

CONGREGATION FOR THE DOCTRINE OF THE FAITH

In 1984 the Congregation for the Doctrine of the Faith published a document entitled Libertatis Nuntius, *which dealt with "Certain Aspects of the Theology of Liberation." The document was critical toward liberation theology, especially as it had developed in Latin America, and it raised strong protest from Latin American theologians as well as from Christians throughout the world. In March 1986, the Congregation published another document called "Instruction on Christian Freedom and Liberation." While claiming continuity with the 1984 instruction, this document was nevertheless much more balanced in tone and much more favorable to the various liberation movements and the theology which was emerging from them.*

This "Instruction on Christian Freedom and Liberation" consists of five chapters. The first (#5-24) is a reflection on "The State of Freedom in the World Today" and is historical and sociological in nature. Chapter II ((#25-42) speaks of the human call to freedom within the context of human sinfulness and rebellion against God's liberating purposes. The third chapter (#43-60) is a biblical-theological reflection on liberation and Christian freedom, and Chapter IV (#61-70) focuses on the liberating mission of the church. The final chapter (#71-96) speaks of this mission within the context of the church's tradition of social teaching.

Published here is Chapter IV (#61-70). What is emphasized in this chapter is the essential link between evangelization and justice (Part I) and the importance of a "preferential option for the poor" (Part II). There is also a cautious approval—but an approval, nonetheless—of basic ecclesial communities. The experience of such communities, if they remain faithful to the Christian tradition and to church authorities, is described as "a treasure for the whole church" (#69).

(From Chapter IV: "The Liberating Mission of the Church")*

---

*Reprinted from Congregation for the Doctrine of the Faith, *Instruction on Christian Freedom and Liberation*, March 22, 1986 (Washington, D.C: United States Catholic Conference, 1986).

THE CHURCH AND THE ANXIETIES OF MANKIND

61. The Church is firmly determined to respond to the anxiety of contemporary man as he endures oppression and yearns for freedom. The political and economic running of society is not a direct part of her mission.[1] But the Lord Jesus has entrusted to her the word of truth which is capable of enlightening consciences. Divine love, which is her life, impels her to a true solidarity with everyone who suffers. If her members remain faithful to this mission, the Holy Spirit, the source of freedom, will dwell in them, and they will bring forth fruits of justice and peace in their families and in the places where they work and live.

I. FOR THE INTEGRAL SALVATION OF THE WORLD

THE BEATITUDES AND THE POWER OF THE GOSPEL

62. The Gospel is the power of eternal life, given even now to those who receive it.[2] But by begetting people who are renewed,[3] this power penetrates the human community and its history, thus purifying and giving life to its activities. In this way it is a "root of culture."[4]

The Beatitudes proclaimed by Jesus express the perfection of evangelical love, and they have never ceased to be lived throughout the history of the Church by countless baptized individuals, and in an eminent manner by the saints.

The Beatitudes, beginning with the first, the one concerning the poor, form a whole which itself must not be separated from the entirety of the Sermon on the Mount.[5] In this Sermon, Jesus, who is the new Moses, gives a commentary on the Decalogue, the Law of the Covenant, thus giving it its definitive and fullest meaning. Read and interpreted in their full context, the Beatitudes express the spirit of the Kingdom of God which is to come. But, in the light of the definitive destiny of human history thus manifested, there simultaneously appear with a more vivid clarity the foundations of justice in the temporal order.

For the Beatitudes, by teaching trust which relies on God, hope of eternal life, love of justice, and mercy which goes as far as pardon and reconciliation, enable us to situate the temporal order in relation to a transcendent order which gives the temporal order its true measure but without taking away its own nature.

In the light of these things, the commitment necessary in temporal tasks of service to neighbour and the human community is both urgently demanded and kept in its right perspective. The Beatitudes prevent us from worshipping earthly goods and from committing the injustices which their unbridled pursuit involves.[6] They also divert us from an unrealistic and ruinous search for a perfect world, "for the form of this world is passing away" (1 Cor. 7:31).

THE PROCLAMATION OF SALVATION

63. The Church's essential mission, following that of Christ, is a mission of evangelization and salvation.[7] She draws her zeal from the divine love. Evangelization is the proclamation of salvation, which is a gift of God. Through the word of God and the Sacraments, man is freed in the first place from the power of sin and the power of the Evil One which oppress him; and he is brought into a communion of love with God. Following her Lord who "came into the world to save

sinners" (1 Tim. 1:15), the Church desires the salvation of all people.

In this mission, the Church teaches the way which man must follow in this world in order to enter the Kingdom of God. Her teaching therefore extends to the whole moral order, and notably to the justice which must regulate human relations. This is part of the preaching of the Gospel.

But the love which impels the Church to communicate to all people a sharing in the grace of divine life also causes her, through the effective action of her members, to pursue people's true temporal good, help them in their needs, provide for their education and promote an integral liberation from everything that hinders the development of individuals. The Church desires the good of man in all his dimensions, first of all as a member of the city of God, and then as a member of the earthly city.

EVANGELIZATION AND THE PROMOTION OF JUSTICE

64. Therefore, when the Church speaks about the promotion of justice in human societies, or when she urges the faithful laity to work in this sphere according to their own vocation, she is not going beyond her mission. She is however concerned that this mission should not be absorbed by preoccupations concerning the temporal order or reduced to such preoccupations. Hence she takes great care to maintain clearly and firmly both the unity and the distinction between evangelization and human promotion: unity, because she seeks the good of the whole person; distinction, because these two tasks enter, in different ways, into her mission.

THE GOSPEL AND EARTHLY REALITIES

65. It is thus by pursuing her own finality that the Church sheds the light of the Gospel on earthly realities in order that human beings may be healed of their miseries and raised in dignity. The cohesion of society in accordance with justice and peace is thereby promoted and strengthened.[8] Thus the Church is being faithful to her mission when she condemns the forms of deviation, slavery and oppression of which people are victims.

She is being faithful to her mission when she opposes attempts to set up a form of social life from which God is absent, whether by deliberate opposition or by culpable negligence.[9]

She is likewise being faithful to her mission when she exercises her judgment regarding political movements which seek to fight poverty and oppression according to theories or methods of action which are contrary to the Gospel and opposed to man himself.[10]

It is of course true that, with the energy of grace, evangelical morality brings man new perspectives and new duties. But its purpose is to perfect and elevate a moral dimension which already belongs to human nature and with which the Church concerns herself in the knowledge that this is a heritage belonging to all people by their very nature.

II. A LOVE OF PREFERENCE FOR THE POOR

JESUS AND POVERTY

66. Christ Jesus, although he was rich, became poor in order to make us rich by means of his poverty.[11] Saint Paul is speaking here of the mystery of the Incarnation

of the eternal Son, who came to take on mortal human nature in order to save man from the misery into which sin had plunged him. Furthermore, in the human condition Christ chose a state of poverty and deprivation[12] in order to show in what consists the true wealth which ought to be sought, that of communion of life with God. He taught detachment from earthly riches so that we might desire the riches of heaven.[13] The Apostles whom he chose also had to leave all things and share his deprivation.[14]

Christ was foretold by the Prophets, as the Messiah of the poor;[15] and it was among the latter, the humble, the "poor of Yahweh", who were thirsting for the justice of the Kingdom, that he found hearts ready to receive him. But he also wished to be near to those who, though rich in the goods of this world, were excluded from the community as "publicans and sinners", for he had come to call them to conversion.[16]

It is this sort of poverty, made up of detachment, trust in God, sobriety and a readiness to share, that Jesus declared blessed.

JESUS AND THE POOR

67. But Jesus not only brought the grace and peace of God; he also healed innumerable sick people; he had compassion on the crowd who had nothing to eat and he fed them; with the disciples who followed him he practiced almsgiving.[17] Therefore the Beatitude of poverty which he proclaimed can never signify that Christians are permitted to ignore the poor who lack what is necessary for human life in this world. This poverty is the result and consequence of people's sin and natural frailty, and it is an evil from which human beings must be freed as completely as possible.

LOVE OF PREFERENCE FOR THE POOR

68. In its various forms—material deprivation, unjust oppression, physical and psychological illnesses, and finally death—human misery is the obvious sign of the natural condition of weakness in which man finds himself since original sin and the sign of his need for salvation. Hence it drew the compassion of Christ the Saviour to take it upon himself[18] and to be identified with the least of his brethren (cf. Mt. 25:40, 45). Hence also those who are oppressed by poverty are the object of a love of preference on the part of the Church, which since her origin and in spite of the failings of many of her members has not ceased to work for their relief, defence and liberation. She has done this through numberless works of charity which remain always and everywhere indispensable.[19] In addition, through her social doctrine which she strives to apply, she has sought to promote structural changes in society so as to secure conditions of life worthy of the human person.

By detachment from riches, which makes possible sharing and opens the gate of the Kingdom,[20] the disciples of Jesus bear witness through love for the poor and unfortunate to the love of the Father himself manifested in the Saviour. This love comes from God and goes to God. The disciples of Christ have always recognized in the gifts placed on the altar a gift offered to God himself.

In loving the poor, the Church also witnesses to man's dignity. She clearly affirms that man is worth more for what he is than for what he has. She bears witness to the fact that this dignity cannot be destroyed, whatever the situation of poverty, scorn, rejection or powerlessness to which a human being has been reduced. She shows her solidarity with those who do not count in a society by which they are rejected spiritually and sometimes even physically. She is particularly drawn with maternal affection toward those children who, through human wickedness, will never be brought forth from the womb to the light of day, as also for the elderly, alone and abandoned.

The special option for the poor, far from being a sign of particularism or sectarianism, manifests the universality of the Church's being and mission. This option excludes no one.

This is the reason why the Church cannot express this option by means of reductive sociological and ideological categories which would make this preference a partisan choice and a source of conflict.

BASIC COMMUNITIES AND OTHER CHRISTIAN GROUPS

69. The new basic communities or other groups of Christians which have arisen to be witnesses to this evangelical love are a source of great hope for the Church. If they really live in unity with the local Church and the universal Church, they will be a real expression of communion and a means for constructing a still deeper communion.[21] Their fidelity to their mission will depend on how careful they are to educate their members in the fullness of the Christian faith through listening to the Word of God, fidelity to the teaching of the Magisterium, to the hierarchical order of the Church and to the sacramental life. If this condition is fulfilled, their experience, rooted in a commitment to the complete liberation of man, becomes a treasure for the whole Church.

THEOLOGICAL REFLECTION

70. Similarly, a theological reflection developed from a particular experience can constitute a very positive contribution, inasmuch as it makes possible a highlighting of aspects of the Word of God, the richness of which had not yet been fully grasped. But in order that this reflection may be truly a reading of the Scripture and not a projection onto the Word of God of a meaning which it does not contain, the theologian will be careful to interpret the experience from which he begins in the light of the experience of the Church herself. This experience of the Church shines with a singular brightness and in all its purity in the lives of the saints. It pertains to the pastors of the Church, in communion with the Successor of Peter, to discern its authenticity.

NOTES

Numbers in parentheses refer to the number of the note in the original text. The note numbers below refer to the text in the present volume.

1. (85) Cf. *Gaudium et Spes*, 42, #2.
2. (86) Cf. Jn. 17:3.
3. (87) Cf. Rom. 6:4; 2 Cor. 5:17; Col. 3:9-11.
4. (88) Cf. Paul VI, Apostolic Exhortation *Evangelii Nuntiandi*, 18 and 20: AAS 68 (1976), pp. 17 and 19.
5. (89) Mt. 5:3.
6. (90) *Gaudium et Spes*, 37.
7. (91) Cf. Dogmatic Constitution on the Church *Lumen Gentium* 17; Church's

Decree on Missionary Activity *Ad Gentes*, 1; Paul VI, Apostolic Exhortation *Evangelii Nuntiandi*, 14: AAS 68 (1976), p. 13.

8. (92) *Gaudium et Spes*, 40, #3.

9. (93) Cf. John Paul II, Apostolic Exhortation *Reconciliatio et Paenitentia*, 14: AAS 77 (1985), pp. 211-212.

10. (94) *Libertatis Nuntius*, XI, 10: AAS 76 (1984), p. 901.

11. (95) Cf. 2 Cor. 8:9.

12. (96) Cf. Lk. 2:7; 9:58.

13. (97) Cf. Mt. 6:19-20; 24-34; 19:21.

14. (98) Cf. Lk. 5:11, 28; Mt. 19:27.

15. (99) Cf. Is. 11:4; 61:1; Lk. 4:18.

16. (100) Cf. Lk. 19:1-10; Mk. 2:13-17.

17. (101) Cf. Mt. 8:6; 14:13-21; Jn. 13:29.

18. (102) Cf. Mt. 8:17.

19. (103) Cf. Paul VI, Encyclical *Populorum Progressio*, 12 and 46: AAS 59 (1967), pp. 262-263 and p. 280; *Document of the Third General Conference of the Latin American Episcopate at Puebla*, 476. [The latter document is found in this volume, Part II Chapter 3—eds.]

20. (104) Cf. Acts 2:44-45.

21. (105) Cf. Second Extraordinary Synod, *Relatio Finalis*, II, C,6: *L'Osservatore Romano*, 10 December 1985, p. 7; Paul VI, Apostolic Exhortation *Evangelii Nuntiandi*, 58: AAS 68 (1976), pp. 46-49.

7

AMECEA Bishops' Message to Catholic Families in Eastern Africa

Moshi, Tanzania, May 2, 1986

ASSOCIATION OF THE MEMBER EPISCOPAL CONFERENCES OF EASTERN AFRICA (AMECEA)

In late April and early May 1986, the Association of Member Episcopal Conferences of Eastern Africa, known by the acronym AMECEA, celebrated its twenty-fifth anniversary and held its ninth Plenary Assembly at Moshi, Tanzania. The theme of the assembly was "Families Truly Christian and Truly African," and at its conclusion the bishops issued a message "to the Catholic families in Eastern Africa." Although the bishops had wrestled with extremely difficult issues, like polygamy and "trial marriages," their conclusions are still very traditional, reflecting a loyalty to reiterated teaching on these topics on the occasion of several papal visits to Africa in the past. Printed here is the major portion of the bishops' message.

AMECEA BISHOPS' MESSAGE*

We, the Bishops of AMECEA, aware of the enormous problems facing Christian families in Eastern Africa today, have spent several days together with representatives of priests, religious and laity, praying and reflecting on solutions best suited to our cultural situations, so as to help these families grow more and more into "Truly Christian and Truly African Families."

We are very grateful to God that he has blessed our countries with many good and happy African Christian families which are the backbone of Christian life in our region. We wish to encourage and support them in their efforts to live up to the challenges of the Gospel message. We pray that such families may increase and through their life witness may act as pastoral agents in solving the problems of marriage and family life we have been studying this week.

With diligence and genuine sense of pastoral concern, we have examined some of the major problems and their root causes which you have been involved in

---

*"The AMECEA Bishops' Message to the Catholic Families in Eastern Africa," Reprinted from *African Ecclesiastical Review* 28, 3/4 (June/August, 1986): 265-69.

identifying over the last six years. The problems include polygamy; broken marriages; migrant labour; cultural differences in cases of transcultural marriages; premarriage cohabitation; mixed marriages, drunkenness and infidelity.

We have examined initatives made hitherto on behalf of families, such as: the promotion of Marriage Encounter Programmes; Natural Family Planning; Christian Family Movement; Pioneer Movement or Alcoholics Anonymous; the discouragement of excessive bride-price, etc.

We have also examined obstacles to these initiatives, including: opposition of governmental and non-governmental agencies which promote unorthodox ways of birth control; disregard of traditional values and adequate preparation for marriage and maintenance of stable families; ignorance about Christian marriage and lack of deep faith; influence of mass media and lack of trained personnel.

It is in view of these that we have come up with new initiatives. We appeal to the whole People of God to be fully involved in making these solutions as effective as possible. For this reason, we have produced, during this session, guidelines for a *Catechesis for Christian Families* in which suggestions are made for deepening sacramental life, biblical nourishment, family spirituality and for the emergence of ministries to deal with these problems according to the needs of our local Church.

MARRIAGE IN PREPARATORY STAGES

On this matter, we observe that African traditional marriage is a developing process which takes various stages before finalisation. With this in mind we recommend that each episcopal conference should undertake a research into traditional customary marriage in order to determine how the Church should be involved. The so-called *trial* marriages are unacceptable for we believe marriage to be a total commitment. We recommend the development of pastoral programmes which will present marriage as a love covenant.

For the couples living in customary marriages we recommend that diocesan pastoral programmes be developed to take care of these couples in the hope of bringing them to celebrate their union as a sacrament.

POLYGAMY

Polygamy is practised both in its traditional and modern forms in Eastern Africa. We take a very firm stand against it because it is incompatible with the Gospel message. At the same time polygamous families are part of our pastoral concern. With the good of these families at heart, we agree that a *Catechesis* be developed in the hope of integrating them into the Christian communities and gradually leading them to freely fulfill the conditions required for full participation in the life of the Church.

MIGRANT LABOUR

We note with grave concern problems caused to marriage and family life through prolonged separation of husband and wife due to migrant labour or any other such employment which can only be found far away from one's home. We appeal to governments and all other employers to try hard to provide adequate housing facilities for entire families of their employees in accordance with the Charter of the Rights of the Family (Art. 12). We call on husbands and wives always to remember that a family can only be strengthened if the two stay together. It is only then that they will be able to deepen their love and give adequate education to their children.

MARRIAGES IN DIFFICULTIES

With pastoral concern to assist families which find themselves in difficulties, we have recommended that each diocese within AMECEA ensure the establishment of a regular marriage tribunal to deal with broken marriages. We have agreed that, as provided for in Canon Law, No. 1425, each episcopal conference within AME-CEA will discuss the issue of allowing one ecclesiastical judge in these tribunals instead of the normal three. We want to involve competent lay people in these tribunals and where possible to select some of them to study Church law to help in this apostolate.

We call on the pastors and the other pastoral workers to make these Church marriage tribunals, their procedures and competence known among the faithful.

Families that seek assistance should be helped early enough by the pastoral workers. Let priests and other pastoral agents listen attentively and sympathetically to couples' difficulties in order to find solutions to them. Let priests work together with the competent lay leaders to solve marriage and family problems in their areas. Prevention is always better than cure. This should be a guiding principle in this regard.

FAMILY PLANNING

Among the many burning issues in the contemporary world is the issue of family planning. We realise that this issue is of great importance in our AMECEA countries. Family planning is being promoted by governmental, world, continental and national organisations. All types of methods of family planning are being promoted by such organizations to bring about their desired aim. In the secular world, family planning has come to mean simply the limiting of the number of children a married couple can get, whereas in the Catholic sense, it is for the benefit of the couple, the entire family and society.

We remind all our faithful that the artificial methods of family planning are unacceptable to the Catholic doctrine and practice. Every local Church within AMECEA should inform the faithful of the grave dangers, both moral and medical, contained in these artificial methods and means. This information should reach all categories of people especially those who are particularly vulnerable either because of ignorance, poverty, or immaturity of age.

CONCLUSION

In our guidelines, you will find three major headings. We have guidelines for married people, for pre-marriage catechesis and for the many people in our region who live a nomadic life and deserve a special apostolate and catechesis, adapted to their culture and world-view.

It is our great conviction that in order to create and promote families which are "Truly Christian and Truly African," family catechesis must start at an early age for every Christian. We outline what Christian children should be taught in this regard. We have also given guidelines for the pre-marriage catechesis for the youth in order to prepare them for solid adult Christian life. The married couples need this family catechesis for their ongoing formation in the vocation and mission of marriage and family life.

We firmly declare that since the Christian family is the *Domestic Church* and indispensable school for Christian values, it is also our pastoral priority within the overall priority of small Christian communities.

We therefore call upon all pastoral agents mentioned in the guidelines to bring these guidelines to the attention of the faithful and to use them in this all-important work of promoting "Families Truly Christian and Truly African."

8

To the Ends of the Earth

Washington, D.C., November 1986

U.S. CATHOLIC BISHOPS

The big news at the National Conference of Catholic Bishops at their November 1986 meeting was the approval and publication of the pastoral letter, Economic Justice for All: Catholic Social Teaching and the U.S. Economy. *At the same meeting, with much less fanfare, the bishops released what they called a "Pastoral Statement on World Mission," for the double purpose of providing "a theological and pastoral instrument for mission animation" (#2) and affirming missionaries in their work.*

The document emphasizes its continuity with Vatican II's Ad Gentes *(the decree on the church's missionary activity) and Paul VI's* Evangelii Nuntiandi *(part of which is printed in this volume). It also tries to make connections between the missionary activity of the church and the ideas of political and economic global interdependence of nations espoused in the pastoral letters on peace and the economy (cf. #6-7). After the Introduction (#1-8), a short first chapter (#9-21) speaks of the "new missionary context" of the post-colonial world. A second, longer chapter (#22-50) reflects on various aspects of mission theology, from its rootedness in the Trinity to the necessity of ecumenism, dialogue, and a holistic attitude toward evangelization. Chapter III (#51-60) sketches out the elements of a missionary spirituality.*

Reprinted here are the Introduction and Chapters I and II. The document does not break a lot of new ground—that could hardly be expected of a magisterial document. It does, however, summarize very succinctly many current trends in the theology of mission. It lays special emphasis not only on the essential missionary nature of the church (#16), but also on the reality of mission in today's world as being a mutual sending and receiving of evangelizers (#15).

TO THE ENDS OF THE EARTH*

INTRODUCTION

1. *Jesus the Missionary*: Jesus was a missionary. As the word of God, he is the light of all nations.[1] As the word made flesh, he brought God's own life into our

---

*To the Ends of the Earth (Washington, D.C.: United States Catholic Conference, 1986).

midst.[2] Before returning to the Father, he sent the church to continue the mission given him by the Father and empowered her with his Spirit: "As the Father has sent me, so I send you" (Jn. 20:21).[3]

2. *A Missionary Church*: The church, therefore, is missionary by her very nature. She continues the mission of the Son and the mission of the Holy Spirit by proclaiming to the ends of the earth the salvation Christ offers those who believe in him.[4] We are faithful to the nature of the church to the degree that we love and sincerely promote her missionary activity. As teachers and pastors we are responsible for keeping alive a vibrant Catholic missionary spirit in the United States.

3. *Purpose of Statement*: Our purpose in writing this pastoral letter is twofold:

First, to provide a theological and pastoral instrument for mission animation in order to stimulate interest in and a personal sense of responsibility for the church's mission to other peoples. Jesus' great commission to the first disciples is now addressed to us. Like them, we must go and make disciples of all the nations, baptize them in the name of the Father, and the Son and the Holy Spirit, and teach them everything that Jesus has commanded.[5] This mission to the peoples of all nations must involve all of us personally in our parishes and at the diocesan and universal levels of the church.

Second, to affirm missionaries and their efforts to proclaim the Gospel and promote the reign of God. Jesus Christ, the Lord of all, is with them as they go forth in his name.[6] So must the entire church in the United States be with them as they carry out our common mission under difficult and often dangerous circumstances. Our focus in this pastoral is the proclamation of the Gospel to peoples outside the United States. While we are acutely conscious of our continuing need to evangelize in our own country, that challenge, as great as it is, must never cause us to forget our responsibility to share the good news of Jesus with the rest of the world.

4. *Documents on Mission*: Over the centuries, the church has frequently reflected on her founding by Christ as a missionary community with a vision of God's reign that stretches beyond the horizon of history. Our own time has seen the promulgation of the Second Vatican Council's Decree on the Missionary Activity of the Church (*Ad Gentes*) and Pope Paul VI's Apostolic Exhortation on Evangelization in the Modern World (*Evangelii Nuntiandi*). These important documents stress the essential missionary nature of the church and outline a contemporary charter for her mission through sensitive adaptation to new conditions.

5. *World Mission*: We commemorate *Ad Gentes* and *Evangelii Nuntiandi* with this pastoral letter on the mission of the church in the United States to other lands. We do so as members of the college of bishops, all of whom "are consecrated not just for one diocese alone, but for the salvation of the whole world."[7] Our concern must be for the whole church, but especially for "those parts of the world where the word of God has not yet been proclaimed."[8]

6. *Mission and "The Challenge of Peace"*: Concern for world mission springs from the same principles we set forth in our pastoral letters "The Challenge of Peace" and "Economic Justice for All: Catholic Social Teaching and the U.S. Economy." These letters offer substantial help for understanding our church's mission to other peoples and nations. As we said in "The Challenge of Peace":

"The theological principle of unity has always affirmed a human interdependence; but today this bond is complemented by the growing political and economic interdependence of the world, manifested in a whole range of international issues."[9]

When the church brings Christ's message to the ends of the earth, she helps foster this unity. As we stated:

"The risen Lord's gift of peace is inextricably bound to the call to follow Jesus and to continue the proclamation of God's reign. Matthew's Gospel (28:16-20; cf. Lk. 24:44-53) tells us that Jesus' last words to his disciples were a sending forth and a promise: 'I shall be with you all days.' In the continuing presence of Jesus, disciples of all ages find the courage to follow him. To follow Jesus Christ implies continual conversion in one's own life as one seeks to act in ways which are consonant with the justice, forgiveness and love of God's reign. Discipleship reaches out to the ends of the earth and calls for reconciliation among all peoples so that God's purpose, 'a plan for the fullness of time, to unite all things in him' (Eph. 1:10) will be fulfilled."[10]

7. *Mission and "Economic Justice for All"*: Our pastoral, "Economic Justice for All: Catholic Social Teaching and the U.S. Economy," shows how the church's mission in an interdependent world has important implications for economic policy. Here we follow the traditional principles of Catholic teaching on interdependence as expressed in the writings of recent popes. These principles affirm the dignity of the human person, the unity of the human family, the right of all of us to share the goods of the earth, the need to pursue the international common good and the imperative of distributive justice in a world ever more sharply divided between rich and poor.[11]

8. *Unity with the Universal Church*: This pastoral letter presents the challenge to the church in the United States with regard to world mission. We write conscious of our unity with John Paul II, our pope and with the church throughout the world.

I. THE NEW MISSIONARY CONTEXT

9. *New Context*: In their publications and personal communications, missionaries emphasize how greatly the missionary context has changed since World War II, and even since the promulgation of *Ad Gentes* and *Evangelii Nuntiandi*.[12] It is important that we understand this change.

HISTORICAL BACKGROUND

10. *Missionary Roots of U.S. Church*: From the earliest days, European missionaries served immigrants to the New World and the native people they found on these shores. Many journeyed from Spain, France, England and other countries to give heroic witness to the Gospel in Colonial America. Missionaries such as Isaac Jogues and Junipero Serra made major contributions to shaping our identity as Catholics with a mission.

11. *Missionaries and Immigrants*: Missionaries accompanied the millions of poor and destitute people who vitalized our growing nation in the 19th and 20th centuries. At this time, too, heroic witness was not uncommon. Two of these missionaries, Mother Frances Xavier Cabrini and Bishop John Neumann, are celebrated as saints.

12. *Missionaries in Our Turn*: In God's providence, our own people have accepted the challenge of sharing the gift of faith we have received. Especially in this century, but even in the last, missionaries were sent to announce the Gospel to other nations and peoples. Religious congregations and missionary societies, some of them founded in our own country, played a prominent part in this work. The bishops of the United States underscored their commitment to world mission when they established Maryknoll as The Catholic Foreign Mission Society of America in 1911.

Dioceses also sent priests, religious and laity to mission lands. This proud tradition continues at the present time.

13. *Pontifical Mission Aid Societies*: People young and old encouraged these missionaries with prayers and sacrifices, assisted them financially and welcomed them on visits home. The Society for the Propagation of the Faith and the Association of the Holy Childhood — the pontifical mission aid societies — have been principally responsible for fostering this popular support, performing the central role in universal missionary cooperation that the Second Vatican Council has affirmed:

"It is right that these works (i.e., the pontifical mission aid societies) be given first place, because they are a means by which Catholics are imbued from infancy with a truly universal and missionary outlook and also as a means for instigating an effective collecting of funds for all the missions, each according to its needs."[13]

The church has commissioned these organizations to awaken and deepen the missionary conscience of the people of God; to inform them about the needs of universal mission; and to encourage local churches to pray for and support one another with personnel and material aid.

CONTEMPORARY DEVELOPMENTS

14. *A New Vitality*: A significant contemporary development in world mission is the shifting of the church's center of gravity from the West, from Europe and North America, toward the East and the South. In Latin America, Africa and Asia the church is experiencing either profound revitalization or enormous growth. Indeed, the Christian energy of these local churches has begun to overflow into missionary service of the Gospel.[14]

15. *Mission Sending, Mission Receiving*: The lands to which missionaries went used to be called "the mission." These countries were seen as mission receiving. Other countries were thought of as mission sending; they did not see themselves in need of receiving missionaries. A deeper understanding of the theology of mission leads us to recognize that these distinctions no longer apply. Every local church is both mission sending and mission receiving.

A NEW SELF-UNDERSTANDING

16. *Church is Mission*: These changes have brought about a new self-understanding, both for the former "mission countries" which have taken the missionary mandate of the church as their own, and for those which have long ceased to think of themselves as "mission countries." Together we are coming to see that any local church has no choice but to reach out to others with the Gospel of Christ's love for all peoples. To say "church" is to say "mission."

17. *Basic Task of Mission*: Missionaries have always seen their principal tasks as preaching the Gospel to those who have not heard it, baptizing them with the waters of salvation, caring for their physical well-being and forming Christian communities. These missionaries were also sent to lend pastoral assistance to other established churches in need. The magnificent work of these men and women has been an invaluable service to the church, and today's missionaries build on their achievements.

18. *Influence of Colonial Attitudes*: At times in the past missionaries brought not only the strengths but also some of the weaknesses of Western civilization. It often happened that they labored in lands where their own country had political and

economic interests. In areas where their home country was the colonial power, those to whom they were sent sometimes found it difficult to distinguish the church's missionary effort from the colonizing effort, which proved critical when the colonial empires were dismantled after World War II.

19. *Solidarity with Local Church*: Today missionaries work primarily in established local churches, to whose life and vitality they want to contribute. The need to cooperate with diocesan bishops and authorized pastoral workers requires adaptation to local institutions and cultures. When missionaries come from a country like the United States, which has great political and economic interests throughout the world, their participation in the life of the local church can place them in conflict with the policies of their own government or, indeed, of their host government. Nevertheless, they must be in union with the diocesan bishop and the local church which they have been sent to serve.[15]

20. *Overcoming Colonial Attitudes*: In the post-colonial era, missionaries inevitably confront the effects of long Western domination in the Third World. As they work with others to promote the reign of God, they face the challenge of clearly distinguishing their Christian mission from colonial and neocolonial practices. Missionaries sometimes work in countries where freedom of conscience, freedom of religion and other basic human rights are either overtly or subtly restricted. These, especially, need to know that we are one with them and understand the very difficult situations in which they labor.

21. *Heroic Witness*: Mission work still calls for heroic witness to the faith. We are proud of Jean Donovan, a lay woman; Ita Ford and Maura Clarke, Maryknoll Sisters; Dorothy Kazel, an Ursuline Sister; James Miller, a De La Salle Christian Brother; William Woods, a Maryknoll priest; Stanley Rother, an Oklahoma diocesan priest; and many others who have died violent deaths serving their brothers and sisters in Christ. Nor can we forget missionaries like Bishops Francis X. Ford and James E. Walsh who have suffered imprisonment or exile because of their Christian witness. May their courageous response to the Gospel inspire us to expand our missionary commitment to all peoples.

II. TODAY'S MISSION TASK

22. *Mission and the Trinity*: The Missionary task of the church is rooted theologically in the Blessed Trinity. The very origin of the church is from the missions of the Son and the Holy Spirit as decreed by the Father, "the fountain of love," who desires the salvation of the whole human race."[16] To continue his mission in time, Christ gave the missionary mandate to his followers to "make disciples of all nations" (Mt. 28:19), and he sent the Holy Spirit, the promised one of the Father,[17] who impels the church to share the Gospel with the world. Like all good news, the Gospel of salvation is irrepressible. The spontaneous need to communicate it comes from the quickening presence of the Holy Spirit in every aspect of church life. The Holy Spirit is the spirit of universal mission[18] and reconciliation.[19] The same Spirit who accompanies and quickens the missionary activity of the church likewise precedes that activity, offering those beyond the church's visible limits a participation in the paschal mystery of Christ.[20]

23. *Urgency of Mission*: We must pray for and earnestly desire a sense of urgency regarding our missionary task. This sense of urgency flows from the demands of being faithful disciples of Jesus, from our responsibility to share his Gospel and from a concern that all our brothers and sisters participate as fully as possible in

his life and saving mystery. We see this urgency in the life of Jesus, God's beloved Son, who was sent to proclaim the good news of the kingdom: "This is the time of fulfillment; the reign of God is at hand! Reform your lives and believe in the Gospel!" (Mk. 1:15).

24. *Coming of the Kingdom*: When the people of Capernaum tried to restrict Jesus' mission to themselves, he answered, "To other towns I must announce the good news of the reign of God, because that is why I was sent" (Lk. 4:43). In his very person, in all that he said and did, and especially in his death and resurrection, that kingdom was already breaking into the world. It will be perfectly established, however, only in the fullness of time.

25. *Foundation of the Church*: Jesus called a small number of men and women to be his disciples, to share intimately in his life and his vision of God's reign, and to spread his word to other times and places.[21] He selected 12 of them to be his apostles,[22] promised them the Holy Spirit as an abiding presence, and commissioned them to be his "witnesses in Jerusalem, throughout Judea and Samaria, yes even to the ends of the earth" (Acts 1:8). These apostles were established as the foundation of the church,[23] which was divinely constituted as the effective sign, the herald, the seed and the promoter of the kingdom, indeed its initial budding forth on earth.[24]

26. *Church Continues Jesus' Mission*: Nearly 20 centuries of Christian history have elapsed, and Jesus' prayer: "Your Kingdom come!" (Mt. 6:9-13; Lk. 11:2-4) is still our prayer. The mission he gave his apostles and disciples continues to be the church's mission. As we read in the preface to the decree *Ad Gentes*:

"Having been divinely sent to the nations that she might be 'the universal sacrament of salvation' (*Lumen Gentium*) the church, in obedience to the command of her Founder (Mk. 16:15), strives to preach the Gospel to all men."[25]

Like the men and women who first responded to Jesus' invitation, those who respond in our time develop a personal relationship with Christ that sustains them in their mission.

27. *Holiest Duty of the Church*: St. Paul expressed the urgency of mission when he wrote to the Corinthians: "Preaching the Gospel is not the subject of a boast; I am under compulsion and have no choice; I am ruined if I do not preach it" (1 Cor. 9:16). And preach the Gospel he did, not only in neighboring towns and cities, but to every nation he was able to reach. Like St. Paul, we are called to share the Gospel by the witness of our lives and the explicit proclamation of salvation in Jesus Christ.[26] The council calls this "the greatest and holiest duty of the church."[27]

28. *Needs of Others*: The human and spiritual needs of peoples beyond our borders call us to the urgency of mission. Mission always expresses a concern for the life of others. Moved by the Spirit, we ardently desire that our brothers and sisters have life, and in abundance,[28] and that they be saved by faith in Christ through the grace of God. This is our prayer in the name of Jesus Christ our Lord.

29. *Ecumenical Cooperation*: We rejoice that Christians of other Churches share and participate in the mission of our Lord. John Paul II has urged that those who share Christ's mission "must show forth his unifying love in action."[29] Today the dangers from proselytizing are real. Nevertheless, where there can be mutual respect among the different religious traditions, there are increasing opportunities in mission work for collaboration in prayer, good works, the use of media, community service and social action. Such collaboration is itself a witness to the reconciling spirit of God.

HUNGRY FOR THE WORD

30. *Spiritual and Material Poverty*: Often those who have not heard the Gospel are doubly poor, doubly hungry, doubly oppressed. They are materially poor, lacking possessions; they are spiritually poor, lacking that home which springs from the knowledge and love of Christ. Their hunger is not only for bread and rice, but also for the word that gives meaning to their existence. They are oppressed not only by social injustice but also by the sin at its root.

31. *Mission to the Whole Person*: By the same token, people are saved not only as individuals but also as members of sociocultural groups. They must experience the redemption not only of their souls but also of their whole bodily existence, not only in a world to come but also beginning here on earth. They must participate in the mystery of Christ not passively or minimally but rather as fully as possible, with intelligence, freedom and a lively sense of responsibility. Those who rejoice in the life poured into their hearts by the Spirit of Christ must be not only receivers of the word but also missionaries to others.

32. *Planting in Holy Ground*: Mission is characterized not by power and the need to dominate, but by a deep concern for the salvation of others and a profound respect for the ways they have already searched for and experienced God. The ground in which we are called to plant the Gospel is holy ground, for before our arrival God has already visited the people he knows and loves.[30] In this ground, sown with the seeds of God's own word, a local church is born, a church that expresses its vitality in the language of its own culture, a church also called to be missionary beyond its own borders.

MUTUALITY IN MISSION

33. *United with the Human Family*: As soon as a local church is established, Christ calls it to share the Gospel it has received. Such sharing is essential for the church's vitality, since those who give life to others find it for themselves. So it was with Jesus throughout his life, and especially in his death and resurrection. Sharing is essential to every level of church life; it applies to dioceses and parishes as well as families and individuals. The local church cannot live in isolation, unconcerned for other peoples. As human beings created by the Father of all, as disciples of the risen Jesus who is Lord of all and as Christians who have received the Holy Spirit, we are united with the entire human family. This union shapes our attitudes and moves us to respect other peoples and their cultures, to make their concerns our own and to share with them the gospel riches we have received.[31]

34. *Missionary Institutes in Other Lands*: The church has now been planted on all the continents and in most nations. It has grown and matured in countries once thought of as mission territories. Local churches in these countries recognized the importance of sharing the unique insights which accompanied the Gospel's flowering in their cultures. Several like Nigeria, South Korea, Mexico, Colombia and the Philippines, have established their own foreign mission societies. Moreover, missionary institutes, orders and congregations are drawing members from former mission countries and sending them to other peoples.

35. *Sharing the Gospel*: Each new incarnation of the Gospel must be shared, even if the growth of the local church is as yet modest. As we have seen, mission is mutual, not one-directional. Christian peoples and local churches will share the Gospel with one another in various ways, from each according to its special gifts and abilities, to each according to its needs.[32]

36. *Openness to Others*: Even as we go out to other nations to announce the Good News, we must remain open to the voice of the Gospel speaking to us in a myriad of cultural and social expressions. We must be willing to welcome new immigrants into our parishes, to respect the cultural treasures of these newcomers and allow ourselves to be enriched and strengthened by their witness of faith. In this we come to see more clearly how the local church expresses the life of the universal church. As Pope John Paul II said in a message to the Curial cardinals, "The church is a communion of churches, and indirectly a communion of nations, languages and cultures. Each of these brings its gifts to the whole."[33] Mission involves mutual ministry and dialogue among the local churches of the world.

37. *Sensitivity in Mission*: Each local church must carry out its mission to other nations and cultures with great sensitivity. Peoples inevitably communicate out of their historical experience. Nevertheless, we must constantly strive to transcend culturally based limitations in our manifestation of the church's life. If we fail to link Christian values with what is already good in a culture, we merely export an expression of faith foreign to that culture, one the people cannot fully accept. It expresses someone else's faith experience, not their own."[34] Mission must therefore humbly imitate the example of Jesus, who did not cling to his divine privileges but became like us in all things save sin.[35]

38. *Common Elements*: There are, it is true, expressions of faith and morals in the Scriptures that are meaningful in every cultural milieu. The Lord's Prayer, the Beatitudes, the commandments, the story of Jesus and the sacraments all tend to bond human beings together in one faith and one church.[36] Cultural differences remain significantly important, however.

39. *Mission Is Not Coercive*: Jesus's call to discipleship was a free invitation. In the same way, the church does not coerce others to accept the Gospel and join her ranks. Mission presupposes love for those being evangelized and, as Paul VI said, "the first sign of this love is respect for the religious and spiritual situation of those being evangelized."[37] The Church extends an invitation, realizing that they may not respond. If we extend our invitation well, witnessing in the love of God and the image of Christ, and with the fire of the Holy Spirit, we have fulfilled Christ's mandate.[38] Acceptance of the Gospel and conversion to Christ is the working of God's grace, a mystery beyond comprehension which we accept in faith.[39]

MISSION AND DIALOGUE

40. *Role of Dialogue*: The way we extend Christ's free invitation to others differs according to local circumstances.[40] The context of mission in Japan or India, for example, is vastly different from that in Bolivia or the Philippines. The recent document on dialogue and mission of the Vatican Secretariat for Non-Christians emphasizes the role of dialogue with adherents to other great religions.[41] While dialogue takes many forms, "before all else, dialogue is a manner of acting, an attitude and a spirit which guides one's conduct. It implies concern, respect and hospitality toward the other. It leaves room for the other person's identity, his modes of expression and his values. Dialogue is thus the norm and necessary manner of every form of Christian mission, as well as of every aspect of it, whether one speaks of simple presence and witness, service or direct proclamation. Any sense of mission not permeated by such a dialogical spirit would go against the demands of true humanity and against the teachings of the Gospel."[42]

41. *Other Great Religions*: Dialogue goes beyond collaboration and discussion

with members of other great religions. It includes the sharing of faith, religious experiences, prayer, contemplation. In such sharing, all parties are mutually enriched.

"The sometimes profound differences between the faiths do not prevent this dialogue. Those differences, rather, must be referred back in humility and confidence to God who 'is greater than our heart' " (1 Jn. 3:20).[43]

42. *Conversion the Goal of Mission*: Though dialogue is a vital characteristic of mission, it is not the goal of missionary proclamation. The Secretariat for Non-Christians goes on to say:

"According to the Second Vatican Council, missionary proclamation has conversion as its goal: 'that non-Christians be freely converted to the Lord under the action of the Holy Spirit who opens their hearts so that they may adhere to him' (*Ad Gentes*, 13)."[44]

43. *Church Offers the Fullness of Revealed Truth*: Pope John Paul II emphasized this same point in his homily in Calcutta: "While esteeming the value of these (non-Christian) religions, and seeing in them at times the action of the Holy Spirit who is like the wind which 'blows where it wills' (Jn. 3:8), the church remains convinced of the need for her to fulfill her task of offering to the world the fullness of revealed truth, the truth of the redemption in Jesus Christ."[45]

The fact that the Holy Father spoke these important words in India, a predominantly non-Christian country, makes them especially significant.

44. *True Inculturation*: In this work of dialogue and evangelization, the church must be a leaven for all cultures, at home in each culture. True inculturation occurs when the Gospel penetrates the heart of cultural experience and shows how Christ gives new meaning to authentic human values. However, the church must never allow herself to be absorbed by any culture,[46] since not all cultural expressions are in conformity with the Gospel. The church retains the indispensable duty of testing and evaluating cultural expressions in the light of her understanding of revealed truth. Cultures, like individual human beings and societies, need to be purified by the blood of Christ.

HOLISTIC APPROACH

45. *Response to Suffering*: Solidarity with others and faithfulness to the Gospel demand that we respond to people's genuine needs and hungers, even those of which they may be unaware. As noted above, human hunger takes two forms. While spiritual hungers reflect our highest aspirations, physical hungers can be so great as to blunt or even block them. Some social hungers may indicate the presence of oppression, preventing people from developing in an atmosphere of peace and justice. In a human being, in a society, in the world, when one member suffers all suffer.

46. *Mission of Jesus Was Liberation*: A holistic approach to mission recognizes that humanity's hungers are so interwoven that the spirit cannot be satisfied without attending to the body.[47] As we read in a recent instruction from the Holy See:

"Liberation is first and foremost from the radical slavery of sin. Its end and its goal is the freedom of the children of God, which is the gift of grace. As a logical consequence, it calls for freedom from many different kinds of slavery in the cultural, economic, social and political spheres, all of which derive ultimately from sin and so often prevent people from living in a manner befitting their dignity."[48]

The church's seriousness about responding to all genuine human needs is further stressed in a subsequent document:

"The church is firmly determined to respond to the anxiety of contemporary man as he endures oppression and yearns for freedom. The political and economic running of society is not a direct part of her mission. But the Lord Jesus has entrusted to her the word of truth which is capable of enlightening consciences. Divine love, which is her life, impels her to a true solidarity with everyone who suffers."[49]

47. *Jesus' Mission Is Now Ours*: Clearly, then, neither the church as a whole nor the church in the United States can remain indifferent to the suffering, inequities and oppression that afflict so much of the world's population. These evils openly contradict Christ's goal. Jesus came to bring Good News to the poor, proclaim liberty to captives, give sight to the blind and release prisoners.[50] His mission became that of the church, and now it is ours.[51]

48. *Liberation Requires Action*: Had Jesus merely said that his mission was to set people free from sin and all forms of oppression,[52] his words would have fallen on deaf ears. He had to work at this task of liberation. He not only talked about freeing the poor and oppressed but, undeterred by criticism, actually welcomed the poor and sinners to share at his table. Like Jesus, we must be able to accompany others in their suffering and be willing to suffer with them.

49. *Special Option for the Poor*: In its openness to all, the church's mission makes a special option for the poor and powerless. "The special option for the poor, far from being a sign of particularism or sectarianism, manifests the universality of the church's being and mission."[53] This special option is deeply rooted in the mission of Jesus, who rejected no one but was especially sensitive to those who needed him most. The poor, destitute and powerless of the world help us see and evaluate the evils of our society and the evils that one society or nation inflicts on another. Accompanying the poor assures us of the relevance of our message of salvation.

50. *Evangelizing the Powerful*: The option for the poor also implies the need to evangelize the powerful and influential. If the gospel call to conversion can reach their hearts, they will help construct a new society. In our option for the poor, we join our aspirations and commitment to those of our brother bishops in Latin America, Africa, Asia and Oceania as expressed in their pastoral statements.[54]

NOTES

1. *Lumen Gentium*.
2. See Jn. 1:1-5, 10-12, 16.
3. See also Jn. 17:18.
4. *Ad Gentes*, 2-3, Mk. 16:15-16.
5. See Mt. 28:16-20.
6. Mt. 28:20.
7. *Ad Gentes*, 38; see also *Lumen Gentium*, 23 and *Christus Dominus*, 6.
8. *Christus Dominus*, 6.
9. "The Challenge of Peace," 240.
10. Ibid., 54.
11. See *Mater et Magistra, Pacem in Terris, Populorum Progressio, Octagesima Adveniens*, and *Laborem Exercens*.
12. See *Mission in Dialogue, the Sedos Research Seminar on the Future of Mission*, March 8-19, 1981, Rome, Italy. Edited by Mary Motte, FMM, and Joseph R. Lang, MM (Maryknoll, N.Y.: Orbis Books, 1982).
13. *Ad Gentes*, 38. See Canon 791, Code of Canon Law (Canon Law Society of America, Washington, D.C: 1983).

14. Omer Degrijse, CICM, *Going Forth: Missionary Consciousness in Third World Catholic Churches* (Maryknoll, N.Y.: Orbis Books, 1984).

15. See *Evangelii Nuntiandi*, 60. "If each individual evangelizes in the name of the church, who herself does so by virtue of a mandate from the Lord, no evangelizer is the absolute master of his evangelizing action, with a discretionary power to carry it out in accordance with the individualistic criteria and perspectives; he acts in communion with the church and her pastors."

16. See *Evangelii Nuntiandi*, 13-15; *Ad Gentes*, 2-3.

17. See Lk. 24:49; Jn. 14:26.

18. See Acts 2:1-11.

19. See Jn. 20:19-23.

20. *Ad Gentes*, 4; *Lumen Gentium*, 16; *Gaudium et Spes*, 22.

21. Mk. 1:16-20.

22. See Lk. 6:12-16.

23. See Eph.2:20.

24. *Lumen Gentium* 5; See "Instruction on Christian Freedom and Liberation," Congregation for the Doctrine of the Faith, March 22, 1986 (Washington, D.C.: USCC), 58.

25. *Ad Gentes*, 1.

26. *Evangelii Nuntiandi*, 40-48.

27. *Ad Gentes*, 29.

28. See Jn. 10:10.

29. Homily, Ecumenical Service, Synod of Bishops, Dec. 5, 1985. Origins, vol 15, p. 454.

30. See Acts 7:33; 10:1-11, 18.

31. *Evangelii Nuntiandi*, 19, 30-31.

32. *Ad Gentes*, 38; Acts 2:42-47; 4:32-35.

33. Pope John Paul II, Message to the Curial Cardinals, Christmas, 1984.

34. See Pope John Paul II, Address to the Amerindians of Canada at the Shrine of St. Anne de Beaupre.

35. See Phil. 2:6-11; Heb. 4:14-15.

36. *Evangelii Nuntiandi*, 20, 25.

37. Ibid., 79.

38. See Mt. 28:16-20.

39. See Mt. 10:16-42; 12:16-24; Jn. 6:61-70.

40. *Ad Gentes*, 6.

41. Secretariat for Non-Christians, "The Attitude of the Church Towards the Followers of Other Religions, Reflections and Orientations on Dialogue and Mission," Pentecost, 1984. See also Paul VI, *Ecclesiam Suam* (Aug. 6, 1964).

42. Ibid., 29.

43. Ibid., 35.

44. Ibid., 37.

45. Pope John Paul II, Homily, Feb. 5, 1986.

46. See Final Report of the Extraordinary Synod of 1985, II, D.4l, *Catechesi Tradendae*, 53, and *Familiaris Consortio*, 10-16. [The first two of these sources are in this volume. — eds.].

47. *Evangelii Nuntiandi*, 33.

48. "Instruction on Certain Aspects of the Theology of Liberation," Origins, vol. 14, no. 13, Introduction.

49. "Instruction on Christian Freedom and Liberation," Congregation for the Doctrine of the Faith, March, 22, 1986 (Washington, D.C.: USCC), 61.

50. See Lk. 4:18.

51. "The evil inequities and oppressions of every kind which afflict millions of men and women today openly contradict Christ's Gospel and cannot leave the conscience of any Christian indifferent." "Instruction on Christian Freedom and Liberation," 57.

52. See Lk. 4:16-19.

53. "Instruction on Christian Freedom and Liberation," 68. [This text is found in this volume. — eds.].

54. See, for example, Second General Conference of Latin American Bishops: "The Church in the Present-Day Transformation of Latin America in the Light of the Council" (Medellín, 1968); Third General Conference of Latin American Bishops: "Evangelization at Present and in the Future of Latin America" (Puebla, 1979); First Plenary Assembly of the Federation of Asian Bishops Conferences, "Evangelization in Modern-Day Asia," Taipei, April 1974.

9

Final Statement of Fourth Plenary Assembly

Tokyo, September, 1986

FEDERATION OF ASIAN BISHOPS' CONFERENCES

Since 1970 the Federation of Asian Bishops' Conferences has held a number of important consultations and Plenary Assemblies dealing with various issues relevant to the church in Asia. In preparation for the 1974 Synod of Bishops which focused on evangelization, the federation held its first Plenary Assembly in Taipei, Taiwan, and published an important document entitled "Evangelization in Asia Today." Since then the federation has met to discuss such topics as catechetics in the Asian context, prayer, the family, and, in 1986, the vocation and mission of the laity.

The sections reprinted below are parts of the 1986 document on the laity. They speak in an eloquent way how the laity—Asia's youth, women, and members of families—need to live out their baptismal commitment and consecration by involvement in the world of education, mass media, labor, business, and the health services. In a real way, the bishops affirm, the laity represents the true future of the Asian church.

THE CHALLENGES OF ASIA*

THE YOUTH OF ASIA

By sheer number alone, the youth of Asia is representative of the continent as a whole. Of the total population, 60% are between 15 and 24 years of age. Moreover, the life of this youth reflects Asia's manifold economic, political, religious and educational problems.

The youth of Asia is Asia today. The convulsive struggles for liberation in Asia are reflected in the pains of growth of its youth and in their agonizing longings for a new world. The People of God in Asia must become, in a certain sense, a "Church

---

*A document prepared by the FABC Fourth Plenary Assembly in Tokyo, Japan. Reprinted from *East Asia Pastoral Review* (1986): 4.

of the Young" if it wants to transform the "face of Asia, the Continent of the Young" (cf. FABC 1970).

THE LAITY AND THE PLIGHT OF ASIAN WOMEN

The international media have highlighted how tourism and the entertainment industries have exploited, degraded and dehumanised Asian women. However, this is but one aspect of the reality of Asian women today. Many are the injustices heaped upon them, because of the traditional societies which discriminate against them and because of the new economic and industrial situations. Dowry, forced marriages, wife-beating, the destruction of the female foetus, weigh heavily on our women's consciousness and may lead to desperation and even suicide. Modern industry exploits them by paying a paltry sum for their hard labor in quarries, construction sites and in local or multinational companies. There is discrimination against them in employment policies and as domestic workers they are also abused. In general, Asian society views them as inferior. Such are some of the tragic realities of Asian women that cry out for drastic change. On the one hand, there is the deep and genuine positive sensitivity of Asians to the feminine presence. Woman is considered the heart of the family. In times of crisis, she is the valiant woman on whose shoulders others lean. The advancement and the contribution that women have made in the professions, as doctors, lawyers, managers, accountants, political leaders, teachers, etc. have been phenomenal, despite the obstacles placed in their path by tradition. In the Church, women contribute significantly in various ministries of teaching, healing, catechizing, administrating, organizing, etc. They serve as members of pastoral teams. In our Assembly we have listened to them and have been made more aware of certain fundamental facts and truths.

But the recognition of women's full personhood has equally to be evident in the Church. For the Church cannot be a sign of the eschatological community if the gifts of the Spirit to its women are not given proper recognition, and if women do not share in the "freedom of the children of God." They expect significant responsibilities in the ministries and decision-making processes of the Church.

Only then shall the entire People of God be a credible sign of the dignity and freedom of woman in the wider Asian society and in the world. The Church will then be able to speak "with power and in truth" about the plight of Asian women and become their voice, a voice that will speak with an authority unlike any other, for it would then be, unambiguously, the Word of God.

THE LAITY AND THE FAMILY

Perhaps the greatest challenge to the Church in Asia is posed by the Asian family. The Asian family is the cellular receptacle of all of Asia's problems — poverty and repression, exploitation and degradation, divisions and conflicts. The family is directly affected by the religious, political, economic, social and cultural problems of Asia, the problems related to women, health, work, business, education, etc.

The Christian family is rightly referred to as the "domestic Church" where members assist one another towards a fullness of life in Christ, through ordinary circumstances and events of life. At home, in the family setting, in the daily events of living and giving, the human person interiorizes culture as well as belief with an easy connaturality.

The values and attitudes necessary for the evangelization of the Asian world are first practiced in the family. Love, justice, peace, truth, freedom, concern for the poor and the needy, faith in God, hope in his liberating goodness and power, responsibility and self-sacrifice and other Gospel values are first learned by precept and example in the family. Here evangelization initially takes place. Here a "civilization of love" begins. Thus evangelized, the Asian family is able to evangelize, to reach out to other families and communities and together journey towards the Kingdom of God.

THE LAITY IN THE WORLD OF EDUCATION

Two important facts in the education scene of Asia immediately strike at us: the illiteracy of vast numbers of Asians, and the visibility and great reputation of the Catholic educational institutions, especially in non-Christian areas. These, indeed, urge us to reflect not only on the role of the laity but also on the role of the entire Church in education.

Two major negative judgements of people are well known to us—that Catholic schools seem to cater mostly to the middle class and to the rich, and that they seem to support traditional structures and values rather than act as vehicles of social change. Rather than setting them aside as invalid and uninformed we prefer rather to take this criticism as a constant reminder of our priority for the poor and for seeking the transformation of society. This criticism may provide us with a scale with which to evaluate our educational service.

We look beyond the formal school system and ask how the laity can carry out the ministry of teaching among the out-of-school youth in urban and rural areas. This is not an easy task, yet we see the beginning of it in literacy, training in skills, and leadership formation programmes through non-formal education. This is particularly true of the educational work that is taking place in Basic Ecclesial Communities. Here again the laity play a major role.

THE LAITY AND THE MASS MEDIA

This is the hour when the laity of Asia is called to evangelise their milieu through those powerful instruments of mass communication created by modern technology.

This vision will require of the People of God and especially of its leadership a supportive stance towards the systematic formation and training of the laity to assume even greater responsibilities in the media. This is a pastoral priority in the light of the Asian situation where the people of God must reach out to millions struggling for social transformation, a struggle that requires inter-faith collaboration. As the educational apostolate, so also the media apostolate depends to a large extent on the laity.

THE LAITY AND THE WORLD OF WORK

When we turn our attention to the world of work, we come to recognize the deep aspirations of vast masses of people of Asia for liberation from sin and its consequences. They participate in God's continual activity of recreating and transforming the world. The development in the life of the human person in Asia is the effect of total human work, in cooperation with the Creator.

It is necessary, therefore, that workers look at the activities that promote and defend their rights within the context of such a spirituality. Some of these activities are the formation of trade unions or agricultural associations, the workers' efforts to ensure their role in decision-making processes, mass action for cheaper agricultural fertilizers, etc. The worker will find the meaning of his life in such a spirituality of work. In the light of the Church's preferential option for the poor, our attention is further directed to certain sectors of young workers in Asia: (1) children who are forced to work endless hours in shops, restaurants, on farms, etc.; (2) young women workers coming from rural areas and often subjected to sexual harassment and inhuman working and living conditions; (3) domestic workers working in countries other than their own who are exploited as cheap labour; (4) migrants from villages to the cities and to other countries, who are uprooted and forced to struggle for survival under the most adverse conditions.

SOCIAL RESPONSIBILITY IN THE WORLD OF BUSINESS

The transformation of the social structures is the mission not only of the workers but also of business people, government officials, managers and policy makers. Cooperation among the different sectors of society is indispensable. This cooperation has to exist at national and global levels, and assumes that all sectors of society believe that the resources of this world belong to the entire human family and that social responsibility means stewardship of the goods of this world.

In this context the laity belonging to the world of business hear the call of God to live out their faith according to Gospel values and the needs of the others. This involves a number of options in their business, ranging from the simple exercise of the values of truth, justice and love to their active participation in transforming the world of business towards greater worker participation, more discerning consumer guidance, more responsible interventions by the governments, and a more equitable society. There is need for guiding principles on the conduct of business, somewhat like a Code of Ethics for Business, to enable people in business to permeate their dealings with the Gospel values.

THE LAITY AND HEALTH SERVICES

At our assembly the laity have shared their concerns in the world of health. We thank the Lord for the marvelous advances of medicine, the product of human creativity and endeavour, in the war against disease. But we are confronted every day with serious problems rising from the practice of modern medicine: the prohibitive costs of medical services, the overconcentration of medical health delivery system in urban areas, the inadequacy of preventive medical services, to name only a few. More seriously, we are today witnessing the emergence of bio-ethical problems important not only by their extent but also by their growing complexity. All these confront the entire Church, but more particularly the laity in medical services.

But even greater than the concern for the renewal of our traditional health institutions should be our concern for the mass of people in the rural areas. The benefits of modern medicine do not reach them adequately, because of their poverty and the lack of appropriate medical services to them.

The forgiving Christ who is also the healing Christ reached out to the poor and the marginalized in order to bring to them the healing power of God. God's people, especially the laity in health services, must likewise reach out to the farmers and workers, the landless and slumdwellers, so that through them the healing touch of

God may be felt by all in need. This is why the resources of the Church must be channeled to outreach health service programmes that are community-based and community-oriented. With joy we note the increasing number of Churches in Asia that respond to this serious need.

10

Sollicitudo Rei Socialis

Rome, December 30, 1987

POPE JOHN PAUL II

To commemorate the twentieth anniversary of Paul VI's 1967 encyclical Populorum Progressio, *John Paul II issued an encyclical of his own which aimed to "emphasize, through a theological investigation of the present world, the need for a fuller and more nuanced concept of development," (#4). In this way, even though the world had changed, sometimes drastically, in the twenty years since Paul VI's work, the pope hoped to continue the spirit of* Populorum Progressio, *and point out its continuing relevance for our day.*

After an introductory section (#1-4), the encyclical devotes a second section to a summary and analysis of Populorum Progressio, *particularly from the viewpoint of its continuity with past church social teaching, but especially its original contribution (#5-10). Thirdly, a long section (#11-26) analyses the positive and (mostly) negative aspects of the contemporary world, and poses the question of the fourth section, which is the true nature of development (#27-34). Development is not merely economic, but is a wider concept including human, social, cultural, and economic elements. The fifth section provides a "theological reading of modern problems" (#35-40), and then, in a final part, a number of specific guidelines are spelled out (#41-45). A short conclusion (#46-49) is added.*

While the whole encyclical touches on what is a "constitutive part of preaching the Gospel," to quote the well-known phrase of the 1971 Synod of Bishops, we have selected several excerpts from the section on the notion of development (IV) and several paragraphs from the encyclical's conclusion.

(From IV: *"Authentic Human Development"*)*

32. The obligation to commit oneself to the development of peoples is not just an *individual* duty and still less an *individualistic* one, as if it were possible to achieve this development through the isolated efforts of each individual. It is an imperative which obliges *each and every* man and woman as well as societies and nations. In particular, it obliges the Catholic Church and the other churches and ecclesial

---

*Encyclical Letter of Pope John Paul II, December 30, 1987. Reprinted from the English version published by the U. S. Catholic Conference, 1987.

communities, with which we are completely willing to collaborate in this field. In this sense, just as we Catholics invite our Christian brethren to share in our initiatives, so too we declare that we are ready to collaborate in theirs, and we welcome the invitations presented to us. In this pursuit of integral human development we can also do much with the members of other religions, as in fact is being done in various places.

Collaboration in the development of the whole person and of every human being is in fact a duty of *all toward all* and must be shared by the four parts of the world: East and West, North and South; or, as we say today, by the different "worlds." If, on the contrary, people try to achieve it in only one part or in only one world, they do so at the expense of the others; and, precisely because the others are ignored, their own development becomes exaggerated and misdirected.

Peoples or *nations*, too, have a right to their own full development, which while including—as already said—the economic and social aspects should also include individual cultural identity and openness to the transcendent. Not even the need for development can be used as an excuse for imposing on others one's own way of life or own religious belief.

33. Nor would a type of development which did not respect and promote *human rights*—personal and social, economic and political, including the *rights of nations and of peoples*—be really *worthy of man*.

Today, perhaps more than in the past, the *intrinsic contradiction* of a development limited only to its economic element is seen more clearly. Such development easily subjects the human person and his deepest needs to the demands of economic planning and selfish profit.

The *intrinsic connection* between authentic development and respect for human rights once again reveals the moral character of development: The true elevation of man in conformity with the natural and historical vocation of each individual is not attained *only* by exploiting the abundance of goods and services or by having available perfect infrastructures.

When individuals and communities do not see a rigorous respect for the moral, cultural and spiritual requirements based on the dignity of the person and on the proper identity of each community, beginning with the family and religious societies, then all the rest—availability of goods, abundance of technical resources applied to daily life, a certain level of material well-being—will prove unsatisfying and in the end contemptible. The Lord clearly says this in the Gospel when He calls the attention of all to the true hierarchy of values: "For what will it profit a man if he gains the whole world and forfeits his life?" (Mt 16:26).

True development, in keeping with the *specific* needs of the human being—man or woman, child, adult or old person—implies, especially for those who actively share in this process and are responsible for it, a lively *awareness* of the *value* of the rights of all and of each person. It likewise implies a lively awareness of the need to respect the right of every individual to the full use of the benefits offered by science and technology.

On the *internal level* of every nation, respect for all rights takes on great importance, especially: the right to life at every stage of its existence; the rights of the family as the basic social community or "cell of society"; justice in employment relationships; the rights inherent in the life of the political community as such; the rights based on the *transcendent vocation* of the human being beginning with the right of freedom to profess and practice one's own religious belief.

On the *international level*, that is, the level of relations between states or, in present-day usage, between the different "worlds," there must be complete *respect* for the identity of each people, with its own historical and cultural characteristics. It is likewise essential, as the encyclical *Populorum Progressio* already asked, "to recognize each people's equal right to be seated at the table of the common banquet,"[1] instead of lying outside the door like Lazarus, while "the dogs come out and lick his sores" (cf. Lk 16:21). Both peoples and individuals must enjoy the *fundamental equality*[2] which is the basis, for example, of the Charter of the United Nations Organization: the equality which is the basis of the right of all to share in the process of full development.

In order to be genuine, development must be achieved within the framework of *solidarity* and *freedom*, without ever sacrificing either of them under whatever pretext. The moral character of development and its necessary promotion are emphasized when the most rigorous respect is given to all the demands deriving from the order of *truth* and good proper to the human person. Furthermore, the Christian who is taught to see that man is the image of God, called to share in the truth and the good which is *God himself*, does not understand a commitment to development and its application which excludes regard and respect for the unique dignity of this "image." In other words, true development must be based on the *love of God and neighbor* and must help to promote the relationships between individuals and society. This is the "civilization of love" of which Paul VI often spoke.

34. Nor can the moral character of development exclude respect *for the beings which constitute* the natural world, which the ancient Greeks—alluding precisely to the order which distinguishes it—called the "cosmos." Such realities also demand respect, by virtue of a threefold consideration which is useful to reflect upon carefully.

The *first consideration* is the appropriateness of acquiring a *growing awareness* of the fact that one cannot use with impunity the different categories of beings, whether living or inanimate—animals, plants, the natural elements—simply as one wishes, according to one's own economic needs. On the contrary, one must take into account *the nature of each being* and of its *mutual connection* in an ordered system, which is precisely the "cosmos."

The *second consideration* is based on the realization—which is perhaps more urgent—that *natural resources* are limited. Some are not, as it is said, *renewable*. Using them as if they were inexhaustible, with *absolute dominion*, seriously endangers their availability not only for the present generation but above all for generations to come.

The *third consideration* refers directly to the consequences of a certain type of developement on the *quality of life* in the industrialized zones. We all know that the direct or indirect result of industrialization is, ever more frequently, the pollution of the environment, with serious consequences for the health of the population.

Once again it is evident that development, the planning which governs it and the way in which resources are used must include respect for moral demands. One of the latter undoubtedly imposes limits on the use of the natural world. The dominion granted to man by the Creator is not an absolute power nor can one speak of a freedom to "use and misuse" or to dispose of things as one pleases. The limitation imposed from the beginning by the Creator himself and expressed symbolically by the prohibition not to "eat of the fruit of the tree" (cf. Gn 2:16-17) shows clearly enough that, when it comes to the natural world, we are subject not only to biological laws but also to moral ones, which cannot be violated with impunity.

A true concept of development cannot ignore the use of the elements of nature, the renewability of resources and the consequences of haphazard industrialization — three considerations which alert our consciences to the *moral dimension* of development.[3]

(From VII: *"Conclusion"*)

46. Peoples and individuals aspire to be free: their search for full development signals their desire to overcome the many obstacles preventing them from enjoying a "more human life."

Recently in the period following the publication of the encyclical *Populorum Progressio*, a new way of confronting the problems of poverty and underdevelopment has spread in some areas of the world, especially in Latin America. This approach makes *liberation* the fundamental category and the first principle of action. The positive values, as well as the deviations and risks of deviation, which are damaging to the faith and are connected with this form of theological reflection and method, have been appropriately pointed out by the Church's Magisterium.[4]

It is fitting to add that the aspiration to freedom from all forms of slavery affecting the individual and society is something *noble* and *legitimate*. This, in fact, is the purpose of development, or rather liberation and development, taking into account the intimate connection between the two.

Development which is merely economic is incapable of setting man free; on the contrary, it will end by enslaving him further. Development that does not include the *cultural, transcendent and religious dimensions* of man and society, to the extent that it does not recognize the existence of such dimensions and does not endeavor to direct its goals and priorities toward the same, is *even less* conducive to authentic liberation. Human beings are totally free only when they are completely *themselves*, in the fullness of their rights and duties. The same can be said about society as a whole.

The principal obstacle to be overcome on the way to authentic liberation is *sin* and the *structures* produced by sin as it multiplies and spreads.[5]

The freedom with which Christ has set us free (cf. Gal 5:1) encourages us to become the *servants* of all. Thus the process of *development* and *liberation* takes concrete shape in the exercise of *solidarity*, that is to say, in the love and service of neighbor, especially of the poorest: "For where truth and love are missing, the process of liberation results in the death of a freedom which will have lost all support."[6]

47. In the context of the *sad experiences* of recent years and of the *mainly negative picture* of the present moment, the Church must strongly affirm the *possibility* of overcoming the obstacles which by excess or by defect stand in the way of development. And she must affirm her confidence in a *true liberation*. Ultimately, this confidence and this possibility are based on the *Church's awareness* of the divine promise guaranteeing that our present history does not remain closed in upon itself but is open to the kingdom of God.

The Church has *confidence also in man*, though she knows the evil of which he is capable. For she well knows that — in spite of the heritage of sin and the sin which each one is capable of committing — there exist in the human person sufficient qualities and energies, a fundamental "goodness" (cf. Gn 1:31), because he is the image of the Creator, placed under the redemptive influence of Christ, who "united himself in some fashion with every man,"[7] and because the efficacious action of the Holy Spirit "fills the earth" (Wis 1:7).

There is no justification, then, for despair or pessimism or inertia. Though it be with sorrow, it must be said that just as one may sin through selfishness and the desire for excessive profit and power, *one may also be found wanting* with regard to the urgent needs of multitudes of human beings submerged in conditions of under-development, through *fear, indecision* and basically through *cowardice.* We are *all* called, indeed *obliged,* to face the *tremendous challenge* of the last decade of the second millennium, also because the present dangers threaten everyone: a world economic crisis, a war without frontiers, without winners or losers. In the face of such a threat, the distinction between rich individuals and countries *will have little value,* except that a greater responsibility rests on those who have more and can do more.

This is not, however, the *sole motive* or *even the most important one.* At stake is the *dignity of the human person,* whose *defense* and *promotion* have been entrusted to us by the Creator, and to whom the men and women at every moment of history are strictly and responsibly *in debt.* As many people are already more or less clearly aware, the present situation *does not seem to correspond* to this dignity. *Every individual* is called upon to play his or her part in this *peaceful* campaign, a campaign to be conducted by *peaceful* means in order to secure *development in peace,* in order to safeguard nature itself and the world about us. The Church, too, feels profoundly involved in this enterprise, and she hopes for its ultimate success.

NOTES

Numbers that appear in parentheses refer to the number of the note in the original text. The note numbers below refer to the text in this volume.

1. (61) Cf. *Populorum Progressio,* 47: "... a world where freedom is not an empty word and where the poor man Lazarus can sit down at the same table as the rich man."

2. Cf. ibid., 47: "It is a question, rather, of building a world where every man, no matter what his race, religion or nationality, can live a fully human life, freed from servitude imposed on him by other men"; cf. also *Gaudium et Spes,* 29. Such *fundamental equality* is one of the basic reasons why the Church has always been opposed to every form of racism.

3. (63) Cf. Homily at Val Visdende (July 12, 1987), 5: *L'Osservatore Romano,* July 13-14, 1987 (English language edition, Aug. 10, 1987; *Octagesima Adveniens,* 21: AAS 63 (1971), pp. 416f.

4. (83) Cf. *Libertatis Conscientia,* Introduction: AAS 76 (1984), pp. 876f.

5. (84) *Reconciliatio et Paenitentia,* 16: AAS 77 (1985), pp. 213-217; *Libertatis Conscientia,* 38, 42: AAS 79 (1987), pp. 569-571.

6. (85) *Libertatis Conscientia,* 24: loc. cit., p. 564.

7. (86) *Gaudium et Spes,* 22; *Redemptor Hominis,* 8: AAS 71 (1979), p. 272.

Faith and Inculturation

Rome, December 1987

INTERNATIONAL THEOLOGICAL COMMISSION

Since its first meeting in 1969, the International Theological Commission has met yearly to discuss various issues as they impinge upon theological doctrine and church teaching. Among issues discussed have been questions about the priesthood, marriage, ecclesiology, human development, and the relationship between theologians and the church's teaching office. In 1988 the commission gave its final approval to a document on the issue of "Faith and Inculturation." It represents an important, though only a quasi-official statement of the church on the inculturation of the Gospel.

Basing its reflections on two themes in the teaching of Pope John Paul II— that of the transcendence of revelation on the one hand and the urgency of the evangelization of cultures on the other—the commission develops the document in three parts. The first part presents a "Christian anthropology," within which the notions of "nature," "culture," and "grace" are described and discussed. Then, in a longer section which treats inculturation as it appears in the history of Israel, the life and work of Jesus and the early church, the biblical roots of the process are made clear. A final, third part discusses various problems involved in the inculturation enterprise: popular piety, dialogue with non-Christian religions, non-Western cultures, and Western secularization. Reprinted here are parts one and three of the document.

I. NATURE, CULTURE AND GRACE*

1. Anthropologists readily return to describe or define culture in terms of the distinction, sometimes even opposition, between nature and culture. The significance of this word *nature* varies moreover with the different conceptions of the natural sciences, of philosophy and of theology. The Magisterium understands this word in a very specific sense: the nature of a being is what constitutes it as such,

---

*A document prepared by the International Theological Commission during its plenary session of December 1987, broadly approved in *forma specifica* during its plenary session of October 1987, and published with the *placet* of Cardinal Joseph Ratzinger, President of the Commission.

with the dynamism of its tendencies towards its proper ends. It is from God that natures possess what they are, as well as their proper ends. They are from that moment, impregnated with a significance in which man, as *the image of God*, is capable of discerning the "creative intention of God."[1]

2. The fundamental inclinations of human nature, expressed by natural law, appear therefore as an expression of the will of the Creator. This natural law declares the specific requirements of *human* nature, requirements which are significant of the design of God for his rational and free creature. Thus all that misunderstanding is avoided which, perceiving nature in a univocal sense, would reduce man to material nature.

3. It is appropriate, at the same time, to consider human nature according to its unfolding in historical time: that is to observe what man, endowed with a fallible liberty, and often subjected to his passions, has made of his humanity. This heritage transmitted to new generations includes simultaneously immense treasures of wisdom, art, and generosity, and a considerable share of deviations and perversions. Attention therefore, as a whole, revolves around human nature and the human condition, an expression which integrates existential elements, of which certain ones—sin and grace—affect the history of salvation. If therefore we use the word "culture" in a primary positive sense—as a synonym of development, for example—as have Vatican II and the recent popes, we will not forget that cultures can perpetuate and favour the choice of pride and selfishness.

4. Culture consists in the extension of the requirements of human nature, as the accomplishment of its ends, as is especially taught in the Constitution *Gaudium et Spes*: It is a fact bearing on the very person of man that he can come to an authentic and full humanity only through culture, that is, through the cultivation of natural goods and values. The word *culture* in its general sense indicates all those factors by which man refines and unfolds his manifold spiritual and bodily qualities.[2] Thus the domain of culture is multiple: by knowledge and work, man applies himself to the taming of the universe; he humanises social life through the progress of customs and institutions, he expresses, communicates and in short conserves in his works, through the course of time, the great spiritual exercises and aspirations of man in order that they may be of advantage to the progress of many, even of all mankind.

5. The primary constituent of culture is the human person, considered in all aspects of his being. Man betters *himself*—this is the first end of all culture—but he does so thanks to the *works* of culture and thanks to a cultural memory. Culture also still designates the *milieu* in which and on account of which persons may grow.

6. The human person is a community being which blossoms in giving and in receiving. It is thus in solidarity with others and across living social relationships that the person progresses. Also those realities of nation, people, society with their cultural patrimony, constitute for the development of persons "a specific historical environment, from which they draw the values which permit them to promote human and civic culture."[3]

7. Culture, which is always a concrete and particular culture, is open to the higher values common to all. Thus the originality of a culture does not signify withdrawal into itself but a contribution to the richness which is the good of all. Cultural pluralism cannot therefore be interpreted as the juxtaposition of a closed universe, but as participation in a unison of realities all directed towards the universal values of humanity. The phenomena of the reciprocal penetration of cultures, frequent in history, illustrates this fundamental openness of particular cultures to the values common to all, and through this their openness one to another.

8. Man is a naturally religious being. The turning towards the Absolute is inscribed in his deepest being. In a general sense, religion is an *integral constituent* of culture, in which it takes root and blossoms. Moreover, all the great cultures include, as the keystone of the edifice they constitute, the religious dimension, the inspiration of the great achievements which have marked the ancient history of civilisations.

9. At the root of the great religions is the transcendent movement of man in search of God. Purified of its deviations and disagreeable aspects, this movement should be the object of sincere respect. It is on this that the Christian faith comes to engraft itself. What distinguishes the Christian faith is that it is free adherence to the proposition of the gratuitous love of God which has been revealed to us, which has given us his only Son to free us from sin and has poured out his Spirit in our hearts. The radical reality of Christianity lies in the gift that God makes of himself to humanity, facing all the aspirations, requests, conquests and achievements of nature.

10. Therefore, because it transcends the entire natural and cultural order, the Christian faith is, on the one hand, compatible with all cultures in so far as they conform to right reasons and goodwill, and, on the other hand, to an eminent degree, is a dynamising factor of culture. A single principle explains the totality of relationships between faith and culture: grace respects nature, healing in it the wounds of sin, comforting and elevating it. Elevation to the divine life is the specific finality of grace, but it cannot realise this unless nature is healed and unless elevation to the supernatural order brings nature, in the way proper to itself, to the plenitude of perfection.

11. The process of inculturation may be defined as the Church's efforts to make the message of Christ penetrate a given socio-cultural *milieu*, calling on the latter to grow according to all its particular values, as long as these are compatible with the Gospel. The term "inculturation" includes the notion of growth, of the mutual enrichment of persons and groups, rendered possible by the encounter of the Gospel with a social milieu. "Inculturation is the incarnation of the Gospel in the hereditary cultures, and at the same time, the introduction of these cultures into the life of the Church."[4]

III. PRESENT PROBLEMS OF INCULTURATION

1. The inculturation of the faith, which we have considered firstly from a philosophical viewpoint (nature, culture and grace), then from the point of view of history and dogma (inculturation of the history of salvation) still poses considerable problems for theological reflection and pastoral action. Thus the questions aroused in the sixteenth century by the discovery of new worlds continue to preoccupy us. How may one harmonise the spontaneous expression of the religiosity of peoples with faith? What attitude should be adopted in the face of non-Christian religions, especially those "bound up with cultural advancement"?[5] New questions have arisen in our time. How should "young Churches", born in our century of the indigenisation of already-existing Christian communities, consider both their Christian past and the cultural history of their respective peoples? Finally how should the Gospel animate, purify and fortify the new world into which we have brought industrialization and urbanization? To us it seems that these four questions should be faced by anyone who reflects on the present conditions of the inculturation of faith.

POPULAR PIETY

2. In the countries which have been affected by the Gospel, we normally understand by *popular piety*, on the one hand, the union of Christian faith and piety with the profound culture, and on the other with the previous forms of religion of populations. It involves those very numerous devotions in which Christians express their religious sentiment in the simple language, among other things, of festival, pilgrimage, dance and song. One could speak of *vital synthesis* with reference to this piety, since it unites "body and spirit, ecclesial communion and institution, individual and community, Christian faith and love of one's country, intelligence and affectivity".[6] The quality of this synthesis stems, as one might expect, from the antiquity and profundity of the evangelisation, as from the compatibility of its religious and cultural antecedents with the Christian faith.

3. In the Apostolic Exhortation "Evangelii Nuntiandi" Paul VI confirmed and encouraged a new appreciation of popular piety. "For long seen as less pure, sometimes scorned, these particular expressions of the quest for God and the faith today have become practically everywhere the object of rediscovery."[7]

4. "If well directed, especially by a pedagogy of evangelisation," continued Paul VI (popular piety) "is rich in value. It communicates a thirst of God which only the simple and the poor can understand. It renders capable generosity and sacrifice, even to the level of heroism, when it is a question of manifesting faith. It includes a sharp sense of the profound attributes of God: paternity, providence, loving and constant presence. It engenders internal attitudes, rarely observed elsewhere to a similar degree: patience, sense of the Cross in daily life, detachment, openness to others, devotion."[8]

5. Moreover the strength and depth of the roots of popular piety clearly manifested themselves in the long period of discredit mentioned by Paul VI. The expressions of popular piety have survived numerous predictions of disappearance of which modernity and the progress of secularity seemed to warn. They have preserved and even increased, in many regions of the globe, the attractions they exercised on the masses.

6. The limits of popular piety have often been condemned. They stem from a certain naivety, are a source of various deformations of religion, even of superstitions. One remains at the level of cultural manifestations without a true adherence in faith as expressed in service of one's neighbour. Badly directed, popular piety can even lead to the formation of sects and thus place true ecclesial community in danger. It also risks being manipulated, be it by political powers or by religious forces foreign to the Christian faith.

7. The taking into account of these dangers invites us to practice an intelligent catechesis attracted to the merits of an authentic popular piety and at the same time capable of discernment. A living and adapted liturgy is equally called to play a major role in the integration of a very pure faith and the traditional forms of the religious life of peoples. Without any doubt whatsoever, popular piety can bring an irreplaceable contribution to a Christian cultural anthropology which would permit the reduction of the often tragic division between the faith of Christians and certain socio-economic institutions, of quite different orientation, which regulate their daily life.

INCULTURATION OF FAITH AND NON-CHRISTIAN RELIGIONS

8. From its origin, the Church has encountered on many levels, the question of the plurality of religions. Even today Christians constitute only about a third of the

world's population. Moreover, they must live in a world which expresses a growing sympathy for pluralism in religious matters.

9. Given the great place of religion in culture, a local or particular Church, implanted in a non-Christian socio-cultural milieu must take seriously into account the religious elements of this milieu. Moreover, this preoccupation should be in accordance with the depth and vitality of these religious elements.

10. If we may consider one continent as an example, we shall speak of Asia, which witnessed the birth of several of the world's great religious movements. Hinduism, Buddhism, Islam, Confucianism, Taoism, Shintoism: each of these religious systems certainly located in distinct regions of the continent are deeply rooted in the people and show much vigour. Individual life, as well as social and community activity, has been marked in a decisive manner by these religious and spiritual traditions. In addition the Asian Churches consider the question of non-Christian religions as one of the most important and most urgent. They have even made it the object of that privileged form of relation: the dialogue.

THE DIALOGUE OF RELIGIONS

11. Dialogue with other religions forms an integral part of Christian life; by exchange, study and work in common, this dialogue contributes to a better understanding of the religion of the other and to a growth of piety.

12. For Christian faith, the unity of all in their origin and destiny, that is in creation and in communion with God in Jesus Christ is accompanied by the universal presence and action of the Holy Spirit. The Church in dialogue listens and learns. "The Catholic Church rejects nothing which is true and holy in these religions. She looks with sincere respect upon those ways of conduct and of life, those rules and teachings which, though differing in many particulars from what she holds and sets forth, nevertheless often reflect a ray of that Truth which enlightens all men."[9]

13. This dialogue possesses something original, since, as the history of religions testifies, the plurality of religions has often given rise to discrimination and jealousy, fanaticism and despotism, all of which drew on religion the accusation of being a source of division in the human family. The Church "universal sacrament of salvation", that is "sign and instrument of intimate union with God and of the unity of all the human race",[10] is called by God to be minister and instrument of unity in Jesus Christ for all men and all peoples.

THE TRANSCENDENCE OF THE GOSPEL IN RELATION TO CULTURE

14. We cannot however, forget the transcendence of the Gospel in relation to all human cultures in which the Christian faith has the vocation to enroot itself and come to fruition according to all its potentialities. However great the respect should be for what is true and holy in the cultural heritage of a people, this attitude does not demand that one should lend an absolute character to this cultural heritage. No-one can forget that, from the beginning, the Gospel was a "scandal for the Jews and foolishness for the pagans".[11] Inculturation which borrows the way of dialogue between religions cannot in any way pledge itself to syncretism.

THE YOUNG CHURCHES AND THEIR CHRISTIAN PAST

15. The Church prolongs and actualises the mystery of the Servant of Yahweh who was promised to be "the light of the nations so that salvation might reach the

ends of the earth"[12] and to be the "Covenant of the Peoples".[13] This prophecy is realised at the Last Supper, when, on the eve of his Passion, Christ surrounded by the Twelve, gives his body and blood to his followers as the food and drink of the New Covenant thus assimilating them into his own body. The Church, people of the New Covenant was being born. She would receive at Pentecost the Spirit of Christ, the Spirit of the Lamb sacrificed from the beginning and who was already working to fulfil this desire so deeply rooted in human beings: a union the more intense with respect to the intense diversity.

16. In virtue of the Catholic Communion, which unites all the particular Churches in one history, the young Churches consider the past of the Churches which gives birth of them, as part of their own history. However, the majority act of interpretation which is the hallmark of their spiritual maturity consists in recognising this precedence as originatory and not only as historical. This signifies that in receiving in faith the Gospel which their elders announced to them, the young Churches welcomed the "initiator of the faith"[14] and the entire Tradition in which the faith is attested, as also the capacity to give birth to new forms in which the unique and common faith would find expression. Equal in dignity, drawing life from the same mystery, authentic sister Churches, the young Churches manifest, in concert with their elders, the fullness of the mystery of Christ.

17. People of the New Covenant: it is in so far as it commemorates the Paschal mystery and ceaselessly announces the return of the Lord that the Church may be called an eschatology that began with the cultural traditions of peoples, on condition, of course, that these traditions had been subjected to the purifying law of death and resurrection in Christ Jesus.

18. Like St. Paul and the Areopagus in Athens, the young Church interprets its ancestral culture in a new and creative manner. When this culture passes through Christ, "the veil falls."[15] At the time of the "incubation" of faith, this Church has discovered Christ as "exegete and exegesis" of the Father in the Spirit:[16] moreover it does not cease to contemplate him as such. Now it is discovering him as "exegete and exegesis" of man, source and destination of culture. To the unknown God, revealed on the Cross, corresponds unknown man, announced by the young Church as the living Paschal mystery inaugurated by grace in the ancient culture.

19. In the salvation it makes present, the young Church endeavours to locate all the traces of God's care for a particular human group, the *semina Verbi*. What the prologue of the letter to the Hebrews says of the Fathers and the prophets may in relation with Jesus Christ be repeated, in an analogical manner of course, for all human culture in so far as it is right and true and bears wisdom.

CHRISTIAN FAITH AND MODERNITY

23. The inculturation of the Gospel in modern societies will demand a methodical effort of concerted research and action. This effort will assure on the part of those responsible for evangelisation 1) an attitude of openness and a critical eye; 2) the capacity to perceive the spiritual expectations and human aspirations of the new cultures; 3) the aptitude for cultural analysis, having in mind an effective encounter with the modern world.

24. A receptive attitude is required among those who wish to understand and evangelise the world of our time. Modernity is accompanied by undeniable progress in many cultural and material domains: well-being, human mobility, science, research, education, a new sense of solidarity. In addition the Church of Vatican

II has taken a lively account of the new conditions in which she must exercise her mission and it is in the cultures of modernity that the Church of tomorrow will be constructed. The traditional advance applicable to discernment is reiterated by Pius XII. "It is necessary to deepen one's understanding of the civilisation and institutions of various peoples and to cultivate their best qualities and gifts ... All in the customs of peoples which are not inextricably bound up with superstitions or errors should be examined with benevolence and if possible, preserved intact."[17]

25. The Gospel raises fundamental questions amongst those who reflect on the behaviour of modern man, how should one make this man understand the radical nature of the message of Christ: unconditional love, evangelical poverty, adoration of the Father and constant yielding to his will? How should one educate towards the Christian sense of suffering and death? How should one arouse faith and hope in the event of the resurrection accomplished by Jesus Christ?

26. We must develop a *capacity to analyse cultures* and to gauge their moral and spiritual indicators. A mobilisation of the whole Church is called for so that the extremely complex task of the inculturation of the Gospel in today's world may be faced with success. We must wed to this topic the preoccupation of John Paul II, "From the beginning of my pontificate I considered that the dialogue of the Church with the cultures of our time was a vital area, whose stake is the fate of the world in this the end of the twentieth century".[18]

NOTES

Numbers in parentheses below refer to the number of the note in the original text. The note numbers below refer to the text in this volume.

1. (12) Paul VI, Encyclical letter *Humanae Vitae* on birth control, in *Documentation Catholique* 65, 1 September 1968, p. 1447.

2. (13) Vatican II Pastoral Constitution *Gaudium et Spes* on the Church in the Modern World, n. 53.

3. (14) Ibid.

4. (15) John Paul II, Encyclical letter *Slavorum Apostoli* for the eleventh centenary of the work of evangelisation of Saints Cyril and Methodius, 2 June 1985, n. 21, in *Documentation Catholique*, 2 June 1985, p. 724. [This text appears in this volume in Part II Chapter 4 — eds.]

5. (56) Vatican II, Declaration *Nostra Aetate* on the Relationship of the Church to Non-Christian Religions, n. 2.

6. (57) The Third Conference of the Bishops of Latin America, The Evangelisation of Latin America in the Present and in the Future, n. 448. [The text can be found in this volume, Part II Chapter 3 — eds.]

7. (58) Paul VI, Apostolic exhortation "Evangelii Nuntiandi" on Evangelisation in the Modern World, 8 December 1975, n. 48.

8. (59) Ibid.

9. (60) Vatican II, Declaration *Nostra Aetate* on the Relationship of the Church to Non-Christian Religions, n. 2.

10. (61) Vatican II, Dogmatica Constitution *Lumen Gentium* on the Church, n. 1.

11. (62) I Co 1:23.

12. (64) Is 49:6.

13. (64) Is 49:8.

14. (65) Heb 12:2.

15. (66) II Co 3:16.

16. (67) Cf. Henri de Lubac "Exégèse mediévale" coll. Théologie, n. 41, Paris, 1959, t.1, p. 322-324.

17. (68) Pius XII, Encyclical letter *Summi Pontificatus* on the feast of Christ the King, 20 October 1939, in "Documentation Catholique," 40, 5 December 1939, c. 1261.

18. (69) John Paul II, Letter of foundation of the Pontifical Council for Culture, 20 May 1982, in "Documentation Catholique," 79, 20 June, 1982, p. 604.

12

Heritage and Hope:
Evangelization in America

Washington, D.C., November, 1990

U.S. BISHOPS

At their semiannual meeting in November 1990, the U. S. Catholic bishops approved a pastoral letter commemorating the fifth centenary of the evangelization of the Americas. While the letter is quite balanced, acknowledging both the negative and destructive as well as the positive and constructive sides of the original evangelization of the Native American peoples, it appeared in the midst of a controversy about the meaning of the fifth centenary and the moral rightness of its celebration. In May 1990, the National Council of Churches in the United States issued a resolution calling not for celebration but for "reflection and penance," and the fifth centenary has been an object of sharp debate in secular circles as well (cf. New York Times, June 2, 1991). On the other side, the Vatican suppressed a catechetical program designed for the quincentenary sponsored by the organization of Latin American religious (CLAR) on the grounds that it was too critical of the methods of the Spanish and Portuguese in their original evangelization; and Pope John Paul II has written that while certain limitations cannot be ignored, neither can contemporary criteria of missionary methods be applied to methods employed five centuries ago. The U.S. bishops' document does not attempt to whitewash or glorify the past, but denies emphatically that the evangelization of the Americas was "a totally negative experience in which only violence and exploitation of the native peoples were present." Because of the objection by several African-American bishops that the document glorified Bartolome de las Casas, who at one time advocated the importation of African slave labor, the document admits this candidly while adding that las Casas "soon repented upon suffering profound moral anguish."

The document is divided into four parts. The first is a frank discussion of the positive and negative aspects of the evangelization of the Americas, and this is followed by a longer second part which tells the "stories" of a large number of women and men who devoted their lives to evangelization. The third part of the document calls for recommitment—at all levels of the church—to the work of evangelization, thus suggesting that the best way of commemorating the quincentenary would be to be renewed in one's Christian commitment. The short fourth section points out three areas—historical research, ceremonial observance and renewal for evangelical action—by which the anniversary can be observed by U. S. Catholics.

Reprinted here is the entire first part of the pastoral letter, together with short sections from the second and third parts.

INTRODUCTION*

As we observe the 500th anniversary of the encounter between Europe and the Americas, we join our fellow citizens in the United States, Canada, Latin America and many European nations in commemorating an event that reshaped the course of world history. Although we share this event with many throughout the world, our primary concern in this letter is with our own land, the United States of America. As pastors and teachers of the people of God, we wish to call attention to the crucial role that evangelization has played in forming the present civilization of our continent. "Evangelization," as Pope Paul VI has said, "means bringing the good news of Jesus Christ into all strata of humanity and through its influence transforming humanity from within and making it new."[1]

It is that process of transformation that we highlight as we observe the quincentennial, the change that results from men and women hearing the proclamation of the good news that, in Christ, God is reconciling the world and bringing to light a kingdom of righteousness, peace and joy. We recall the history of that process on our own continent, rejoicing in its successes and lamenting and learning from its failures. As Pope John Paul II has indicated, the church wishes to approach the quincentenary "with the humility of truth, without triumphalism or false modesty, but looking only at the truth, in order to give thanks to God for its successes and to draw from its errors motives for projecting herself renewed toward the future."[2] As church, we have often been unconscious and insensitive to the mistreatment of our Native American brothers and sisters and have at times reflected the racism of the dominant culture of which we have been a part. In this quincentennial year, we extend our apology to the native peoples and pledge ourselves to work with them and to ensure their rights, their religious freedom and the preservation of their cultural heritage.

Mindful of the valuable contribution of other Christians in bringing the Gospel to our hemisphere, we nevertheless focus in this statement on the legacy of Catholics. We wish to gain from an examination of our past a firm sense of our identity as an evangelized and evangelizing church.

But beyond that we wish to speak to the present, to look at the challenges we face here and now. We wish, as well, to look to the future to see how to continue the work of evangelization and to promote what Pope John Paul II has described as "a new evangelization: new in its ardor, its methods, its expression."[3]

We challenge all those who hear our message to respond, to be part of the process by which the word of God takes root and bears fruit that nourishes every part of life. The story of the Americas is our story, not only in the sense that there have been millions of Christians who have populated this hemisphere, but also in the sense that, as the Second Vatican Council has taught, there is nothing genuinely human that does not touch the followers of Christ.[4] All the joys, the hopes, the

---

Heritage and Hope (Washington, D.C.: U.S. Catholic Conference, 1991).

griefs, the anxieties that make up the story of the last half-millennium are our heritage as Catholics and members of the American community.

THE DRAMA OF EVANGELIZATION

Human history is the drama of humanity's search for God and God's loving revelation. God has made women and men, placing deep within their souls a hunger for the divine. God has established within creation signs that manifest the Creator's love. In the great event of the incarnation that drama reached its high point. "The Word of God became flesh and dwelt among us."[5] Christ is the light that "enlightens everyone who comes into the world."[6] He is the fullness of the Godhead from whom we have all received grace and truth.[7] To spread the good news of his coming, Jesus called to himself a people and sent them forth as witnesses of the great things that they had seen and heard.[8] Compelled by the love of Christ they went forth to the ends of the earth to proclaim the message of Jesus. The church, as the people of God, stands on that "foundation of the apostles and prophets."[9] The Spirit also has been at work outside the visible church, scattering among the nations what the church fathers of the second and third centuries called the "seeds of the word," inspiring men and women through their discoveries, their aspirations, their sufferings and their joys.

Men and women have responded in various ways to God's loving revelation, often cooperating with God's grace and also in their weakness falling short of the invitation to abundant life. At times the seeds of the word sown on good ground have been choked by the cares of this world. The struggle to allow the word to blossom in our lives is an acute one that was no less arduous in the past than today. The failures, which often have tragic consequences, are likewise not new but part of our heritage as imperfect, yet graced daughters and sons of God.

The fundamental unity of the human race stems from the fact that it has been made in "God's image and likeness." Christ's Gospel of love and redemption transcends national boundaries, cultural differences and divisions among peoples. It cannot be considered foreign anywhere on earth; nor can it be identical with any one culture.[10]

The faith, however, finds expression in the particular values, customs and cultural institutions of those who respond to God's revelation. This means that both the message and the people to whom it is addressed must be viewed with respect and dignity.[11] The story of the coming of faith to our hemisphere must begin, then, not with the landing of the first missionaries, but centuries before with the history of the Native American peoples.

Migrating across this great continent, the peoples settled over thousands of miles from the mountains of the Pacific Northwest to the tropical swamps of the Southeast, developing distinct languages and cultures, and carefully planned social systems to meet the demanding needs of a vast, challenging environment. The Creator walked with the first Americans, giving them a realization of the sacredness of creation, manifested in their rites of chant, dance and other rituals. The sun dance and the vision quest spoke of their understanding of the importance of prayer and spiritual growth. The sweat lodge, the traditions of fasting and keeping silence illustrated an understanding of the values of self-humiliation and deprivation for the sake of something greater. Their respect for unborn life, for the elderly and for children told of a refined sense of the value of life. These prayers, practices and sacred celebrations showed the wonder and awe with which the native peoples carried out their stewardship of the earth.

The encounter with the Europeans was a harsh and painful one for the indigenous peoples. The introduction of diseases to which the Native Americans had no immunities led to the death of millions.[12] Added to that were the cultural oppression, the injustices, the disrespect for native ways and traditions that must be acknowledged and lamented.[13] The great waves of European colonization were accompanied by destruction of Indian civilization, the violent usurpation of Indian lands and the brutalization of their inhabitants. Many of those associated with the colonization of the land failed to see in the natives the workings of the same God that they espoused. Confronted with a vastly different culture, European Christians were challenged to re-examine how their own culture shaped their faith. Often they failed to distinguish between what was crucial to the Gospel and what were matters of cultural preference. That failure brought with it catastrophic consequences for the native peoples, who were at times forced to become European at the same time they became Christian.

Yet, that is not the whole picture. The effort to portray the history of the encounter as a totally negative experience in which only violence and exploitation of the native peoples were present is not an accurate interpretation of the past. The notion, traditionally known as the "black legend," that Catholic Spain was uniquely cruel and violent in the administration of its colonies is simply untrue. Spanish monarchs, through the Patronato Real, financed the ministries of thousands of missionaries and made extensive efforts to support the church's efforts in the newly encountered lands. Also through Spain many of the cultural refinements and scientific advances of Renaissance Europe were brought to the Americas.

There was, in fact, a deeply positive aspect of the encounter of European and American cultures. Through the work of many who came in obedience to Christ's command to spread the Gospel and through the efforts of those who responded to the word—the Native Americans and peoples of the new race that resulted from the mingling of the European and American peoples—the Gospel did in fact take root. The encounter engendered an unprecedented missionary effort on the part of European Christians that was to reshape the map of the church. It represented a widening of the frontiers of humanity and a vigorous effort on the part of the church to bring about the universality that Christ desired for his message. It cannot be denied that the interdependence of the cross and the crown that occurred during the first missionary campaigns brought with it contradictions and injustices. But neither can it be denied that the expansion of Christianity into our hemisphere brought to the peoples of this land the gift of the Christian faith with its power of humanization and salvation, dignity and fraternity, justice and love.

From the earliest days there were Catholic missionaries who exercised a humanizing presence in the midst of colonization. Many of the missionaries made an effort at adapting the forms and symbols of Christianity to the customs of the indigenous American peoples. They learned the languages, the ceremonies and the traditions of the native peoples, attempting to show how Christianity complemented their beliefs and challenged those things in their culture that conflicted with Christ's message. They labored for the spiritual and material welfare of those to whom they ministered.

Perhaps the most significant moral problem the church faced in the Americas was that of human dignity and slavery. Some spoke out energetically for the rights of the native peoples and against the mistreatment of imported slaves. Bartolome de las Casas, a Dominican, bishop and friend of the Columbus family, was a tireless defender of Indian rights. While for a time he advocated the practice of importing

African peoples to replace the Indian slaves, he soon repented upon suffering profound moral anguish. As bishop of Chiapas he ordered the denial of absolution to those who persisted in holding slaves. This mandate earned him the opposition of so many in his diocese that he resigned as bishop. Las Casas went on to become one of the earliest opponents of the enslavement of peoples of any race.

Las Casas inspired the work of the Spanish theologians Francisco de Vitoria and Francisco Suarez, who were pioneers in the creation of a philosophy of universal human rights based on the dignity of the person. Spanish rulers like Charles I responded to the call for reform and instituted new laws to protect the rights of natives. The pontiffs also responded, condemning any efforts at the enslavement of the native population. Pope Paul III in 1537 issued his bull *Sublimis Deus*, in which he denounced those that held that "the inhabitants of the West Indies and the southern continents ... should be treated like irrational animals and used exclusively for our profit and service." He declared that "Indians, as well as any other peoples which Christianity will come to know in the future, must not be deprived of their freedom and their possessions ... even if they are not Christians; on the contrary, they must be left to enjoy their freedom and possessions." Later Urban VIII declared that anyone who kept Indian slaves would incur excommunication."[14]

STORIES OF EVANGELIZATION

For 500 years the Gospel of Jesus Christ informed the life of the Americas, attempting to complete and fulfill that which was good in both the native and immigrant cultures and confront what was not. The stories of the many evangelizers—men and women, clergy, religious and lay—who strove to spread the good news are numerous and varied. In what follows we tell only a few of those stories, not necessarily the most important, but ones that illustrate the range and depth of the evangelizing process in our history. It is not intended to be a list of the most famous or the best but of significant voices that can inspire us today.

(There follow short stories about, among others, Christopher Columbus, Early Spanish Missionaries, Juan Diego and Guadalupe, Jacques Marquette, Marie of the Incarnation, Kateri Tekawitha, Isaac Jogues, Alsonso de Sandoval, Mary Elizabeth Lange, Elizabeth Seton, Pierre DeSmet, Felix Varela, Katharine Drexel, John Neumann, Frances Xavier Cabrini, Thomas Price and James Walsh).

A CALL TO THE CIVILIZATION OF LOVE

America for these 500 years has stood as a sign of hope for many peoples. The moment calls for Christians, faithful to the Gospel, to realize the hope that a people renewed by the saving presence of Christ may help build a better society. May the new evangelization stimulate holiness, integrity and tireless activity to promote the dignity of all human life, thus witnessing more fully to the presence of the kingdom of God in our midst. May we all, through a fresh commitment to the Gospel, engage in a new "discovery," a new creation of a world still being sought: a community of faith, a culture of solidarity, a civilization of love. The future is struggling to be born as the word of God entreats men and women to respond more fully to its message. It is one in which a "new inspired synthesis of the spiritual and temporal, of the ancient and modern" might be brought forth.[15]

All of the people of God must do their part in this new evangelization. Scholars and teachers, in reverence for the truth, should see their work as contributing to the good of humanity in the light of the Gospel. Parents, in their trying but immeasurably important task, should work to build the "domestic church" in which faith and virtue are nurtured. The young, who have a special vocation to hope, should spread among their peers the message of light and life that is in Christ. Artists, who toil to create works of beauty and meaning, should view their art as a medium through which others may see something of the transcendent. Public servants, who struggle in an environment of utilitarianism, should spread the justice of Christ's kingdom by their way of life. Laborers and mechanics, those working in commerce and law, those who care for the sick and those who engage in scientific research: The Gospel calls them all to a special witness in our society. It calls each of us to incarnate the good news of Christ in the midst of our labors.

We are each called to become salt and light for the world, and at all times a sign of contradiction that challenges and transforms the world according to the mind of Christ. While we are not called to impose our religious beliefs on others, we are compelled to give the example of lives of faith, goodness and service. On issues of fundamental moral importance it is at times necessary to challenge publicly the conscience of society—as did our sisters and brothers in other ages—to uphold those basic human values that advance fundamental human rights and promote the spiritual aspirations of every person.

It is our hope that during 1992 and thereafter our nation will give special attention to the condition of Native Americans. We encourage all Americans to better understand the role of native peoples in our history and to respond to the just grievances of our Native American brothers and sisters.

We hope that this will be a graced time for rejecting all forms of racism. The negative consequences of slavery are still painfully felt in both the African-American culture of today and throughout society in the Americas. We acknowledge and lament this and pledge ourselves during this quincentennial year to redress those injustices.

The church in this country is truly multicultural. Our many peoples, each in their uniqueness, are gifts of God. May we at this time renew our appreciation of this as we welcome the new immigrants to our land, many of whom came to our shores with a vibrant Catholic Faith. Asians, Europeans, Africans and citizens of the Americas each enrich our faith community.

It is our hope that during this time we recognize and give thanks for the birth of the Hispanic people, a beautiful fruit of the coming together of diverse peoples and cultures. Theirs was indeed a painful birth, but the result was five centuries of transformation affecting both church and society. The Hispanic presence is now more evident than ever as we move into the second half-millennium of the Gospel in America.

We wish to strive for a new reconciliation in the spirit of the Gospel among all Americans and to recognize more fully our solidarity with the nations of this hemisphere. Evangelization is unfinished if exploitation of the weak, of minorities and of peoples of the Third World countries still exists. The quincentenary calls us to a new commitment as Christians to right the evils of the past and the present, and to be forceful advocates of the peace and justice proclaimed by the Gospel. May we stand with our sisters and brothers of Latin America in their struggles for dignity, freedom and peace with justice.

May the church of the United States also not forget its commitment to the universal dimension of evangelization. May we continue as a church to share our human and material resources with those evangelizers of other lands who strive to bring the Gospel to their peoples.[16] With Pope Paul VI may we say as we witness a growing number of Catholics proclaiming the faith: "We cannot but experience a great inner joy when we see so many pastors, religious and lay people fired with their mission to evangelize, seeking more suitable ways of proclaiming the Gospel effectively."[17]

NOTES

Numbers in parentheses refer to the number of the note in the original text. The note numbers below refer to the text in the present volume.

1. (1) Paul VI, *Evangelii Nuntiandi*, 1975, 18.

2. John Paul II, "Building a New Latin America," *Origins* 14:20 (Nov. 1, 1984), p. 308.

3. Cf. ibid., p. 307.

4. Cf. *Gaudium et Spes*, 1.

5. Jn. 1:14.

6. Jn. 1:9.

7. Cf. Jn. 1:14.

8. Cf. Acts 4:20.

9. Eph. 2:20.

10. "Statement of the U.S. Catholic Bishops on American Indians" (U.S. Catholic Conference Office for Publishing and Promotion Services, 1977), 6.

11. *Evangelii Nuntiandi*, 4.

12. Cf. Alfred Crosby, *The Columbian Exchange* (Greenwood Press, 1972).

13. (13) John Paul II, "Meeting with Native Americans," in *Unity in the Work of Service* (USCC, 1987), p. 109.

14. (14) Cf. Pontifical Commission Justice and Peace, "The Church and Racism: Toward a More Fraternal Society" (USCC, 1988), p. 11.

15. (40) Paul VI, "Homily in St. Peter's Basilica," July 4, 1964.

16. (41) Cf. National Conference of Catholic Bishops, *To the Ends of the Earth: A Pastoral Statement on World Mission* (USCC, 1987). [The text of this document can be found in Part II Chapter 8—eds.]

17. (42) *Evangelii Nuntiandi*, 73.

13

Redemptoris Missio

Rome, December 7, 1990

POPE JOHN PAUL II

To commemorate the twenty-fifth anniversary of Vatican II's Decree on Missionary Activity, John Paul II published his eighth encyclical, entitled Redemptoris Missio. *The Latin title of the council document,* Ad Gentes *("to all peoples"), is the major theme of the encyclical: the pope distinguishes sharply among missionary activity, pastoral care, and the re-evangelization of people "who no longer consider themselves members of the church and live a life far removed from Christ and his Gospel" (#33). Only the mission* ad gentes *is missionary activity proper; missionary activity consists in proclaiming Christ as the only Savior (#4) and working toward the establishment of the church in all parts of the world.*

In emphasizing the geographical aspect of mission and its Christological and ecclesiological content, the pope's intention was to counter various movements in the church which were de-emphasizing, he felt, Christ and the church's central role in the history of salvation. Among these movements were certain theologies which emphasized a theocentric theology of creation at the expense of a Christocentric theology of redemption (cf. #19), theologies which focused on the kingdom rather than on the church (cf. #12-20), and practices of interreligious dialogue which stressed the commonalities among religions rather than Christian uniqueness (#55-57). The pope makes it quite clear that church teaching holds that, though other followers of other religious ways can find salvation, such salvation is found finally and fully in Christ and his church (cf. #55).

Without denying this firm and emphatic orientation, however, the reader can sense another spirit at work in the document. While there is a strong stress on the geographical concept of mission, it is tempered somewhat by an admission that mission goes "beyond the frontiers of race and religion" (#25), that it needs to be developed in urban situations, as well as in the "modern equivalents of the Areopagus" (#37) where Christians work for peace, development, liberation, human rights, ecological wholeness, and within contemporary scientific and secular realities. While interreligious dialogue is certainly recommended with caution, it is acknowledged that dialogue is indeed "part of the Church's evangelizing mission" (#55).

This long document—over two hundred pages in the original Latin edition—is divided into eight chapters. Chapters I and II deal respectively with the Christocentric and ecclesial focus of Christian mission, and Chapter III reflects on the

Holy Spirit as the "Principal Agent of Mission." Chapter IV speaks of the various senses of the mission ad gentes *and is in many ways the most original chapter in the encyclical. Chapter V, the longest chapter, deals with various aspects of mission: witness, proclamation, conversion, the role of the local church and basic communities, inculturation, dialogue, and liberation. Chapters VI and VII deal with missionaries and cooperation in mission, and the document concludes with an eighth chapter on missionary spirituality.*

We have reprinted several important parts of the encyclical: the first section reprints the Christocentric sections of the document, along with its treatment of the Reign (kingdom) of God. Also included are the pope's important reflections on the new kinds of Areopagus that today's world presents to evangelizers and his cautious appraisal of interreligious dialogue.

(From Chapter I: "Jesus Christ, The Only Savior")*

(From Paragraph 4) The church's universal mission is born of faith in Jesus Christ as is stated in our Trinitarian profession of faith: "I believe in one Lord, Jesus Christ, the only Son of God, eternally begotten of the Father .... . For us men and for our salvation he came down from heaven: By the power of the Holy Spirit he was born of the Virgin Mary and became man."[1] The redemption event brings salvation to all, "for each one is included in the mystery of the redemption and with each one Christ has united himself forever through this mystery."[2] It is only in faith that the church's mission can be understood and only in faith that it can find its basis.

Nevertheless, also as a result of the changes which have taken place in modern times and the spread of new theological ideas, some people wonder: Is missionary work among non-Christians still relevant? Has it not been replaced by interreligious dialogue? Is not human development an adequate goal of the church's mission? Does not respect for conscience and for freedom exclude all efforts at conversion? Is it not possible to attain salvation in any religion? Why then should there be missionary activity?

"NO ONE COMES TO THE FATHER BUT BY ME" (JN. 14:6)

5. If we go back to the beginnings of the church, we find a clear affirmation that Christ is the one savior of all, the only one able to reveal God and lead to God. In reply to the Jewish religious authorities who question the apostles about the healing of the lame man, Peter says: "By the name of Jesus Christ of Nazareth whom you crucified, whom God raised from the dead, by him this man is standing before you well. ... And there is salvation in no one else, for there is no other name under heaven given among men by which we must be saved" (Acts 4:10,12). This statement, which was made to the Sanhedrin, has a universal value, since for all people—Jews and Gentiles alike—salvation can only come from Jesus Christ.

(From Paragraph 6) Thus, although it is legitimate and helpful to consider the various aspects of the mystery of Christ, we must never lose sight of its unity. In the process of discovering and appreciating the manifold gifts—especially the spir-

---

*Reprinted from the English translation of *Redemptoris Missio* published by the Vatican Polyglot Press, Vatican City State, 7 December 1990.

itual treasures—that God has bestowed on every people, we cannot separate those gifts from Jesus Christ, who is at the center of God's plan of salvation. Just as "by his incarnation the Son of God united himself in some sense with every human being," so too "we are obliged to hold that the Holy Spirit offers everyone the possibility of sharing in the paschal mystery in a matter known only to God."³ God's plan is "to unite all things in Christ, things in heaven and things on earth" (Eph. 1:10).

THE KINGDOM IN RELATION TO CHRIST AND THE CHURCH

17. Nowadays the kingdom is much spoken of, but not always in a way consonant with the thinking of the church. In fact, there are ideas about salvation and mission which can be called *anthropocentric* in the reductive sense of the word inasmuch as they are focused on man's earthly needs. In this view, the kingdom tends to become something completely human and secularized; what counts are programs and struggles for a liberation which is socioeconomic, political and even cultural, but within a horizon that is closed to the transcendent. Without denying that on this level too there are values to be promoted, such a notion nevertheless remains within the confines of a kingdom of man, deprived of its authentic and profound dimensions. Such a view easily translates into one more ideology of purely earthly progress. The kingdom of God, however, "is not of this world . . . is not from the world" (Jn. 18:36).

There are also conceptions which deliberately emphasize the kingdom and which describe themselves as "kingdom centered." They stress the image of a church which is not concerned about herself, but which is totally concerned with bearing witness to and serving the kingdom. It is a "church for others" just as Christ is the "man for others." The church's task is described as though it had to proceed in two directions: on the one hand promoting such "values of the kingdom" as peace, justice, freedom, brotherhood, etc., while on the other hand fostering dialogue between peoples, cultures and religions so that through a mutual enrichment they might help the world to be renewed and to journey ever closer toward the kingdom.

Together with positive aspects, these conceptions often reveal negative aspects as well. First, they are silent about Christ: The kingdom of which they speak is "theocentrically" based, since, according to them, Christ cannot be understood by those who lack Christian faith, whereas different peoples, cultures and religions are capable of finding common ground in the one divine reality, by whatever name it is called. For the same reason they put great stress on the mystery of creation, which is reflected in the diversity of cultures and beliefs, but they keep silent about the mystery of redemption. Furthermore, the kingdom, as they understand it, ends up either leaving very little room for the church or undervaluing the church in reaction to a presumed "ecclesiocentrism" of the past and because they consider the church herself only a sign, for that matter a sign not without ambiguity.

18. This is not the kingdom of God as we know it from revelation. The kingdom cannot be detached either from Christ or from the church.

MISSION *AD GENTES* RETAINS ITS VALUE

33. The fact that there is a diversity of activities in the church's one mission is not intrinsic to that mission, but arises from the variety of circumstances in which that mission is carried out.⁴ Looking at today's world from the viewpoint of evangelization, we can distinguish three situations.

First, there is the situation which the church's missionary activity addresses: peoples, groups and sociocultural context in which Christ and his Gospel are not known or which lack Christian communities sufficiently mature to be able to incarnate the faith in their own environment and proclaim it to other groups. This is mission *ad gentes* in the proper sense of the term.[5]

Second, there are Christian communities with adequate and solid ecclesial structures. They are fervent in their faith and in Christian living. They bear witness to the Gospel in their surroundings and have a sense of commitment to the universal mission. In these communities the church carries out her activity and pastoral care.

Third, there is an intermediate situation, particularly in countries with ancient Christian roots and occasionally in the younger churches as well, where entire groups of the baptized have lost a living sense of the faith or even no longer consider themselves members of the church and live a life far removed from Christ and his Gospel. In this case what is needed is a "new evangelization" or a "re-evangelization."

34. Missionary activity proper, namely the mission *ad gentes*, is directed to "peoples or groups who do not yet believe in Christ," in whom the church "has not yet taken root"[6] and whose culture has not yet been influenced by the Gospel.[7] It is distinct from other ecclesial activities inasmuch as it is addressed to groups and settings which are non-Christian, because the preaching of the Gospel and the presence of the church are either absent or insufficient. It can thus be characterized as the work of proclaiming Christ and his Gospel, building up the local church and promoting the values of the kingdom. The specific nature of this mission *ad gentes* consists in its being addressed to "non-Christians." It is therefore necessary to ensure that this specifically "missionary work that Jesus entrusted and still entrusts each day to his church"[8] does not become an indistinguishable part of the overall mission of the whole people of God and as a result become neglected or forgotten.

On the other hand, the boundaries between pastoral care of the faithful, new evangelization and specific missionary activity are not clearly definable, and it is unthinkable to create barriers between them or to put them into watertight compartments. Nevertheless, there must be no lessening of the impetus to preach the Gospel and to establish new churches among peoples or communities where they do not yet exist, for this is the first task of the church, which has been sent forth to all peoples and to the very ends of the earth. Without the mission *ad gentes*, the church's very missionary dimension would be deprived of its essential meaning and of the very activity that exemplifies it.

Also to be noted is the real and growing interdependence which exists between these various saving activities of the church. Each of them influences, stimulates and assists the others. The missionary thrust fosters exchanges between the churches and directs them toward the larger world, with positive influences in every direction. The churches in traditionally Christian countries, for example, involved as they are in the challenging task of new evangelization, are coming to understand more clearly that they cannot be missionaries to non-Christians in other countries and continents unless they are seriously concerned about the non-Christians at home. Hence missionary activity *ad intra* is a credible sign and a stimulus for missionary activity *ad extra* and vice versa.

PARAMETERS OF THE CHURCH'S MISSION *AD GENTES*

37. By virtue of Christ's universal mandate, the mission *ad gentes* knows no boundaries. Still, it is possible to determine certain parameters within which that

mission is exercised in order to gain a real grasp of the situation.

(a) *Territorial limits.* Missionary activity has normally been defined in terms of specific territories. The Second Vatican Council acknowledged the territorial dimension of the mission *ad gentes*[9] a dimension which even today remains important for determining responsibilities, competencies and the geographical limits of missionary activity. Certainly a universal mission implies a universal perspective. Indeed, the church refuses to allow her missionary presence to be hindered by geographical boundaries or political barriers. But it is also true that missionary activity *ad gentes*, being different from the pastoral care of the faithful and the new evangelization of the non-practicing, is exercised within well-defined territories and groups of people.

The growth in the number of new churches in recent times should not deceive us. Within the territories entrusted to these churches — particularly in Asia, but also in Africa, Latin America and Oceania — there remain vast regions still to be evangelized. In many nations entire peoples and cultural areas of great importance have not yet been reached by the proclamation of the Gospel and the presence of the local church.[10] Even in traditionally Christian countries there are regions that are under the special structures of the mission *ad gentes*, with groups and areas not yet evangelized. Thus, in these countries too there is a need not only for a new evangelization, but also, in some cases, for an initial evangelization.[11]

Situations are not, however, the same everywhere. While acknowledging that statements about the missionary responsibility of the church are not credible unless they are backed up by a serious commitment to a new evangelization in the traditionally Christian countries, it does not seem justified to regard as identical the situation of a people which has never known Jesus Christ and that of a people which has known him, accepted him and then rejected him while continuing to live in a culture which in a large part has absorbed Gospel principles and values. These are two basically different situations with regard to the faith.

Thus the criterion of geography, although somewhat imprecise and always provisional, is still a valid indicator of the frontiers toward which missionary activity must be directed. There are countries and geographical and cultural areas which lack indigenous Christian communities. In other places, these communities are so small as not to be a clear sign of a Christian presence, or they lack the dynamism to evangelize their societies or belong to a minority population not integrated into the dominant culture of the nation. Particularly in Asia, toward which the church's mission *ad gentes* ought to be chiefly directed, Christians are a small minority even though sometimes there are signficant numbers of converts and outstanding examples of Christian presence.

(b) *New worlds and new social phenomena.* The rapid and profound transformations which characterize today's world, expecially in the Southern Hemisphere, are having a powerful effect on the overall missionary picture. Where before there were stable human and social situations, today everything is in flux. One thinks, for example, of urbanization and the massive growth of cities, especially where demographic pressure is greatest. In not a few countries, over half the population already lives in a few "megalopolises," where human problems are often aggravated by the feeling of anonymity experienced by masses of people.

In the modern age, missionary activity has been carried out especially in isolated regions which are far from centers of civilization and which are hard to penetrate because of difficulties of communication, language or climate. Today the image of mission *ad gentes* is perhaps changing: Efforts should be concentrated on the big cities, where new customs and styles of living arise together with new forms of culture and communication, which then influence the wider population. It is true that the "option for the neediest" means that we should not overlook the most abandoned and isolated human groups, but it is also true that individuals or small groups cannot be evangelized if we neglect the centers where a new humanity, so to speak, is emerging and where new models of development are taking shape. The future of the younger nations is being shaped in the cities.

Speaking of the future, we cannot forget the young, who in many countries comprise more than half the population. How do we bring the message of Christ to non-Christian young people, who represent the future of entire continents? Clearly, the ordinary means of pastoral work are not sufficient: What are needed are associations, institutions, special centers and groups, and cultural and social initiatives for young people. This is a field where modern ecclesial movements have ample room for involvement.

Among the great changes taking place in the contemporary world, migration has produced a new phenomenon: Non-Christians are becoming very numerous in traditionally Christian countries, creating fresh opportunities for contacts and cultural exchanges, and calling the church to hospitality, dialogue, assistance and, in a word, fraternity. Among migrants, refugees occupy a very special place and deserve the greatest attention. Today there are many millions of refugees in the world and their number is constantly increasing. They have fled from conditions of political oppression and inhuman misery, from famine and drought of catastrophic proportions. The church must make them part of her overall apostolic concern.

Finally, we may mention the situations of poverty—often on an intolerable scale—which have been created in not a few countries and which are often the cause of mass migration. The community of believers in Christ is challenged by these inhuman situations: The proclamation of Christ and the kingdom of God must become the means for restoring the human dignity of these people.

(c) *Cultural sectors: the modern equivalents of the Areopagus.* After preaching in a number of places, St. Paul arrived in Athens, where he went to the Areopagus and proclaimed the Gospel in language appropriate to and understandable in those surroundings (cf. Acts 17:22-31). At that time the Areopagus represented the cultural center of the learned people of Athens, and today it can be taken as a symbol of the new sectors in which the Gospel must be proclaimed.

The first Areopagus of the modern age is the world of communications, which is unifying humanity and turning it into what is known as a "global village." The means of social communication have become so important as to be for many the chief means of information and education, of guidance and inspiration in their behavior as individuals, families and within society at large. In particular, the younger generation is growing up in a world conditioned by the mass media. To some degree perhaps this Areopagus has been neglected. Generally, preference has been given to other means of preaching the Gospel and of Christian education, while the mass media are left to the initiative of individuals or small groups and enter into pastoral planning only in a secondary way. Involvement in the mass media, however, is not meant merely to strengthen the preaching of the Gospel. There is a deeper reality involved here: Since the very evangelization of modern culture depends to a great extent on the influence of the media, it is not enough to use the media simply to spread the Christian message and the church's authentic teaching. It is also necessary to integrate the message into the "new culture" created by modern communications. This is a complex issue, since the "new culture" originates not just from whatever context is eventually expressed, but from the very fact that there exist new ways of communicating, with new languages, new techniques and a new psychology. Pope Paul VI said that "the split between the Gospel and culture is undoubtedly the tragedy of our time,"[12] and the field of communications fully confirms this judgement.

There are many other forms of the "Areopagus" in the modern world toward which the church's missionary activity ought to be directed; for example, commitment to peace, development and the liberation of peoples; the rights of individuals and peoples, especially those of minorities; the advancement of women and children; safeguarding the created world. These too are areas which need to be illuminated with the light of the Gospel.

We must also mention the important "Areopagus" of culture, scientific research and international relations which promote dialogue and open up new possibilities. We would do well to be attentive to these modern areas of activity and to be involved in them. People sense that they are, as it were, travelling together across life's sea and that they are called to ever greater unity and solidarity. Solutions to pressing problems must be studied, discussed and worked out with the involvement of all. That is why international organizations and meetings are proving increasingly important in many sectors of human life, from culture to politics, from the economy to research. Christians who live and work in this international sphere must always remember their duty to bear witness to the Gospel.

38. Our times are both momentous and fascinating. While on the one hand people seem to be pursuing material prosperity and to be sinking ever deeper into consumerism and materialism, on the other hand we are witnessing a desperate search for meaning, the need for an inner life and a desire to learn new forms and methods of meditation and prayer. Not only in cultures with strong religious elements, but also in secularized societies the spiritual dimension of life is being sought after as an antidote to dehumanization. This phenomenon — the so-called "religious revival" — is not without ambiguity, but it also represents an opportunity. The church has an immense spiritual patrimony to offer mankind, a heritage in Christ, who called himself "the way, and the truth and the life" (Jn. 14:6): It is the Christian path to meeting God, to prayer, to asceticism and to the search for life's meaning. Here too there is an "Areopagus" to be evangelized.

DIALOGUE WITH OUR BROTHERS AND SISTERS OF OTHER RELIGIONS

55. Interreligious dialogue is a part of the church's evangelizing mission. Understood as a method and means of mutual knowledge and enrichment, dialogue is not in opposition to the mission *ad gentes*; indeed it has special links with that mission and is one of its expressions. This mission, in fact, is addressed to those who do not know Christ and his Gospel, and who belong for the most part to other religions. In Christ, God calls all peoples to himself, and he wishes to share with them the fullness of his revelation and love. He does not fail to make himself present in many ways, not only to individuals but also to entire peoples through their spiritual riches, of which their religions are the main and essential expression even when they contain "gaps, insufficiencies and errors."[13] All of this has been given ample emphasis by the council and the subsequent magisterium, without detracting in any way from the fact that salvation comes from Christ and that dialogue does not dispense from evangelization.[14]

In the light of the economy of salvation, the church sees no conflict between proclaiming Christ and engaging in interreligious dialogue. Instead, she feels the need to link the two in the context of her mission *ad gentes*. These two elements must maintain both their intimate connection and their distinctiveness; therefore they should not be confused, manipulated or regarded as identical as though they were interchangeable.

I recently wrote to the bishops of Asia: "Although the church gladly acknowledges whatever is true and holy in the religious traditions of Buddhism, Hinduism and Islam as a reflection of that truth which enlightens all men, this does not lessen her duty and resolve to proclaim without fail Jesus Christ, who is 'the way and the truth and the life.' ... The fact that the followers of other religions can receive God's grace and be saved by Christ apart from the ordinary means which he has established does not thereby cancel the call to faith and baptism which God wills for all people."[15] Indeed, Christ himself, "while expressly insisting on the need for faith and baptism, at the same time confirmed the need for the church, into which people enter through baptism as through a door."[16] Dialogue should be conducted and implemented with the conviction that the church is the ordinary means of salvation and that she alone possesses the fullness of the means of salvation.[17]

NOTES

Numbers in parentheses refer to the number of notes in the original text. The note numbers below refer to the text in the present volume.

1. (5) Nicene-Constantinopolitan Creed, Denz. – Schon., 150.
2. (6) *Redemptor Hominis*, 13.
3. (8) Second Vatican Council, *Gaudium et Spes*, 22.
4. (51) *Ad Gentes*, 6.
5. (52) Cf. ibid.
6. (53) Cf. ibid., 6, 23, 27.
7. (54) Cf. *Evangelii Nuntiandi*, 18-20.
8. (55) *Christifideles Laici*, 35.
9. (59) *Ad Gentes*, 6.
10. (60) Cf. ibid., 20.
11. (61) Cf. Address to the members of the symposium of the Council of the European Episcopal Conference, Oct. 11, 1985: AAS 78 (1986), 178-189.
12. (62) *Evangelii Nuntiandi*, 20.
13. (98) Paul VI, Address at the opening of the Second Vatican Council, September 29, 1963: AAS 55 (1963), 858; cf. Second Vatican Council, *Nostra Aetate*, 2; *Lumen Gentium*, 16; *Ad Gentes*, 9; *Evangelii Nuntiandi*, 53.
14. (99) Cf. Paul VI, encyclical *Ecclesiam Suam* (Aug. 6, 1964): AAS 56 (1964), 609-659; *Ad Gentes*, 11, 41; Secretariate for Non-Christians, document *L'atteggiamento della Chiesa di Fronte ai Seguaci di Altre Religioni: Reflessioni e orientamenti su dialogo e missione* (Sept. 4, 1984): AAS 76 (1984), 816-828.
15. (100) Letter to the fifth plenary assembly of Asian bishops' conferences (June 23, 1990), 4, *L'Osservatore Romano*, July 18, 1990.
16. (101) *Lumen Gentium*, 14; cf. *Ad Gentes*, 7.
17. (102) *Unitatis Redintegratio*, 3; *Ad Gentes*, 7.

14

Dialogue and Proclamation

Rome, June 20, 1991

*PONTIFICAL COUNCIL FOR INTERRELIGIOUS DIALOGUE AND
CONGREGATION FOR THE EVANGELIZATION OF PEOPLES*

During the Second Vatican Council, Paul VI established the Secretariat for Non-Christians, to be headed by the venerable former rector of the Pontifical Biblical Institute, Cardinal Augustine Bea. Following its plenary assembly in 1984, the secretariat issued "The Attitude of the Church Toward the Followers of Other Religions: Reflections and Orientations on Dialogue and Mission," a document which laid down a number of principles regarding encounters between Catholic Christians and women and men of other religious ways. One of the cardinal principles of this document was that the direct proclamation of the gospel and interreligious dialogue were each essential and interrelated elements of the overall Mission of the church. In the words of the document: "The fact that Christian mission can never be separated from love and respect for others is proof for Christians of the place of dialogue within that mission" (1984 Document, #19). In June, 1990, a document entitled Dialogue and Proclamation *was issued in a joint publication of the Secretariat—now called the Pontifical Council for Interreligious Dialogue—and the Congregation for the Evangelization of Peoples. Its purpose was to give reflection to the two interrelated elements of dialogue and proclamation, and it does this in three parts. A first part deals with dialogue; a second deals with proclamation; and a third reflects on their interrelationship. The document makes it clear that, even if dialogue is treated first, it has no priority over proclamation; dialogue, rather, represents an essential but not exclusive aspect of missionary proclamation of the gospel (cf. #3).*

As the text of the document was in its final preparatory stages, John Paul II published his Redemptoris Missio, *and in several paragraphs (cf. the encyclical, #55-57, included in this volume, Part 2, chapter 13) the pope deals specifically with the issues discussed here more at length. The present document recommends that it be read in this encyclical's light (#4), but it is significant that the treatment of dialogue here is more nuanced and somewhat more open. This is so quite possibly because "Dialogue and Proclamation" was much longer in preparation by a very balanced group of experts and itself went through dialogue and numerous revisions until it met the approval of its drafters and the Congregation for the Doctrine of Faith.* Redemptoris Missio, *on the other hand, was not circulated widely prior to its publication and shows a good deal of polemics against mis-*

siological positions viewed negatively by certain Vatican officials. For instance, in the encyclical, conversion is defined as "accepting, by a personal decision, the saving sovereignty of Christ and becoming his disciple" (encyclical, #46); in "Dialogue and Proclamation" conversion is "the humble and penitent return of the heart to God in the desire to submit one's life more generously to him" (#11, quoting the 1984 document of the then Secretariat for Non-Christians, "Dialogue and Mission," #37). Except for the reference to Redemptoris Missio *in #4, "Dialogue and Proclamation" does not refer to it at all, partly because the drafters of the encyclical kept it secret.*

Whether or not this document becomes, in effect, a refining of the pope's strongly stated ideas, "Dialogue and Proclamation" represents a significant contribution to official Catholic thought on the question of the validity of other religious ways in the face of the traditional Christian claim that, outside of Christ, there is "no other name . . . by which we are to be saved" (cf. Acts 4:12).

INTRODUCTION*

1. It is 25 years since *Nostra Aetate,* the declaration of the Second Vatican Council on the Church's relationship to other religions, was promulgated. The document stressed the importance of interreligious dialogue. At the same time it recalled that the Church is in duty bound to proclaim without fail Christ, the Way, the Truth, and the Life, in whom all people find their fulfillment (cf. *Nostra Aetate,* 2).

2. To foster the work of dialogue, Pope Paul VI set up in 1964 the Secretariat for Non-Christians, recently renamed the Pontifical Council for Interreligious Dialogue. Following its Plenary Assembly of 1984, the Secretariat issued a document entitled "The Attitude of the Church towards the Followers of Other Religions: Reflections and Orientations on Dialogue and Mission." This document states that the evangelizing mission of the Church is a "single but complex and articulated reality." It indicates the principal elements of this mission: presence and witness; commitment to social development and human liberation; liturgical life, prayer and contemplation; interreligious dialogue; and finally, proclamation and catechesis.[1] Proclamation and dialogue are thus both viewed, each in its own place, as component elements and authentic forms of the one evangelizing mission of the Church. They are both oriented towards the communication of salvific truth.

3. The present document gives further consideration to these two elements. It first puts forward the characteristics of each, and then studies their mutual relationship. If dialogue is treated first, this is not because it has any priority over proclamation. It is simply due to the fact that dialogue is the primary concern of the Pontifical Council for Interreligious Dialogue which initiated the preparation of the document. The document in fact was first discussed during the Plenary Assembly of the Secretariat in 1987. The observations made then, together with further consultation, have led to this text, which was finalized and adopted at the Plenary Assembly of the Pontifical Council for Interreligious Dialogue in April 1990. In the process there has been close collaboration between the Pontifical Council for Interreligious Dialogue and the Congregation for the Evangelization of Peoples. Both dicasteries are offering these reflections to the universal Church.

---

*Reprinted from the Bulletin of the Pontifical Council on Interreligious Dialogue, vol. 26, no. 2, 1991 (Rome: Vatican Polyglot Press).

4. Among the reasons which make the relationship between dialogue and proclamation a relevant theme for study, the following may be mentioned:

a) In the world of today, characterized by rapid communications, mobility of peoples, and interdependence, there is a new awareness of the fact of religious plurality. Religions do not merely exist, or simply survive. In some cases they give clear evidence of a revival. They continue to inspire and influence the lives of millions of their adherents. In the present context of religious plurality, the important role played by religious traditions cannot be overlooked.

b) Interreligious dialogue between Christians and followers of other religious traditions, as envisaged by the Second Vatican Council, is only gradually coming to be understood. Its practice remains hesitant in some places. The situation differs from country to country. It can depend on the size of the Christian community, on which other religious traditions are present, and on various other cultural, social and political factors. A further examination of the question may help to stimulate dialogue.

c) The practice of dialogue raises problems in the minds of many. There are those who would seem to think, erroneously, that in the Church's mission today dialogue should simply replace proclamation. At the other extreme, some fail to see the value of interreligious dialogue. Yet others are perplexed and ask: if interreligious dialogue has become so important, has the proclamation of the Gospel message lost its urgency? Has the effort to bring people into the community of the Church become secondary or even superfluous? There is a need therefore for doctrinal and pastoral guidance to which this document wishes to contribute, without pretending to answer fully the many and complex questions which arise in this connection.

As this text was in its final stages of preparation for publication, the Holy Father, Pope John Paul II, offered to the Church his Encyclical Letter *Redemptoris Missio* in which he addressed these questions and many more. The present document spells out in greater detail the teaching of the Encyclical on dialogue and its relationship to proclamation (cf. *Redemptoris Missio*, 55-57). It is therefore to be read in the light of this Encyclical.

5. The World Day of Prayer for Peace in Assisi, on 27 October 1986, held at the initiative of Pope John Paul II, provides another stimulus for reflection. Both on the day itself and after, especially in his address to the Cardinals and to the Roman Curia in December, 1986, the Holy Father explained the meaning of the Assisi celebration. He underlined the fundamental unity of the human race, in its origin and its destiny, and the role of the Church as an effective sign of this unity. He brought out forcibly the significance of interreligious dialogue, while at the same time reaffirming the Church's duty to announce Jesus Christ to the world.[2]

6. The following year, in his address to the members of the Plenary Assembly of the Pontifical Council for Interreligious Dialogue, Pope John Paul II declared: "Just as interreligious dialogue is one element in the mission of the Church, the proclamation of God's saving work in Our Lord Jesus Christ is another . . . There can be no question of choosing one and ignoring or rejecting the other."[3] The lead given by the Pope encourages us to give further attention to the present theme.

7. This document is addressed to all Catholics, particularly to all who have a leadership role in the community or are engaged in formation work. It is offered as well for the consideration of Christians belonging to other Churches or ecclesial communities who themselves have been reflecting on the questions it raises.[4] It is hoped that it will receive attention also from the followers of other religious traditions.

Before proceeding it will be useful to clarify the terms being used in this document.

8. *Evangelizing mission,* or more simply *evangelization,* refers to the mission of the Church in its totality. In the Apostolic Exhortation *Evangelii Nuntiandi* the term evangelization is taken in different ways. It means "to bring the Good News into all areas of humanity, and through its impact, to transform that humanity from within, making it new" (EN, 18). Thus, through evangelization the Church "seeks to convert solely through the divine power of the Message she proclaims, both the personal and collective consciences of people, the activities in which they engage, their ways of life, and the actual milieux in which they live" (EN, 18). The Church accomplishes her *evangelizing mission* through a variety of activities. Hence there is a broad concept of evangelization. Yet in the same document, evangelization is also taken more specifically to mean "the clear and unambiguous proclamation of the Lord Jesus" (EN, 22). The Exhortation states that "this proclamation—*kerygma,* preaching or catechesis—occupies such an important place in evangelization that it has often become synonymous with it; and yet it is only one aspect of evangelization" (EN, 22). In this document the term evangelizing mission is used for evangelization in its broad sense, while the more specific understanding is expressed by the term *proclamation.*

9. *Dialogue* can be understood in different ways. Firstly, at the purely human level, it means reciprocal communication, leading to a common goal or, at a deeper level, to interpersonal communion. Secondly, dialogue can be taken as an attitude of respect and friendship, which permeates or should permeate all those activities constituting the evangelizing mission of the Church. This can appropriately be called "the spirit of dialogue." Thirdly, in the context of religious plurality, dialogue means "all positive and constructive interreligious relations with individuals and communities of other faiths which are directed at mutual understanding and enrichment" (DM, 3), in obedience to truth and respect for freedom. It includes both witness and the exploration of respective religious convictions. It is in this third sense that the present document uses the term dialogue for one of the integral elements of the Church's evangelizing mission.

10. *Proclamation* is the communication of the Gospel message, the mystery of salvation realized by God for all in Jesus Christ by the power of the Spirit. It is an invitation to a commitment of faith in Jesus Christ and to entry through baptism into the community of believers which is the Church. This proclamation can be solemn and public, as for instance on the day of Pentecost (cf. Acts 2:5-41), or a simple private conversation (cf. Acts 8:30-38). It leads naturally to catechesis which aims at deepening this faith. Proclamation is the foundation, center, and summit of evangelization (cf. EN, 27).

11. Included in the idea of *conversion* there is always a general movement towards God, "the humble and penitent return of the heart to God in the desire to submit one's life more generously to him" (DM, 37). More specifically, conversion may refer to a change of religious adherence, and particularly to embracing the Christian faith. When the term conversion is used in this document, the context will show which sense is intended.

12. The terms *religions* or *religious traditions* are used here in a generic and analogical sense. They cover those religions which, with Christianity, are wont to refer back to the faith of Abraham,[5] as well as the religious traditions of Asia, Africa, and elsewhere.

13. Interreligious dialogue ought to extend to all religions and their followers.

This document, however, will not treat of dialogue with the followers of "New Religious Movements" due to the diversity of situations which these movements present and the need for discernment on the human and religious values which each contains.[6]

I. INTERRELIGIOUS DIALOGUE

A. CHRISTIAN APPROACH TO RELIGIOUS TRADITIONS

14. A just appraisal of other religious traditions normally presupposes close contact with them. This implies, besides theoretical knowledge, practical experience of interreligious dialogue with the followers of these traditions. Nevertheless, it is also true that a correct theological evaluation of these traditions, at least in general terms, is a necessary presupposition for interreligious dialogue. These traditions are to be approached with great sensitivity, on account of the spiritual and human values enshrined in them. They command our respect because over the centuries they have borne witness to the efforts to find answers "to those profound mysteries of the human condition" (*Nostra Aetate*, 1) and have given expression to the religious experience and the longings of millions of their adherents, and they continue to do so today.

15. The Second Vatican Council has given the lead for such a positive assessment. The exact meaning of what the Council affirms needs to be carefully and accurately ascertained. The Council reaffirms the traditional doctrine according to which salvation in Jesus Christ is, in a mysterious way, a reality open to all persons of good will. A clear enunciation of this basic conviction in Vatican II is found in the Constitution *Gaudium et Spes*. The Council teaches that Christ, the New Adam, through the mystery of his incarnation, death and resurrection, is at work in each human person to bring about interior renewal:

> This holds true not for Christians only but also for all persons of good will in whose hearts grace is active invisibly. For since Christ died for all, and since all are in fact called to one and the same destiny, which is divine, we must hold that the Holy Spirit offers to all the possibility of being made partners, in a way known to God, in the Paschal mystery (GS, 22).

16. The Council proceeds further. Making its own the vision and the terminology of some early Church Fathers, *Nostra Aetate* speaks of the presence in these traditions of "a ray of that Truth which enlightens all" (*Nostra Aetate*, 2). *Ad Gentes* recognizes the presence of "seeds of the word", and points to "the riches which a generous God has distributed among the nations" (no. 11). Again, *Lumen Gentium* refers to the good which is "found sown" not only "in minds and hearts," but also "in the rites and customs of peoples" (no. 17).

17. These few references suffice to show that the Council has openly acknowledged the presence of positive values not only in the religious life of individual believers of other religious traditions, but also in the religious traditions to which they belong. It attributed these values to the active presence of God through his Word, pointing also to the universal action of the Spirit: "Without doubt," *Ad Gentes* affirms, "the Holy Spirit was at work in the world before Christ was glorified" (no. 4). From this it can be seen that these elements, as a preparation for the Gospel (cf. *Lumen Gentium*, 16), have played and do still play a providential role

in the divine economy of salvation. This recognition impels the Church to enter into "dialogue and collaboration" (*Nostra Aetate,* 2; cf. *Gaudium et Spes,* 92-93): "Let Christians, while witnessing to their own faith and way of life, acknowledge, preserve and encourage the spiritual and moral good found among non-Christians, as well as their social and cultural values" (*Nostra Aetate,* 2).

18. The Council is not unaware of the necessity of the missionary activity of the Church in order to perfect in Christ these elements found in other religions. The Council states very clearly: "Whatever truth and grace are to be found among the nations, as a sort of secret presence of God, this activity frees from all taint of evil and restores to Christ its Maker, who overthrows the devil's domain and wards off the manifold malice of vice. And so, whatever good is found to be sown in the hearts and minds of men, or in the rites and cultures peculiar to various peoples, is not lost. More than that, it is healed, ennobled, and perfected for the glory of God, the shame of the demon, and the bliss of men" (*Ad Gentes,* 9).

19. The Old Testament testifies that from the beginning of creation God made a Covenant with all peoples (Gen 1-11). This shows that there is but one history of salvation for the whole of humankind. The Covenant with Noah, the man who "walked with God" (Gen 6:9), is symbolic of the divine intervention in the history of the nations. Non-Israelite figures of the Old Testament are seen in the New Testament as belonging to this one history of salvation. Abel, Enoch and Noah are proposed as models of faith (cf. Heb 11:4-7). They knew, adored and believed in the one true God who is identical with the God who revealed himself to Abraham and Moses. The Gentile High Priest Melchisedek blesses Abraham, the father of all believers (cf. Heb 7:1-17). It is this history of salvation which sees its final fulfillment in Jesus Christ in whom is established the new and definitive Covenant for all peoples.

20. The religious consciousness of Israel is characterized by a deep awareness of its unique status as God's Chosen People. This election, accompanied by a process of formation and continuous exhortations to preserve the purity of monotheism, constitutes a mission. The prophets continually insist on loyalty and fidelity to the One True God and speak about the promised Messiah. And yet these prophets, particularly at the time of the Exile, bring a universal perspective, for God's salvation is understood to extend beyond and through Israel to the nations. Thus Isaiah foretells that in the final days the nations will stream to the house of the Lord, and they will say: "Come, let us go up to the mountain of the Lord, to the house of the God of Jacob; that he may teach us his ways and that we may walk in his paths" (Is 2:3). It is also said that "all the ends of the earth shall see the salvation of our God" (Is 52:10). In the Wisdom literature also, which bears witness to cultural exchanges between Israel and its neighbors, the action of God in the whole universe is clearly affirmed. It goes beyond the boundaries of the Chosen People to touch both the history of nation and the lives of individuals.

21. Turning to the New Testament, we see that Jesus professes to have come to gather the lost sheep of Israel (cf. Mt 15:24) and forbids his disciples for the moment to turn to the Gentiles (cf. Mt 10:5). He nevertheless displays an open attitude towards men and women who do not belong to the chosen people of Israel. He enters into dialogue with them and recognizes the good that is in them. He marvels at the centurion's readiness to believe, saying that he has found no such faith in Israel (cf. Mt 8:5-13). He performs miracles of healing for "foreigners" (cf. Mk 7:24-30; Mt 15:21-28), and these miracles are signs of the coming of the Kingdom. He converses with the Samaritan woman and speaks to her of a time when worship

will not be restricted to any one particular place, but when true worshippers will "worship the Father in spirit and truth" (Jn 4:23). Jesus is thus opening up a new horizon, beyond the purely local, to a universality which is both Christological and Pneumatological in character. For the new sanctuary is now the body of the Lord Jesus (cf. Jn 2:21) whom the Father has raised up in the power of the Spirit.

22. Jesus' message, then, proved by the witness of his life, is that in his own person the Kingdom of God is breaking through to the world. At the beginning of his public ministry, in Galilee of the nations, he can say: "The time has come, and the Kingdom of God is close at hand." He also indicates the conditions for entry into this Kingdom: "Repent, and believe the Good News" (Mk 1:15). This message is not confined only to those who belong to the specially chosen people. Jesus in fact explicitly announces the entry of the Gentiles into the Kingdom of God (cf. Mt 8:10-11; Mt 11:20-24; Mt 25:31-32, 34), a Kingdom which is to be understood as being at one and the same time historical and eschatological. It is both the Father's Kingdom, for the coming of which it is necessary to pray (cf. Mt 6:10), and Jesus' own Kingdom, since Jesus openly declares himself to be king (cf. Jn 18:33-37). In fact in Jesus Christ, the Son of God made man, we have the fullness of revelation and salvation and the fulfillment of the desires of the nations.

23. References in the New Testament to the religious life of the Gentiles and to their religious traditions may appear to be contrasting, but can be seen as complementary. There is, on the one hand, the negative verdict of the Letter to the Romans against those who have failed to recognize God in his creation and have fallen into idolatry and depravity (cf. Rom 1:18-32). On the other hand, the Acts testify to Paul's positive and open attitude towards the Gentiles, both in his discourse to the Lycaonians (cf. Acts 14:8-18) and in his Areopagus speech at Athens, in which he praised their religious spirit and announced to them the one whom unknowingly they revered as the "unknown God" (cf. Acts 17:22-34). Nor must it be forgotten that the Wisdom tradition is applied in the New Testament to Jesus Christ as the Wisdom of God, the Word of God that enlightens every man (cf: Jn 1:9) and who in his Incarnation pitches his tent among us (cf. Jn 1:14).

24. The post-Biblical tradition also contains contrasting data. Negative judgements on the religious world of their time can easily be gleaned from the writings of the Fathers. Yet the early tradition shows a remarkable openness. A number of Church Fathers take up the sapiential tradition reflected in the New Testament. In particular, writers of the second century and the first part of the third century such as Justin, Irenaeus and Clement of Alexandria, either explicitly or in an equivalent way, speak about the "seeds" sown by the Word of God in the nations.[7] Thus it can be said that for them, prior to and outside the Christian dispensation, God has already, in an incomplete way, manifested himself. This manifestation of the *Logos* is an adumbration of the full revelation in Jesus Christ to which it points.

25. In fact, these early Fathers offer what may be called a theology of history. History becomes salvation history, inasmuch as through it God progressively manifests himself and communicates with humankind. This process of divine manifestation and communication reaches its climax in the incarnation of the Son of God in Jesus Christ. For this reason, Irenaeus distinguishes four "covenants" given by God to the human race: in Adam, in Noah, in Moses, and in Jesus Christ.[8] The same patristic current, whose importance is not to be underestimated, may be said to culminate in Augustine who in his later works stressed the universal presence and influence of the mystery of Christ even before the Incarnation. In fulfillment of his plan of salvation, God, in his Son, has reached out to the whole of humankind.

Thus, in a certain sense, Christianity already existed "at the beginning of the human race."⁹

26. It was to this early Christian vision of history that the Second Vatican Council made reference. After the Council, the Church's Magisterium, especially that of Pope John Paul II, has proceeded further in the same direction. First the Pope gives explicit recognition to the operative presence of the Holy Spirit in the life of the members of other religious traditions, as when in *Redemptor Hominis* he speaks of their "firm belief" as being "an effect of the Spirit of truth operating outside the visible confines of the Mystical Body" (no. 6). In *Dominum et Vivificantem,* he takes a further step, affirming the universal action of the Holy Spirit in the world before the Christian dispensation, to which it was ordained, and referring to the universal action of the same Spirit today, even outside the visible body of the Church (cf. no. 53).

27. In his address to the Roman Curia after the World Day of Prayer for Peace in Assisi, Pope John Paul II stressed once more the universal presence of the Holy Spirit, stating that "every authentic prayer is called forth by the Holy Spirit, who is mysteriously present in the heart of every person," Christian or otherwise. But again, in the same discourse, the Pope, going beyond an individual perspective, articulated the main elements which together can be seen as constituting the theological basis for a positive approach to other religious traditions and the practice of interreligious dialogue.

28. First comes the fact that the whole of humankind forms one family, due to the common origin of all men and women, created by God in his own image. Correspondingly, all are called to a common destiny, the fullness of life in God. Moreover, there is but one plan of salvation for humankind, with its center in Jesus Christ, who in his incarnation "has united himself in a certain manner to every person" (*Redemptor Hominis,* 13; cf. *Gaudium et Spes,* 22.2). Finally there needs to be mentioned the active presence of the Holy Spirit in the religious life of the members of the other religious traditions. From all this the Pope concludes to a "mystery of unity" which was manifested clearly at Assisi, "in spite of the differences between religious professions."¹⁰

29. From this mystery of unity it follows that all men and women who are saved share, though differently, in the same mystery of salvation in Jesus Christ through his Spirit. Christians know this through their faith, while others remain unaware that Jesus Christ is the source of their salvation. The mystery of salvation reaches out to them, in a way known to God, through the invisible action of the Spirit of Christ. Concretely, it will be in the sincere practice of what is good in their own religious traditions and by following the dictates of their conscience that the members of other religions respond positively to God's invitation and receive salvation in Jesus Christ, even while they do not recognize or acknowledge him as their saviour (cf. *Ad Gentes,* 3, 9, 11).

30. The fruits of the Spirit of God in the personal life of individuals, whether Christian or otherwise, are easily discernible (cf. Gal 5:22-23). To identify in other religious traditions elements of grace capable of sustaining the positive response of their members to God's invitation is much more difficult. It requires a discernment for which criteria have to be established. Sincere individuals marked by the Spirit of God have certainly put their imprint on the elaboration and the development of their respective religious traditions. It does not follow, however, that everything in them is good.

31. To say that the other religious traditions include elements of grace does not

imply that everything in them is the result of grace. For sin has been at work in the world, and so religious traditions, notwithstanding their positive values, reflect the limitations of the human spirit, sometimes inclined to choose evil. An open and positive approach to other religious traditions cannot overlook the contradictions which may exist between them and Christian revelation. It must, where necessary, recognize that there is incompatibility between some fundamental elements of the Christian religion and some aspects of such traditions.

32. This means that, while entering with an open mind into dialogue with the followers of other religious traditions, Christians may have also to challenge them in a peaceful spirit with regard to the content of their belief. But Christians, too, must allow themselves to be questioned. Notwithstanding the fullness of God's revelation in Jesus Christ, the way Christians sometimes understand their religion and practice it may be in need of purification.

B. THE PLACE OF INTERRELIGIOUS DIALOGUE
IN THE EVANGELIZING MISSION OF THE CHURCH

33. The Church has been willed by God and instituted by Christ to be, in the fullness of time, the sign and instrument of the divine plan of salvation (cf. *Lumen Gentium,* 1), the center of which is the mystery of Christ. She is the "universal sacrament of salvation" (LG, 48)) and is "necessary for salvation" (LG, 14). The Lord Jesus himself inaugurated her mission "by preaching the good news, that is, the coming of God's Kingdom" (LG, 5).

34. The relationship between the Church and the Kingdom is mysterious and complex. As Vatican II teaches, "principally the Kingdom is revealed in the person of Christ himself." Yet the Church, which has received from the Lord Jesus the mission of proclaiming the Kingdom" is, on earth, the seed and the beginning of that Kingdom." At the same time the Church "slowly grows to maturity (and) longs for the completed Kingdom" (*Lumen Gentium,* 5). Thus "the Kingdom is insepa-rable from the Church, because both are inseparable from the person and work of Jesus himself . . . It is therefore not possible to separate the Church from the Kingdom as if the first belonged exclusively to the imperfect realm of history, while the second would be the perfect eschatological fulfillment of the divine plan of salvation."[11]

35. To the Church, as the sacrament in which the Kingdom of God is present "in mystery," are related or oriented (*ordinantur*) (cf. *Lumen Gentium,* 16) the members of other religious traditions who, inasmuch as they respond to God's calling as perceived by their conscience, are saved in Jesus Christ and thus already share in some way in the reality which is signified by the Kingdom. The Church's mission is to foster "the Kingdom of our Lord and his Christ" (Rev 11:15), at whose service she is placed. Part of her role consists in recognizing that the inchoate reality of this Kingdom can be found also beyond the confines of the Church, for example in the hearts of the followers of other religious traditions, insofar as they live evangelical values and are open to the action of the Spirit. It must be remembered nevertheless that this is indeed an inchoate reality, which needs to find completion through being related to the Kingdom of Christ already present in the Church yet realized fully only in the world to come.

36. The Church on earth is always on pilgrimage. Although she is holy by divine institution, her members are not perfect; they bear the mark of their human limi-tations. Consequently, her transparency as sacrament of salvation is blurred. This

is the reason why the Church herself, "insofar as she is an institution of men here on earth," and not only her members, is constantly in need of renewal and reform (cf. *Unitatis Redintegratio,* 6).

37. With regard to divine Revelation the Council taught that "the most intimate truth which this revelation gives us about God and the salvation of man shines forth in Christ, who is himself both the mediator and the sum total of revelation" (*Dei Verbum,* 2). Faithful to the command received from Christ himself, the apostles handed on this Revelation. Yet "the Tradition that comes from the apostles makes progress in the Church, with the help of the Holy Spirit. There is growth in insight into the realities and words that are being passed on" (*Dei Verbum,* 8). This happens through study and spiritual experience. It also comes about through the teaching of the bishops who have received a sure charism of truth. Thus the Church "is always advancing towards the plenitude of divine truth, until eventually the words of God are fulfilled in her" (*Dei Verbum,* 8). This in no way contradicts the Church's divine institution nor the fullness of God's Revelation in Jesus Christ which has been entrusted to her.

38. Against this background it becomes easier to see why and in what sense interreligious dialogue is an integral element of the Church's evangelizing mission. The foundation of the Church's commitment to dialogue is not merely anthropological but primarily theological. God, in an age-long dialogue, has offered and continues to offer salvation to humankind. In faithfulness to the divine initiative, the Church too must enter into a dialogue of salvation with all men and women.

39. Pope Paul VI taught this clearly in his first Encyclical *Ecclesiam Suam.* Pope John Paul II too has stressed the Church's call to interreligious dialogue and assigned to it the same foundation. Addressing the 1984 Plenary Assembly of the Pontifical Council for Interreligious Dialogue, the Pope declared: "(Interreligious) dialogue is fundamental to the Church, which is called to collaborate in God's plan with her methods of presence, respect and love towards all persons." He went on to call attention to a passage from *Ad Gentes:* "closely united to men in their life and work, Christ's disciples hope to render to others true witness of Christ and to work for this salvation, even where they are not able to proclaim Christ fully" (*Ad Gentes,* 12). He prefaced this by saying: "dialogue finds its place within the Church's salvific mission; for this reason it is a dialogue of salvation."[12]

40. In this dialogue of salvation, Christians and others are called to collaborate with the Spirit of the Risen Lord who is universally present and active. Interreligious dialogue does not merely aim at mutual understanding and friendly relations. It reaches a much deeper level, that of the spirit, where exchange and sharing consist in a mutual witness to one's beliefs and a common exploration of one's respective religious convictions. In dialogue Christians and others are invited to deepen their religious commitment, to respond with increasing sincerity to God's personal call and gracious self-gift which, as our faith tells us, always passes through the mediation of Jesus Christ and the work of his Spirit.

41. Given this aim, a deeper conversion of all towards God, interreligious dialogue possesses its own validity. In this process of conversion "the decision may be made to leave one's previous spiritual or religious situation in order to direct oneself towards another" (DM, 37). Sincere dialogue implies, on the one hand, mutual acceptance of differences, or even of contradictions, and on the other, respect for the free decision of persons taken according to the dictates of their conscience (cf. DH, 2). The teaching of the Council must nevertheless be borne in mind: "All men are bound to seek the truth, especially in what concerns God and his Church, and to embrace it and to hold on to it as they come to know it" (DH, 1).

C. FORMS OF DIALOGUE

42. There exist different forms of interreligious dialogue. It may be useful to recall those mentioned by the 1984 document of the Pontifical Council for Interreligious Dialogue (cf. DM, 28-35). It spoke of four forms, without claiming to establish among them any order of priority:

a) The *dialogue of life,* where people strive to live in an open and neighborly spirit, sharing their joys and sorrows, their human problems and preoccupations.

b) The *dialogue of action,* in which Christians and others collaborate for the integral development and liberation of people.

c) The *dialogue of theological exchange,* where specialists seek to deepen their understanding of their respective religious heritages, and to appreciate each other's spiritual values.

d) The *dialogue of religious experience,* where persons, rooted in their own religious traditions, share their spiritual riches, for instance with regard to prayer and contemplation, faith and ways of searching for God or the Absolute.

43. One should not lose sight of this variety of forms of dialogue. Were it to be reduced to theological exchange, dialogue might easily be taken as a sort of luxury item in the Church's mission, a domain reserved for specialists. On the contrary, guided by the Pope and their bishops, all local Churches, and all the members of these Churches, are called to dialogue, though not all in the same way. It can be seen, moreover, that the different forms are interconnected. Contacts in daily life and common commitment to action will normally open the door for cooperation in promoting human and spiritual values; they may also eventually lead to the dialogue of religious experience in response to the great questions which the circumstances of life do not fail to arouse in the minds of people (cf. *Nostra Aetate,* 2). Exchanges at the level of religious experience can give more life to theological discussions. These in turn can enlighten experiences and encourage closer contacts.

44. The importance of dialogue for integral development, social justice and human liberation needs to be stressed. Local Churches are called upon, as witnesses to Christ, to commit themselves in this respect in an unselfish and impartial manner. There is need to stand up for human rights, proclaim the demands of justice, and denounce injustice not only when their own members are victimized, but independently of the religious allegiance of the victims. There is need also to join together in trying to solve the great problems facing society and the world, as well as in education for justice and peace.

45. Another context in which interreligious dialogue seems urgent today is that of culture. Culture is broader than religion. According to one concept, religion can be said to represent the transcendent dimension of culture and in a certain way its soul. Religions have certainly contributed to the progress of culture and the construction of a more humane society. Yet religious practices have sometimes had an alienating influence upon cultures. Today, an autonomous secular culture can play a critical role with regard to negative elements in particular religions. The question is complex, for several religious traditions may coexist within one and the same cultural framework while, conversely, the same religion may find expression in different cultural contexts. Again, religious differences may lead to distinct cultures in the same region.

46. The Christian message supports many values found and lived in the wisdom and the rich heritage of cultures, but it may also put in question culturally accepted values. Attentive dialogue implies recognizing and accepting cultural values which

respect the human person's dignity and transcendent destiny. It may happen, nevertheless, that some aspects of traditional Christian cultures are challenged by the local cultures of other religious traditions (cf. EN, 20). In these complex relationships between culture and religion, interreligious dialogue at the level of culture takes on considerable importance. Its aim is to eliminate tensions and conflicts, and potential confrontations by a better understanding among the various religious cultures of any given region. It may contribute to purifying cultures from any dehumanizing elements, and thus be an agent of transformation. It can also help to uphold certain traditional cultural values which are under threat from modernity and the levelling down which indiscriminate internationalization may bring with it.

D. DISPOSITIONS FOR INTERRELIGIOUS DIALOGUE AND ITS FRUITS

47. Dialogue requires, on the part of Christians as well as of the followers of other traditions, a balanced attitude. They should be neither ingenuous nor overly critical, but open and receptive. Unselfishness and impartiality, acceptance of differences and of possible contradictions, have already been mentioned. The will to engage together in commitment to the truth and the readiness to allow oneself to be transformed by the encounter are other dispositions required.

48. This does not mean that in entering into dialogue the partners should lay aside their respective religious convictions. The opposite is true: the sincerity of interreligious dialogue requires that each enters into it with the integrity of his or her own faith. At the same time, while remaining firm in their belief that in Jesus Christ, the only mediator between God and man (cf. 1 Tim 2:4-6), the fullness of revelation has been given to them, Christians must remember that God has also manifested himself in some way to the followers of other religious traditions. Consequently, it is with receptive minds that they approach the convictions and values of others.

49. Moreover, the fullness of truth received in Jesus Christ does not give individual Christians the guarantee that they have grasped that truth fully. In the last analysis, truth is not a thing we possess, but a person by whom we must allow ourselves to be possessed. This is an unending process. While keeping their identity intact, Christians must be prepared to learn and to receive from and through others the positive values of their traditions. Through dialogue, they may be moved to give up ingrained prejudices, to revise preconceived ideas, and even sometimes to allow the understanding of their faith to be purified.

50. If Christians cultivate such openness and allow themselves to be tested, they will be able to gather the fruits of dialogue. They will discover with admiration all that God's action through Jesus Christ in his Spirit has accomplished and continues to accomplish in the world and in the whole of humankind. Far from weakening their own faith, true dialogue will deepen it. They will become increasingly aware of their Christian identity and perceive more clearly the distinctive elements of the Christian message. Their faith will gain new dimensions as they discover the active presence of the mystery of Jesus Christ beyond the visible boundaries of the Church and of the Christian fold.

E. OBSTACLES TO DIALOGUE

51. Already on a purely human level it is not easy to practice dialogue. Interreligious dialogue is even more difficult. It is important to be aware of the obstacles

which may arise. Some would apply equally to the members of all religious traditions and impede the success of dialogue. Others may affect some religious traditions more specifically and make it difficult for a process of dialogue to be initiated. Some of the more important obstacles will be mentioned here.

52. a) Insufficient grounding in one's own faith.

b) Insufficient knowledge and understanding of the belief and practices of other religions, leading to a lack of appreciation for their significance and even at times to misrepresentation.

c) Cultural differences, arising from different levels of instruction, or from the use of different languages.

d) Socio-political factors or some burdens of the past.

e) Wrong understanding of the meaning of terms such as conversion, baptism, dialogue, etc.

f) Self-sufficiency, lack of openness leading to defensive or aggressive attitudes.

g) A lack of conviction with regard to the value of interreligious dialogue, which some may see as a task reserved to specialists, and others as a sign of weakness or even a betrayal of the faith.

h) Suspicion about the other's motives in dialogue.

i) A polemical spirit when expressing religious convictions.

j) Intolerance, which is often aggravated by association with political, economic, racial and ethnic factors, a lack of reciprocity in dialogue which can lead to frustration.

k) Certain features of the present religious climate, e.g., growing materialism, religious indifference, and the multiplication of religious sects, which creates confusion and raises new problems.

53. Many of these obstacles arise from a lack of understanding of the true nature and goal of interreligious dialogue. These need therefore to be constantly explained. Much patience is required. It must be remembered that the Church's commitment to dialogue is not dependent on success in achieving mutual understanding and enrichment; rather it flows from God's initiative in entering into a dialogue with humankind and from the example of Jesus Christ whose life, death and resurrection gave to that dialogue its ultimate expression.

54. Moreover, the obstacles, though real, should not lead us to underestimate the possibilities of dialogue or to overlook the results already achieved. There has been a growth in mutual understanding, and in active cooperation. Dialogue has had a positive impact on the Church herself. Other religions have also been led through dialogue to renewal and greater openness. Interreligious dialogue has made it possible for the Church to share Gospel values with others. So despite the difficulties, the Church's commitment to dialogue remains firm and irreversible.

II. PROCLAIMING JESUS CHRSIST

A. THE MANDATE FROM THE RISEN LORD

55. The Lord Jesus gave to his disciples a mandate to proclaim the Gospel. This fact is reported by all four Gospels and by the Acts of the Apostles. There are however certain nuances in the different versions. In Matthew Jesus says to his disciples: "All authority in heaven and earth has been given to me. Go therefore and make disciples of all nations, baptizing them in the name of the Father and of the Son and of the Holy Spirit, teaching them to observe all that I have commanded

you; and lo, I am with you always, to the close of the age" (Mt 28: 18-20).

In Mark the command is given more succinctly: "Go into all the world and preach the Gospel to the whole creation. He who believes and is baptized will be saved; but he who does not believe will be condemned" (Mk 16:15-16).

In Luke the expression is less direct: "Thus it is written that the Christ should suffer and on the third day rise from the dead, and that repentance and forgiveness of sins should be preached in his name to all the nations, beginning from Jerusalem. You are witnesses of these things" (Lk 24:46-48).

In Acts the extent of this witness is emphasized: "But you shall receive power when the Holy Spirit has come upon you; and you shall be my witnesses in Jerusalem and in all Judea and Samaria and to the end of the earth" (Acts 1:8).

In John again the mission is expressed differently: "As you sent me into the world, I have sent them into the world" (Jn 17:18); "As the Father sent me, so am I sending you" (Jn 20:21).

Announcing the Good News to all, witnessing, making disciples, baptizing, teaching, all these aspects enter into the Church's evangelizing mission, yet they need to be seen in the light of the mission accomplished by Jesus himself, the mission he received from the Father.

56. Jesus proclaimed the Gospel from God saying: "The time is fulfilled, and the Kingdom of God is at hand; repent and believe in the Gospel" (Mk 1:14-15). This passage sums up the ministry of Jesus. Jesus does not proclaim this Good News of the Kingdom by word alone, but also by his actions, attitudes and options, indeed by means of his whole life and finally through his death and resurrection. His parables, his miracles, the exorcisms he works, all are related to the Kingdom of God which he announces. This Kingdom moreover is not just something to be preached, quite unrelated to his own person. Jesus makes it clear that it is through him and in him that the Reign of God is breaking through into the world (cf. Lk 17:20-22), that in him the Kingdom has already come upon us, even though it still needs to grow to its fullness.[13]

57. His teaching is confirmed by his life. "Even if you refuse to believe in me, at least believe in the work I do" (Jn 10:38). Similarly, his deeds are explained by his words which spring from his awareness of being one with the Father. "I tell you most solemnly, the Son can do nothing by himself, he can only do what he sees the Father doing" (Jn 5:19). In the trial before Pilate, Jesus says that he has come into the world "to bear witness to the truth" (Jn 18:37). The Father also bears witness to him, both in words spoken from heaven and in the mighty works, the signs, which Jesus is enabled to perform. It is the Spirit who "seals" Jesus' witness, authenticating it as true (cf. Jn 3:32-35).

B. THE ROLE OF THE CHURCH

58. It is against this background that the mandate given by the Risen Lord to the Apostolic Church needs to be understood. The Church's mission is to proclaim the Kingdom of God established on earth in Jesus Christ, through his life, death and resurrection, as God's decisive and universal offer of salvation to the world. For this reason "there is no true evangelization if the name, the teaching, the life, the promises, the Kingdom and the mystery of Jesus of Nazareth, the Son of God are not proclaimed" (EN, 22). There is continuity between the Kingdom preached by Jesus and the mystery of Christ announced by the Church.

59. Continuing the mission of Jesus, the Church is "the seed and beginning" of

the kingdom (cf. LG, 5). She is at the service of this Kingdom and "witnesses" to it. This includes witness to faith in Christ, the Saviour, since this is the very heart of the Church's own faith and life. In the history of the Church, all the Apostles were "witnesses" to the life, death and resurrection of Christ.[14] Witness is given by words and deeds which are not to be set one against the other. The deed validates the word, but without the word the deed may be misinterpreted. The witness of the Apostles, both in words and signs, is subordinate to the Holy Spirit, sent by the Father to fulfil this talk of witness.[15]

C. THE CONTENT OF PROCLAMATION

60. On the Day of Pentecost, in fulfillment of Christ's promise, the Holy Spirit came down on the Apostles. At that time "there were devout men living in Jerusalem from every nation under heaven" (Acts 2:5) — the list of people present, given in the book of Acts, serves to underline the universal import of this first ecclesial event. In the name of the Eleven Peter addressed those assembled, announcing Jesus, commended by God with miracles and portents, crucified by men but raised to life again by God. He concluded: "For this reason the whole house of Israel can be certain that God has made this Jesus, whom you crucified, both Lord and Christ" (Acts 2:36). This was followed by the invitation to his hearers to repent, to become disciples of Jesus by being baptized in his name for the forgiveness of sins, and thus to receive the gift of the Holy Spirit. A little later, before the Sanhedrin, Peter bore witness to his faith in the risen Christ, stating clearly: "Only in him is there salvation, for of all names in the world given to men this is the only one by which we can be saved" (Acts 4:11-12). The universal nature of the Christian message of salvation is brought out again in the account of the conversion of Cornelius. When Peter witnessed to the life and work of Jesus, from the beginning of his ministry in Galilee right up to his Resurrection, "the Holy Spirit came down on all the listeners" so that those who had accompanied Peter were astonished "that the gift of the Holy Spirit should be poured out on gentiles too" (Acts 10:44-45).

61. The Apostles therefore, following the Pentecost event, present themselves as witnesses to Christ's resurrection (cf. Acts 1:22; 4:33; 5:32-33), or, in a more concise formula, simply as witnesses to Christ (cf. Acts 3:15; 13:31). Nowhere is this clearer than in Paul, "called to be an apostle, set apart for the service of the Gospel" (Rom 1:1), who received from Jesus Christ the "apostolic mission of winning the obedience of faith among all the nations for the honor of his name" (Rom 1:5). Paul preaches "the Gospel that God promised long ago through his prophets in the holy scriptures" (Rom 1:2), the "Gospel of his Son" (Rom 1:9). He preaches a crucified Christ: "a stumbling block to Jews and folly to Gentiles" (1 Cor 1:23; cf. 2:2), "for no other foundation can any one lay than that which is laid" (1 Cor 3:11). The whole message of Paul is, as it were, summed up in his solemn declaration to the Ephesians:

I, who am less than the least of all God's holy people, have been entrusted with this special grace, of proclaiming to the gentiles this unfathomable treasure of Christ and of throwing light on the inner workings of the mystery kept hidden through all the ages in God, the Creator of everything," [this many-sided wisdom of God which he has now revealed through the Church] "according to the plan which he had formed from all eternity in Christ Jesus our Lord" (Eph 3:8-11).

The same message is found in the Pastoral Letters. God

> desires all men to be saved and to come to the knowledge of the truth. For there is one God, and there is one mediator between God and men the man Christ Jesus, who gave himself as a ransom for all (1 Tim 2:4-6).

This "mystery of our religion" which is "very deep" finds expression in a liturgical fragment: "He was manifested in the flesh, vindicated in the spirit, seen by angels, preached among the nations, believed on in the world, taken up in glory" (1 Tim 3:16).

62. Turning to the apostle John, we find that he presents himself above all as a witness, one who has seen Jesus and discovered his mystery (cf. Jn 13:23-25; 21:24). "We are declaring to you what we have seen and heard"—of the Word of life— "so that you too may share our life" (1 Jn 1:3). "We ourselves have seen and testify that the Father sent his Son as saviour of the world" (1 Jn 4:14). Central to the message of John is the Incarnation: "The Word became flesh, he lived among us, and we saw his glory, the glory that he has from the Father as only Son of the Father, full of grace and truth" (Jn 1:14). Through Jesus, therefore, the Father can be seen (cf. Jn 14:9) he is the way to the Father (cf. Jn 14:6). Lifted up on the cross he draws all people to himself (cf. Jn 12:32). He is truly "the Saviour of the World" (Jn 4:42).

63. "Proclaim the word", Paul writes to Timothy (2 Tim 4:2). The content of this word is expressed in different ways: it is the Kingdom (cf. Acts 20:25), the Gospel of the Kingdom (cf. Mt 24:14), the Gospel of God (cf. Mk 1:14; 1 Thess 2:9). But these different formulations really mean the same thing: to preach Jesus (cf. Acts 9:20; 19:13), to preach Christ (cf. Acts 8:5). Just as Jesus spoke God's own words (cf. Jn 3:34), so the apostles preach the word of God, for Jesus whom they preach is the Word.

The Christian message therefore is a powerful one, to be welcomed for what it really is, "not the word of any human being, but God's word" (1 Thess 2:13). Accepted in faith the word will be "alive and active," cutting "more incisively than any two-edged sword" (Heb 4:12). It will be a word which purifies (cf. Jn 15:3), it will be the source of the truth which brings freedom (cf. Jn 8:31-32). The word will become an interior presence: "Anyone who loves me will keep my word, and my Father will love him, and we shall come to him and make a home in him" (Jn 14:23). This is the word of God which is to be proclaimed by Christians.

D. THE PRESENCE AND POWER OF THE HOLY SPIRIT

64. In proclaiming this word, the Church knows that she can rely on the Holy Spirit, who both prompts her proclamation and leads the hearers to obedience of faith.

It is the Holy Spirit who today, just as at the beginning of the Church, acts in every evangelizer who allows himself to be possessed and led by him. The Holy Spirit places on his lips the words which he could not find by himself, and at the same time the Holy Spirit predisposes the soul of the hearer to be open and receptive to the Good News and to the Kingdom being proclaimed (EN, 75).

65. The force of the Spirit is attested by the fact that the most powerful witness is often given precisely at that point where the disciple is most helpless, incapable of word or deed, and yet remains faithful. As Paul says:

I will all the more gladly boast of my weaknesses, that the power of Christ may rest upon me. For the sake of Christ, then, I am content with weaknesses, insults, hardships, persecutions, and calamities; for when I am weak, then I am strong (2 Cor 12:9-10).

The witness by which the Spirit brings men and women to know Jesus as Lord is no human achievement but God's own work.

E. THE URGENCY OF PROCLAMATION

66. Pope Paul VI said in his exhortation *Evangelii Nuntiandi*:

The presentation of the Gospel message is not optional for the Church. It is her duty, by command of the Lord Jesus, so that men may believe and be saved. This message is indeed a necessary one. It is unique and irreplaceable. It allows of neither indifference, syncretism, nor compromise, for it concerns the salvation of mankind (EN, 5).

The urgency had been indicated by Paul.

How then are they to call upon him if they have not come to believe in him? And how can they believe in him if they have never heard of him? And how will they hear of him unless there is a preacher for them? ... But it is in that way that faith comes, from hearing, and that means hearing the word of Christ (Rom 10:14ff).

"This law, set down one day by the Apostle Paul, maintains its full force today ... it is through listening to the Word that one is led to believe" (EN, 42). It is fitting to remember also that other word of Paul: "For if I preach the Gospel, that gives me no ground for boasting. For necessity is laid upon me. Woe to me if I do not preach the Gospel" (1 Cor 9:16).

67. Proclamation is a response to the human aspiration for salvation. Wherever God opens a door for the word in order to declare the mystery of Christ, then the living God and he whom he has sent for the salvation of all, Jesus Christ, are confidently and perseveringly proclaimed to all men. And this is in order that non-Christians, whose hearts are being opened by the Holy Spirit, might, while believing, freely turn to the Lord who, since he is "the Way, the Truth, and the Life" (Jn 14:6), will satisfy all their inner hopes, or rather infinitely surpass them (AG, 13).

F. THE MANNER OF PROCLAMATION

68. While proclaiming the message of God in Jesus Christ, the evangelizing Church must always remember that her task is not exercised in a complete void. For the Holy Spirit, the Spirit of Christ, is present and active among the hearers of the Good News even before the Church's missionary action comes into operation (cf. RH, 12, DV, 53). They may in many cases have already responded implicitly to God's offer of salvation in Jesus Christ, a sign of this being the sincere practice of their own religious traditions, insofar as these contain authentic religious values. They may have already been touched by the Spirit and in some way associated unknowingly to the paschal mystery of Jesus Christ (cf. GS, 22).

69. Mindful of what God has already accomplished in those addressed, the Church seeks to discover the right way to announce the Good News. She takes her lead from divine pedagogy. This means learning from Jesus himself, and observing the times and seasons as prompted by the Spirit. Jesus only progressively revealed to his hearers the meaning of the Kingdom, God's plan of salvation realized in his own mystery. Only gradually, and with infinite care, did he unveil for them the implications of his message, his identity as the Son of God, the scandal of the Cross. Even his closest disciples, as the Gospels testify, reached full faith in their Master only through their Easter experience and the gift of the Spirit. Those who wish to become disciples of Jesus today will pass through the same process of discovery and commitment. Accordingly the Church's proclamation must be both progressive and patient, keeping pace with those who bear the message, respecting their freedom and even their "slowness to believe" (EN, 79).

70. Other qualities must also characterize the Church's proclamation. It should be:

a) Confident, in the power of the Spirit, and in obedience to the mandate received from the Lord.[16]

b) Faithful in the transmission of the teaching received from Christ and preserved in the Church, which is the depository of the Good News to be proclaimed (cf. EN, 15). "Fidelity to the message whose servants we are . . . is a pivotal point of proclamation" (EN, 4). "Evangelization is for no one an individual and isolated act; it is one that is deeply ecclesial" (EN, 60).

c) Humble, in the awareness that the fullness of revelation in Jesus Christ has been received as a free gift (Eph 3:2), and that the messengers of the Gospel do not always fully live up to its demands.

d) Respectful, of the presence and action of the Spirit of God in the hearts of those who listen to the message, in the recognition that the Spirit is the "principal agent of evangelization" (EN, 75).

e) Dialogical, for in proclamation the hearer of the Word is not expected to be a passive receiver. There is progress from the "seeds of the Word" already present in the hearer to the full mystery of salvation in Jesus Christ. The Church must recognize a process of purification and enlightenment in which the Spirit of God opens the mind and heart of the hearer to the obedience of faith.

f) Inculturated, incarnated in the culture and the spiritual tradition of those addressed, so that the message is not only intelligible to them, but is conceived as responding to their deepest aspirations, as truly the Good News they have been longing for (cf; EN, 20, 62).

71. To maintain these qualities the Church must not only bear in mind the circumstances of life and the religious experience of those addressed. She must also live in constant dialogue with her Lord and Master through prayer and penance, meditation and liturgical life, and above all in the celebration of the Eucharist. Only then will both proclamation and celebration of the Gospel message become fully alive.

G. OBSTACLES TO PROCLAMATION

72. The Church's proclamation of the Good News makes serious demands both on the evangelizing Church and her members engaged in evangelization and on those called by God to the obedience of Christian faith. It is no easy task. Some of the principal obstacles she can meet with are mentioned here.

73. Difficulties from within:

a) It can happen that Christian witness does not correspond to belief; there is a gap between word and deed, between the Christian message and the way Christians live it.

b) Christians may fail to proclaim the Gospel through negligence, human respect, or shame, which Saint Paul called "blushing for the Gospel," or because of false ideas about God's plan of salvation (cf. EN, 80).

c) Christians who lack appreciation and respect for other believers and their religious traditions are ill-prepared to proclaim the Gospel to them.

d) In some Christians, an attitude of superiority, which can show itself at the cultural level, might give rise to the supposition that a particular culture is linked with the Christian message and is to be imposed on converts.

74. Difficulties from outside:

a) The weight of history makes proclamation more difficult, as certain methods of evangelization in the past have sometimes aroused fear and suspicion on the part of the followers of other religions.

b) The members of other religions may fear that the Church's evangelizing mission will result in the destruction of their religion and culture.

c) A different conception of human rights or a lack of respect for them in practice can result in a lack of religious freedom.

d) Persecution can render the Church's proclamation especially difficult or well-nigh impossible. It must be remembered, however, that the cross is a source of life: "The blood of martyrs is the seed of Christians."

e) The identification of a particular religion with the national culture or with a political system creates a climate of intolerance.

f) In some places, conversion is forbidden by law or converts to Christianity meet with serious problems, such as ostracism by their religious community of origin, social milieu or cultural environment.

g) In pluralistic contexts, the danger of indifferentism, relativism, or of religious syncretism creates obstacles to the proclamation of the Gospel.

H. PROCLAMATION IN THE EVANGELIZING MISSION OF THE CHURCH

75. The Church's evangelizing mission has sometimes been understood as consisting simply in inviting people to become disciples of Jesus in the Church. Gradually a broader understanding of evangelization has been developed, in which proclamation of the mystery of Christ nevertheless remains central. The Second Vatican Council's decree on the Missionary Activity of the Church, when dealing with missionary work, mentions solidarity with mankind, dialogue and collaboration, before speaking about witness and the preaching of the Gospel (cf. AG, 11-13). The 1974 Synod of Bishops and the Apostolic Exhortation *Evangelii Nuntiandi* which followed it have both taken evangelization in a broad sense. In evangelization, the whole person of the evangelizer is involved: words, actions, witness of life (cf. EN, 21-22). Likewise its aim extends to all that is human, as it seeks to transform human culture and cultures with the power of the Gospel (cf. EN, 18-20). Yet Pope Paul VI made it quite clear that

evangelization will always entail as the simultaneous foundation, core and summit of its dynamism a clear proclamation that in Jesus Christ, the Son of God made man, who died and rose from the dead, salvation is offered to all as a gift of God's kindness and mercy (EN, 27).

It is in this sense that the 1984 document of the Pontifical Council for Interreligious Dialogue lists proclamation among the various elements which make up the Church's evangelizing mission (cf. DM, 13).

76. Still it is useful to point out once again that to proclaim the name of Jesus and to invite people to become his disciples in the Church is a sacred and major duty which the Church cannot neglect. Evangelization would be incomplete without it (EN, 22), for without this central element the others, though in themselves genuine forms of the Church's mission, would lose their cohesion and vitality. It is clear therefore that in situations where, for political or other reasons, proclamation as such is practically impossible, the Church is already carrying out her evangelizing mission not only through presence and witness but also through such activities as work for integral human development and dialogue. On the other hand, in other situations where people are disposed to hear the message of the Gospel and have the possibility of responding to it, the Church is duty bound to meet their expectations.

III. INTERRELIGIOUS DIALOGUE AND PROCLAMATION

A. INTERRELATED YET NOT INTERCHANGEABLE

77. Interreligious dialogue and proclamation, though not on the same level, are both authentic elements of the Church's evangelizing mission. Both are legitimate and necessary. They are intimately related, but not interchangeable: true interreligious dialogue on the part of the Christian supposes the desire to make Jesus Christ better known, recognized and loved, proclaiming Jesus Christ is to be carried out in the Gospel spirit of dialogue. The two activities remain distinct but, as experience shows, one and the same local Church, one and the same person, can be diversely engaged in both.

78. In actual fact the way of fulfilling the Church's mission depends upon the particular circumstances of each local Church, of each Christian. It always implies a certain sensitivity to the social, cultural, religious and political aspects of the situation, as also attentiveness to the "signs of the times" through which the Spirit of God is speaking, teaching and guiding. Such sensitivity and attentiveness are developed through a spirituality of dialogue. This requires a prayerful discernment and theological reflection on the significance in God's plan of the different religious traditions and the experience of those who find in them their spiritual nourishment.

B. THE CHURCH AND RELIGIONS

79. In fulfilling her mission, the Church comes into contact with people of other religious traditions. Some become disciples of Jesus Christ in his Church, as a result of a profound conversion and through a free decision of their own. Others are attracted by the person of Jesus and his message, but for various reasons do not enter the fold. Yet others seem to have but little or no interest in Jesus. Whatever the case may be, the Church's mission extends to all. Also in relation to the religions to which they belong, the Church in dialogue can be seen to have a prophetic role. In bearing witness to Gospel values, she raises questions for these religions. Similarly, the Church, insofar as she bears the mark of human limitations, may find herself challenged. So in promoting these values, in a spirit of emulation and of respect for the mystery of God, the members of the Church and the followers of

other religions find themselves to be companions on the common path which humanity is called to tread. At the end of the day of prayer, fasting, and pilgrimage for peace in Assisi, Pope John Paul II said: "Let us see in it an anticipation of what God would like the developing history of humanity to be: a fraternal journey in which we accompany one another towards the transcendental goal which he sets for us."[17]

80. The Church encourages and fosters interreligious dialogue not only between herself and other religious traditions, but even among these religious traditions themselves. This is one way in which she fulfills her role as "sacrament, that is, a sign and instrument of communion with God and unity among all people" (LG, 1). She is invited by the Spirit to encourage all religious institutions and movements to meet, to enter into collaboration, and to purify themselves in order to promote truth and life, holiness, justice, love and peace, dimensions of that Kingdom which, at the end of time, Christ will hand over to his Father (cf. 1 Cor 15:24). Thus, interreligious dialogue is truly part of the dialogue of salvation initiated by God.[18]

C. PROCLAIMING JESUS CHRIST

81. Proclamation, on the other hand, aims at guiding people to explicit knowledge of what God has done for all men and women in Jesus Christ, and at inviting them to become disciples of Jesus through becoming members of the Church. When, in obedience to the command of the risen Lord and the Spirit's promptings, the Church fulfills this task of proclamation, this will often need to be done in a progressive manner. A discernment is to be made concerning how God is present in each one's personal history. The followers of other religions may discover, as may Christians also, that they already share many values. This can lead to a challenge in the form of the witness of the Christian community or a personal profession of faith, in which the full identity of Jesus is humbly confessed. Then, when the time is right, Jesus' decisive question can be put: "Who do you say that I am?" The true answer to this question can come only through faith. The preaching and the confession, under the movement of grace, that Jesus of Nazareth is the Son of God the Father, the Risen Lord and Saviour, constitutes the final stage of proclamation. One who freely professes this faith is invited to become a disciple of Jesus in his Church and to take a responsible part in her mission.

D. COMMITMENT TO THE ONE MISSION

82. All Christians are called to be personally involved in these two ways of carrying out the one mission of the Church, namely proclamation and dialogue. The manner in which they do this will depend on the circumstances and also on their degree of preparation. They must nevertheless always bear in mind that dialogue, as has already been said, does not constitute the whole mission of the Church, that it cannot simply replace proclamation, but remains oriented towards proclamation in so far as the dynamic process of the Church's evangelizing mission reaches in it its climax and its fullness. As they engage in interreligious dialogue they will discover the "seeds of the Word" sown in people's hearts and in the religious traditions to which they belong. In deepening their appreciation of the mystery of Christ they will be able to discern the positive values in the human search for the unknown or incompletely known God. Throughout the various stages of dialogue, the partners will feel a great need both to impart and to receive information, to

give and to receive explanations, to ask questions of each other. Christians in dialogue have the duty of responding to their partners' expectations regarding the contents of the Christian faith, of bearing witness to this faith when this is called for, of giving an account of the hope that is within them (1 Pet 3:15). In order to be able to do this, Christians should deepen their faith, purify their attitudes, clarify their language and render their worship more and more authentic.

83. In this dialogical approach, how could they not hope and desire to share with others their joy in knowing and following Jesus Christ, Lord and Saviour? We are here at the heart of the mystery of love. Insofar as the Church and Christians have a deep love for the Lord Jesus, the desire to share him with others is motivated not merely by obedience to the Lord's command, but by this love itself. It should not be surprising, but quite normal, that the followers of other religions should also desire sincerely to share their faith. All dialogue implies reciprocity and aims at banishing fear and aggressiveness.

84. Christians must always be aware of the influence of the Holy Spirit and be prepared to follow wherever in God's providence and design the Spirit is leading them. It is the Spirit who is guiding the evangelizing mission of the Church. It belongs to the Spirit to inspire both the Church's proclamation and the obedience of faith. It is for us to be attentive to the promptings of the Spirit. Whether proclamation be possible or not, the Church pursues her mission in full respect for freedom, through interreligious dialogue, witnessing to and sharing Gospel values. In this way the partners in dialogue proceed in response to the divine call of which they are conscious. All, both Christians and the followers of other religious traditions, are invited by God himself to enter into the mystery of his patience, as human beings seek his light and truth. Only God knows the times and stages of the fulfillment of this long human quest.

E. JESUS OUR MODEL

85. It is in this climate of expectation and listening that the Church and Christians pursue proclamation and interreligious dialogue with a true Gospel spirit. They are aware that "all things work together for the good of those who love God" (Rom 8:28). By grace they have come to know that he is the Father of all, and that he has revealed himself in Jesus Christ. Is not Jesus their model and guide in the commitment to both proclamation and dialogue? Is he not the only one who even today can say to a sincere religious person: "You are not far from the Kingdom of God" (Mk 12:34).

86. Christians are not only to imitate Jesus, but to be closely united to him. He invited his disciples and friends to join him in his unique offering on behalf of the whole of humanity. The bread and wine for which he gave thanks symbolized the entire creation. They became his body "given" and his blood "poured out for the forgiveness of sins". Through the ministry of the Church, the one Eucharist is offered by Jesus in every age and place, since the time of his passion, death and resurrection in Jerusalem. It is here that Christians unite themselves to Christ in his offering which "brings salvation to the whole world" (Eucharistic Prayer IV). Such a prayer is pleasing to God who "desires all men to be saved and to come to the knowledge of the truth" (1 Tim 2:4). Thus they offer thanks for "everything that is true, everything that is honorable, everything that is upright and pure, everything that we love and admire, whatever is good and praiseworthy" (Phil 4:8). Here they draw the grace of discernment, to be able to read the signs of the Spirit's

presence and to recognize the favorable time and right manner of proclaiming Jesus Christ.

CONCLUSION

87. The aim of these reflections on interreligious dialogue and proclamation has been to provide some basic clarifications. However, it is important to remember that the various religions differ from one another. Special attention should therefore be given to relations with the followers of each religion.

88. It is also important that specific studies on the relationship between dialogue and proclamation be undertaken, taking into account each religion within its geographical area and its socio-cultural context. Episcopal Conferences could entrust such studies to the appropriate commissions and theological and pastoral institutes. In the light of the results of these studies, these institutes could also organize special courses and study sessions in order to train people for both dialogue and proclamation. Special attention is to be given to young people living in a pluralistic environment, who meet the followers of other religions at school, at work, in youth movements and other associations and even within their own families.

89. Dialogue and proclamation are difficult tasks, and yet absolutely necessary. All Christians, according to their situations, should be encouraged to equip themselves so that they may better fulfil this two-fold commitment. Yet more than tasks to be accomplished, dialogue and proclamation are graces to be sought in prayer. May all continually implore the help of the Holy Spirit so that he may be "the divine inspirer of their plans, their initiatives and their evangelizing activity" (EN, 75).

Pentecost, 19 May 1991

Francis Cardinal Arinze
President Pontifical Council
Interreligious Dialogue

Josef Cardinal Tomko
Prefect Congregation for the
Evangelization of Peoples

NOTES

1. "The Attitude of the Church towards the Followers of Other Religions (Reflections and Orientations on Dialogue and Mission)" AAS, 76 (1984) pp. 816-828, also *Bulletin Secretariatus pro non Christianis,* n. 56 (1984/2), art. 13. (This document will be referred to henceforth as DM).

2. *Insegnamenti di Giovanni Paolo II,* vol. 9, 2 (1986) pp. 1249-73; 2019-29 (hereafter referred to as *Insegnamenti.* Cf. *Bulletin* no. 64 (1987/1), which contains all the Pope's discourses before, during, and after the day of prayer in Assisi.

3. *Insegnamenti,* vol. 10,1 (1987) pp. 1449-52. Cf. *Bulletin* no. 66 (1987/3) pp. 223-25.

4. *Guidelines on Dialogue with People of Living Faiths and Ideologies,* World Council of Churches, Geneva 1979; "Mission and Evangelism—an Ecumenical Affirmation," *International Review of Mission* 71 (1982), pp. 427-51.

5. Because the spiritual patrimony common to Christians and Jews is so great (*Nostra Aetate,* 4), dialogue between Christians and Jews has its own special requirements. These are not dealt with in this document. For a full treatment, cf. Commission on Religious Relations with Jews, see "Guidelines on Religious Relations

with Jews," 1 December 1974 (in Austin P. Flannery, ed., *Documents of Vatican II,* 1984, pp. 743-49); "Notes for a Correct Presentation of Jews and Judaism in Catholic Preaching and Catechesis," 24 June 1985, *Origins,* vol. 15, n. 2 (4 July 1985), pp. 102-7.

6. The question of New Religious Movements has been treated in a recent document published in collaboration by the following Pontifical Councils: PC for Promoting Christian Unity, PC for Interreligious Dialogue, PC for Dialogue with Nonbelievers and PC for Culture. The complete text can be found in *Origins,* vol. 16, no. 1 (22 May 1986).

7. Justin speaks about the "seeds" sown by the *Logos* in the religious traditions. Through the incarnation the manifestation of the *Logos* becomes complete (*1 Apol.* 46,1-4; *2 Apol.* 8,1; 10:1-3; 13:4-6). For Irenaeus, the Son, the visible manifestation of the Father, has revealed himself to mankind "from the beginning;" yet the Incarnation brings about something entirely new (*Adv. Haer.* 4, 6, 5-7; 4, 7, 2; 4, 20, 6-7). Clement of Alexandria explains that "philosophy" was given to the Greeks by God as a "covenant", as a "stepping-stone to the philosophy which is according to Christ," as a "schoolmaster" bringing the Hellenistic mind to him (*Stromata,* 1, 5; 6, 8; 7, 2).

8. *Adv. Haer.,* 3, 11, 8.

9. *Retract.,* 1, 13, 3; cf. *Enarr. in Ps. 118* (*Sermo* 29, 9), 142, 3.

10. *Insegnamenti,* vol. 9, 2 (1986) pp. 2019-29; English text in *L'Osservatore Romano* weekly edition in English, 5 January 1987, and Bulletin n. 64 (1987/1) pp. 54-62.

11. John Paul II, "Discourse to Indian Bishops on 'ad limina' Visit," 14 April 1989 (AAS, vol. 81) p. 1126; *Bulletin,* n. 71 (1989/2) p. 149.

12. *Insegnamenti,* vol. 7, 1 (1984) pp. 595-99; English text in *Bulletin,* no. 56 (1984/2) pp. 122-25.

13. In the early Church the Kingdom of God is identified with the Reign of Christ (cf. Eph 5:5; Rev 11:15; 12:10). See also Origen, *In Mt 14:7; Hom. in Lc 36,* where he calls Christ *autobasileia,* and Tertullian, *Adv. Marc.* IV, 33,8: "In evangelio est Dei Regnum, Christus ipse." On the correct understanding of the term "kingdom," see the report of the International Theological Commission (8 October 1985), *Selected Themes in Ecclesiology,* n. 10, 3.

14. Cf. Acts 2:32; 3:15; 10:39; 13:31; 23:11.

15. Cf. Jn 15:26ff.; 1 Jn 5:7-10; Acts 5:32.

16. Cf. 1 Thess 2:2; 2 Cor 3:12; 7:4; Phil 1:20; Eph 3:12; 6:19-20; Acts 4:13,29,31; 9:27, 28 etc.

17. *Insegnamenti,* vol. 9, 2 (1986) p. 1262; *Bulletin,* n. 64 (1987/1) p. 41.

18. *Ecclesiam Suam,* chapter 3; cf. also *Insegnamenti* 7, 1 (1984) p. 598; English text in *Bulletin,* n. 56 (1984/2).

Part III

EASTERN ORTHODOX AND ORIENTAL CHURCH STATEMENTS

1

Go Forth in Peace:
Orthodox Perspectives on Mission

1986

ORTHODOX ADVISORY GROUP TO WCC-CWME

*Beginning in 1973 and virtually every year since, representatives of Eastern Ortho-
dox Churches have met regularly to consider the meaning of mission in Orthodoxy
and to discuss the Orthodox contribution to ecumenical mission and evangelism.
Organized in cooperation with the WCC's Commission on World Mission and
Evangelism, which in recent years has had a desk for Orthodox Studies, an
Orthodox Advisory Group has met at the invitation of some local Orthodox
Church to define a topic of interest to Orthodoxy or to provide input and critique
for a scheduled ecumenical meeting, e.g., Nairobi (1975), Melbourne (1980),
Vancouver (1983), San Antonio (1989), and Canberra (1991). Representatives
of Eastern Oriental Churches, though not yet formally in communion with the
Orthodox group, have also been invited.*

*The essays which follow were prepared over a period of years and re-edited by
Professor Ion Bria for publication in the volume* Go Forth in Peace. *They testify
to the rich theological and spiritual legacy which Orthodoxy brings to "Common
Witness" and to the dialogue about mission today. A comparison of these Orthodox texts with the ecumenical texts in Part I gives striking evidence of the extent
of Orthodox influence on the ecumenical missionary discussion since Nairobi.*

I. THE THEOLOGICAL FOUNDATIONS FOR MISSION*

THE IMPORTANCE OF TRINITARIAN THEOLOGY

The mission of the church is based on Christ's mission. A proper understanding
of this mission requires, in the first place, an application of trinitarian theology.
Christ's sending of the apostles is rooted in the fact that Christ himself is sent by
the Father in the Holy Spirit (John 20:21-33). The significance of this scriptural
assertion for the concept of mission is commonly recognized, but the trinitarian

---

*Reprinted from Ion Bria, comp. and ed., *Go Forth in Peace: Orthodox Perspectives on Mission*,
WCC Mission Series No. 7 (Geneva: WCC, 1986), 3-9.

theology, which is implied in it, deserves more attention than it normally receives.

Trinitarian theology points to the fact that God is in God's own self a life of communion and that God's involvement in history aims at drawing humanity and creation in general into this communion with God's very life. The implications of this assertion for understanding mission are very important: mission does not aim primarily at the propagation or transmission of intellectual convictions, doctrines, moral commands, etc., but at the transmission of the life of communion that exists in God. The "sending" of mission is essentially the sending of the Spirit (John 14:26), who manifests precisely the life of God as communion (I Cor. 13:13).

The salvation of the world should be seen as a "programme" of the holy trinity for the whole of creation. The kingdom of God is the inner movement and final goal not only of every human adventure, but of all the dynamic of the universe. True life is life in the holy trinity, in Christ by the Spirit coming from and oriented towards the Father.

THE CENTRALITY OF CHRIST

In our faith, Christ occupies the central place in the act of confessing, for he is the dynamic factor in Christian confession in the world. Following the biblical and kerygmatic tradition of the church, we confess the incarnation of the Logos of God the Father, the mediator through the work of the Paraclete — for our regeneration and the restoration of our communion with God — in the divine-human person of Christ. Thus the Logos of God is not only saviour but also creator. He is our *centre* in a double sense: as divine Logos, source and model of our reason, and as initiating partner of our dialogue with him. As the divine-human hypostasis, the centre of everybody and everything, he is the *partner* with the creative and generative *source* of the dialogue with him and among human beings. He is the Logos of all things and the Logos is the image of the Father. The world has an ontological basis in God, because all things are linked to the Logos. They represent the diversification of the reason of the Logos. At the same time their link and their unity in a harmonious whole are grounded in the nondifferentiated unity of the personal Logos. While things are material, tangible and intelligible images of the diversified reasons and thoughts of the Logos, the human being is the image of the Logos himself as a person who thinks.

The Son of God has assumed the fullness of our humanity into himself; in that process, he affirms, he heals and restores humanity by placing it in himself, and therefore in the holy trinity. It is the great mystery of the perfect divine-human unity that becomes the source-spring of the new life of the world. In making Christ central in our theological understanding, however, the trinitarian and incarnational aspects of the new life should always be held together, in a christocentric but not in a christomonistic manner.

THE INCARNATION

In order to establish the communion between God and humanity, broken because of the fall in its cosmic dimension, the Logos, in his capacity as a person, has introduced himself more intimately into creation and into human history. He is incarnate through the Holy Spirit. Through his incarnation he has revealed the meaning of things. He has restored the bond with us and has renewed the human being. In Christ we find not only reason as the source of our common human reason, but *our total being* is lifted up to the image of God through participation in the Spirit. Through the same act the Logos has established a new relationship between the creator and the human being, an ontological relationship, dynamic not static, which is created and perfected through the energies of God, effected by the Holy Spirit. By restoring us to our function the incarnate Logos communicates to us the power to liberate ourselves from our egotism, in order to understand others and to enter into communion with them and with him. This is the interpersonal function of the Logos. Christ is thus the human being par excellence, the centre of creation, the central human who relates to all. He calls us to make humanity understand that it should not be content with its insufficient rationality and to help people to find the personal origin of reason that is to be found precisely in Christ.

In spite of the humanization of the Logos, we are still free to refuse communion with God. Hence also the presence of sin and evil, which have a real existence and which are opposed to the regenerative work of the Logos. Evil is at the root of the divisions and the passions that have separated us. But the incarnate Logos who effectively unites us establishes in the Holy Spirit the communion in the church that is the body of Christ. The church realizes the unifying message of the divine Logos, for the Logos is its centre and therefore the unifying basis for all humanity.

THE CROSS

Christ is sent into the world not as teacher, example, etc., but as a bearer of this divine life that aims at drawing the world into the way of existence that is to be found in the trinity. The understanding of Christ as the Logos of God in the early church served at that time to illustrate two things that are significant for mission. On the one hand it meant that Christ as the Logos, eternally existing in God as one of the trinity, is sent to the world as a bearer of the trinitarian life and not as a separate individual. On the other hand, it meant that as the cosmic Logos, the power that sustains the world, Christ was sent for no lesser purpose than to bring the world into the life of God. Christ's mission is, therefore, essentially the self-giving of the trinity so that the world may become a participant in the divine life.

This mission of Christ takes place in a "fallen" world and is met by the resistance of the "powers and principalities" of evil and sin. This has made the cross the inevitable passage of Christ's mission. Mission, therefore, takes place in the context of struggle and implies a conversion, a paschal and baptismal passage of the world into a "new creation." This is not a fight that manifests itself simply in the souls of individuals; it permeates all of social life through injustice, oppression, etc., and even the whole of natural existence through sickness and death.

THE RESURRECTION

While the reality of the cross represents the inevitable context of mission as a clash between the trinitarian way of existence and the "powers and principalities" of sin, the resurrection of Christ throws light on mission in two fundamental ways. In the first place it points to the fact that the outcome of mission is beyond any doubt the defeat of the powers of sin in both its social and natural implications (the overcoming of death). Christ's ascension and constant intercession at the right hand of God sustain this assurance. Equally, however, the resurrection points to the fact that this outcome of mission is not controlled by historical forces but is eschatological in nature. It is the Spirit of God that raised Christ from the dead (Rom. 8:11). The church's mission cannot build up or bring about the kingdom. It can only announce its coming through the kerygma of the resurrection and point to it in a sacramental way.

Everything will be fully revealed and realized in the eschaton; meanwhile the church already participates in it through the first-fruits of the Holy Spirit. Therefore, it confesses this eschaton to be open, through the Logos, in the first-fruits of the Spirit, which are the source and power for advancing the whole of humanity towards the coming kingdom, and for giving to the world a joyful hope of the authentic and eternal life that follows the sacrifice of the cross.

It is important not only to keep the cross and resurrection together, but to keep the whole incarnate life of Christ as a single unit. There can be no Christian "theology of the cross" divorced from the annunciation to the Blessed Virgin, the birth, the baptism, and the public ministry ending in the resurrection, ascension, Pentecost and second coming. It would be equally misleading to contrast a "theology of glory" and a "theology of the cross." The cross is where Christ was glorified ("Now is the Son of Man glorified," John 13:31). The glory of Christ was manifested also in the washing of the disciples' feet as in the cross and resurrection and in all the acts of the economy of salvation.

THE WORK OF THE HOLY SPIRIT

Christians are often tempted to confine the activity of God the Holy Spirit to the church, or to individual human hearts or to the inspiration and illumination of the Bible.

But the Spirit was with Christ from the beginning of creation, brooding upon it, giving life to it, bringing form and perfection to all things. Long before human beings appeared on the face of the earth, the Spirit has been at work in the world, proceeding eternally from the Father.

The church glorifies the Holy Spirit along with the Father and the Son, for the Spirit is creator, life-giver and perfector. He is with Christ always. It was the Spirit of the Lord who abode upon Jesus at baptism, and who anointed him to preach the good news (Luke 4:18-19). It is the Spirit who gives life (John 6:63), because it is the Spirit of him who raised Jesus from the dead (Rom. 8:11). To set the mind on the Spirit is life and peace (Rom. 8:6).

It is important to affirm these three elements about the work of the Spirit:

a) The whole saving activity of Christ is inseparable from the work of the Holy Spirit, and the christological and pneumatological affirmations should be kept integrally related to each other in a fully trinitarian context.

b) The work of the Holy Spirit as life-giver and perfector should be seen in its wider cosmic sense and not just in a narrow ecclesiastical or individual sense. It is the Spirit who makes *all* things new — the Spirit of the new creation.

c) The bread of life, the body and blood of our Lord, becomes that by the invocation of the Holy Spirit. The Holy Spirit is not an impersonal force, but the living Spirit of God, who is also the Spirit of the community, the Spirit who perfects and completes all the sacramental mysteries of the church.

SYNERGIA

This is the deep foundation for the patristic teaching on salvation. It is not the case that we are equal partners with God or that God cannot act independently of us. *Synergia* means that God has chosen to work through us. God calls us to surrender ourselves to Christ in order that God may unite us to God's self and work through us, enhancing our freedom and in no way abolishing our personal subjectivity.

Our flesh is weak, but we are not daunted by the weakness of the flesh, for the word of God has become flesh. The life of Jesus Christ includes our bodies of flesh, our minds and wills and all our human faculties.

It is precisely in our weakness that the strength of God is manifested. The Spirit helps us in our weakness. When we acknowledge our natural limitations in humility and repentance, then God takes us and does his mighty acts through us. Where there is faith, God works through the feeble and the powerless. The apostles were not chosen because they were wise or learned, wealthy or powerful. The people of Israel were chosen when they were an enslaved people in Egypt. Not many of us Christians were chosen because we were wise and strong.

But weakness remains weakness where there is no repentance or faith. Our problem today is that we are so preoccupied with our past failures and present powerlessness that we do not set our minds on the Spirit of God, who is wise and powerful. So long as we put our trust in our own wisdom and resources, the Spirit of God does not do his mighty acts through us. "We have this treasure in earthen vessels, to show that the transcendent power belongs to God and not to us" (II Cor. 4:7). That transcendent power is not limited by our limitations, but only waits for our repentance and faith to receive that power.

THE CALL TO REPENTANCE AND TO OBEDIENCE TO THE WILL OF GOD

It is obvious that throughout history Christians have failed to be faithful and have obstructed the work of God in the world. God in Christ has equipped the church with all the gifts of the Spirit necessary for its upbuilding and its ministry; the eucharist and the other sacramental mysteries of the church as well as the provision of bishops, presbyters, and deacons, are all for this purpose. The fasts and feasts, the liturgical calendar and offices, the churches (parishes) and monasteries, the various ways of sanctifying different times and places, the growth of saints in the church, all these exist both for the healing of Christians, and for the mediation of the new life to the world. A rich tradition of iconography makes the unseen world of the holy events and persons physically present in the church.

In the church, the Spirit of God is at work despite our failures as Christians. Those who have the Spirit can discern the work of the Spirit in the church and in the world, despite human unbelief and disobedience. The Spirit has not abandoned the church or the world. Along with our confession of faith in God the Holy Spirit, we confess our belief also in the one, holy, catholic and apostolic church.

Yes, despite our failures—and they are many—God is at work. But that is no ground for complacency. Neither does that fact justify our failures. Our lack of love, however, hinders the Spirit. Our indiscipline makes the heart of God grieve. Because of our unbelief God does not do his great work of healing the sick, cleansing the leper, opening the eyes of the blind, as Christ did where there was faith.

So, the first step in effectively mediating the life of Christ to the world is to call ourselves to repentance and to a life of renewed faith and disciplined obedience to the will of God. The healing of nations demands that Christians be disciplined healers. We have to put to death the old Adam in us, and be clothed with the new man in Christ. The deep spiritual *askesis,* or discipline, of daily dying to ourselves and being born anew in Christ by the Spirit, has to be practised by all Christians, whether living in a monastery or not. *Theosis* is a continuing state of adoration, prayer, thanksgiving, worship, and intercession, as well as meditation and contemplation of the triune God and God's infinite love. This life of participation in the life and worship of the church and the "inner liturgy of the heart" constitute a foretaste of *theosis,* for all Christians, as they walk their pilgrim way through life. "Be still and know that I am God," says the Lord. We need to practise that deep silence of the Spirit, in order to receive the life of God and to mediate it to the world. We need also to "put on the whole armour of God, for our struggle is not against flesh and blood, but against the powers of darkness, against the spiritual hosts of evil" (Eph. 6:10-16).

II. CHURCH AND MISSION

It is in the fulfilment of our Lord's mandate to "Go and make disciples of all nations" (Matt. 28:16-20) that we find an authentic understanding of the church. The meaning of the Greek word for church, ecclesia (from '*Ek-kalo*), is to call out, to gather the people of God as a sign and manifestation of the kingdom of God.

Through the individual members of the body of Christ, the church is unequivocally committed to communicating the good *news* and to striving towards the growth, sanctification and wellbeing of this one body. Since the Pentecost event, when the first disciples were filled with God's Holy Spirit, this communication was no longer an option but rather an obligation, a necessity: "For I am compelled to preach. Woe to me if I do not preach the gospel!" (I Cor. 9:16).

Thus, by definition, the church can never remain static nor satisfied with the status quo. It must continually be in mission, proclaiming, announcing and teaching the good news to the oikoumene, the whole inhabited earth: "You will receive power when the Holy Spirit comes on you, and you will be my witnesses in Jerusalem, and in all Judea and Samaria, and to the ends of the earth" (Acts 1:8).

The gospel, in order to be good news, must be communicated. All the people of God, together and individually, bear the responsibility for witnessing to the good news and for maintaining and preserving the catholicity of God's revelation to his people in every local church.

THE APOSTOLICITY OF THE CHURCH

The kingdom of God which has come and is coming is presented to the world by the community of repentant and pardoned sinners, which is the body of Christ, the church. Despite the sins of its members and because the word lives in it, the church proclaims the kingdom of God to the world. Because the church is given the presence of the Holy Spirit as guarantee, the kingdom is in our midst, the end— the eschaton—is already accessible to the world. The kingdom is already at work in the world, a joyful hope. Therefore the church is an eschatological community, a pilgrim people, which lives in the ardent expectation of the return of its Lord and bears witness to him before the world.

Mission means the proclamation of the good news, i.e. of the coming of the kingdom: "The time is fulfilled, the kingdom of God is at hand; repent and believe in the gospel" (Mark 1:15). But Jesus only proclaims this good news to the "lost sheep of the house of Israel" (Matt. 15:24). Not until after his resurrection did he send his disciples beyond the frontiers of Israel: "Go forth, therefore, and make all nations my disciples; baptize men everywhere in the name of the Father and the Son and the Holy Spirit" (Matt. 28:19). But he commands them to wait in Jerusalem until he sends upon them the "Father's promised gift" and they are "clothed with power from on high" (Luke 24:29), and then he sends them "to be witnesses . . . to the end of the earth" (Acts 1:8).

The church thus discovers the splendour of the kingdom of God in the person of the risen Christ, revealed to the disciples of all times by the coming of the Holy Spirit, and in this way it finds the power to proclaim the kingdom to the ends of the earth. Rejoicing, therefore, in the communion of the Holy Spirit and marvelling at the resurrection, the church proclaims to the world the reign of "Jesus Christ crucified" (I Cor. 2:2), the reign of "Him who is and who was and who is to come" (Rev. 1:4; 1:8; 4:8).

MISSION AS PART OF THE NATURE OF THE CHURCH

The proclamation of the kingdom of God lies at the very heart of the church's vocation in the world. Mission belongs to the very nature of the church, whatever the conditions of its life, for without mission there is no church, because the church continues the work of humankind's salvation revealed and achieved by Jesus Christ our saviour. Only by the Pentecostal outpouring of the Holy Spirit is the mission of the church possible and the apostolic community endowed with the power of the Spirit for the announcement of the gospel of the Christ who died and rose again for our salvation. The coming of the Holy Spirit in the church is not an isolated historic event in the past but a permanent gift which gives life to the church, ensuring its existence in the history of humanity, making possible its witness to the inaugurated kingdom of God. The Holy Spirit is the divine power whereby the church is able to obey the command of the risen Lord: "Go forth to every part of the world and proclaim the good news to the whole creation" (Mark 16:15; cf. Luke 24:47 and Acts 1:8). This permanent Pentecostal outpouring of the Spirit on the church is a reality in the church's worship, in its public prayer, in the Sunday celebration of the eucharist, but it overflows the limits of ecclesial worship and constitutes the inner dynamic that gives character to all expressions of and all activities in the life of the church.

Mission is not related exclusively to the "apostolicity," but to all the *notae* of the church, including unity, holiness and catholicity. This affects the concept of mission in a decisive way, since it removes it from the realm of quantity to become a qualitative reality; it is not the number of "converts" or the statistical membership of the church that can point to the existence of mission; the holiness, unity and catholicity (which is not to be confused with geographical expansion and universality) determine the notion of mission more than any success in numbers (Matt. 18:20).

THE EUCHARISTIC COMMUNITY

The goal and aim of the proclamation of the gospel, and thus of mission, is the establishment of eucharistic communities in every locality, within its own context and culture and in its own language. These eucharistic communities, centred around worship and the celebration of the holy eucharist, will initiate the kingdom of God and become the focal point for active and concrete Christian witness, for mutual spiritual and material support and for teaching the members "to observe all that I have commanded you."

The local church, both clergy and laity in possession of the fulness of catholicity, must respond in obedience to the gospel and to the specific needs of its own situation and circumstances. The eucharistic community will witness most effectively through its own example of openness and unity, as well as through the spirituality and holiness of its individual members. These will be communicated through their active participation in the sacramental life of the community and through concrete expressions of love and concern for one another and for the whole body of Christ, in accordance with the teaching of our Lord in his parable of the last judgement (Matt. 25:36-41).

CHALLENGES TO THE MISSIONARY CALLING OF THE CHURCH

Within

Mission suffers and is seriously distorted or disappears whenever it is not possible to point to a community in history that reflects this trinitarian existence of communion. This happens whenever the church is so distorted or divided that it is no longer possible to recognize it as such a communion, or whenever mission is exercised without reference to the church, but with reference simply to the individuals or the social realities of history. Ecclesiological heresy, therefore, renders mission impossible or distorted.

Without

The church in our time should resist the temptation to insure itself, or even to enter into partnership with the authorities and powers of this world, lest it betray the most precious gift of the Spirit, namely, the liberty of the children of God. In all the struggles and conflicts that rend asunder the human family, the church should seek to reflect the sufferings, injustices and forms of violence (open or concealed), and to reverberate the cries and appeals of all those—Christians and non-Christians—who are persecuted for their faith and brutally treated in violation of human dignity and the basic principles of justice.

While weaknesses and betrayals of which the members of the church are guilty may all too easily obscure the witness, they cannot cancel out the fundamental calling of the church: "Heaven and earth will pass away, but my words will not pass away" (Matt. 24:35). This summons remains even if some of us are deaf to it; the power of death, the gates of Hades will not prevail against the church (cf. Matt. 16:18).

THE PEOPLE OF GOD IN MISSION

It is the privilege of all the members of the eucharistic communities, clergy and laity, young and old, women and men, to participate in the ongoing mission of God. By virtue of their baptism, charismation and reception of the new life of the gospel as experienced in prayer, worship and communion, all have an apostolic calling to witness through the quality of their lives to the experience of the risen Christ. The emphasis, therefore, lies on the realization of the vocation of the whole people of God to live as a corporate witnessing community.

In order to understand Orthodoxy, we must remember that all believers are consecrated so as to live the good news inside as well as outside the temple of God: "The priesthood of believers is no longer limited to places of worship, to liturgical time and space. It is rather an immersion into the life of the human community through an evangelical witness" (*The Future of Orthodox Witness*). The believers enjoy the wondrous freedom of proclaiming the good news and witnessing to the Lord in a variety of ways best suited to the circumstances and the particular needs of the society in which they live.

Therefore, all categories of the people of God must be enabled to fulfill their potentials, exercise their manifold gifts and be involved in mission, as St. Paul says in I Corinthians 12:27-31.

THE INVOLVEMENT OF WOMEN

Each member of the body of Christ must take on a full share of the mission of the church. To more effectively meet the needs of the church and its work in society, use must be made of the different charismata and contributions of both men and women.

Theological schools and church leadership are encouraged to examine at all levels the possibilities for new vocations for theologically trained women who can serve the emerging needs of the church.

Special courses also need to be given so as to make the training of women for church service more relevant and meaningful. These courses would also be open to women who seek to be better trained as laypersons capable of participating in the local, regional or national policy-making bodies of the church. Particular attention should be given to the vocation of the wives of priests.

Women who are called to full-time ministry in the church may consider a ministry in the sphere of the diaconate, remembering that in the early centuries of the church the deaconess played a significant role in fulfilling the true diakonia of the church. The role of the deaconesses in the Coptic Orthodox Church of Egypt and the Armenian Church in Constantinople could serve as an example for other Orthodox churches. The mother of God is the permanent point of reference for the mission of women in the Orthodox Church.

YOUTH AND MISSION

The revival of interest in mission and of missionary work within the Orthodox Church in recent years has been the result of the vision and efforts of Orthodox youth movements, notably through the Porefthendes, an Inter-Orthodox Missionary Centre related to Syndesmos, the fellowship of Orthodox youth organizations.

Today we must encourage this prophetic and apostolic role of youth by stimulating their full participation in the church and in missionary activities. Orthodox youth, whether in local or international movements, should be called upon to bring their fresh enthusiasm, vigour and new perspectives to Orthodox missionary efforts. Moreover, special attention should be given to the educating of young persons for mission.

COMMON CHRISTIAN WITNESS

We are constantly confronted by situations in the secular society that require common Christian witness. Many of the Christian values are under attack. Only if we confront together the sinister influences of secularism will we be successful in asserting the way of life we believe to be essential for the wellbeing of the people of God.

On issues such as the sanctity of marriage, the stability of the family, human rights, abortion, peace, nuclear disarmament, etc., which affect all of us and not simply the Orthodox, we must speak and act together.

Other issues, such as the increase of migrant workers in certain areas of the world and the mobility of people as tourists, students and political refugees, call for common witness and solutions.

Our Orthodox churches and our people should be encouraged whenever possible to take part in and even initiate such a common witness. Two recent ecumenical texts may be of assistance in guiding our efforts: *Common Witness* and *Mission and Evangelism—An Ecumenical Affirmation*. (Published by the Commission on World Mission and Evangelism of the World Council of Churches, Geneva, Switzerland.)

PRINCIPLES OF MISSION

Inspired by the Holy Spirit, several principles have been followed in the church's witness from the very inception of the Christian church on the day of Pentecost.

a) The principle of the use of different languages. Through the action of the Holy Spirit, the disciples "began to speak in other tongues," and the multitude that gathered on that occasion was bewildered, "because each one heard them speaking in his own language" (Acts 2:1-9). On that day it was revealed that the gospel, so as to be understood by those who are the hearers, must be proclaimed in their "own language."

We know that the church has not always and in every place been obedient to this revelation. Even today language is often a significant obstacle to the hearing and understanding of the gospel. At times the institutional church *insists* on the proclamation of the good news in a language that is foreign and unknown to the hearers. This is a direct and deliberate contradiction of the spirit of Pentecost.

b) The second principle deals with race. When some questions arose among the first disciples about preaching to and baptizing gentiles, a vision revealed to Peter by our Lord forced him to affirm: "Truly I perceive that God shows no particularity, but in every nation anyone who fears him and does what is right is acceptable to him" (Acts 10:34-35).

Again we must admit our failure through the ages to be obedient to this affirmation of the apostle Peter. Racism is rampant in the world today and often finds Christians among its strongest advocates. The church must continually reaffirm its opposition to racism and proclaim more forcefully and convincingly the gospel of love and justice for all.

c) The third principle deals with culture and was best expressed by St. Paul: "To the Jews I became like a Jew, to win the Jews. To those under the law I became like one under the law, though I myself am not under the law, so as to win those under the law ... To the weak I became weak to win the weak. I have become all things to all men so that by all possible means I might save some. I do all this for the sake of the gospel, that I may share in its blessings" (I Cor. 9:20-23).

Too often those bringing the gospel to a new context made no attempt to understand and immerse themselves in the culture. They rather sought to uproot and radically change that culture without any regard for its positive values. We must repeatedly reassert that this is in contradiction to the apostolic tradition.

III. LITURGY AND MISSION[1]

Throughout history, the worship of the church has been the expression and guardian of divine revelation. Not only does it express and represent the saving events of Christ's life, death, resurrection and ascension to heaven, but it is also, for the members of the church, the living anticipation of the kingdom to come. In worship, the church, being the body of Christ enlivened by the Holy Spirit, unites the faithful as the adopted sons and daughters of God, the Father.

Liturgical worship is an action of the church and is centred around the eucharist. Although the sacrament of the eucharist, since the very origin of the church, was a celebration closed to outsiders, and full participation in the eucharist remains reserved for the members of the church, liturgical worship as a whole is an obvious form of witness and mission.

THE EUCHARISTIC LITURGY AS A MISSIONARY EVENT

The eucharistic liturgy is the full participation of the faithful in the salvation brought about by the incarnation of the divine Logos and through them into the whole cosmos. By the mutual self-giving of Christ and of his people, by sanctification of the bread and wine and the "christification" of the communicants, it is the place where we experience the fullness of salvation, the communion of the Holy Spirit, heaven on earth. Through the humble and "kenotic" hiding of the divine word in the mystery of the bread, offered, broken, and given, "we proclaim his death and confess his resurrection until he comes again."

It is the role of the eucharistic liturgy to initiate us into the kingdom, to enable us to "taste ... and see that the Lord is good" (Ps. 34:8, quoted by I Pet. 2:3). It is the function of the liturgy to transform us as individuals into "living stones" of the church and as a community into an authentic image of the kingdom.

The liturgy is our thanksgiving for—and on behalf of—the created world, and the restoration in Christ of the fallen world. It is the image of the kingdom; it is the *cosmos* becoming *ecclesia*.

LITURGY AS PREPARATION FOR WITNESS

The divine liturgy—divine because, though celebrated by human beings, it is essentially the work of God—begins with a cry of joy and gratitude: "Blessed is the kingdom of the Father, Son and Holy Spirit." The entire eucharistic liturgy unfolds within the horizon of the kingdom, which is its *raison d'etre* and its goal.

This kingdom is a dynamic reality: it has come and it is coming, because Christ has come and Christ is coming. The mission of the church will therefore be to summon people of all nations and of all ages to become a pilgrim people. The liturgy is an invitation to join with the Lord and to travel with him. This appears at the beginning of the Orthodox liturgies in the Little Entrance with the gospel and in the Great Entrance with the offering of bread and wine: "In thy kingdom. Remember us, O Lord, when thou comest in thy kingdom ... May the Lord God remember us all in his kingdom ... " This movement of the liturgy carries us along with Christ towards the promised land.

The kingdom, prepared for us before the creation of the world (Matt. 25:34) and proclaimed in the whole of Christ's preaching, was given to the world by the Lamb of God offering himself on the cross and by his rising again from the dead. In its liturgy, the church gives thanks ("makes eucharist,") for this gift, in the words: "Thou ... hast left nought undone till thou hadst brought us into heaven and bestowed upon us thy kingdom for to come." By its thanksgiving, by its eucharist, the church receives the gift of the kingdom.

In the liturgy, we all "by participating in the one bread and one chalice" ask "to be united in the communion of the one Holy Spirit" (Lit. St. Basil) standing before the one holy table led by one bishop, we pray together as brothers and sisters of Christ to our common Father. Our distinct persons, united by love, confess with one mind the unity of the three divine persons, Father, Son and Holy Spirit, consubstantial and indivisible trinity.

The gift given by the Son in his self-offering on the cross is communicated to people of all times by the Holy Spirit who receives what belongs to the Son and communicates it to us (cf. John 16:14). When the Holy Spirit is invoked in the prayer of epiclesis, the celebrant prays: "that thy Holy Spirit may come upon us and upon these gifts . . . that they may be to them that partake thereof unto sobriety of soul, the remission of sins, the participation of thy Holy Spirit, the fulfillment of the kingdom of heaven . . . " In the course of the liturgy, the radiance of the Holy Spirit projects the full image of the kingdom onto the church gathered together by him. The liturgy is the continuation of Pentecost. When all the faithful come to communicate, they enter into the splendour of the kingdom.

Immediately after we have in this way met with him who has come but whom we also expect to come again, we cry out: "Grant that we may partake of thee more truly, in that day of thy kingdom which shall have no night." Everything is given to us in this communion yet everything is not yet accomplished. The efficacy of the church's missionary witness depends on the authenticity of our communion. Our ability to present the light of the kingdom to the world is proportionate to the degree in which we receive it in the eucharistic mystery.

Although the eucharist is the most perfect access to the economy of salvation, it is the goal—and also the springboard—of mission, rather than the means of mission. The eucharist reveals the iconic function of the church. The church as an institution points to the eucharistic assembly as its sole genuine image, as the transparent icon of Christ.

WORSHIP AS THE MOTIVATING FACTOR OF LIFE

Worship is the centre of the life of the church, but it should also determine the whole life of every Christian. "Every tree that does not bear good fruit is cut down and thrown into the fire. Thus you will know them by their fruits. Not every one who says to me 'Lord, Lord' shall enter the kingdom of heaven, but he who does the will of my Father who is in heaven" (Matt. 7:20-23). The realization of these words of Christ has a great significance for the success of Christian mission.

The human person, through membership in the worshipping community, in spiritual poetry, in church music, in iconography, with body and soul (I Cor. 6:20), actively participates in the gifts of grace. This involvement of human nature in its fullness—and not only of reason—in glorifying God, is an essential factor of Orthodox worship. It must be preserved and developed, as a powerful means of Christian witness.

THE PRIEST AND THE LITURGY

In order to become a really powerful expression of the church's mission in the world, worship must be meaningfully understood by its participants (I Cor. 14:6-15). It is through a full participation in the liturgy that the people realize both the teaching and then the life, death and resurrection of Jesus Christ, which is the very reality of what we are attempting to proclaim. In other words, the liturgy itself is the proclamation of the gospel in an existential and experiential manner. This has certain implications for the Orthodox priest.

— The liturgy is not for the priest alone, i.e. it is not he alone who celebrates, but rather the entire people of God (clergy and laity) who celebrate. It is in his *function* only, given in ordination, that he is to lead the people in the liturgy.

— The priest must never separate the *kerygma* of Christ, i.e. the teaching, proclamation, and exhortation of the scripture, from the liturgy; this kerygma is part of the very fabric of the liturgy. There is an analogy of this link between the teaching and the sacrifice (*anaphora*) and the eating (*koinonia*), to be seen in the life of our Lord when he *first* taught the people and then offered himself in his body and blood on behalf of all.

— Thus, preaching, being an essential part of worship, should never be omitted, whatever the number of those present at every occasion.

— Through sermons and homilies, the priest must adapt the words of the Scripture to the reality of the circumstances. Noting the difference between relativity and relevance, it is important that this adaptation be made without changing the essential, lifegiving, and salvatory message. For this, there is thus a constant need for proper training and preparation vis-à-vis the sermon.

THE PARTICIPATION OF THE FAITHFUL

Because the liturgy is proclamation, it is imperative that the people of God participate in this reality.

— The parish members must be educated to understand what it is that is happening in the divine liturgy, and in this way to comprehend the proclamation in the liturgy.

— Among the means of achieving the participation of a greater number of faithful in the liturgical life of the church, there should be, wherever possible, a greater involvement of the laity, including women, in those forms of worship that are allowed to them by the church, especially in congregational singing. All people, children and adults, men and women, should learn the hymns of the liturgy. In order to facilitate this, the liturgy should be in the language of the land (which is comprehensive and contemporary) and thus encourage the active and conscientious participation of the people.

— There are aspects of the liturgy that may make it appear frozen and irrelevant. It is thus necessary to make the liturgical language more accessible to the average faithful, and it might be desirable to take initiatives (with the blessing of ecclesiastical authorities) that would make our forms of worship more comprehensible to young people (for example, catechetical explanations could precede the services).

— The important educative role of the icon and of liturgical art in general, in an initiation into an understanding of the mysteries of the church and of faith, cannot be overstressed.

— The church seeks to order our whole life by the sanctification of time, by the liturgical cycles, the celebration of the year's festivals, the observance of fasts, the practice of ascesis, and regular visitation. An effort must be made to bring into everyday life the liturgical rhythm of the consecration of time (matins, hours, vespers, saints' days, feast days).

— New forms of worship patterned on the old ones should be developed, having in mind the special needs of contemporary society (i.e. of travellers, youth, children, people in industry). Also, wherever is possible, the establishment of new worshipping communities, outside the existing parishes and temples, could be considered.

— The church should seriously study the renewal of the ancient tradition of the Order of Deaconess, as is mentioned in early ecumenical councils.

As in the days following Pentecost, a sharing "community" must be created to make the whole church a practising "community of the saints and a holy nation," for it is in the ever-living communion of the saints that the church's faith is experienced and passed on in its most intense and purest form.

LITURGICAL SPIRITUALITY AND WITNESS

It belongs to the very nature of the church to bear witness to the gospel in the world. This witness is rooted in the coming of the Spirit at Pentecost. From Pentecost until the parousia, the risen Christ is made manifest and present by the Holy Spirit in liturgical life, through word and sacraments. The whole life and prayer of the church's members, whether meeting together for common worship or celebrating each one "in the temple of the heart," centres on the eucharist. Here all the prayers and liturgical acts of the people of God converge; here the church discovers its true identity. In all of Christian spirituality, eucharistic spirituality creates a dynamic piety, mystical bonds with Christ that overcome evil by realizing fully the mystery of incarnation and divinization in all its dimensions. The eucharistic human being is in fact a human being who overcomes the conditioning of our fallen nature.

In the liturgical celebration, which extends into the daily life of the church's members, the church announces and achieves the advent of the kingdom of the holy trinity. In all things, it commemorates the glorified Christ and gives thanks to God in Jesus Christ. The entire tradition of the church, its worship, its theology, and its preaching, is a doxology, a continual thanksgiving, a confession of faith in Christ's Easter triumph and our liberation from all the forces that oppress and degrade us.

— Prayer and the eucharist, whereby Christians overcome their selfish ways, impel them also to become involved in the social and political life of their respective countries.

— The faithful should, as well, establish personal contact with non-believers, in order to transmit the spiritual experiences gained by a meaningful participation in the liturgy.

— Orthodox spirituality is a spirituality that embraces the great variety of ways whereby human life is sanctified and which, through fasting and ascesis, makes it possible for us to participate in the divine life both physically and with the whole range of our faculties. This sanctification also includes the human mind, in which its arrogant self-sufficiency is conquered and illumination granted to it in the confession of faith and in the act of praise. Orthodox spirituality is thus a tried and tested school in which human beings are initiated into the mystery of God, the mystery of God's love and of God's salvation accomplished and communicated. This understanding is given and received by various forms of spiritual and pastoral guidance, by confession, and it culminates in the authentic creation of a new life by the Holy Spirit, a life in which "it is no longer I that live but Christ lives in me."

— The common spirituality of the people of God and monastic spirituality must not be treated as if these were mutually opposed. Nor must we restrict to just a few people the continual invocation of the blessed name of Jesus. In Orthodoxy great value is attached to the plurality of forms and expressions of Christian devotion. At every stage in their spiritual journey, Christians receive the gifts of the Holy Spirit in rich measure and can achieve the perfection to which they are called.

IV. HOLY SCRIPTURE, PROCLAMATION AND LITURGY[2]

The Bible and the liturgy must not be isolated as self-contained, autonomous entities. They were established to remain together, united forever.

THE INTERACTION OF THE BIBLE AND LITURGICAL LIFE

The liturgical life of the church is one of the most fundamental ways in which it proclaims the word of God to the world. It is especially in and through the liturgy and divine services that people come to know God as manifested and still being manifest to the world in Jesus Christ. Our Lord Jesus Christ, crucified, risen and ascended, is the unchanging content and message of the gospel and of the liturgy (I Cor. 1:23; I Cor. 15:20; Mark 16:19).

Holy scripture is the source and basis of the whole liturgical and spiritual life of the church. The Bible contains the revealed message of the old and new covenants. This message finds its liturgical actualization in the worship of the church, especially in the eucharist, the sacrament of the new covenant. In the course of the liturgical year, through feasts, readings, sermons, biblical instruction, hymnography, symbols and iconography, the church actualizes the mystery of the history of salvation and renews the covenant between God and God's people.

—The biblical content and understanding of the liturgy must constantly be affirmed, so that they are not distorted by merely folkloristic, ritualistic or cultural attitudes. Within the liturgy, the proclamation of the good news is not just an evangelistic event. It also becomes an ecclesial reality through the eucharistic communion. The church is the eucharistic manifestation of the history of salvation, which is witnessed to and made evident in the New Testament. It is therefore crucial for Christians to understand their life and history in the perspective of the holy scriptures. This points to the ecclesial reality itself and to the eucharistic status of the church. Orthodoxy cannot dissociate the biblical vision of the church from its liturgical manifestation.

—The proclamation of the word receives its full theological significance and power within the assembly, the visible manifestation of the eucharistic community. The incarnate word of God nourishes the church in the liturgy, as good news and as spiritual bread. Indeed, one cannot share in the eucharistic part of the liturgy without fully sharing in its kerygmatic part (biblical reading, sermons, etc.). In the liturgy the participant is guided by the book of life on the way to a full knowledge of divine revelation.

—Both in the gospel and in the liturgy, Jesus Christ is continually offering himself as "the way, the truth, and the life" (John 14:6). Because the liturgy is founded on the word of God and is permeated by it, it is of particular importance for evangelistic witness.

—The Bible occupies a unique place in the liturgy, filling it with deep meaning. The liturgy becomes a living word of God addressed to people; it creates an atmosphere of dialogue between a person and God and between persons. In the liturgy we talk with God and God talks with us; we pray to God, we thank and glorify God. Through our prayer, thanksgiving and praise we proclaim God. Therefore the liturgy is indeed a proclamation.

BIBLICAL AND LITURGICAL LANGUAGE

Because of the special place of the Bible in the liturgical life of the church, it should become more understandable and accessible to the people: " ... the sheep hear his voice, and he calls his own sheep by name and leads them out ... and the sheep will follow him, for they know his voice. A stranger they will not follow, but they will flee from him, for they do not know the voice of strangers" (John 10:3-5).

Attention must be given to both biblical and liturgical language, for this is a crucial challenge for the Orthodox witness of today. This problem has two aspects: on the one hand, in many Orthodox churches, through the old biblical and liturgical texts, a national language and culture was shaped and is still protected. On the other, the old liturgical language limits the very possibilities of the contemporary faithful to identify themselves with the liturgy, which is their prayer, and handicaps the church in communicating with the younger generation.

Thus, in preaching and in the liturgy, it is of utmost importance that the Bible be communicated to people in their mother tongue and in a language they can understand. " ... But if I do not know the meaning of the language, I shall be a foreigner to the speaker and the speaker a foreigner to me" (I Cor. 14:11). "I could wish to be present with you now and to change my tone ... " (Gal. 4:20). Every Christian should have direct access to the text of the holy scriptures both through private and liturgical readings.

Finally, in renewing the question of language, each Orthodox Church should take into account its local, cultural, historical and psychological setting as well as pastoral needs.

A GREATER ACCESS TO THE WORD OF GOD

— It is important that the faithful have a better knowledge of, and a more direct access to, the biblical texts printed wholly or in part in the language they speak. The translation and distribution of the Bible remains an important task and responsibility of the church.

— It would be worthwhile to have the entire text of the Bible (Old and New Testaments) read during the liturgical Sunday synaxes and to improve the pericopes of evangelical and apostolic readings prescribed for the Sundays and feasts of the year. For in these days multitudes of God's people assemble who, because of the incompleteness and monotony of the pericope, are deprived of the possibility to listen to the word of God and its interpretation in its fullness. This will not only result in a better common knowledge of the Bible but in the enrichment and renewal of the topics treated in the homilies.

— So that we might participate more fully in the all-sanctifying and illuminating power of divine grace which is communicated in the liturgy and through the word of God, a more extensive reading of the Bible in liturgies not combined directly with the eucharist should be promoted. In this respect, the church should consider reinstituting the old practice of using a variety of liturgies, whose styles reflect the missionary milieux and the culture of the participants.

— All possible assistance should be provided to those who stimulate interest for Bible studies among people, under the guidance of the church.

— Another way of bringing the good news closer to people is to illustrate the various important Bible stories by using icons that are venerated by the people: " ... every scribe who has been trained for the kingdom of heaven is like a householder who brings out of his treasure what is new and what is old" (Matt. 13:52).

—In order to communicate with a society where contacts with the church's liturgical life are becoming increasingly rare, churches can use the methods and means offered by modern technology. Their use should be carefully studied as well as the message that is communicated through them.

PROCLAMATION AND INTERPRETATION

Throughout its history, the church has continued the ministry of the apostles by following the command of Jesus Christ (Matt. 28:19-20). It has been called to celebrate the holy mysteries and to proclaim the gospel to all nations. Thus, the duty to preach is part of the Christian priesthood just as are both sacramental actions and pastoral ministry.

The Bible is alive in the liturgy. It is opened to the people through the lips of the praying church. The word of God becomes alive and effective through proclamation and interpretation in the sermon, which is an integral part of the liturgy, and it transforms the inner life of the listener.

—One of the principal aims of preaching the word of God is to give an interpretation, under the guidance of the Holy Spirit, of biblical events in ways which meet the spiritual needs of people today and which speak to problems confronting them.

—In his preaching, the priest should respond not only to the personal and religious questions of the faithful, but also to their present social concerns.

—There is a need for the renewal of the preaching and teaching ministry, especially in view of the concerns and problems of the new audience of the worship services. Because the celebrant is both priest and preacher, the church should give the utmost importance, in the education of the clergy, to the teaching of the Bible, homiletics, catechetics and liturgics in view of the ministry of the word (Acts 6:4). The priest must learn to adapt his proclamation and teaching to his listeners, avoiding ecclesiastical verbiage, and taking into account the language used in his missionary environment.

—As an example of this, the patristic homilies are an excellent model for preaching today. This type of sermon actualizes the message of the biblical text in a pastoral and communal perspective and puts the emphasis on God's action in the history and life of men and women. Such homilies should be simple, short, authentic, and reflect the inner dialogue between the preacher and the faithful. They should enable the truth of God to manifest itself in and through the weakness of human language.

—Any other creative ways of preaching the Bible already existing within local Orthodox churches should be regarded as valuable and as deserving further dissemination.

PROCLAMATION TO THE WORLD

We must remain conscious of our responsibility before God, the church and all humanity to fulfil the commandment of our Lord Jesus Christ. ". . . Go, therefore, and make disciples of all peoples . . ." (Matt. 28:19). It also follows from the way the great apostle to the Gentiles felt about it in saying ". . . Woe to me if I do not preach the gospel!" (I Cor. 9:16). ". . . He who speaks in a tongue, should pray for the power to interpret. For if I pray in a tongue, my spirit prays but my mind is unfruitful" (I Cor. 14:13-14).

Today, however, our witness is handicapped by the erosion of the sense of the sacred in the contemporary world. The proclamation and the teaching of holy scripture must take into account the social and cultural realities of society in order to become accessible and understandable. The hearers of this proclamation and teaching will then be able to discover, through the liturgy, the true spiritual and sacred dimension of this world, which is often hidden by difficult terminology.

LITURGY AND PROCLAMATION

Proclamation should not be taken only in the narrow sense of an informative preaching of the truth, but rather of incorporating humanity into the mystical union with God. At every step of the liturgy we encounter the word of God. Although they belong chronologically to the past, the saving events of divine economy, through the Holy Spirit's action, transcend time's limitation, become really present, and the faithful in the here and now live that which historically belongs to the past, as well as to the eschaton. In the liturgy we do not have simply a memorial, but a living reality. It is an epicletic contemporization and consecration. A continuous parousia, a real presence of Christ emerges through the liturgy.

TO WHOM IS THE GOSPEL PROCLAIMED?

The incarnation was for the whole people of all ages and for the redemption of the whole cosmos. The holy eucharist was instituted, among other things, to proclaim the death and the resurrection of our Lord "until he comes again." Thus, the following categories of people should directly or indirectly hear the message of the holy eucharist.

— The members of the church who try sincerely to practise the faith should be made true evangelists by the gospel proclaimed to them. St. John Chrysostom said: "I do not believe in the salvation of anyone who does not try to save others."

— The nominal Christians who attend the church just as a routine.

— The mobile population, migrant workers, refugees, etc., some of whom have no permanent roots under the sun.

— People of the diaspora of our modern age.

— The non-Christians in the vicinity of our congregations and churches who are still to a large extent strangers to the healing and radiating power of the gospel.

— The fields where no one has ever preached the gospel.

HOW DO WE PROCLAIM THE GOSPEL?

During the liturgy the readings from the Bible are done not as self-centred service and action, but in the service of the liturgical life of the church. To accomplish the mission of the church in proclaiming the gospel, a variety of methods and approaches must be used, according to the possibilities and the needs of the local church.

— The faithful should have continual education in understanding the meaning of the liturgy and the message of the gospel.

— Meaningful literature should be published, such as: informative pamphlets; pictorial and illustrated publications; volumes of new homilies and sermons, etc.

— The mass media of television, radio, and newspapers should be employed.

— Theological training of priests must emphasize the importance of an awareness of the needs for pastoral care, missionary zeal, and the proclamation of the word.

V. THE GOOD NEWS AND EVANGELISTIC WITNESS[3]

WHAT IS EVANGELISTIC WITNESS?

Evangelistic witness is not the whole mission of the church, which has many other dimensions. Evangelistic witness is here understood to be the communication of Christ to those who do not consider themselves Christian, wherever these people may be found. This includes the need of the church to witness to some of its own nominal members.

By its nature, however, evangelistic witness is first of all and primarily a confrontation of humankind by the message, judgement, love, presence, redemption, command and transfiguring power of the energies of the one, holy and undivided trinity.

Evangelistic witness is a call to salvation, which means the restoration of the relationship of God and humanity, as understood in the Orthodox teaching of *theosis*. This message has its source in the scriptures, which witness to the redemption of humankind in Christ Jesus, yet it also includes a worldview which locates each of us vis-à-vis God, our fellows as individuals and in society, as well as our own personhood and destiny. It includes both the relationship of God and each person, and the relationship of human being to fellow human being (vertical and horizontal).

Evangelistic witness brings to each the true response to the essential need *qua* human being. It is the bringing of the divine response to the real need of persons as individuals and of persons in community. It is the message of human restoration and the divinization of the human. As such it speaks to the most profound human need, yet it also meets and overcomes the felt needs of human beings in more specific and concrete dimensions.

Because human beings are fallen, evangelistic witness will also appear to have an element of foolishness (*moria*), and will always contain within it an element of *skandalon* simply because human wisdom cannot fully comprehend the transcendent wisdom of God. Yet, evangelistic witness does more than provide a message of divine dimensions; it also conveys a way of living applicable in full within the community of the body of believers, the church, and in part in the world at large.

WHY ARE WE REQUIRED TO MAKE EVANGELISTIC WITNESS?

We do not have the option of keeping the good news to ourselves. Sharing the word and communicating the word and confessing the faith once given to the saints is an integral part of fulfilling the image and likeness of God and the achievement of *theosis*. Like St. Paul, the believer must be able to say about all who do not know the life in Christ what he said about his fellow countrymen: " . . . my heart's desire and prayer to God for them is that they may be saved" (Rom. 10:1). The uncommunicated gospel (good news) is a patent contradiction.

The goal of evangelistic witness—though it may pass through many stages and pause at many intermediate places—is finally one: conversion from a life characterized by sin, separation from God, submission to evil and the unfulfilled potential of God's image, to a new life characterized by the forgiveness of sins, obedience to the commands of God, renewed fellowship with God in the trinity, growth in the restoration of the divine image, and the realization among us of the prototype of the love of Christ. More briefly and succinctly put, the final goal of evangelistic witness is conversion and baptism. Conversion is a wilful turning from sin, death and the evil to true life in God. Baptism is the reception of a new member into the new life of the community of God's people, the church.

Though the conversion and baptism of all is the final goal of evangelistic witness, there is a need to identify many intermediate goals also, such as:

—the increase of love and dialogue among Christians and non-Christians;

—the formation of the gospel message into the language and thought-forms of the non-Christian neighbour;

—the interpenetration of the structures of society;

—the promulgation of the will of God in reference to the injustice among us; and

—the prophetic challenge to the world's values.

All these share in the task of evangelistic witness and in part serve as a motive to speak the word of Christ to all.

WHO PERFORMS THE TASK OF EVANGELISTIC WITNESS?

The most true and profound response to this question would be that it is God, through the power of the Holy Spirit, who does the work of evangelistic witness. We are made *diakonoi* of the gospel, "according to the gift of God's grace which was given [us] by the working of his power" (Eph. 3:7). In a further sense, it is the whole community of God which does this work.

The Clergy

More particularly, four groups or classes of Christians are charged, each in their own way, with the task of evangelistic witness. First are those ordained in the Lord's service. The chief evangelist of the church is the bishop with his presbyterion and diaconate as well as the monastic establishment. In the history of the church, these "professionals" of evangelistic witness have carried on this work for the church with great success. And inasmuch as they still lead the worship, preach the word of God, visit the oppressed and suffering, speak the word of truth in the tribunals of power, proclaim the gospel before vast audiences electronically present, communicate the Orthodox truth through the printed word, or walk the foreign mission trails, they continue to do so. Yet, we are all too conscious of our lethargy and deafness to the divine commission. Theological schools of all levels are challenged to heal that deafness through proper and full education for evangelical witness of the candidates for Holy Orders. There is a need to restore the claim of evangelical witness upon the priestly conscience of these servants of God.

The Priest as Evangelist

"Evangelist," which differs from catechist, here means one who must "go forth and proclaim the gospel," i.e. to both nominal Christians, the "potential parish," and to non-believers. This, however, presents various problems with which the Orthodox must deal.

It is within the very nature of the faith that the *Evangelion* as a "witness" to Jesus Christ must be emphasized. In various cultures, this must be done with whatever means are available to the priest.

Here the personality of the priest is crucial in the sense that he must have proper respect for others, possess an integrity of character, and allow others to use their free will in coming to the Orthodox faith.

Thus, coercion of any sort in the name of Christ does not lead to a faith development but to a desire for spiritual aggressiveness. A distinction must be made between proselytism, which is a corruption of Christian witness, and an evangelistic witness, which seeks to demonstrate the Orthodox faith to the world as an "active presence." By this "active presence," the Orthodox roots in the land are strengthened. This presence, however, can only come forth through a deep missionary consciousness on the part of the priest and, in turn, by the people of God.

The Laity

The second group specifically charged with the work of evangelical witness is the laity. We have just rediscovered the theology of the laity in the Orthodox Church. They are part of the "royal priesthood" of the church. We are all—clergy and laity—called to be "a holy priesthood, to offer spiritual sacrifices acceptable to God through Jesus Christ" (I Pet. 2:5). As such, we are all "a chosen race, a royal priesthood, a holy nation, God's own people." Thus, the laity shares in the whole work of the church, including that of evangelistic witness. Part of the task of the clergy is to "raise the consciousness" of the laity regarding their roles in the fulfillment of the work of the church. The primary means of evangelical witness today is the authentic Christian life to which every layperson is called. Also necessary to an effective witness are:
—a vital and living participation in the divine liturgy;
—the personal witness of faith; and
—Christian involvement of the believer in the social, political, educational, cultural and intellectual life of his or her nation and society.
Orthodoxy of doctrine, combined with evangelical behaviour are the conditions of true evangelical witness by the laity.

The Martyrs

There are those among us called against our will to mission. Some of us become evangelistic witnesses suddenly when the principalities and powers of the age force us into situations of martyrdom, when compromise and accommodation are not possible. Today, the ancient experience of expropriation, prison and arena is frequently repeated. When called, we must be ready for the special witness of martyrdom.

The Prophets

Others of us are called from among the members of the body of Christ to evangelistic witness because of the special gifts of the Holy Spirit. Throughout the ages persons have been touched by the Holy Spirit and provided with gifts of unique character. These persons may do the work of evangelistic witness. It is incumbent upon them, however, always to do so from within the faith and truth of the body of the church. In turn, the church must look upon these members seized of the Holy Spirit with the wisdom of Gamaliel (Acts 5:34-39).

FOR WHOM IS THE EVANGELISTIC WITNESS?

It would be true to say that evangelistic witness is directed toward all of the *ktisis* that groans and travails in search of adoption and redemption (Rom. 8:22). But what, specifically, does this mean?

Nominal Christians

First of all, the church's evangelistic witness is for the Christian who is not a Christian. There are many who have been baptized, and yet have put off Christ, either deliberately or through indifference. Often such people still find it possible sociologically or culturally or ethnically to relate in some manner to the Christian community. The re-Christianization of Christians is an important task of the church's evangelistic witness.

Evangelistic witness is, consequently, also directed to those who superficially identify Orthodox Christianity with their national culture. We cannot be content with a process of indigenization which leaves much of our national and cultural lives untouched by the spirit of the gospel. The transfiguring power of the holy trinity is meant to reach into every nook and cranny of our national life. Those who live in or come from the traditional Orthodox lands are especially sensitive to this challenge of evangelistic witness.

Contemporary Humanity

Evangelistic witness is directed to the new secularized humanity in an ever more secularized world. The forces of technology, scientific success, and control over the environment have provided humankind with an enviable control over the conditions of life. Yet that control has had many undesirable consequences, also. It has taught people to think of themselves primarily as consumers; they are *homo economicus*. Their circumscribed goals of life require no transcendent referent, no forgiveness, no restoration of relationship, no sacramental life, no *theosis*, no God. Yet, exactly because they sit in that darkness, they are the object of the church's evangelistic witness.

Institutions of Modern Society

Evangelistic witness will also speak to the structures of this world, its economic, political and societal institutions. Especially necessary is the witness of social justice in the name of the poor and the oppressed. We must re-learn the patristic lesson that the church is the mouth and voice of the poor and the oppressed in the presence of the powers that be.

In our own way we must learn once again "how to speak to the ear of the King," on the people's behalf.

HOW DO WE MAKE OUR EVANGELISTIC WITNESS?

It is the task of evangelistic witness to lead persons to the acknowledgement of God's saving power in their lives. "[He] is the Lord of all and bestows his riches upon all who call upon him." Yet, "how are men to call upon him in whom they have not believed? And how are they to believe in him of whom they have never heard? And how are they to hear without a preacher? And how can men preach unless they are sent?" (Rom. 10:12, 14-15). After two thousand years this Pauline injunction retains its urgency and timeliness.

Yet those same intervening years require us to review our conceptions of the methods of evangelistic witness. On the one hand it is clear that proclamation alone is not the only way in which evangelistic witness is made. Further, in this day and age mere preaching may no longer be the most effective way of evangelistic witness. Paul does not tell us what we are to do when the gospel has been proclaimed and rejected, or even worse, simply ignored! Yet, of one thing we are sure. We are sent by Christ to bear witness to him and his saving truth for all of humankind.

PREREQUISITES FOR WITNESS

Faith and Humility

How is it to be done today? In the first instance this question must be directed to the attitudes and motives of "those who are sent." Those who are sent must first be conscious of their own repentance, conversion and salvation. Those who are fully aware of the new life of grace in the community of the holy trinity and in the reality of the community of the church alone are able to communicate the saving witness. This comes about above all with the knowledge that nothing we do is of effect without the energizing power of the trinity. No matter what it is that we do in evangelistic witness we know that it is "God making his appeal through us" (II Cor. 5:20).

As difficult and beyond our capabilities as the work of evangelistic witness may seem, then, we undertake the task with a spirit not of fear or of inadequacy or of insufficiency—though all these in truth exist in us—but with hope that through our meagre efforts this witness may be empowered by the gracious energies of the triune God, in whose name we undertake the task.

And so it is that "those who are sent" to be evangelistic witnesses do so as ones having experienced the redemption of God and who then work with the full understanding of their own insufficiency, fully expecting the grace of God to "provide the growth." Thus it is in a constant spirit of *metanoia* (repentance), with a full sense of our own limitations that we make our evangelistic witness.

Koinonia and Love

How is evangelistic witness to be made today objectively? The chief means of witness for the church today is not the bold announcement of Christ as saviour to a world which has already heard the words and still remains unresponsive. The first and chief method of evangelistic witness is the same as that of the early church. Those who saw the quality of life of those early believers were so attracted by its power and beauty that they sought to find its power and its source (e.g. Epistle of Diognetus; Libanus' praise of Chrysostom's mother).

Thus, the first method of evangelistic witness is the sharing of love by those who have acknowledged the love of God for them. "We love because he first loved us" (I John 4:19). It was an injunction to evangelistic witness when the apostle of love instructed: "Beloved, let us love one another; for love is of God, and he who loves is born of God and knows God" (I John 4:7).

More specifically, the same apostle says, " . . . this is the victory that overcomes the world, our faith" (I John 5:3-4). Our obedience to God's will is a powerful form of evangelistic witness as well. We have cheapened the gospel in the past by much talking and little practice. Our obedience to God's will must now be the vehicle for our message.

The Call to Justice and Truth

But the word of God cannot be contained only in the personal sphere. Evangelistic witness must also be made before the social and political tribunal. Christians must address the word of God to contemporary issues of justice with all available means. Evangelistic witness must keep a vigilant eye upon all emergent social movements and concerns (women's liberation, racial consciousness, sexual freedom, etc.) in order to spread the word of truth. But it should seek to do its task toward and in these situations not by parroting words of another age, but by reformulating the unchanging truth with an eye to its contemporization. Certainly, in doing this it will also respond creatively in the patristic spirit to the ever-new and ever-changing phenomena of our times.

VI. MISSION AS "LITURGY AFTER THE LITURGY"[4]

THE LITURGY AS A MEANS OF PERSONAL GROWTH

The liturgy is not an escape from life, but a continuous transformation of life according to the prototype of Jesus Christ, through the power of the Spirit.

If it is true that in the liturgy we do not only hear a message but we also anticipate in the great event of liberation from sin our communion with the person of Christ through the real presence of the Holy Spirit, then this event of our personal incorporation into the body of Christ, this transfiguration of our little being into a member of Christ, must be evident and be proclaimed in all our life. The liturgy has to be continued in personal everyday situations. Every one of the faithful is called upon to continue a secret devotion, on the secret altar of the heart, to realize a living proclamation of the good news "for the sake of the whole world." Without this continuation the liturgy remains half finished. Since by the eucharistic event we are incorporated in Christ to serve the world and be sacrificed for it, we have to express in concrete *diakonia,* in community life, our new being in Christ, who is the servant of all. The sacrifice of the eucharist must be extended in personal sacrifices for people in need, the brothers and sisters for whom Christ died. Since the liturgy is the participation in the great event of liberation from the demonic powers, then the continuation of liturgy in life means a continuous liberation from the powers of evil that are working inside us (e.g. the terrible complex of egoism), a continual re-orientation and openness to insights and efforts aiming at liberating human persons from all demonic structures of injustice, exploitation, agony and loneliness, and aiming at creating real communion of persons in love.

THE WITNESS OF THE COMMUNITY IN THE WORLD

The liturgy does not end when the eucharistic assembly disperses. "Let us go forth in peace"; the dismissal is a sending off of every believer to mission in the world where he or she lives and works, and of the whole community into the world, to witness by what they are that the kingdom is coming. Christians who have heard the word and received the bread of life should henceforth be living prophetic signs of the coming kingdom. Having been sanctified, for they have become temples of the Holy Spirit, and deified, because they have been kindled by the fire descended from heaven, they hear the exhortation: "Heal the sick ... and say to them, 'the kingdom of God has come near to you ... behold, I have given you authority to tread upon ... all the power of the enemy' " (Luke 10:9-19). Every Christian is called to proclaim the kingdom and to demonstrate its power. Hence a manifold function:

— The exorcism of demons: the struggle against the idols of racism, money, nationalism, ideologies, and the robotization and exploitation of human beings.

— The healing of the sick: the church exercises this function not only in the sacraments of penance and the anointing of the sick but also by tackling all the ills and disorders of the human being and society. It does this in the power of the cross: self-effacing service of the sick and prisoners; solidarity with the tortured and the oppressed, especially with those who suffer for their opinions. As the voice of the voiceless, the church must, in the discharge of its calling, teach and practice respect for every human being, with the aim of restoring the divine image in each individual and communion among all. It should encourage respect for the whole of creation and everything in nature. A kingdom of priests, it offers up the whole of creation—obedient to Christ and renewed by the Spirit—to God the Father.

—Voluntarily accepted poverty in demonstration of solidarity with the poor king (cf. Zech. 9:9).

—Fasting with him who said that "man does not live by bread alone," "for the kingdom of God does not mean food and drink but righteousness and peace and joy, in the Holy Spirit" (Rom. 14:17).

—Identification with all those who go hungry.

—Chastity not only in monastic life but also in conjugal love and procreation.

—Revaluation of the humility which makes it possible for the other person to be renewed.

—Mutual submission (cf. Eph. 5:21) in listening to the Spirit who speaks through the church.

—A liberty which refuses to let itself be intimidated by threats or taken in by false promises.

—Constant interior prayer throughout all the vicissitudes of daily life.

All these are aspects of a life based on an eschatological vision of existence, on an evangelical life worthy of the children of the kingdom.

THE PARISH AND MISSION

Although the essence of Christian mission is the proclamation to each human being of the gospel of forgiveness, resurrection and life eternal, such proclamation is valid, credible and effective only if it is not isolated from the gospel of love, by which Christians are recognized as Christ's disciples, from involvement and sharing in suffering wherever it may appear. For mission is the work of the same Holy Spirit that anointed Christ "to preach good news to the poor, to proclaim release to the captives and recovering of sight to the blind, to set at liberty those who are oppressed, to proclaim the acceptable year of the Lord" (Luke 4:18-19).

While preaching the gospel of the eternal kingdom that is yet to come, we know that this kingdom is already present in our midst and is realized every time we sacrifice ourselves for the will of God to be done on earth as it is in heaven.

The missionary character of the parish is rooted in its very nature. Although administratively and institutionally it is a part of the church, sacramentally and spiritually it possesses the fulness of the gifts of the Holy Spirit; it is indeed the presence and epiphany of the whole church, of the whole faith, and of the whole grace. As the whole church, the parish is called to preach and to teach the saving gospel of Christ in the world and to be the witness of Christ in the particular conditions set for it by God. In this sense the entire life of the parish is a mission, for it exists not merely for the religious edification of its members, but above all for the salvation of the whole world from the power of the "prince of this world."

The living source of the fulfillment by the parish of this mission is the liturgy whose very essence is the epiphany and the communication of the kingdom of God revealed in the life, the teaching, the death, the resurrection, and the glorification of Jesus Christ. The meaning of the liturgy has often been obscured by one-sided interpretations, in which it was presented almost exclusively as a means of individual sanctification. It is urgent, therefore, that we rediscover the initial *lex orandi* of the church in its cosmic, redemptive and eschatological dimensions. Behind this static and individualistic understanding of the liturgy we must recover its dynamic nature and power. It edifies and fulfils the church as the sacrament of the kingdom; it transforms us, the members of the church, into the witness of Christ, and his co-workers.

THE ROLE OF THE LAITY

Together with the rediscovery of the essential meaning of the liturgy, we must rediscover the true nature and vocation of the laity in the church. For too long the very term *laikos* carried with it connotations of passivity, of not belonging to the active, i.e. clerical, stratum in the church. But we know that initially the term meant the belonging to the laos, the people of God—to "a chosen race, a royal priesthood, a holy nation, God's own people," whom God "has called out of darkness into his marvelous light" (I Pet. 2:9). In the sacraments of baptism and holy chrismation, each member of the church was made into the temple of the Holy Spirit, dedicated, consecrated to God and called to serve him. In other terms, each laikos is, above all, called to be a witness, i.e. an active participant in the church's mission in the world.

Today, in several parts of the world, the task of bearing testimony to Christ, of bringing new people from darkness into the marvellous light of knowing Christ, is performed primarily by the laity. This alone should encourage us to rediscover the true nature and vocation of the laity, their unique place in the overall missionary ministry of the church. And again, there is no better way to that discovery than the study of the church's *leitourgia* as truly *concelebration,* a corporate act in which each member of the church finds his or her place in the edification of the body of Christ.

"We are fellow-workers for God," declares St. Paul (I Cor. 3:9). Through human voices and human lives, Christ's call to follow him reverberates throughout the centuries. For those who take it seriously, this "service" of the divine word and the divine love entails a deep and permanent surrender of their lives. Christians who obey the word of their Lord must resist the temptation to overrate their own importance and to come between God and God's children. The service of God and God's word demands a radical exercise in self-renunciation and spiritual poverty, the better to be able to serve God and one's brothers and sisters. What St. John the Baptist said of himself in relation to Christ must also be true of us: "He must increase, but I must decrease" (John 3:30). This way of voluntary impoverishment following the pattern of the "Poor Man" thus helps to liberate the inner person and to make him or her capable of receiving the diverse charisms of the Holy Spirit so that through this sanctification, community and communion are strengthened and developed among human beings.

This is the basis of the Orthodox theology of mission, to acquire the dynamic, the power of the Spirit of Christ. It is the Spirit who creates the languages, forms and methods of mission. With this in mind, the whole people of God is summoned to be a true sign of the kingdom of God. It must confess courageously that the future of the church will come only as a gift of him who is the Lord of the future.

INTERNAL MISSION

The Life of Love

If the missionary proclamation of the gospel of the kingdom is to reach human hearts, there must be a palpable and real correspondence between the word preached in the power and joy of the Holy Spirit and the actual life of the Christian community. The gap between the message and the life of the historical church and its members constitutes the most massive obstacle to the credibility of the gospel for our contemporaries. "See how these Christians love one another," declared an ancient Christian apologist. The love of Christians is the very substance as well as the radiance of the gospel. In the apostolic community of Jerusalem as well as in the communities founded by St. Paul, the sharing of material things and concern for the poor became the spontaneous and necessary expression of their experience of the trinitarian love which is disclosed in the life of the church. The sharing of material things and of life itself thus flows from eucharistic communion and constitutes one of its radical requirements. When the church identifies itself with the prayer of its saviour, "Your kingdom come," it must above all ask itself in a spirit of penitence how much the unworthiness of Christians acts as a screen hindering the radiance of Christ himself from shining through.

The efficacy of missionary witness will be directly proportional to the Christian experience of the love of Christ. This love, says St. Paul, "controls us" (II Cor. 5:14). Once this flame of love sets one's heart ablaze, it prevents one from isolating oneself comfortably in one's own personal existence or that of one's community. The dismissal of the faithful at the end of the liturgy with the words "Go forth in peace!" does not mean that the liturgy is over, but that it is transposed into another form in which it continues, in the inner worship of the heart, in a life immersed in the daily life of human society. It is high time we overcame the very real temptation to make an absolute distinction between a spiritual life and a secular life. All human existence is sacred and remains within God's sight. It is within that existence that Christ's sovereignty purposes to be installed, so that no realm or aspect of human life may be abandoned to the forces of evil.

Christians thus experience in their own flesh and blood the inevitable tension between existence in the world and not belonging to the world. It is precisely because of the Christian's heavenly citizenship (cf. Heb. 13:14) that he or she is able to enter fully into the whole life of human society and to bring the light of Christ to bear on that life.

Service

Christ said, "Go ye therefore and make disciples of all nations, baptizing them in the name of the Father, and of the Son, and of the Holy Spirit" (Matt. 28:19). This means that together with worship other forms of Christian activity have great importance for mission, such as:
- preaching;
- publications;
- personal contacts;
- welfare;
- religious education;
- youth movements; and
- renewal of monastic life.

Each church should take advantage of these forms of mission if they are available to it.

Asceticism

Those who practice a spirituality of "Christian maximalism," renewal groups, religious orders, set us an example of mission. A joyful asceticism, whereby the old self is crucified with Christ so that the new self may rise with him and live for God (Rom. 6:5-11) carries the cross and resurrection of Christ into daily life; it develops all the potentialities of baptism and constitutes an essential sign of the coming kingdom.

Theological Education

There is a need for a deep change in the very understanding of the place of theology in our church. For centuries theology was thought of as an exclusively clerical task. But the time has come for a declericalization of theology. If theology is, above all, the study of the saving truth, it is needed by all members of the church; it is their essential spiritual food. To become this, however, it must revise its language, forms, and methods; it must be made into a common concern of the church. This change is needed by both clergy and laity, so that edification in the church— in a manner still to be defined—might become a continuous process of absorbing the saving truth and thereby entering it.

Spiritual Life

The church ensures the continuity and authenticity of prayer by the variety and richness of its liturgical and sacramental life. The life of the Christian, renewed by the Holy Spirit, is founded on prayer. Through prayer, Christians rediscover their deepest roots, their bond with life. In the spiritual life that it nourishes and prepares, the liturgical celebration finds its indispensable continuation.

Participation in the Eucharist

Of particular importance is the lay participation in the eucharist, and, in general, the sacramental discipline of the church. There are divergences and discrepancies in the churches, however, which reflect different theological traditions and require for their elimination deep theological, pastoral and spiritual investigation and effort. No revival of the parish as a truly liturgical community fulfilling itself at Christ's table in his kingdom is possible without a eucharistic revival, which alone can give life and integrate with one another the gifts and charisms of all members of the body of Christ.

Development of Individual Gifts

The whole church bears witness to the good news of the renewal of divine life in our fallen world. When the church rediscovers its essence as a fellowship, we begin to live as the church and not simply in the church. The church then ceases to be an oppressive structure and becomes again for its members the Father's house, providing them with shelter and with the heavenly bread. Here individual gifts are developed in all their rich diversity—prayer, love, wisdom, testimony—all contributing to the upbuilding of the one body of Christ.

SPECIFIC AREAS OF INTERNAL MISSION

The Role of Women

What is the proper place of women in this church of Christ that is essentially a fellowship? In a time when equal rights are being affirmed, do we not have to remember that it is in the body of Christ that woman finds both her true place and the forms of service that accord with her nature and her gifts?

The church today cannot ignore the question that presses on the universal human conscience concerning the place and role of woman in society in general, the special difficulties that she faces in an industrial society in which she participates as man's equal in the development of society, but in which, in virtue of her special charisms, she helps to uphold and carry the church and bears children both for life and for the Spirit. The church cannot be content to leave to others the burden of solving these questions about the distinctive dignity of woman in keeping with her nature, and about her liberation from all bondage by the Spirit of Christ.

Human Relationships

The problems presented by marriage, by the growing incidence of divorce, by the difficulties of human love in a hedonistically oriented society, can only be solved in the spirituality of a transfiguration of human nature, by the path of asceticism and spiritual combat, for this is the only way in which the demons by which our society is possessed can be exorcized.

Family

It must be emphasized that it is in large measure within the family cell that Christian life becomes a reality and the health of all nations is thus renewed. In face of contemporary threats to the very existence of the family, it should be remembered that it is within its setting that the spiritual worship and the proclamation of the word of God takes place day by day, that the priesthood of the parents, who offer their children to the divine light and who are thus the provisional representatives and mirrors of the divine parenthood and compassion, is exercised.

Youth

The confusion and difficulties of young people cannot fail to concern the church at the deepest levels of its pastoral mission. Because of the vulnerability of the young but also because of the dynamism and vigour that is naturally theirs, special care needs to be given to the guidance of young people as they face up to the immense problems of life, love, suffering, and the struggle for existence. The Orthodox Church has a vision and a profound experience of the problems of childhood and youth that it should share with all people of good will.

NOTES

1. *Go Forth in Peace*, 17-23.
2. *Go Forth in Peace*, 24-29.
3. *Go Forth in Peace*, 30-37. Originally printed in *International Review of Mission* 64: 253 (1975), 86-92.
4. *Go Forth in Peace*, 38-46.

2

Final Report of CWME Consultation of Eastern Orthodox and Oriental Orthodox Churches

Neapolis, 1988

In preparation for the WCC-CWME World Conference on Mission and Evangelism held at San Antonio, Texas (1989), a consultation of the Orthodox Advisory Group was convened at Neapolis, near Thessaloniki, from April 16-24, 1988, on the theme "Your Will Be Done—Orthodoxy in Mission." The consultation undertook a systematic analysis of the situation of the Orthodox churches, along with a further study of the theological problem of mission, in preparation for San Antonio. Situational reports were presented on Orthodoxy in Eastern Europe, the Islamic world, and other regions, and attention was devoted to the Orthodox approach to youth. The close collaboration of members of Eastern Oriental Churches in this consultation is a sign of growing rapprochement between the two Orthodox families of churches.

FINAL REPORT OF THE NEAPOLIS CONSULTATION (1988)*

More than sixty representatives of the Eastern Orthodox and Oriental Orthodox Churches, with the blessings and encouragement of their spiritual leaders, met and worked together in Neapolis, Greece from 16 to 24 April 1988 under the theme "Your Will Be Done: Orthodoxy in Mission," in order to prepare their contribution to the World Mission Conference to be held in San Antonio, Texas, under the theme "Thy Will Be Done: Mission in Christ's Way."

The participants found their participation in the life of the diocese and the parish during the consultation to be a deeply rewarding and enriching experience that brought them closer together as brothers and sisters in Christ.

The meeting was rich in testimony and experience. Papers and reports prepared by the brothers and sisters reflected the *martyria* of the Orthodox churches in their particular environments and served as a basis for broad and constructive discussion, implemented through panel discussions, which widened the scope of witnessing

*Reprinted from *Mission from Three Perspectives* (Geneva: WCC-CWME, 1989), 32-47; also found in *Your Will Be Done: Orthodoxy in Mission,* CWME Consultation of Eastern Orthodox and Oriental Orthodox Churches, Neapolis, Greece, April 16-24, 1988 (Katerini: Tertios, 1989), 43-60.

through the testimonies provided by youth, women and clergy involved in mission.

The harmonious collaboration and constructive discussions among the members of both Orthodox families, Eastern and Oriental, was highly appreciated and is a hopeful sign for the success of the on-going official bilateral theological dialogue of the Orthodox churches.

I. WITNESSING IN THE OIKOUMENE TODAY

THE APOSTOLIC WITNESS

God offers salvation to all human beings of all eras without limitation or exception because God wants all to be saved and to come to the knowledge of truth (I Tim. 2:4). As a result of his unlimited love for humankind, which submitted to evil, distortion and death by abusing the free will, God sent his only begotten Son "that whoever believes in him should not perish but have eternal life" (John 3:16).

Christ conquered sin and death, reconciled and granted peace to all things on earth and in heaven (cf. Col. 1:20), and granted the joy and the hope of the resurrection, which is the heart of the Christian message. "If Christ be not raised, our faith is in vain; you are yet in your sins" (I Cor. 15:17).

Christ ordered his disciples and apostles to proclaim the good news of salvation to all nations (Matt. 28:19), to the whole world and to all of creation (Mark 16:15) so that the salvific grace of Christ should be revealed to all who "sit in the darkness and the shadow of death" (Luke 1:79). The apostles had to be and to become witnesses of all salvific events of Christ's life (cf. Luke 24:48; Acts 10:39). The apostles considered this very witness to be their main mission. In replacing Judas they elected someone who, like they, was a witness to Christ's resurrection (Acts 1:22). Preaching the resurrection, they assured all that they were its witnesses (Acts 3:16). They could not avoid the obligation to proclaim all that they had seen and all that they had heard (Acts 4:20) because the joy of such an experience is only "fulfilled" when it is shared and transmitted to others so that they also might become communicants and participants (I John 1:4).

Throughout the centuries, the Orthodox Church had offered its apostolic witness to the crucified, buried and resurrected Christ. This same witness is continued by Christian mission today in the midst of such challenging conditions as secularization, pluralism, dialogue with other faiths and ideologies.

WITNESS IN A SECULAR WORLD

The mission of the church has cosmic dimensions. Its aim is to embrace and to renew the whole world, to transfigure it into God's kingdom. Mission is to approach and draw near, to sanctify and to renew the world, to give new content to old ways of life, to accept local cultures and their ways of expression that do not contradict the Christian faith, transforming them into means of salvation.

During the first centuries of its existence, the church managed to transfigure the face of the oikoumene in spite of resistance by the world, which attempted to make the church conform to the world. The church responded to these tendencies towards secularization by entering into dialogue with Greek philosophy and pagan culture, which resulted in the production of creative theological patristic literature, the intensification of the ascetic elements of the Christian life of its communities and monasteries as a new means of martyria, and the expanding and enriching of its worship. Within the boundaries of liturgical life the church sanctified the activities and creative talents of human beings in all forms of art (literature, architecture, painting, music).

In Orthodox worship the Christian message is proclaimed through all the senses. The entire human being participates with soul and body, mind and heart; hearing, smelling and touching. The icons, incense, the embrace of peace, the partaking of the eucharistic bread and wine enrich and fulfil the teaching and the preaching.

Education is more successful when influenced by the good news of salvation and a life in Christ in which the principle components are asceticism and eschatological expectation. Ascesis, as a voluntary withdrawal from a consumerist enjoyment of material goods, together with the desire to offer these goods to the poor and the needy, makes the passion and the cross of Christ more conscious in the life of Christians.

Mission is closely related to ascesis. For example, the Thessalonian Saints, Cyril and Methodius, before departing for Moravia, planned their missionary program and prepared themselves in a monastery of Olympos in Bithinia. Their missionary team was composed of priests, deacons, monks and lay persons. From the Saints of the Oriental Orthodox Non-Chalcedonian family, seven monks left the monastery of St. Minas in Egypt, formed a mission and evangelized Ireland. Their relics are still to be found in Belimina (near Belfast). Christian mission in Switzerland has been greatly affected by St. Verena, from Egypt. In all Orthodox countries, monasteries assisted in the proclamation and witness of the Christian message.

Unfortunately, in recent centuries, especially following the Enlightenment and the French Revolution, the Christian message was gradually marginalized and humanism became an autonomous anthropology leading to atheism. In such a context, links with the church are severed and the principles of state ideologies and education, as well as consumerism, dominate, satisfying industrial ambitions both in the east and the west. Secularization torments Christian communities in the whole world because the task of different ideologies is to separate human beings from the influence of the church. This separation is caused by destructive forces against the church, thus diminishing the church's diakonia in the world.

Some, who are not satisfied with secularized society, turn not to Christianity but to eastern cults. Islam, in confronting secularization, often turns to a more conservative lifestyle; the reaction to western humanism sometimes leads to an extreme theocracy, which demeans the human being.

The abundance of material goods and economic conformism, dechristianized state power and education, the lack of Christian perspective in the mass-media, the weakness of the family in exercising Christian pedagogical work and the diminishing of the spiritual and apostolic role of motherhood leads to secularism. The contradiction between words and deeds in the life of Christians further contributes to the development of a secular way of life.

Nevertheless, many human beings continue to be attracted to Orthodox Christianity through its asceticism and mysticism, the joy of the resurrection in its worship, the presence of ascetics and saints, and the proof through holiness that Christians are not conformed to the world (cf. Rom. 12:2; I Pet. 1:14).

WITNESS WITHIN A PLURALISTIC SOCIETY AND AMONG BELIEVERS OF OTHER FAITHS

Today, Christianity is in a situation similar to that of the apostolic era when it faced syncretism and different philosophies or religions. A pluralistic world brings

Christianity into confrontation and dialogue with other teachings and faiths. Despite intolerance and fanaticism, Christians can use the immense potential offered by contemporary technology to witness to and evangelize others, to lead them in Christ's way. Christianity sees in a positive way the creative work of human beings when it leads to the uplifting of humanity and to the glory of God. To understand the cultural particularities of the evangelized, we must speak their language, respond with love to both spiritual and material deprivation and bring life and brilliance to each eucharistic community. The love we owe to those of other faiths makes more imperative our duty to confirm, as did the early Christian Apologists, whatever truth may be found in them while affirming the fullness and authenticity of the salvific truth of Christianity, even under pressure of persecution. The Orthodox churches, continuing the apostolic witness, have given tangible proof of endurance through the cloud of witnesses and new martyrs.

The awareness of the real needs of other people in this world helps us in the fulfilment of our missionary work and diakonia. Here, the basic missionary principle does not lose its eternal significance for a consistent and holy Christian life, which impresses and is beneficial to the awakening of those outside the church. In the midst of peoples and cultures where Christians live with all other persons, mission in Christ's way ought to lead towards sanctity of life, as an early Christian text of the second century states:

> Christians are not distinguished from others because of their homelands, their languages and their customs. Moreover, they do not live in separate towns, neither do they use a different dialect. . . . However, while living in Greece and barbarian (non-Greek) cities, following the indigenous customs pertaining to clothing, food, and lifestyle, they provide an admirable and extraordinary way of life (Epistle to Diognetos, 5).

II. MISSION AND UNITY

ECCLESIOLOGICAL PERSPECTIVES

The apostolic community was gathered into one body by the Holy Spirit in the power and joy of the resurrection (cf. John 20:22). Members of this community were called to be witnesses to the risen Christ "to the ends of the earth" (Acts 1:8). The ground of unity of the church, the body of Christ, is the love and unity eternally manifested in the life of the Holy Trinity. The church, as the presence of the kingdom of God, is called to manifest this trinitarian communion and love within its fold and towards the world. The church's mission is the expression of this unity and love.

God's love for the world is manifested in the incarnation of the word of God (John 1:1), in the supreme sacrifice on the cross and in the power of the resurrection. It was his mission from the Father, the accomplishment of his will (cf. Luke 22:42; John 5:30). The church, as the body of Christ, is called to this missionary act of self-giving sacrifice and to proclaim the good news of salvation to the world.

In the eucharistic celebration every local church experiences the fullness of the church catholic and prepares itself to address the world through words and deeds of love. The church gathers into one body the whole creation and the joy and the sufferings of all people as it stands in the presence of God in the eucharistic act of praise, thanksgiving and intercession. This inward movement of gathering into one body is accompanied by the outward movement of going forth in mission and service to God's creation. Together, these movements constitute the church's witness to the crucified and risen Christ in whom the unity and the love of the Triune God is manifested in a unique way.

COMMON WITNESS

In the church's "ecclesial" (ek-kalo) movement of calling out, incorporating and building up process, the following major aspects are necessary for its realization today:

(1) As Eastern Orthodox and Oriental Orthodox Non-Chalcedonian churches, we need to fully restore the unity in communion of our two families of churches. While we gratefully acknowledge the steps recently taken by our churches towards coming together in mutual love and communion in the one apostolic faith, we wish to emphasize the urgency of the matter for our common witness today. We need to reaffirm our unity in faith above all historic, ethnic, racial, linguistic, national or political loyalties.

(2) As active members of the wider ecumenical family of churches, we pray and work for the unity of all in accordance with the will of God expressed in the high-priestly prayer of our Lord. It is our special mission to witness to the apostolic faith of the one undivided church as all churches seek to grow more and more in "one Lord, one faith and one baptism."

(3) It is God's oikoumene that is the wider context of our unity. Our theological and spiritual heritage is filled with the cosmic dimension of God's salvation. Nothing in the created realm is excluded from this sanctifying and transfiguring power of the Spirit of God. As the liturgical experience shows, the one eucharistic bread stands at the same time for the one church and the totality of creation that we offer to God in thanksgiving. While joyfully celebrating the marvellous gift of creation, we have to commit ourselves to humanity's struggles for human dignity, justice and peace. As Orthodox churches we can witness to the integrity of creation by dedicating ourselves to acts of healing, reconciling, enlightening and saving.

The outgoing ("processional") movement of the church's witness is what we usually call mission. This mission of the church has several points of reference, such as the eternal unity in the Triune God, unity between the divine and human in the incarnate word of God and the unity between Christ, the head of the church and the church his body. All these dimensions of unity are constitutively qualified by love. The same divine love is the motivating power behind the sending of the Son by the Father and the mission of the comforter Spirit to the church. Thus, the mission of the church is in fact an outreaching processional movement of unity and love.

Therefore, the church, the people of God in the communion of the Holy Spirit, is missionary in its very being, ever proceeding and ever gathering, pulsating with God's all-embracing love and unity. The church, as the presence of the kingdom of God in the world, illuminates in one single reality the glory of God and the eschatological destiny of creation.

The missionary character of the church is expressed in diverse ways and forms: liturgical witness to the transcendent dimension of reality, direct evangelistic witness, witness in secular and pluralistic situations, witness through prayer and asceticism, witnessing the life-giving gospel to the poor and oppressed, witness through committed sharing of the struggle for justice and peace, etc. These are some of the expressions of the outreaching movement of the church's mission.

The constitutive character of mission as the expression of unity calls for a common witness. The situation of our world makes it imperative that what the churches can do together they should not do separately. The search for a common witness helps the churches to come out of their parochial loyalties and encourages them to seek together God's will for our contemporary world.

The Orthodox churches, living in diverse cultures, challenged by their sociopolitical, economic and linguistic situations, are called upon to engage in a common witness to the one apostolic faith in Christ in new missionary situations. By responding to these challenges creatively and in the unity of the Spirit, without catering to the narrow interests of each individual church, the churches are responding to the will of God.

A serious effort towards creating Orthodox missionary centres and a global missionary strategy will inspire and enable our local Orthodox churches not only to witness along with other Orthodox churches, but also to contribute substantially, from the Orthodox perspective, to other Christian churches engaged in similar forms of witness.

PROSELYTISM

Proselytism, along with the actual disunity among the churches, creates major obstacles for our common witness. Some Christian churches and evangelical bodies are actively engaged in proselytizing Christians already belonging to Orthodox churches. All proselytism by any church should be condemned, and all antagonism and unhealthy competition in mission work should be avoided, as constituting a distorted form of mission.

Unfortunately, well-financed resources and the power of the media in western Europe and America, often play a key role in maintaining the unchristian missionary zeal of those involved in proselytizing efforts. The Orthodox churches have to continue efforts to persuade those churches and agencies involved in proselytism not to engage in dubious missionary activities detrimental to God's will for unity, and to seek the path of true Christian charity and unity.

At the same time, our Orthodox churches have to pay closer attention to the pastoral, educational and spiritual needs of our people and foster in every possible way a continual spiritual renewal in our parishes and monastic communities. It is especially important to develop ways of strengthening family life and caring for the special needs of youth that they might realize the communal love and concern of the church for their well-being and salvation.

One impetus for the modern ecumenical vision was originally inspired by the committed search for a common witness to the good news of salvation. It still remains the primary objective of our ecumenical involvement—to offer common witness in love to the power of Christ, crucified and risen, so that those who are caught up in this world of division, conflict and death may believe and be transfigured.

III. SOCIAL IMPLICATIONS OF SACRAMENTAL LIFE

THE SACRAMENTAL DIMENSION OF LIFE

In the sacrament—*mysterion*—of the church, human beings are restored to their proper relationship to God: to communion in Christ with God in the Holy Trinity. Through baptism, chrismation and eucharist, persons receive a new birth in Christ, are anointed in the Spirit and are fully incorporated into the body of Christ—the church. The gift of this new life in Christ implies a commitment to the renewal of all of life, a conversion of mind and heart, so that God's will may be done, so that the world itself may be transformed and raised up by the witness and work of his children.

In Christ's life, death and resurrection, all creation is restored and sanctified (cf. Eph. 1:10). Our life in Christ, therefore, must become a sacramental life, a life that continues the process of sanctifying all life and all time given to us as God's gift. The church, in the fullness of this sacramental and diaconal life, is and manifests dynamically Christ's presence to the world. Thus, as we participate in the church's life, through fasting, prayer, the celebration of feasts and sacraments, and active service to the poor, we renew ourselves and the entire cosmos, to the extent that our life conforms to Christ in the Holy Spirit.

The struggle to renew all things in God is a daily effort. It involves not merely individuals working for their own salvation, but the corporate work of persons seeking to unite all creation in communion with the living God. Such a life requires humility and sacrifice, self-emptiness, the giving of ourselves to others in love and service, as the Lord gave himself up for us "for the life of the world" (John 6:51). It is life lived in community with others and for others. This is the ecclesial, sacramental reality of life in Christ.

THE EUCHARIST AND RENEWAL OF LIFE

How is this sacramental life developed and nurtured today in the midst of a secular, broken and suffering world? How can all things be united once again in the love and sovereignty of God's kingdom?

For Orthodox Christians, the centre and vivifying force of renewal is the eucharist, where all persons and all creation are gathered together, lifted up, and united in the once-and-for-all offering of Christ himself. The eucharist gives us not only the bread of life necessary for our spiritual sustenance and growth, but lifts up our hearts and minds, enabling us to see with a new vision the life that God has prepared for us from all eternity.

It is in the eucharist that we come to know one another as members of one body, united in the love of Christ in the image of the Holy Trinity. It is in and through this communion in the Spirit that we are given the strength and the power to fulfill Christ's mission in the world.

But this same eucharist is also a judgement for Christians, for we may also partake of it "unto our judgement or condemnation" if this gift of communion is not personally appropriated and realized in our daily lives. We know that through our own weakness and sin, we continue to deny God's love and power in the world. When we ignore the sufferings of our brothers and sisters, when we misuse the gifts of creation through pollution, destruction and waste of natural resources, we create new idols of and for ourselves. Isolated in egocentric self-will and self-indulgence, we cause our own spiritual death and that of our neighbours by indifference, conflict, division and lack of love. We also realize that amidst the joyful unity revealed and given to us within our own church, the awareness of the continuing division of Christians saddens and challenges us.

PRAYER AND REPENTANCE

Consequently, the eucharist and the whole liturgical life of the church calls us to prayer and repentance. Through our common prayer in the church, we learn to pray personally, to offer glory and thanksgiving to God, to pray for ourselves and others, to consider the needs of the whole world, to keep one another alive in Christ through our remembrance of the sick and suffering, those in captivity and persecution, those who have departed this life before us, and especially the martyrs, saints and spiritual fathers and mothers whose witness provides an example for our lives, teaching us the true meaning of the words "Your will be done."

This prayer of Christ to the Father is a continual reminder of the need for repentance and forgiveness of sins. It is a call to re-examine our lives in the light of Christ's life. It is a call addressed personally to each of us for *metanoia* and conversion, a call to literally "turn around" our lives and recommit ourselves to Christ.

WITNESS AND THE SACRAMENTAL LIFE

Finally, for those who have strayed from the communion of the church, as well as for those who have never experienced the newness of her life and joy, the sacraments and the entire life of the church offer opportunities for witness to the truth about God and his relationship to us. Baptisms, marriages, visitations to the sick and dying, ordinations, funerals and rites of blessing, as well as the actual diakonia of the church in social concern and justice, provide unique occasions to proclaim God's message of hope, peace and joy in the crucified and resurrected Lord. It is at these moments, when lives are touched by joy or sorrow, suffering and compassion, that the truths about the ultimate questions of life can awaken minds and hearts to the love of God. It is at these times also that the best witness is the personal witness and presence of the church, through the love and care of her members as a supportive community renewed in faith, love and freedom.

Only in this way, through a sacramental awareness and commitment to the world and a personal offering of ourselves to God, all his children, can we carry on Christ's mission in the world: that all may know "what is the breadth and length and height and depth of the love of Christ. . . . so (that we) may attain to fullness of being, the fullness of God himself" (Eph. 3:18-19).

IV. THE MISSIONARY IMPERATIVE AND RESPONSIBILITY IN THE LOCAL CHURCH

THE MISSION OF THE LOCAL CHURCH

The mission of everyone is to know Christ, to live in him and witness to him by word and deed. When our eucharistic assembly experiences this truth, the necessity to share the joy of the resurrection with all people is a natural consequence. This mission includes even those who are baptized, yet ignorant of the calling and election they have received through baptism. It is essential that contemporary means be developed to help them return to the fellowship of the church. The church's mission also calls us to the task of peacemaking, reconciling and defending justice for everyone, especially in contexts where the people of God suffer from injustice, violence, oppression and war. When the eucharistic assembly does not engage in such outreaches it fails to realize its missionary responsibility.

CATHOLICITY OF THE LOCAL CHURCH

According to Orthodox ecclesiology, the building up (*oikodome*) of the body of Christ is an essential part of evangelization. Although there are normative forms of local communities, new forms of Christian communities may be necessary due to many social and cultural factors. In the process of building up new communities, the church, through its bishops, must be flexible in their creation.

The mission of the local church suffers when its "catholic" dimension, its ecumenical openness, is not sufficiently underlined and expressed. The local community must not only pray for the *oikoumene,* but must be aware of the necessity to preach the gospel to the whole world. It is the task of each local church to educate missionaries for this work wherever needed.

Some churches have already organized missionary departments to undertake the responsibility of sending missionaries. But the sending of missionaries is an ecclesiological act of establishing a concrete Christian presence in a given nation and culture. The indigenous church must be assisted to develop its own identity and local structure as part of a global fellowship. Every mission outreach should aim to create self-sufficient churches in fellowship with the whole church.

ENCOURAGING VARIOUS MINISTRIES

The church has always recognized the vocation of great missionaries and evangelists. It has also recognized the missionary vocation of the whole people of God, each member of the body of Christ being called in and by the Holy Spirit to mission.

The local bishop has the duty to identify, encourage, help and actualize various forms of lay ministry. The church needs for its evangelistic work catechists, readers, preachers, chanters and all those who participate in the service of the church. In this regard, it is necessary to renew the tradition of deaconesses. In lay movements and associations, the church possesses an extraordinary missionary network for encouraging the participation of the people of God in mission: men, women, youth, scholars, workers and children.

OTHER MISSION CHALLENGES

(1) The rise of various extremist Christian sects.

(2) The dominating attitude of wealthy and powerful churches towards minority local churches.

(3) The resurgence of other religions and various secular ideologies.

(4) The disintegration of the family as the basic unit of church and society and problems resulting from broken families and single-parent situations.

(5) The emergence of new cultures, which influence — positively or negatively — the spirituality of today's youth.

(6) The search for a contemporary code of communication to transmit the message of eternal truth.

RECOMMENDATIONS TO ORTHODOX CHURCHES

The participants in this consultation acknowledge the missionary involvement of their respective churches and the work already done in the mission field. With the following recommendations they aim to encourage the churches to continue, to enlarge and to enrich their missionary efforts all around the world for the sake of a most efficient evangelistic witness today.

(1) That the missionary vocation must become a major concern and responsibility in the life of the church and that special programs for mission awareness be organized for men, women and children in various walks of life to help them fulfil their missionary obligation.

(2) That Christian education and catechetical material must incorporate the missionary imperative.

(3) That theological schools and other educational institutions incorporate missiological studies in their programs, and the training and skills needed for mission.

(4) That Orthodox institutes and training centres for mission be established to accept and prepare candidates for work in the mission field. That experienced and qualified Orthodox missionaries be utilized as teachers.

(5) That the church institute diaconal ministries, along with liturgical petitions and intercessions with emphasis on mission, for use in local parishes.

(6) That special collections in every parish be offered for mission and that a special place be established for mission information and promotion.

(7) That Associations or Friends of Missionaries be organized for moral and material support of those engaged in mission.

(8) That regional forums be established for coordination, cooperation and sharing of the Orthodox mission resources of the various churches.

(9) That Orthodox publications — especially translations — be utilized for the support of mission work.

(10) That the church renew the vocations of the deaconesses, catechists, readers, musicians and preachers for particular service in the mission field.

(11) That the churches call monks and nuns to establish a monastic witness, in places where missions are being established, as spiritual centers.

(12) That all churches set aside a special time each year for the promotion and support of missions.

(13) That Orthodox churches join with other Christian churches in increasing their moral and financial support for the work of the World Council of Churches in general and the Commission on World Mission and Evangelism (CWME) in particular.

3

Final Report of CWME Orthodox Advisory Group

Boston, 1990

The meeting of the Orthodox Advisory Group at Holy Cross Orthodox School of Theology near Boston, June 17-24, 1990, was convened for the purpose of attempting an Orthodox missiological reflection on the theme of the WCC Seventh Assembly (Canberra, 1991), "Come, Holy Spirit—Renew the Whole Creation." The meeting also provided an opportunity to review ongoing Orthodox participation in the work of CWME and the life of the WCC. Reports from various countries and regions were received. Both before and after Canberra, Orthodox theologians engaged in sharp exchanges with WCC leaders on a variety of theological issues, attesting to Orthodoxy's deep conviction that ecumenical activity must continuously be grounded in scripture and Christian tradition if it is to endure. The text expresses the Orthodox view that the church's participation in God's mission for the salvation and life of the whole creation is enabled by the power of the Holy Spirit.

THE HOLY SPIRIT AND MISSION*

The WCC-CWME Orthodox Advisory Group met at Holy Cross Greek Orthodox School of Theology in Boston, MA, USA, 17-24 June 1990. The purpose of the meeting was to reflect on certain missiological implications of the Canberra Assembly theme, "Come, Holy Spirit—Renew the Whole Creation." Enriched and challenged by the presence of Orthodox priests, lay persons and young students of theology from fifteen countries, the Advisory Group also reviewed and assessed Orthodox missionary efforts in a variety of countries and regions. The San Antonio Report, as well as the reflection on the assembly theme as expressed in the report of the Eastern Orthodox and Oriental Orthodox Consultation at the Orthodox Academy of Crete, Greece, 1989, constituted a solid background for the theological presentations, the panel discussions and the sincere exchange of ideas, information, and experiences.

---

*Reprinted from George Lemopoulos, ed., *The Holy Spirit and Mission,* Report of the CWME Orthodox Advisory Group, Holy Cross Orthodox School of Theology, Boston, June 17-24, 1990 (Geneva: WCC-CWME, 1990), 89-100.

REFLECTING ON THE ASSEMBLY THEME

1. The Assembly theme, "Come, Holy Spirit—Renew the Whole Creation," expresses in prayer the longing of all Christians for the coming of the Holy Spirit to bring the world into communion with God in Christ. It is, therefore, of a particular missiological significance to the Orthodox Church, as we consider the starting point of all missionary activities to be the promise and command of the risen Lord in its trinitarian perspective: "As the Father has sent me, even so I send you ... Receive the Holy Spirit" (John 20:21-22).

2. "When the Paraclete comes, whom I shall send to you from the Father, even the Spirit of truth, who proceeds from the Father, he will bear witness to me; and you are also witnesses" (John 15:26). "When the Spirit of truth comes, he will guide you into all the truth ... He will glorify me, for he will take what is mine and declare it to you" (John 16:13-14). The church in mission bears witness to what the Holy Spirit declares and announces. The Holy Spirit not only interprets Christ's words but transmits his life and power. He grafts us into Christ, so that we may dwell in him and he in us (John 6:53-55).

3. Through the outpouring of the Holy Spirit, the formation of the church and the continuous presence of the Spirit in the world, a process of transfiguration of human life begins that raises humanity and transforms the universe. Mission, therefore, aims to incorporate humankind into Christ by building up his body (cf. Eph. 4:12), forming eucharistic communities wherever people accept the truth of the gospel and come into communion with the Triune God through baptism by the power of the Holy Spirit. Through this communion, the world is purified and liberated from the forces of evil and death. Renewed and sanctified by God's Spirit, humanity moves from disunity into unity, from falsehood into truth, from hatred into love, from self-centredness into a life of communion with God, and, consequently, with all of God's creation.

4. The prayer "Come, Holy Spirit" is uttered by those who believe that the world, in spite of technological and scientific advances and pretensions of self-sufficiency, cannot exist or develop its full potential apart from God's presence and action in it. As humanity moves freely towards God, all life begins to be experienced as a communion of love, reflecting the life of the Holy Trinity.

5. From the scriptures and tradition of our church, by the power of the Holy Spirit, we learn of and experience God's unconditional love for his creation. The Triune God, because of his love, is "God-in-mission." The Spirit teaches us that the purpose of God's involvement in creation and in history is to offer human beings, and, through them, to the entire creation, the possibility of transcending their limitations and entering into the glory and life of God (Rom. 8:20-21). The church finds its true vocation in God's mission for the salvation of the whole world.

6. The Holy Spirit constitutes the church as the body of Christ. The church manifests the fullness of its true nature whenever it gathers to celebrate the eucharist and goes out into the world to proclaim the gospel to all who seek redemption. Mission and evangelism are constitutive of the church's being. They are indispensable expressions of its catholicity and they manifest also the church's participation in God's mission for the salvation of the entire world. In addition, the Spirit of God through its constant, renewing power, challenges all kinds of inertia and stagnation within the church that limits Christian witness of God's love for the whole creation.

7. Christians must be aware that the Spirit of God cannot be domesticated. At every moment and circumstance of their lives, they must learn to pray to the Spirit for guidance and wisdom in order to live according to God's will and to receive God's gifts. It is only through the power of the Holy Spirit that we begin to live in Christ and experience life as communion of love in him (I Cor. 12:3), identifying our existence with him in the suffering of his cross and in the glory of his resurrection. This identification with Christ and the empowerment by the Spirit of God are visibly expressed at Pentecost, when the disciples of Jesus became the church to proclaim "the good news through the Holy Spirit" (cf. I Pet. 1:12).

8. Participating actively in God's mission through the power of the Holy Spirit means that the church prays and acts for the salvation and life of the entire creation. Through its sacramental life, the church invokes God to send his Spirit upon all for the sanctification and unity in Christ of the faithful, as well as to sustain, redeem and sanctify the whole created world. Whatever is positive, creative, communal, just and peaceful in the world must be attributed to God's providential love for his creation. For, as St. Ambrose of Milan said: "All truth, no matter where it comes from, is from the Holy Spirit" (PL 144,919). The church prays for this active and saving presence of God in creation. The awareness of such presence should evoke in the hearts of all Christians praise and thanksgiving to God for his love of the world.

9. From a missiological perspective, the presence of God's Spirit in creation makes the study of cultural, social and physical realities imperative. Such knowledge leads to an appreciation of particular cultural images and symbols by which the Christian faith can be communicated in an existential and meaningful manner. Respect for a particular culture, however, does not necessarily elevate all its expressions to legitimate vehicles for communicating the Christian gospel. Some elements of a particular culture may need to be transformed, and new cultural expressions should or can be developed by the presence of God's Spirit in them.

10. On the other hand, sensitivity and respect for particular cultural expressions of the Christian faith should not be idealized. This can lead to provincialism, destroy the universality of the Christian gospel, and constitute a denial of the Holy Spirit, who moves everything into unity (Eph. 1:10) by transcending all kinds of self-sufficiency.

11. If the Holy Spirit is at work—albeit hiddenly—in culture, then his unexpected ways of judging, testing and re-fashioning Christian witness may be blocked by our lack of confidence in his work, as he acts in the church and in the world. We are called to study the strange and sometimes offensive voices in various cultural milieus not only for the purpose of combatting or converting them, but also to learn from them and to deepen our insights and understanding of the gospel. Thus, in its explicit dialogue with the cultural setting, the faith of the church acquires an existential meaning and a transforming power. In this dialogue, the Holy Spirit helps us to discern the ever newness of the gospel, enlightens us to receive it and empowers us to proclaim it.

12. The awareness that the Spirit of God is present everywhere liberates Christian mission and witness from fanaticism and a narrow understanding of God's salvific presence and action in history. What is expected of us today is to be a missionary church that, in its catholicity, embraces the whole world. Like St. Paul, when he proclaimed the gospel to the Athenians, we need not fear for our salvation when we enter into dialogue with people of other faiths and ideologies. It is our duty to claim confidently that God's Spirit acts in all of his creation, manifesting actively and salvifically God's love for it.

13. Ultimately, as the fundamental criterion for the discernment of the *logos* in all things is the *logos made flesh,* similarly, the criterion of the Spirit at work in the world is and must be the Spirit revealed in and given through the risen Christ.

14. The fact that other destructive, deceitful spirits operate in the world must not abstract our ability to discern God's Spirit at work in the world. The Holy Spirit is at work in the life of the world so that he may ultimately unite everything with God in Christ. This work is accomplished in inscrutable ways since the Holy Spirit "blows where it wills, and you hear the sound of it, but you do not know whence it comes or whither it goes" (John 3:8).

II. STUDYING SOME OF OUR HISTORICAL CONTEXTS

The theme "Holy Spirit and Mission" led the participants of this meeting to reflect on some contextual situations and recent socio-political developments in countries where Orthodox churches live and witness today. The following thoughts and suggestions constitute an attempt to draw concrete missiological implications from the enriching exchange of information and concerns.

(A) CENTRAL AND EASTERN EUROPE

The radical changes taking place today in central and eastern Europe have tremendous missiological consequences for the Orthodox Church. Much has been said about the need for repentance, the new possibilities for evangelistic work and the great challenge of participating in the building up of a renewed society. However, it would be of great missiological importance to attempt an evaluation and to draw strength from the past in the light of both failures and martyrdom.

The most crucial task of the church, in its faithfulness to its inner life of Spirit and Gospel, could be a genuine effort to become visibly that power which unmasks all false messianic expectations or utopian illusions, and resists all forms of idolatry.

In its efforts to proclaim God's unlimited love and share the liberating and reconciling power of the Holy Spirit, the church would have to express Christian conviction and Orthodox vision in public forums and work in groups seeking to improve and transform the conditions of life. Thus, for example, we welcome the effort by the Russian Orthodox Church to enter into dialogue with civil authorities and secular academic circles on the crucial issue of social ethics. This is a form of Christian witness, from which the church was excluded for several decades, and to which it now returns as it shoulders the great missionary task of education and diaconal service leading to social justice.

(B) THE MIDDLE EAST

The Middle East is confronted today with a resurgence of religious conservative trends requiring a unique historical Orthodox witness. This phenomenon could generate pressure, fear and uncertainty in the relationship among all the religious communities if they do not reinforce their experiences in sharing with each other a common way of thinking, lifestyle and culture. As indigenous to the Middle East, the Orthodox need to manifest solidarity with all religious communities in all aspects of life. It is only through such sharing that all religious communities can face together the sinister influences of an imported secularization that is threatening the common local culture — especially the Islamic one — very often leading to aggressive fundamentalism.

It is essential for all Orthodox churches, in the Middle East as well as around the world, to support justice, peace and human rights in the burning local situations and to condemn any interpretation of the scriptures aiming primarily at political purposes. Orthodoxy implies opening up and sharing in the suffering of the poor, far from any sectarian approach. In the Middle East, for example, Orthodox med-ico-social and diaconal services, as a means of Christian witness, aim at expressing true inter-personal relations and love towards all brothers and sisters without any distinction. Any new western missionary enterprise that endeavours to create a Christian population hostile to Muslims—such as the aggressive missionary efforts of certain western Evangelical groups—should be denounced and rejected, because this is a counter-witness to the Christian gospel.

All Orthodox churches are called to be inspired by the unique experience of common witness and common Christian involvement in the Eastern and Oriental Orthodox churches of the Middle East. It is imperative for the Orthodox Church to be united in response to this concrete missionary endeavour.

Finally, all Orthodox churches, in cooperation with the concerned local churches, should help and support the Orthodox presence and witness in the region in order not to lose this historical and living witness of the Holy Spirit's work.

(C) THE WESTERN HEMISPHERE

The planting of Orthodox communities in continents and countries that are new for the Orthodox church has created new opportunities and challenges for Orthodox life and witness. This is especially true in western Europe, North and South America as well as in Australia. One of the points of theological and missiological tension is to be found in the term "diaspora" itself. From the point of view of the Orthodox churches in the Middle East and eastern Europe, Orthodox Christians in the "new lands" are living in diaspora. From the point of view of increasing numbers of clergy and laity in these countries, the Orthodox Church, in its new contexts of life and witness, is a permanent presence, one that calls the church to mission. Conse-quently, "diaspora" is not a term in which they recognize themselves. To be fruitful, the present Orthodox discussion on this matter will need to enter more deeply into the cultural experience of the "new" Orthodox churches and communities by draw-ing their representatives into inter-Orthodox discussion and reflection.

It was noted, furthermore, that the ability of the Orthodox Church, as a whole, to meet the dangers and opportunities of the present moment in coherent and credible ways is being tested day by day, not least in the new countries of Orthodox life and mission. If Orthodox unity in mission and witness is not fully operative in the diaspora, it will not be credible elsewhere. Thus, we consider it to be a primary mission duty that the theological schools make concrete theological proposals in this field to the competent ecclesiastical authorities.

(D) THE YOUNGER ORTHODOX CHURCHES

Though small in number, the missionary Orthodox churches of Africa and Asia inaugurate an important chapter in the history of Orthodoxy and become a hopeful sign for the future. The growing Orthodox missionary activities in Africa and Asia, even if their results are poor compared to other churches, constitute a double challenge to the Orthodox churches. On the one hand, they raise the church's consciousness of the importance of missionary work, even reminding them of the "forgotten commandment." On the other hand, they compel all to know well, appreciate and understand the present realities that are at work in these younger mission churches.

These activities, however, inevitably pose the crucial missionary questions: (a) the relation between gospel and culture, and (b) the encounter of different cultures in the new setting and context. Efforts have already been made to avoid conflicts between proclaiming the gospel and local cultural realities. Concrete experiences show, nevertheless, that the acceptance of a local culture and its ways of expression that do not contradict the Christian faith is not always an easy task. The challenge addressed here to the Orthodox churches is to revitalize, in these efforts, their patristic and missionary tradition.

The spectrum of missionary work in Africa and Asia is wide. And it grows even wider when we meditate on the responsibility that every local church has for assisting its people in matters of sanitation, education and development. In addition, the permanent struggles of the younger Orthodox churches in the third world could forge the Orthodox awareness of the problems of injustice, poverty, oppression and—sometimes—political bondage, and reinforce the Orthodox commitment within the common Christian effort for justice, peace and the integrity of creation.

The prayer and vision of all—ultimately, our aim—is to see the establishment of true local Orthodox churches in Africa and Asia. Therefore, in order to consolidate these churches, there is need of serious and continuous assistance to be offered by the older Orthodox churches.

(E) AN INTERNATIONAL PERSPECTIVE: ORTHODOX YOUTH

Involved in the very life of the church, both on local and international levels, Orthodox youth is an integral part of church's mission. Authentic prophetic voices, such as those among the youth, challenge the churches to engage themselves heavily in mission. Their idealism, enthusiasm and energy are a constant reminder to all that a practical, lived theology is the most effective Christian witness.

In some regions of the world, young people are often the first victims of unjust socio-economic, political and cultural situations. An effort to find adequate means to assist them in overcoming these difficulties is an important missionary responsibility.

The role of "Syndesmos" within the Orthodox church could be considered unique. A unifying force that gathers and binds together Orthodox youth from all parts of the world, it has at the heart of its many concerns a deep appreciation of and a keen interest in missionary activity. In fact, it provides a forum for prayer, reflection and Christian witness. Encouraging the work undertaken by this organization of Orthodox youth could be considered as an important contribution to the missionary activities of youth.

III. ENABLING LOCAL CONGREGATIONS FOR MISSION

The centre of Orthodox spiritual and missionary life is the sacrament of the eucharist, by which, in the power of the Holy Spirit, we become "one body with Christ." Thus, every local congregation, celebrating the eucharist and sharing in Christ's life, shares in Christ's mission. Indeed, it is primarily in the context of the local congregation, the eucharistic gathering, that the good news of salvation is proclaimed.

However, it is a fundamental requirement for every local congregation to experience simultaneously both the universal and local dimension of the church. Each local congregation—and, consequently, each local church—to be genuinely catholic, should pray for and be ready to serve in the most needy regions. In this way, the church remains faithful to its apostolicity and catholicity.

Realizing that the context of the local congregation will vary from region to region, and from nation to nation, and even within a nation, we nevertheless recommend the following as ways to reinforce and empower the local congregation for more active engagement in mission work.

(A) CLERGY

Since the clergy are the most influential and, usually, the most theologically informed leaders within the local congregation, their commitment to mission should be reinforced through:

—required mission concerns during seminary training;

—a period of required training in a mission situation as a prerequisite to ordination;

—the provision of adequate financial support for the priest and his family, thus freeing him for mission work;

—the establishment of mission training centres and, through them, the encouragement of mission vocations;

—the production of mission literature, videos, etc., geared to assist clergy.

(B) LAITY

Mission knowledge and action among adult Orthodox lay Christians must be promoted through:

—Bible studies leading to the discovery of the mission imperative within scripture;

—the integration of mission into worship, i.e., the reintroduction into the divine liturgy of the petitions concerning catechumens;

—seminars, retreats, mission leadership training sessions, etc., to train men and women to share their experience of the Resurrected Lord with the great numbers of people on the periphery of parish life;

—lectures and presentations by visiting missionaries;

—the production of appropriate mission literature, tracts, newsletters, videos, etc.

(C) CHILDREN AND YOUTH

Mission awareness should be instilled among children and youth through:

—the integration of mission teaching into the church school curriculum;

—the lives of great saints, such as Cyril and Methodios, Gregory the Armenian and others, offered as role models;

—the production of mission literature, videos, etc., geared to the young.

(D) OTHER WAYS

Among many other ways to increase mission awareness, zeal and action within the Orthodox churches could be the following:

—help educate indigenous clergy by providing scholarships, especially for persons from developing nations as well as from central and eastern Europe (this should not always mean bringing students to seminaries in the west);

—establish chairs of missiology at the leading Orthodox theological schools, east and west;

—send mission teams to support, encourage and give hope to struggling young churches;

—use fund-raising for mission as an opportunity to teach about mission;

—promote exchange visits among Orthodox lay people of various nations;

—encourage Orthodox churches, where there is a multiplicity of jurisdictions in a single nation, to cooperate in mission work.

(E) SHARING OUR CONCERNS WITH CWME

We would like, first, to express our thanks to CWME for providing opportunities for Orthodox mission persons to gather and for producing publications such as "Martyria—Mission." While we encourage the production of more volumes of this calibre, we would like to recommend:

—that CWME initiate the gathering of Orthodox documents and statements of goals from the various Orthodox Mission Centers and Mission Bodies existing today;

—that CWME help convene, at Holy Cross School of Theology in Brookline, MA, a consultation of persons teaching mission in Orthodox theological schools and persons involved in Orthodox mission structures, to offer a definitive document on the goals, strategies and implementation of Orthodox mission work in the world today;

—that CWME help promote the establishment of endowed chairs of missiology at Orthodox seminaries; and

—that CWME encourage the inclusion of more mission courses at the Ecumenical Institute of Bossey and help provide scholarships for Orthodox students from developing nations.

IV. CONCLUDING REFLECTIONS

Instead of drawing up a conclusion, the Orthodox Advisory Group would like to highlight here two important insights from the WCC/CWME world mission conference, held in San Antonio, Texas, USA, 1989. These insights inspired and guided the work of the group during this meeting and challenged the participants to take into consideration that the key to any mission activity is to act in a local context with a universal-eschatological perspective.

The fact that the will of God refers to the whole world, the whole universe, excludes any isolating of ourselves in an individual piety, in a sort of private Christianity. The will of God covers the whole human reality; it is accomplished in the whole history. . . . But if one temptation is for us not to see the universal duty when we pray 'thy will be done,' the reverse is for us to be occupied only with universal themes, indifferent to concrete reality (San Antonio Report—Address by the Conference Moderator).

The two most important trends of the San Antonio conference were the spirit of universality (catholicity) of the gathering, and its concern for the fullness of the gospel, namely: to hold in creative tension spiritual and material needs, prayer and action, evangelism and social responsibility, dialogue and witness, power and vulnerability, local and universal (San Antonio Report—Message of the Conference).

Part IV

EVANGELICAL PROTESTANT
STATEMENTS

1

The Lausanne Covenant

Lausanne, 1974

LAUSANNE COMMITTEE FOR WORLD EVANGELIZATION

The International Congress on World Evangelization (ICOWE), which met in Lausanne, Switzerland, from July 16-25, 1974, brought together 2,700 participants from 150 countries—half of them from the nonwestern world—and was the largest meeting devoted to the furtherance of mission and evangelism in modern times.

While Lausanne dealt with a great variety of theological and practical issues, its enduring legacy is undoubtedly the Lausanne Covenant, *a statement in fifteen articles by which its signatories sought to affirm their evangelical faith as well as their commitment to the unfinished evangelistic task.*

"We believe that the gospel is God's good news for the whole world, and we are determined by his grace to obey Christ's commission to proclaim it to every person and to make disciples of every nation" (Introduction). "In the light of this our faith and our resolve, we enter into a solemn covenant with God and with each other, to pray, to plan, and to work together for the evangelization of the whole world" (Conclusion).

Among the Covenant's *most important statements are those which affirm the missionary purpose of the Triune God (LC1), the divine inspiration and authority of the scriptures (LC2), the uniqueness of Christ and of the gospel of salvation (LC3), the nature of evangelism and its distinction from dialogue (LC4), the affirmation of "evangelism and socio-political involvement [as] both part of our Christian duty" (LC5), and the church as God's appointed means of spreading the gospel (LC6). Other articles deal with cooperation and partnership between churches and Christian groups in all parts of the world and define other aspects of global mission. The* Lausanne Covenant *has become the ongoing basis for cooperation in mission among evangelicals the world over, and remains the benchmark statement for evangelical mission theology.*

INTRODUCTION*

We, members of the Church of Jesus Christ, from more than 150 nations, participants in the International Congress on World Evangelization at Lausanne, praise

---

*Reprinted from *The Manila Manifesto: An Elaboration of the Lausanne Covenant Fifteen Years Later* (Pasadena, Calif.: LCWE, 1989), 43-57.

God for his great salvation and rejoice in the fellowship he has given us with himself and with each other. We are deeply stirred by what God is doing in our day, moved to penitence by our failures and challenged by the unfinished task of evangelization. We believe the gospel is God's good news for the whole world, and we are determined by his grace to obey Christ's commission to proclaim it to every person and to make disciples of every nation. We desire, therefore, to affirm our faith and our resolve, and to make public our covenant.

1. THE PURPOSE OF GOD

We affirm our belief in the one eternal God, Creator (Isa. 40:28) and Lord of the world, Father, Son and Holy Spirit (Mt. 28:19), who governs all things according to the purpose of his will (Eph.1:11). He has been calling out from the world a people for himself (Ac. 15:14), and sending his people back into the world (Jn. 17:18) to be his servants and his witnesses, for the extension of his kingdom, the building up of Christ's body, and the glory of his name (Eph. 4:12). We confess with shame that we have often denied our calling and failed in our mission, by becoming conformed to the world (Ro. 12:2) or by withdrawing from it (1 Co. 5:10). Yet we rejoice that even when borne by earthen vessels (2 Co. 4:7) the gospel is still a precious treasure. To the task of making that treasure known in the power of the Holy Spirit we desire to dedicate ourselves anew.

2. THE AUTHORITY & POWER OF THE BIBLE

We affirm the divine inspiration (2 Ti. 3:16; 2 Pe. 1:21), truthfulness and authority of both Old and New Testament Scriptures in their entirety as the only written word of God, without error in all that it affirms, and the only infallible rule of faith and practice. We also affirm the power of God's word to accomplish his purpose of salvation (Isa. 55:11; Ro. 1:16; 1 Co. 1:21). The message of the Bible is addressed to all men and women. For God's revelation in Christ and in Scripture is unchangeable (Jn. 10:35; Mt. 5:17, 18; Jude 3). Through it the Holy Spirit still speaks today. He illumines the minds of God's people in every culture to perceive its truth freshly through their own eyes (Eph. 1:17, 18) and thus discloses to the whole Church ever more of the many-coloured wisdom of God.

3. THE UNIQUENESS & UNIVERSALITY OF CHRIST

We affirm that there is only one Saviour and only one gospel (Gal. 1:6-9), although there is a wide diversity of evangelistic approaches. We recognise that everyone has some knowledge of God through his general revelation in nature. But we deny that this can save, for people suppress the truth by their unrighteousness (Ro. 1:18-32). We also reject as derogatory to Christ and the gospel every kind of syncretism and dialogue which implies that Christ speaks equally through all religions and ideologies. Jesus Christ, being himself the only God-man, who gave himself as the only ransom for sinners, is the only mediator between God and people (1 Ti. 2:5, 6). There is no other name by which we must be saved (Ac. 4:12). All men and women are perishing because of sin, but God loves everyone, not wishing that any should perish (Jn. 3:16-19; 2 Pe. 3:9) but that all should repent. Yet those who reject Christ repudiate the joy of salvation and condemn themselves to eternal separation from God (2 Th. 1:7-9). To proclaim Jesus as "the Saviour of the world"

(Jn. 4:42) is not to affirm that all people are either automatically or ultimately saved, still less to affirm that all religions offer salvation in Christ. Rather it is to proclaim God's love for a world of sinners and to invite everyone to respond to him (Mt. 11:28) as Saviour and Lord in the wholehearted personal commitment of repentance and faith. Jesus Christ has been exalted (Eph. 1:20, 21) above every other name; we long for the day when every knee shall bow to him and every tongue shall confess him Lord (Php. 2:9-11).

4. THE NATURE OF EVANGELISM

To evangelise is to spread the good news that Jesus Christ died for our sins and was raised from the dead according to the Scriptures (1 Co. 15:3, 4), and that as the reigning Lord he now offers the forgiveness of sins (Ac. 2:32-39) and the liberating gift of the Spirit to all who repent and believe (Jn. 20:21). Our Christian presence in the world is indispensable to evangelism, and so is that kind of dialogue whose purpose is to listen sensitively in order to understand. But evangelism itself is the proclamation of the historical, biblical Christ as Saviour (1 Co. 1:23; 2 Co. 4:5) and Lord, with a view to persuading people to come to him personally and so be reconciled to God (2 Co. 5:11, 20). In issuing the gospel invitation we have no liberty to conceal the cost of discipleship (Lk. 14:25-33). Jesus still calls all who would follow him to deny themselves, take up their cross (Mk. 8:34), and identify themselves with his new community. The results of evangelism include obedience to Christ, incorporation into his Church (Ac. 2:40, 47) and responsible service in the world (Mk. 10:43-45).

5. CHRISTIAN SOCIAL RESPONSIBILITY

We affirm that God is both the Creator and the Judge of all (Ac. 17:26, 31). We therefore should share his concern for justice (Ge. 18:25) and reconciliation throughout human society and for the liberation of men and women from every kind of oppression (Ps. 45:7; Isa. 1:17). Because men and women are made in the image of God (Ge. 1:26, 27), every person, regardless of race, religion, colour, culture, class, sex or age (Lev. 19:18; Lk. 6:27, 35), has an intrinsic dignity because of which he or she should be respected and served, not exploited (Jas. 3:9). Here too we express penitence both for our neglect and for having sometimes regarded evangelism and social concern as mutually exclusive. Although reconciliation with other people is not reconciliation with God, nor is social action evangelism, nor is political liberation salvation, nevertheless we affirm that evangelism and socio-political involvement are both part of our Christian duty. For both are necessary expressions of our doctrines of God and man, our love for our neighbour and our obedience to Jesus Christ. The message of salvation implies also a message of judgment upon every form of alienation, oppression and discrimination, and we should not be afraid to denounce evil and injustice wherever they exist. When people receive Christ they are born again (Jn. 3:3, 5) into his kingdom and must seek not only to exhibit but also to spread its righteousness (Mt. 5:20; Mt. 6:33) in the midst of an unrighteous world. The salvation we claim should be transforming us (2 Co. 3:18) in the totality of our personal and social responsibilities. Faith without works is dead (Jas. 2:14-26).

6. THE CHURCH & EVANGELISM

We affirm that Christ sends his redeemed people into the world (Jn. 17:18; 20:21; Mt. 28:19, 20) as the Father sent him, and that this calls for a similar deep and costly penetration of the world. We need to break out of our ecclesiastical ghettos and permeate non-Christian society. In the Church's mission of sacrificial service evangelism is primary. World evangelization requires the whole Church to take the whole gospel to the whole world (Ac. 1:8; 20:27). The Church is at the very centre of God's cosmic purpose (Eph. 1:9, 10; 3:9-11) and is his appointed means of spreading the gospel. But a church which preaches the cross must itself be marked by the cross (Ga. 6:14, 17). It becomes a stumbling block (2 Co. 6:3, 4) to evangelism when it betrays the gospel or lacks a living faith in God, a genuine love for people, or scrupulous honesty (2 Ti. 2:19-21) in all things including promotion and finance. The Church is the community of God's people (Php. 1:27) rather than an institution, and must not be identified with any particular culture, social or political system, or human ideology.

7. COOPERATION IN EVANGELISM

We affirm that the Church's visible unity (Eph. 4:3, 4) in truth is God's purpose (Jn. 17:21, 23). Evangelism also summons us to unity (Jn. 13:35), because our oneness strengthens our witness, just as our disunity undermines our gospel of reconciliation. We recognise, however, that organisational unity may take many forms and does not necessarily forward evangelism. Yet we who share the same biblical faith should be closely united in fellowship, work and witness. We confess that our testimony has sometimes been marred by sinful individualism and needless duplication (Php. 1:27). We pledge ourselves to seek a deeper unity in truth, worship, holiness and mission. We urge the development of regional and functional cooperation for the furtherance of the Church's mission, for strategic planning, for mutual encouragement, and for the sharing of resources and experience.

8. CHURCHES IN EVANGELISTIC PARTNERSHIP

We rejoice that a new missionary era has dawned. The dominant role of western missions is fast disappearing. God is raising up from the younger churches a great new resource for world evangelization, and is thus demonstrating that the responsibility to evangelise belongs to the whole body of Christ. All churches should therefore be asking God and themselves what they should be doing both to reach their own area and to send missionaries to other parts of the world (Ro. 1:8; Php. 1:5; 4:15; Ac. 13:1-3; 1 Th. 1:6-8). A reevaluation of our missionary responsibility and role should be continuous. Thus a growing partnership of churches will develop and the universal character of Christ's Church will be more clearly exhibited. We also thank God for agencies which labour in Bible translation, theological education, the mass media, Christian literature, evangelism, missions, church renewal and other specialist fields. They too should engage in constant self-examination to evaluate their effectiveness as part of the Church's mission.

9. THE URGENCY OF THE EVANGELISTIC TASK

More than 2,700 million people, which is more than two-thirds of all humanity, have yet to be evangelised. We are ashamed that so many have been neglected

(Mk. 16:15); it is a standing rebuke to us and to the whole Church. There is now, however, in many parts of the world an unprecedented receptivity to the Lord Jesus Christ. We are convinced that this is the time (Jn. 9:4) for churches and parachurch agencies to pray earnestly for the salvation of the unreached and to launch new efforts to achieve world evangelization. A reduction of foreign missionaries and money in an evangelised country may sometimes be necessary to facilitate the national church's growth in self-reliance and to release resources for unevangelised areas (Mt. 9:35-38). Missionaries should flow ever more freely from and to all six continents in a spirit of humble service. The goal should be, by all available means and at the earliest possible time, that every person will have the opportunity to hear, understand, and receive the good news. We cannot hope to attain this goal without sacrifice. All of us are shocked by the poverty of millions and disturbed by the injustices which cause it (Isa. 58:6, 7; Jas. 2:1-9). Those of us who live in affluent circumstances accept our duty to develop a simple life-style (1 Co. 9:19-23; Jas. 1:27; Mt. 25:31-46; Ac. 2:44, 45; 4:34, 35) in order to contribute more generously to both relief and evangelism.

10. EVANGELISM & CULTURE

The development of strategies for world evangelization calls for imaginative pioneering methods. Under God, the result will be the rise of churches deeply rooted in Christ and closely related to their culture. Culture must always be tested and judged by Scripture (Mk. 7:8, 9, 13). Because men and women are God's creatures (Ge. 4:21, 22), some of their culture is rich in beauty and goodness. Because they are fallen, all of it is tainted with sin and some of it is demonic. The gospel does not presuppose the superiority of any culture to another, but evaluates all cultures according to its own criteria of truth and righteousness, and insists on moral absolutes in every culture (1 Co. 9:19-23). Missions have all too frequently exported with the gospel an alien culture and churches have sometimes been in bondage to culture rather than to Scripture. Christ's evangelists must humbly seek to empty themselves (Php. 2:5-7) of all but their personal authenticity in order to become the servants (2 Co. 4:5) of others, and churches must seek to transform and enrich culture, all for the glory of God.

11. EDUCATION & LEADERSHIP

We confess that we have sometimes pursued church growth at the expense of church depth, and divorced evangelism from Christian nurture. We also acknowledge that some of our missions have been too slow to equip and encourage national leaders to assume their rightful responsibilities (Col. 1:27, 28; Ac. 14:23). Yet we are committed to indigenous principles, and long that every church will have national leaders (Tit. 1:5, 9) who manifest a Christian style of leadership in terms not of domination but of service (Mk. 10:42-45). We recognise that there is a great need to improve theological education, especially for church leaders. In every nation and culture there should be an effective training programme for pastors and laity in doctrine, discipleship, evangelism, nurture and service (Eph. 4:11, 12). Such training programmes should not rely on any stereotyped methodology but should be developed by creative local initiatives according to biblical standards.

12. SPIRITUAL CONFLICT

We believe that we are engaged in constant spiritual warfare with the principalities and powers of evil (Eph. 6:12), who are seeking to overthrow the Church and frustrate its task of world evangelization (2 Co. 4:3, 4). We know our need to equip ourselves with God's armour (Eph. 6:11, 13-18) and to fight this battle with the spiritual weapons (2 Co. 10:3-5) of truth and prayer. For we detect the activity of our enemy, not only in false ideologies outside the Church, but also inside it in false gospels (1 Jn. 2:18-26; 4:1-3; Gal. 1:6-9; 2 Co. 2:17; 4:2) which twist Scripture and put people in the place of God. We need both watchfulness and discernment to safeguard the biblical gospel. We acknowledge that we ourselves are not immune to worldliness of thought and action, that is, to a surrender to secularism. For example, although careful studies of church growth, both numerical and spiritual, are right and valuable, we have sometimes neglected them. At other times, desirous to ensure a response to the gospel, we have compromised our message, manipulated our hearers through pressure techniques, and become unduly preoccupied with statistics or even dishonest in our use of them. All this is worldly. The Church must be in the world (Jn. 17:15); the world must not be in the Church.

13. FREEDOM & PERSECUTION

It is the God-appointed duty of every government (1 Ti. 2:1-4) to secure conditions of peace, justice and liberty in which the Church may obey God, serve the Lord Christ (Col 3:24), and preach the gospel without interference. We therefore pray for the leaders of the nations and call upon them (Ac. 4:19; 5:29) to guarantee freedom of thought and conscience, and freedom to practise and propagate religion in accordance with the will of God and as set forth in The Universal Declaration of Human Rights. We also express our deep concern for all who have been unjustly imprisoned (Heb. 13:1-3), and especially for those who are suffering for their testimony to the Lord Jesus. We promise to pray and work for their freedom (Lk. 4:18). At the same time we refuse to be intimidated by their fate (Ga. 5:11; 6:12). God helping us, we too will seek to stand against injustice and to remain faithful to the gospel, whatever the cost. We do not forget the warnings of Jesus that persecution is inevitable (Mt. 5:10-12; Jn. 15:18-21).

14. THE POWER OF THE HOLY SPIRIT

We believe in the power of the Holy Spirit (Ac. 1:8; 1 Co. 2:4). The Father sent his Spirit to bear witness (Jn. 15:26, 27) to his Son; without his witness ours is futile (Jn. 16:8-11; 1 Co. 12:3; Jn. 3:6-8; 2 Co. 3:18). Conviction of sin, faith in Christ, new birth and Christian growth are all his work. Further, the Holy Spirit is a missionary spirit; thus evangelism should arise spontaneously from a Spirit-filled church. A church that is not a missionary church is contradicting itself and quenching the Spirit (Jn. 7:37-39; 1 Th. 5:19). Worldwide evangelization will become a realistic possibility only when the Spirit renews (Ps. 85:4-7) the Church in truth and wisdom, faith, holiness, love and power. We therefore call upon all Christians to pray for such a visitation of the sovereign Spirit of God that all his fruit (Ga. 5:22, 23) may appear in all his people and that all his gifts (Ro. 12:3-8; 1 Co. 12:4-31) may enrich the body of Christ. Only then will the whole Church become a fit instrument in his hands, that the whole earth may hear his voice (Ps. 67:1-3).

15. THE RETURN OF CHRIST

We believe that Jesus Christ will return personally and visibly, in power and glory (Mk. 14:62), to consummate his salvation and his judgment (Heb. 9:28). This promise of his coming is a further spur to our evangelism, for we remember his words that the gospel must first be preached to all nations (Mk. 13:10). We believe that the interim period between Christ's ascension and return is to be filled with the mission of the people of God (Mt. 28:20; Ac. 1:8-11), who have no liberty to stop before the end. We also remember his warning that false Christs and false prophets will arise as precursors of the final Antichrist (Mk. 13:21-23; 1 Jn. 2:18; 4:1-3). We therefore reject as a proud, self-confident dream the notion that people can ever build a utopia on earth. Our Christian confidence is that God will perfect his kingdom (Lk. 12:32), and we look forward with eager anticipation to that day, and to the new heaven and earth (Rev. 21:1-5; 2 Pe. 3:13) in which righteousness will dwell and God will reign forever. Meanwhile, we rededicate ourselves to the service of Christ and of people in joyful submission to his authority (Mt. 28:18) over the whole of our lives.

CONCLUSION

Therefore, in the light of this our faith and our resolve, we enter into a solemn covenant with God and with each other, to pray, to plan and to work together for the evangelization of the whole world. We call upon others to join us. May God help us by his grace and for his glory to be faithful to this our covenant! Amen, Alleluia!

2

Consultation on Homogeneous Units

Pasadena, 1977

LAUSANNE COMMITTEE FOR WORLD EVANGELIZATION

Following the first Lausanne Congress (1974), the LCWE set up a Theology and Education Group (LTEG) to promote theological reflection on issues related to world evangelization and explore implications of the Lausanne Covenant. *The first issue to be explored was the "homogeneous unit principle," a basic assumption of the philosophy of "church growth" strongly advocated at that time by Dr. Donald McGavran of the School of World Mission of Fuller Theological Seminary, Pasadena, California.*

Advocates and critics of the theory met at Pasadena from May 31-June 2, 1977, to discuss areas of agreement and points of tension. Dr. McGavran argued that people "like to become Christians without crossing racial, linguistic or class barriers," and therefore the churches which grow most rapidly are those in which people feel most at home. Opponents of the "homogeneous unit" (HU) principle replied that the unity of the church amid cultural diversity had to be safeguarded, and that vital ethical principles could not be sacrificed.

In this consultation and the one which follows, LCWE theologians wrestle with the relation between gospel and culture.

Excepts from the Pasadena statement follow.

THE PASADENA CONSULTATION—HOMOGENEOUS UNIT PRINCIPLE*

4. THE RICHES OF CULTURAL DIVERSITY

The arguments advanced to support the concept of the importance of culture are not only pragmatic ("churches grow fastest that way") but biblical ("God desires it that way") . . . We are unanimous in celebrating the colorful mosaic of the human race that God has created. This rich variety should be preserved, not destroyed, by the gospel. The attempt to impose another culture on people who have their own is cultural imperialism. The attempt to level all cultures into a colorless uniformity is a denial of the Creator and an affront to his creation. The preservation of cultural

---

*Reprinted from *The Pasadena Consultation—Homogeneous Unit,* Lausanne Occasional Paper No. 1 (Wheaton, Ill.: LCWE, 1978), 4-5.

diversity honors God, respects man, enriches life, and promotes evangelization. Each church, if it is to be truly indigenous, should be rooted in the soil of its local culture.

5. THE CHURCH, THE CHURCHES AND THE HOMOGENEOUS UNIT PRINCIPLE

We are all agreed that, as there is one God and Father, one Lord Jesus, and one Holy Spirit, so he has only one church. The unity of the church is a given fact (Eph. 4:4-6). At the same time, we have the responsibility to maintain this unity (v. 3), to make it visible, and to grow up into the fullness of unity in Christ (vv. 13-16).

How then can the unity of the church ... and the diversity of cultures ... be reconciled with one another? More particularly, how can separate HU churches express the unity of the Body of Christ?

We are all agreed that the dividing wall which Jesus Christ abolished by his death was *echthra*, "enmity" or "hostility." This ... Jesus abolished in order to "create in himself one new man in place of two, so making peace" (Eph. 2:15).

This did not mean that Jews ceased to be Jews, or Gentiles to be Gentiles. It did mean, however, that their racial differences were not barriers to their fellowship, for through their union with Jesus Christ both groups were now "joint heirs, joint members of the same body and joint partakers of the promise" (Eph. 3:6) ... Thus the church as the single new humanity or God's new society is central to the gospel. Our responsibility is both to preach it and to exhibit it before the watching world.

What did this mean in practice in the early church? It seems probable that, although there were mixed Jewish-Gentile congregations, there were also homogeneous Jewish congregations (who still observed Jewish customs) and homogeneous Gentile congregations (who observed no Jewish customs). Nevertheless, Paul clearly taught them that they belonged to each other in Christ, that they must welcome one another as Christ welcomed them (compare Romans 15:7), and that they must respect one another's consciences and not offend one another. He publicly rebuked Peter in Antioch for withdrawing from table fellowship with Gentile believers, and argued that his action was a denial of the truth of the gospel ...

All of us are agreed that in many situations a homogeneous unit church can be a legitimate and authentic church. Yet we are also agreed that it can never be complete in itself. Indeed, if it remains in isolation, it cannot reflect the universality and diversity of the Body of Christ. Nor can it grow to maturity ...

In our commitment to evangelism, we all understand the reasons why homogeneous unit churches usually grow faster than heterogeneous or multicultural ones. Some of us, however, do not agree that the rapidity with which churches grow is the only or even always the most important Christian priority. We know that an alien culture is a barrier to faith. But we also know that segregation and strife in the church are barriers to faith. If, then, we have to choose between apparent acquiescence in segregation for the sake of numerical church growth and the struggle for reconciliation at the expense of numerical church growth, we find ourselves in a painful dilemma. Some of us have had a personal experience of the evils of tribalism in Africa, racism in America, caste in India, and economic injustice in Latin America, and elsewhere, and all of us are opposed to these things. In such situations none of us could with a good conscience continue to develop HU churches which seem to ignore the social problems and even tolerate them in the church, while some of us believe that the development of HU churches can often contribute to their solution.

We recognize that both positions can be defended in terms of obedience — obedience to Christ's commission to evangelize on the one hand, and obedience to the commands to live in love and justice on the other. The synthesis between the two still eludes us, although we all accept our Lord's own words that it is through the brotherly love and unity of Christians that the world will come to believe in him (John 13:35; 17:21, 23).

3

Consultation on Gospel and Culture

Willowbank, 1978

LAUSANNE COMMITTEE FOR WORLD EVANGELIZATION

From January 6-13, 1978, the LCWE Theology and Education Group, in cooperation with the Lausanne Strategy Working Group, co-sponsored a significant
consultation on the cross-cultural communication of the gospel at Willowbank,
Bermuda. Theologians, anthropologists, linguists, and missionaries dealt with
such matters as the biblical understanding of culture, barriers to gospel communication, the nature of conversion, and cultural implications for the local church
and for Christian life-styles.

The report breaks with past overly negative evangelical views of human culture
and strives for a more nuanced appreciation of culture as reflecting both divine
creation and human fallenness. The following excerpt from the section on
"Church and Culture" argues strongly for the contextualization of the gospel
message and the contextualization of the church in the missionary situation.

THE WILLOWBANK REPORT—GOSPEL AND CULTURE*

8. CHURCH AND CULTURE

In the process of church formation, as in the communication and reception of
the gospel, the question of culture is vital. If the gospel must be contextualized, so
must the church. Indeed, the sub-title of our Consultation has been "the contextualization of Word and Church in a missionary situation."

(A) OLDER, TRADITIONAL APPROACHES

During the missionary expansion of the early part of the 19th century, it was
generally assumed that churches "on the mission field" would be modelled on
churches "at home." The tendency was to produce almost exact replicas. Gothic
architecture, prayer book liturgies, clerical dress, musical instruments, hymns and
tunes, decision-making processes, synods and committees, superintendents and

1. Reprinted from *The Willowbank Report—Gospel and Culture,* Lausanne Occasional Paper
No. 2 (Wheaton, Ill.: LCWE, 1978), 23-28.

archdeacons—all were exported and unimaginatively introduced into the new mission-founded churches. It should be added that these patterns were also eagerly adopted by the new Christians, determined not to be at any point behind their western friends, whose habits and ways of worship they had been attentively watching. But all this was based on the false assumptions that the Bible gave specific instructions about such matters and that the home churches' pattern of government, worship, ministry and life were themselves exemplary.

In reaction to this monocultural export system, pioneer missionary thinkers like Henry Venn and Rufus Anderson in the middle of the last century and Roland Allen earlier in this century popularized the concept of "indigenous" churches, which would be "self-governing, self-supporting and self-propagating." They argued their case well. They pointed out that the policy of the apostle Paul was to plant churches, not to found mission stations. They also added pragmatic arguments to biblical ones, namely that indigeneity was indispensable to the church's growth in maturity and mission. Henry Venn confidently looked forward to the day when missions would hand over all responsibility to national churches, and then what he called "the euthanasia of the mission" would take place. These views gained wide acceptance and were immensely influential.

In our day, however, they are being criticized, not because of the ideal itself, but because of the way it has often been applied. Some missions, for example, have accepted the need for indigenous leadership and have then gone on to recruit and train local leaders, indoctrinating them (the word is harsh but not unfair) in western ways of thought and procedure. These westernized local leaders have then preserved a very western-looking church, and the foreign orientation has persisted, only lightly cloaked by the appearance of indigeneity.

Now, therefore, a more radical concept of indigenous church life needs to be developed, by which each church may discover and express its selfhood as the body of Christ within its own culture.

(B) THE DYNAMIC EQUIVALENCE MODEL

Using the distinction between "form" and "meaning," and between "formal correspondence" and "dynamic equivalence" which have been developed in translation theory . . . an analogy may be drawn between Bible translation and church formation. "Formal correspondence" speaks of a slavish imitation, whether in translating a word into another language or exporting a church model to another culture. Just as a "dynamic equivalence" translation, however, seeks to convey to contemporary readers meanings equivalent to those conveyed to the original readers, by using appropriate cultural forms, so would a "dynamic equivalence" church. It would look in its culture as a good Bible translation looks in its language. It would preserve the essential meanings and functions which the New Testament predicated of the church, but would seek to express these in forms equivalent to the originals but appropriate to the local culture.

We have all found this model helpful and suggestive, and we strongly affirm the ideals it seeks to express. It rightly rejects foreign imports and imitations, and rigid structures. It rightly looks to the New Testament for the principles of church formation, rather than to either tradition or culture, and it equally rightly looks to the local culture for the appropriate forms in which these principles should be expressed. All of us (even those who see limitations in the model) share the vision which it is trying to describe.

Thus, the New Testament indicates that the church is always a worshipping community, "a holy priesthood to offer spiritual sacrifices to God through Jesus Christ" (I Pet. 2:5), but forms of worship (including the presence or absence of different kinds of liturgy, ceremony, music, colour, drama, etc.) will be developed by the church in keeping with indigenous culture. Similarly, the church is always a witnessing and a serving community, but its methods of evangelism and its programme of social involvement will vary. Again, God desires all churches to have pastoral oversight (*episkope*), but forms of government and ministry may differ widely, and the selection, training, ordination, service, dress, payment, and accountability of pastors will be determined by the church to accord with biblical principles and to suit the local culture ...

The test of this or any other model for helping churches develop appropriately, is whether it can enable God's people to capture in their hearts and minds the grand design of which their church is to be the local expression. Every model presents only a partial picture. Local churches need to rely ultimately on the dynamic pressure of the Living Lord of history. For it is he who will guide his people in every age to develop their church life in such a way as both to obey the instructions he has given in Scripture and to reflect the good elements of their local culture.

(C) THE FREEDOM OF THE CHURCH

If each church is to develop creatively in such a way as to find and express itself, it must be free to do so. This is an inalienable right. For each church is God's church. United to Christ, it is a dwelling place of God through his Spirit (Eph. 2:22). Some missions and missionaries have been slow to recognize this, and to accept its implications in the direction of indigenous forms and an every-member ministry. This is one of the main causes which have led to the formation of Independent Churches, notably in Africa, which are seeking new ways of self-expression in terms of local culture.

Although local church leaders have also sometimes impeded indigenous development, the chief blame lies elsewhere. It would not be fair to generalize. The situation has always been diverse. In earlier generations there were missions which never manifested a spirit of domination. In this century some churches have sprung up which have never been under missionary control, having enjoyed self-government from the start. In other cases missionaries have entirely surrendered their former power, so that some mission-founded churches are now fully autonomous, and many missions now work in genuine partnership with churches.

Yet this is not the whole picture. Other churches are still almost completely inhibited from developing their own identity and programme by policies laid down from afar, by the introduction and continuation of foreign traditions, by the use of expatriate leadership, by alien decision-making processes, and especially by the manipulative use of money. Those who maintain such control may be genuinely unaware of the way in which their actions are regarded and experienced at the other end. They may be felt by the churches concerned to be a tyranny ... We strongly oppose such "foreignness", wherever it exists, as a serious obstacle to maturity and mission, and a quenching of the Holy Spirit of God.

It was in protest against the continuance of foreign control that a few years ago the call was made to withdraw all missionaries. In this debate some of us want to avoid the word "moratorium" because it has become an emotive term and sometimes betrays a resentment against the very concept of "missionaries." Others of us wish to retain the word in order to emphasize the truth it expresses. To us it means not a rejection of missionary personnel and money in themselves, but only of their misuse in such a way as to suffocate local initiative. We all agree with the statement of the Lausanne Covenant that "a reduction of foreign missionaries and money . . . may sometimes be necessary to facilitate the national church's growth in self-reliance . . . " (LC9).

(D) POWER STRUCTURES AND MISSION . . .

(E) THE DANGER OF PROVINCIALISM

We have emphasized that the church must be allowed to indigenize itself and to "celebrate, sing and dance" the gospel in its own cultural medium. At the same time, we wish to be alert to the dangers of this process. Some churches in all six continents go beyond a joyful and thankful discovery of their local cultural heritage, and either become boastful and assertive about it (a form of chauvinism) or even absolutize it (a form of idolatry). More common than either of these extremes, however, is "provincialism," that is, such a retreat into their own culture as cuts them adrift from the rest of the church and from the wider world. This is a frequent stance in western churches as well as in the Third World. It denies the God of creation and redemption. It is to proclaim one's freedom, only to enter into another bondage. We draw attention to the three major reasons why we think this attitude should be avoided.

First, each church is part of the universal church. The people of God are by his grace a unique multi-racial, multi-national, multi-cultural community . . . We must always remember that our primary identity as Christians is not in our particular culture but in the one Lord and his one body (Eph. 4:3-6).

Secondly, each church worships the living God of cultural diversity. If we thank him for our cultural heritage, we should thank him for others' also . . . We believe it is enriching for Christians, if they have the opportunity, to develop a bicultural and even a multi-cultural existence, like the apostle Paul . . .

Thirdly, each church should enter into a "partnership . . . in giving and receiving" (Phil. 4:15). No church is, or should try to become, self-sufficient. So churches should develop with each other relationships of prayer, fellowship, interchange of ministry and cooperation . . . A church should be free to reject alien cultural forms and develop its own; it should also feel free to borrow from others. This way lies maturity.

One example of this concerns theology. Cross-cultural witnesses must not attempt to impose a ready-made theological tradition on the church in which they serve, either by personal teaching or by literature or by controlling seminary and Bible college curricula. For every theological tradition both contains elements which are biblically questionable and have been ecclesiastically divisive and omits elements which, while they might be of no great consequence in the country where they originated, may be of immense importance in other contexts . . . Moreover, although the theological controversies of the older churches should not be exported to the younger churches, yet an understanding of the issues, and of the work of the Holy Spirit in the unfolding history of Christian doctrine, should help to protect them from unprofitable repetition of the same battles.

Thus we should seek with equal care to avoid theological imperialism or theological provincialism. A church's theology should be developed by the community of faith out of the Scripture in interaction with other theologies of the past and present, and with the local culture and its needs.

4

Consultation on Simple Life-Style

High Leigh, 1980

LAUSANNE COMMITTEE FOR WORLD EVANGELIZATION AND WORLD EVANGELICAL FELLOWSHIP

Concern for poverty and injustice in the Third World in sharp contrast to growing affluence in the west prompted the convening of an international evangelical consultation on simple life-style at High Leigh, a suburb of London, March 17-21, 1980. The meeting was jointly sponsored by the LCWE Theology and Education Working Group (TEWG) and by the unit on Ethics and Society of the Theological Commission of the World Evangelical Fellowship.

The aim of the consultation was to study Christian living in relation to evangelism, relief, and justice, against the background of God's Word and the world's need. The four-day period, described as "historic and transforming," resulted in a statement of "commitment" which stands as one of the most prophetic evangelical documents on record. The commitment is notable for its attack on the systemic causes of injustice and its call for structural change in society.

THE COMMITMENT*

PREAMBLE

For four days we have been together, eighty-five Christians from twenty-seven countries, to consider the resolve expressed in the Lausanne Covenant (1974) to "develop a simple lifestyle". We have tried to listen to the voice of God, through the pages of the Bible, through the cries of the hungry poor, and through each other. And we believe that God has spoken to us.

We thank God for his great salvation through Jesus Christ, for his revelation in Scripture which is a light for our path, and for the Holy Spirit's power to make us witnesses and servants in the world.

We are disturbed by the injustice of the world, concerned for its victims, and

---

1. Reprinted from Ronald J. Sider, ed., *Lifestyle in the Eighties: An Evangelical Commitment to Simple Lifestyle* (Philadelphia: Westminster, 1982), 13-19. Also found in *An Evangelical Commitment to Simple Life-style,* exposition and commentary by Alan Nichols, Lausanne Occasional Paper No. 20 (Wheaton, Ill.: LCWE, 1980).

moved to repentance for our complicity in it. We have also been stirred to fresh resolves, which we express in this Commitment.

1. CREATION

We worship God as the Creator of all things, and we celebrate the goodness of his creation. In his generosity he has given us everything to enjoy, and we receive it from his hands with humble thanksgiving (1 Timothy 4:4, 6:17). God's creation is marked by rich abundance and diversity, and he intends its resources to be husbanded and shared for the benefit of all.

We therefore denounce environmental destruction, wastefulness and hoarding. We deplore the misery of the poor who suffer as a result of these evils. We also disagree with the drabness of the ascetic. For all these deny the Creator's goodness and reflect the tragedy of the fall. We recognize our own involvement in them, and we repent.

2. STEWARDSHIP

When God made man, male and female, in his own image, he gave them dominion over the earth (Genesis 1:26-28). He made them stewards of its resources, and they became responsible to him as Creator, to the earth which they were to develop, and to their fellow human beings with whom they were to share its riches. So fundamental are these truths that authentic human fulfilment depends on a right relationship to God, neighbour and the earth with all its resources. People's humanity is diminished if they have no just share in those resources.

By unfaithful stewardship, in which we fail to conserve the earth's finite resources, to develop them fully, or to distribute them justly, we both disobey God and alienate people from his purpose for them. We are determined, therefore, to honour God as the owner of all things, to remember that we are stewards and not proprietors of any land or property that we may have, to use them in the service of others, and to seek justice with the poor who are exploited and powerless to defend themselves.

We look forward to "the restoration of all things" at Christ's return (Acts 3:21). At that time our full humanness will be restored; so we must promote human dignity today.

3. POVERTY AND WEALTH

We affirm that involuntary poverty is an offense against the goodness of God. It is related in the Bible to powerlessness, for the poor cannot protect themselves. God's call to rulers is to use their power to defend the poor, not to exploit them. The church must stand with God and the poor against injustice, suffer with them and call on rulers to fulfil their God-appointed role.

We have struggled to open our minds and hearts to the uncomfortable words of Jesus about wealth. "Beware of covetousness" he said, and "a person's life does not consist in the abundance of his possessions" (Luke 12:15). We have listened to his warnings about the danger of riches. For wealth brings worry, vanity and false security, the oppression of the weak and indifference to the sufferings of the needy. So it is hard for a rich person to enter the kingdom of heaven (Matthew 19:23), and the greedy will be excluded from it. The kingdom is a free gift offered to all, but it is especially good news for the poor because they benefit most from the changes it brings.

We believe that Jesus still calls some people (perhaps even us) to follow him in a lifestyle of total, voluntary poverty. He calls all his followers to an inner freedom from the seduction of riches (for it is impossible to serve God and money) and to sacrificial generosity ("to be rich in good works, to be generous and ready to share" — 1 Timothy 6:18). Indeed, the motivation and model for Christian generosity are nothing less than the example of Jesus Christ himself, who, though rich, became poor that through his poverty we might become rich (2 Corinthians 8:9). It was a costly, purposeful self-sacrifice; we mean to seek his grace to follow him. We resolve to get to know poor and oppressed people, to learn issues of injustice from them, to seek to relieve their suffering, and to include them regularly in our prayers.

4. THE NEW COMMUNITY

We rejoice that the church is the new community of the new age, whose members enjoy a new life and a new lifestyle. The earliest Christian church, constituted in Jerusalem on the Day of Pentecost, was characterized by a quality of fellowship unknown before. Those Spirit-filled believers loved one another to such an extent that they sold and shared their possessions. Although their selling and giving were voluntary, and some private property was retained (Acts 5:4), it was made subservient to the needs of the community. "None of them said that anything he had was his own" (Acts 4:32). That is, they were free from the selfish assertion of proprietary rights. And as a result of their transformed economic relationships, "there was not a needy person among them" (Acts 4:34).

This principle of generous and sacrificial sharing, expressed in holding ourselves and our goods available for people in need, is an indispensable characteristic of every Spirit-filled church. So those of us who are affluent in any part of the world are determined to do more to relieve the needs of less privileged believers. Otherwise, we shall be like those rich Christians in Corinth who ate and drank too much while their poor brothers and sisters were left hungry, and we shall deserve the stinging rebuke Paul gave them for despising God's church and desecrating Christ's body (1 Corinthians 11:20-24). Instead, we determine to resemble them at a later stage when Paul urged them out of their abundance to give to the impoverished Christians of Judea "that there may be equality" (2 Corinthians 8:10-15). It was a beautiful demonstration of caring love and of Gentile-Jewish solidarity in Christ.

In this same spirit, we must seek ways to transact the church's corporate business together with minimum expenditure on travel, food and accommodation. We call on churches and para-church agencies in their planning to be acutely aware of the need for integrity in corporate lifestyle and witness.

Christ calls us to be the world's salt and light, in order to hinder its social decay and illumine its darkness. But our light must shine and our salt must retain its saltiness. It is when the new community is most obviously distinct from the world — in its values, standards and lifestyle — that it presents the world with a radically attractive alternative and so exercizes its greatest influence for Christ. We commit ourselves to pray and work for the renewal of our churches.

5. PERSONAL LIFESTYLE

Jesus our Lord summons us to holiness, humility, simplicity and contentment. He also promises us his rest. We confess, however, that we have often allowed unholy desires to disturb our inner tranquility. So without the constant renewal of Christ's peace in our hearts, our emphasis on simple living will be one-sided.

Our Christian obedience demands a simple lifestyle, irrespective of the needs of others. Nevertheless, the facts that 800 million people are destitute and that about 10,000 die of starvation every day make any other lifestyle indefensible.

While some of us have been called to live among the poor, and others to open our homes to the needy, all of us are determined to develop a simpler lifestyle. We intend to re-examine our income and expenditure, in order to manage on less and give away more. We lay down no rules or regulations, for either ourselves or others. Yet we resolve to renounce waste and oppose extravagance in personal living, clothing and housing, travel and church buildings. We also accept the distinction between necessities and luxuries, creative hobbies and empty status symbols, modesty and vanity, occasional celebrations and normal routine, and between the service of God and slavery to fashion. Where to draw the line requires conscientious thought and decision by us, together with members of our family. Those of us who belong to the West need the help of our Third World brothers and sisters in evaluating our standards of spending. Those of us who live in the Third World acknowledge that we too are exposed to the temptation to covetousness. So we need each other's understanding, encouragement and prayers.

6. INTERNATIONAL DEVELOPMENT

We echo the words of the Lausanne Covenant: "We are shocked by the poverty of millions, and disturbed by the injustices which cause it." One quarter of the world's population endures grinding poverty. This gross disparity is an intolerable injustice; we refuse to acquiesce in it. The call for a New International Economic Order expresses the justified frustration of the Third World.

We have come to understand more clearly the connection between resources, income and consumption: people often starve because they cannot afford to buy food, because they have no income, because they have no opportunity to produce, and because they have no access to power. We therefore applaud the growing emphasis of Christian agencies on development rather than air. For the transfer of personnel and appropriate technology can enable people to make good use of their own resources, while at the same time respecting their dignity. We resolve to contribute more generously to human development projects. Where people's lives are at stake, there should never be a shortage of funds.

But the action of governments is essential. Those of us who live in the affluent nations are ashamed that our governments have mostly failed to meet their targets for official development assistance, to maintain emergency food stocks or to liberalize their trade policy.

We have come to believe that in many cases multi-national corporations reduce local initiative in the countries where they work, and tend to oppose any fundamental change in government. We are convinced that they should become more subject to controls and more accountable.

7. JUSTICE AND POLITICS

We are also convinced that the present situation of social injustice is so abhorrent to God that a large measure of change is necessary. Not that we believe in an earthly utopia. But neither are we pessimists. Change can come, although not through commitment to simple lifestyle or human development projects alone.

Poverty and excessive wealth, militarism and the arms industry, and the unjust distribution of capital, land and resources are issues of power and powerlessness. Without a shift of power through structural change these problems cannot be solved.

The Christian church, along with the rest of society, is inevitably involved in politics which is "the art of living in community". Servants of Christ must express his lordship in their political, social and economic commitments and their love for their neighbours by taking part in the political process. How, then, can we contribute to change?

First, we will pray for peace and justice, as God commands. Secondly, we will seek to educate Christian people in the moral and political issues involved, and so clarify their vision and raise their expectations. Thirdly, we will take action. Some Christians are called to special tasks in government, economics or development. All Christians must participate in the active struggle to create a just and responsible society. In some situations obedience to God demands resistance to an unjust established order. Fourthly, we must be ready to suffer. As followers of Jesus, the Suffering Servant, we know that service always involves suffering.

While personal commitment to change our lifestyle without political action to change systems of injustice lacks effectiveness, political action without personal commitment lacks integrity.

8. EVANGELISM

We are deeply concerned for the vast millions of unevangelized people in the world. Nothing that has been said about lifestyle or justice diminishes the urgency of developing evangelistic strategies appropriate to different cultural environments. We must not cease to proclaim Christ as Saviour and Lord throughout the world. The church is not yet taking seriously its commission to be his witnesses "to the ends of the earth" (Acts 1:8).

So the call to a responsible lifestyle must not be divorced from the call to responsible witness. For the credibility of our message is seriously diminished whenever we contradict it by our lives. It is impossible with integrity to proclaim Christ's salvation if he has evidently not saved us from greed, or his lordship if we are not good stewards of our possessions, or his love if we close our hearts against the needy. When Christians care for each other and for the deprived, Jesus Christ becomes more visibly attractive.

In contrast to this, the affluent lifestyle of some Western evangelists when they visit the Third World is understandably offensive to many.

We believe that simple living by Christians generally would release considerable resources of finance and personnel for evangelism as well as development. So by our commitment to a simple lifestyle we recommit ourselves wholeheartedly to world evangelization.

9. THE LORD'S RETURN

The Old Testament prophets both denounced the idolatries and injustices of God's people and warned of his coming judgement. Similar denunciations and warnings are found in the New Testament. The Lord Jesus is coming back soon to judge, to save and to reign. His judgement will fall upon the greedy (who are idolaters) and upon all oppressors. For on that day the King will sit upon his throne and separate the saved from the lost. Those who have ministered to him by ministering to one of the least of his needy brothers and sisters will be saved, for the reality of saving faith is exhibited in serving love. But those who are persistently indifferent to the plight of the needy, and so to Christ in them, will be irretrievably lost (Matthew 25:31-46). All of us need to hear again this solemn warning of Jesus, and resolve afresh to serve him in the deprived. We therefore call on our fellow Christians everywhere to do the same.

OUR RESOLVE

So then, having been freed by the sacrifice of our Lord Jesus Christ, in obedience to his call, in heartfelt compassion for the poor, in concern for evangelism, development and justice, and in solemn anticipation of the Day of Judgement, we humbly commit ourselves to develop a just and simple lifestyle, to support one another in it and to encourage others to join us in this commitment.

We know that we shall need time to work out its implications and that the task will not be easy. May Almighty God give us his grace to be faithful! Amen.

5

Consultation on World Evangelization

Pattaya, 1980

LAUSANNE COMMITTEE FOR WORLD EVANGELIZATION

The Consultation on World Evangelization (COWE), sponsored by the LCWE at Pattaya, Thailand, from June 16-27, 1980, was smaller in scale than the 1974 Lausanne Congress and had a different purpose. COWE's purposes were to assess the progress of world evangelization since Lausanne 1974, to develop new strategies for cross-cultural evangelism in specific contexts, and to seek fresh vision and power for the task.

One of Pattaya's greatest achievements was the holding of seventeen "miniconsultations" on Christian witness to particular people groups, resulting in a series of published reports. The Thailand Statement issued at COWE was in principle an endorsement of the Lausanne Covenant *as the continuing basis of the Lausanne movement, a reminder of the unfinished task, and a reflection on attitudes requisite for Christlike evangelization. One crucial issue which Pattaya failed to resolve—the relationship between evangelism and social responsibility—was to become the focus of later consultations.*

THE THAILAND STATEMENT*

We have gathered at Pattaya, Thailand for the Consultation on World Evangelization, over 800 Christians from a wide diversity of backgrounds, nations and cultures ... We have become freshly burdened by the vast numbers who have never heard the good news of Christ and are lost without him. We have been made ashamed of our lack of vision and zeal, and of our failure to live out the gospel in its fulness ... We believe that there is only one living and true God, the Creator of the universe and the Father of our Lord Jesus Christ ... As his witnesses he has

---

*"The Thailand Statement," in E. R. Dayton and S. Wilson, eds., *The Future of World Evangelization: The Lausanne Movement* (Monrovia, Calif.: MARC, 1984). Fifteen of the miniconsultations gave rise to printed reports (Lausanne Occasional Pamphlets Nos. 5-19) entitled "Christian witness to ... " as follows: 5. refugees; 6. Chinese people; 7. Jewish people; 8. secularized people; 9. large cities; 10. nominal Roman Catholics; 11. new religious movements; 12. Marxists; 13. Muslims; 14. Hindus; 15. Buddhists; 16. traditional religionists (Asia and Oceania); 17. traditional religionists (Latin America and Caribbean); 18. African traditional religionists; 19. nominal Orthodox.

commanded us to proclaim his good news in the power of the Holy Spirit to every person of every culture and nation, to summon them to repent, to believe and follow him. This mandate is urgent, for there is no other Saviour but Jesus Christ. It is also binding on all Christian people ... We are also the servants of Jesus Christ who is himself both "the servant" and "the Lord." He calls us, therefore, not only to obey him as Lord in every area of our lives, but also to serve as he served ... All God's people "should share his concern for justice and reconciliation throughout human society and for the liberation of men from every kind of oppression" (LC5). Although evangelism and social action are not identical, we gladly reaffirm our commitment to both, and we endorse the Lausanne Covenant in its entirety. It remains the basis for our common activity ... The Lausanne Covenant declares that "in the church's mission of sacrificial service evangelism is primary" (LC6) ... If therefore we do not commit ourselves with urgency to the task of evangelization, we are guilty of an inexcusable lack of human compassion ... We have divided into 17 mini-consultations all of which have concentrated on how to reach particular peoples for Christ ... Many of the reports have called for a change in our personal attitudes. The following four have been particularly emphasized:

The first is *love*. Group after group has asserted that "we cannot evangelize if we do not love" ...

Secondly, *humility.* Our study has led us to confess that other people's resistance to the gospel has sometimes been our fault ...

Thirdly, *integrity* ... Our witness loses credibility when we contradict it by our life or life-style ...

The fourth emphasis has to do with *power.* We know that we are engaged in battle with demonic forces ...

We joyfully affirm the unity of the Body of Christ and acknowledge that we are bound together with one another and with all true believers ... We must nevertheless strive for a visible expression of our oneness. This witnesses to Christ's reconciling power and demonstrates our common commitment to serve him. In contrast, competitive programs and needless duplication of effort both waste resources and call into question our profession to be one in Christ. So we pledge ourselves again, in the words of the Lausanne Covenant, "to seek a deeper unity in truth, worship, holiness and mission" (LC7). It is imperative that we work together to fulfill the task of world evangelization ...

6

Consultation on the Relation of Evangelism and Social Responsibility

Grand Rapids, 1982

LAUSANNE COMMITTEE ON WORLD EVANGELIZATION AND WORLD EVANGELICAL FELLOWSHIP

The Thailand Statement (1980) had reaffirmed the Lausanne Covenant *conviction that "evangelism and sociopolitical involvement are both part of our Christian duty" (LC5), a conviction at least partly qualified by a further statement that "in the Church's mission of sacrificial service evangelism is primary" (LC6). Such ambiguities were deeply troubling to many evangelicals who felt that LCWE was insufficiently concerned with social justice. Persons holding this view circulated a "Statement of Concern" at Pattaya, signed by nearly a third of the participants, arguing strenuously against the separation of sociopolitical involvement from evangelism.*

In this charged atmosphere of "considerable controversy and confusion among evangelicals," LCWE, in cooperation with the World Evangelical Fellowship, jointly sponsored an International Consultation of the Relationship Between Evangelism and Social Responsibility (CRESR) at Grand Rapids, June 19-25, 1982. The CRESR papers and consultation report led to clarification but failed to dissolve the tension between evangelical advocates of social justice and the more traditional evangelical supporters of mission. We reproduce here a key excerpt from the extended CRESR report.

4. THE RELATIONSHIP BETWEEN EVANGELISM AND SOCIAL RESPONSIBILITY*

(A) HISTORICAL BACKGROUND

It appears to us that evangelism and social concern have been intimately related to one another throughout the history of the church, although the relationship has been expressed in a variety of ways. Christian people have often engaged in both

---

*Reprinted from *Evangelism and Social Responsibility: An Evangelical Commitment,* Lausanne Occasional Paper No. 21 (LCWE and WEF, 1982), 19-25.

activities quite unself-consciously, without feeling any need to define what they were doing or why. So the problem of their relationship, which led to the convening of this Consultation, is comparatively new, and for historical reasons is of particular importance to evangelical Christians.

The Great Awakening in North America, the Pietistic Movement in Germany, and the Evangelical Revival under the Wesleys in Britain, which all took place in the early part of the 18th century, proved a great stimulus to philanthropy as well as evangelism. The next generation of British evangelicals founded missionary societies and gave conspicuous service in public life, notably Wilberforce in the abolition of the slave trade and of slavery itself, and Shaftesbury in the improvement of conditions in the factories.

But at the end of the 19th century and the beginning of the 20th, the so-called "social gospel" was developed by theological liberals. Some of them confused the Kingdom of God with Christian civilization in general, and with social democracy in particular, and they went on to imagine that by their social programmes they could build God's Kingdom on earth. It seems to have been in over-reaction to this grave distortion of the Gospel that many evangelicals became suspicious of social involvement. And now that evangelicals are recovering a social conscience and rediscovering our evangelical social heritage, it is understandable that some of our brothers and sisters are looking askance at us and suspecting us of relapsing into the old heresy of the social gospel. But the responsible social action which the biblical Gospel lays upon us, and the liberal "social gospel" which was a perversion of the true Gospel, are two quite different things. As we said in the Lausanne Covenant, "we ... reject as a proud self-confident dream the notion that man can ever build a utopia on earth" (Paragraph 15).

Another cause of the divorce of evangelism and social responsibility is the dichotomy which has often developed in our thinking. We tend to set over against one another in an unhealthy way soul and body, the individual and society, redemption and creation, grace and nature, heaven and earth, justification and justice, faith and works. The Bible certainly distinguishes between these, but it also relates them to each other, and it instructs us to hold each pair in a dynamic and creative tension. It is as wrong to disengage them, as in "dualism", as it is to confuse them, as in "monism". It was for this reason that the Lausanne Covenant, speaking of evangelism and socio-political involvement, affirmed that they "are both part of our Christian duty" (Paragraph 5).

(B) PARTICULAR SITUATIONS AND GIFTS

In wanting to affirm that evangelism and social responsibility belong to each other, we are not meaning that neither can ever exist in independence of the other. The Good Samaritan, for example, if we may characterize him as a Christian, could not have been blamed for tending the wounds of the brigands' victim and failing to preach to him. Nor is Philip to be blamed for preaching the Gospel to the Ethiopian eunuch in his chariot and failing to enquire into his social needs. There are still occasions when it is legitimate to concentrate on one or the other of these two Christian duties. It is not wrong to hold an evangelistic crusade without an accompanying programme of social service. Nor is it wrong to feed the hungry in a time of famine without first preaching to them, for, to quote an African proverb, "an empty belly has no ears". It was similar in the days of Moses. He brought the Israelites in Egypt the good news of their liberation, "but they did not listen to him, because of their broken spirit and their cruel bondage" (Exod. 6:9).

There is another justification for sometimes separating evangelism and social action, in addition to the existential demands of a particular situation: namely, the distribution of spiritual gifts. The church is a charismatic community, the Body of Christ, whose members are endowed by the Holy Spirit with different gifts for different forms of ministry. Some are gifted to be "evangelists" (Eph. 4:11), while others are called to "service" (Rom. 12:7; I Pet. 4:11), or to "acts of mercy" (Rom. 12:8). Whatever our gifts may be, we are neither to depreciate them nor to boast of them (I Cor. 12:14-26), but rather to use them for the common good.

The best example of the outworking of this principle occurs in Acts 6 where the apostles, who had been called to "prayer and the ministry of the Word", were in danger of becoming preoccupied with "serving tables", that is, with caring for the material needs of the church's widows. So seven men were appointed to perform this social service, although Stephen and Philip also did some preaching (Acts 6:8-15; 8:5-13). This left the apostles free to concentrate on the pastoral ministry for which they had been commissioned, although they also retained a social concern (e.g., Gal. 2:10). Still today, Christ calls some to pastoral, others to social, others to evangelistic ministries; in fact, there is a wide diversity of spiritual gifts, callings and ministries within the Body of Christ.

(C) THREE KINDS OF RELATIONSHIPS

Having seen that both particular situations and specialist callings can legitimately separate our evangelistic and social responsibilities, we are now ready to consider how in general they relate to one another. What has emerged from our discussion is that there is no one relationship in which they are joined, but that there are at least three equally valid relationships.

First, social activity is a consequence of evangelism. That is, evangelism is the means by which God brings people to new birth, and their new life manifests itself in the service of others. Paul wrote that "faith works through love" (Gal. 5:6), James that " I will show you my faith by my works" (James 2:18), and John that God's love within us will overflow in serving our needy brothers and sisters (I John 3:16-18). As Robert E. Speer wrote about the Gospel in 1900: "wherever it goes, it plants in the hearts of men forces that create new social combinations." We have heard of evangelists in our own day who, during their missions or crusades, actively encourage Christians (including new converts) to become involved in programmes to meet specific local, human needs. This effectively highlights the serving dimension of Christian conversion and commitment.

We can go further than this, however. Social responsibility is more than the consequence of evangelism; it is also one of its principal aims. For Christ gave himself for us not only "to redeem us from all iniquity" but also "to purify for himself a people of his own who are zealous for good deeds" (Tit. 2:14). Similarly, through the Gospel we are "created in Christ Jesus for good works which God prepared beforehand, that we should walk in them" (Eph. 2:10). Good works cannot save, but they are an indispensable evidence of salvation (James 2:14-26).

In saying this, we are not claiming that compassionate service is an automatic consequence of evangelism or of conversion, however. Social responsibility, like evangelism, should therefore be included in the teaching ministry of the church. For we have to confess the inconsistencies in our own lives and the dismal record of evangelical failure, often as a result of the cultural blindspots to which we have already referred. This has grave consequences. When we do not allow the Word of God to transform us in all areas of our personal and social life, we seem to validate the Marxist criticism of religion.

Secondly, social activity can be a bridge *to evangelism.* It can break down prejudice and suspicion, open closed doors, and gain a hearing for the Gospel. Jesus himself sometimes performed works of mercy before proclaiming the Good News of the Kingdom. In more recent times, we were reminded, the construction of dams by the Basel missionaries in Northern Ghana opened a way for the Gospel, and much missionary medical, agricultural, nutritional and educational work has had a similar effect. To add a contemporary western example, a recent crusade in an American city was preceded and accompanied by a "Love in Action" programme, with the evangelist's encouragement. Several "social uplift" groups cooperated and were able to extend their ministries to the inner city poor. As a result, we were told, a number of people came under the sound of the Gospel who would not otherwise have come to the crusade.

Further, by seeking to serve people, it is possible to move from their "felt needs" to their deeper need concerning their relationship with God. Whereas, as another participant put it, "if we turn a blind eye to the suffering, the social oppression, the alienation and loneliness of people, let us not be surprised if they turn a deaf ear to our message of eternal salvation." We are aware of the danger of making "rice Christians", that is, of securing converts only because of the physical benefits we offer. But we have to take this risk, so long as we retain our own integrity and serve people out of genuine love and not with an ulterior motive. Then our actions will be "not bribes but bridges—bridges of love to the world."

Thirdly, social activity not only follows evangelism as its consequence and aim, and precedes it as its bridge, but also accompanies it as its partner. They are like the two blades of a pair of scissors or the two wings of a bird. This partnership is clearly seen in the public ministry of Jesus, who not only preached the Gospel but fed the hungry and healed the sick. In his ministry, *kerygma* (proclamation) and *diakonia* (service) went hand in hand. His words explained his works, and his works dramatized his words. Both were expressions of his compassion for people, and both should be of ours. Both also issue from the lordship of Jesus, for he sends us out into the world both to preach and to serve. If we proclaim the good news of God's love, we must manifest his love in caring for the needy. Indeed, so close is this link between proclaiming and serving, that they actually overlap.

This is not to say that they should be identified with each other, for evangelism is not social responsibility, nor is social responsibility evangelism. Yet, each involves the other.

To proclaim Jesus as Lord and Saviour (evangelism) has social implications, since it summons people to repent of social as well as personal sins, and to live a new life of righteousness and peace in the new society which challenges the old.

To give food to the hungry (social responsibility) has evangelistic implications, since good works of love, if done in the name of Christ, are a demonstration and commendation of the Gospel.

It has been said, therefore, that evangelism, even when it does not have a primarily social intention, nevertheless has a social dimension, while social responsibility, even when it does not have a primarily evangelistic intention, nevertheless has an evangelistic dimension.

Thus, evangelism and social responsibility, while distinct from one another, are integrally related in our proclamation of and obedience to the Gospel. The partnership is, in reality, a marriage.

(D) THE QUESTION OF PRIMACY

This brings us to the question of whether the partnership between evangelism and social responsibility is equal or unequal, that is, whether they are of identical importance or whether one takes precedence over the other. The Lausanne Covenant affirms that "in the church's mission of sacrificial service evangelism is primary" (Paragraph 6). Although some of us have felt uncomfortable about this phrase, lest by it we should be breaking the partnership, yet we are able to endorse and explain it in two ways, in addition to the particular situations and callings already mentioned.

First, evangelism has a certain priority. We are not referring to an invariable *temporal* priority, because in some situations a social ministry will take precedence, but to a *logical* one. The very fact of Christian social responsibility presupposes socially responsible Christians, and it can only be by evangelism and discipling that they have become such. If social activity is a consequence and aim of evangelism (as we have asserted), then evangelism must precede it. In addition, social progress is being hindered in some countries by the prevailing religious culture; only evangelism can change this.

Secondly, evangelism relates to people's eternal destiny, and in bringing them Good News of salvation, Christians are doing what nobody else can do. Seldom if ever should we have to choose between satisfying physical hunger and spiritual hunger, or between healing bodies and saving souls, since an authentic love for our neighbour will lead us to serve him or her as a whole person. Nevertheless, if we must choose, then we have to say that the supreme and ultimate need of all humankind is the saving grace of Jesus Christ, and that therefore a person's eternal, spiritual salvation is of greater importance than his or her temporal and material well-being (cf. II Cor. 4:16-18). As the Thailand Statement expressed it, "of all the tragic needs of human beings none is greater than their alienation from their Creator and the terrible reality of eternal death for those who refuse to repent and believe." Yet this fact must not make us indifferent to the degradations of human poverty and oppression. The choice, we believe, is largely conceptual. In practice, as in the public ministry of Jesus, the two are inseparable, at least in open societies. Rather than competing with each other, they mutually support and strengthen each other in an upward spiral of increased concern for both.

7

Consultation on the Church in Response to Human Need

Wheaton, 1983

WORLD EVANGELICAL FELLOWSHIP

Even before COWE (Pattaya, 1980) and CRESR (Grand Rapids, 1982), evangelicals belonging to the World Evangelical Fellowship had been embarked on an intensive study process, seeking to define the biblical relationship among working with the poor, global relief and development, and evangelization. The "Evangelical Commitment to Simple Life-style" (High Leigh, 1980) was a step in that direction, but the Wheaton 1983 statement on "Transformation: The Church in Response to Human Need" remains the landmark evangelical document on the biblical relationship between gospel ministry and the kingdom of God.

"According to the biblical view of human life, then, transformation is the change from a condition of human existence contrary to God's purposes to one in which people are able to enjoy fullness of life in harmony with God." In the wider context of both divine creation and eschatology, Wheaton 1983 relates the goal of transformation to the biblical vision of the kingdom of God. The statement has ramifications for a whole range of Christian activities, not merely evangelization. The full text of the statement is reproduced below.

TRANSFORMATION: THE CHURCH IN RESPONSE TO HUMAN NEED*

THE WHEATON '83 STATEMENT

INTRODUCTION

For two weeks during June 1983 we have come together from local churches and Christian mission and aid agencies at Wheaton College in the USA from 30 nations to pray about and reflect upon the church's task in response to human need. Some of us belong to churches which are situated among marginalized peoples who

---

*Reprinted from V. Samuel and C. Sugden, eds., *The Church in Response to Human Need*, The Wheaton 1983 Consultation (Grand Rapids, Mich.: Eerdmans; Oxford: Regnum, 1987), 254-265.

live in situations of poverty, powerlessness, and oppression. Others come from churches situated in affluent areas of the world. We are deeply grateful to our heavenly Father for allowing us the privilege of sharing our lives with one another, studying the Scriptures in small groups, considering papers on aspects of human development and transformation, and looking closely at the implications of case studies and histories which describe different responses to human need. Because God hears the cries of the poor, we have sought each other's help to respond (Exod. 3:7-9; James 5:1-6). We rejoice at what we believe the Holy Spirit has been teaching us concerning God's specific purpose and plans for His distressed world and the part the church has to play in them.

As we have faced the enormous challenge before God's people everywhere to alleviate suffering and, in partnership together, to eliminate its causes, we are more than ever aware of the liberating and healing power of the Good News of Jesus. We gladly reaffirm, therefore, our conviction that Jesus Christ alone is the world's peace, for He alone can reconcile people to God and bring all hostilities to an end (Eph. 2:14-17).

We acknowledge, furthermore, that only by spreading the Gospel can the most basic need of human beings be met: to have fellowship with God. In what follows we do not emphasize evangelism as a separate theme, because we see it as an integral part of our total Christian response to human need (Matt. 28:18-21). In addition, it is not necessary simply to repeat what the Lausanne Covenant and the Report of the Consultation on the Relationship between Evangelism and Social Responsibility (CRESR, Grand Rapids, 1982) have already expressed.

What we have discovered we would like to share with our brothers and sisters throughout the world. We offer this statement, not as an attempt to produce a final word, but as a summary of our reflections.

Both Scripture and experience, informed by the Spirit, emphasize that God's people are dependent upon His wisdom in confronting human need. Local churches and mission agencies, then, should act wisely, if they are to be both pastoral and prophetic. Indeed the whole human family with its illusions and divisions needs Christ to be its Wisdom as well as its Savior and King.

Conscious of our struggle to find a biblical view of transformation that relates its working in the heart of believers to its multiplying effects in society, we pray that the Spirit will give us the discernment we need. We believe that the wisdom the Spirit inspires is practical rather than academic, and the possession of the faithful rather than the preserve of the elite. Because we write as part of a world full of conflict and a church easily torn by strife we desire that the convictions expressed in this document be further refined by God's pure and peaceable wisdom.

Some may find our words hard. We pray, however, that many will find them a help to their own thinking and an encouragement to "continue steadfast, immovable, always abounding in the work of the Lord, knowing that in the Lord your labor is not in vain" (1 Cor. 15:58).

I. CHRISTIAN SOCIAL INVOLVEMENT

1. As Christians reflect on God's intention for the world they are often tempted to be either naively optimistic or darkly pessimistic. Some, inspired by a utopian vision seem to suggest that God's Kingdom, in all its fullness, can be built on earth. We do not subscribe to this view, since Scripture informs us of the reality and pervasiveness of both personal and societal sin (Isa. 1:10-26; Amos 2:6-8; Mic. 2:1-

10; Rom. 1:28-32). Thus we recognize that utopianism is nothing but a false dream (see the CRESR Report, IV, A).

2. Other Christians become pessimistic because they are faced with the reality of increasing poverty and misery, of rampant oppression and exploitation by powers of the right and the left, of spiralling violence coupled with the threat of nuclear warfare. They are concerned, too, about the increasing possibility that planet earth will not be able to sustain its population for long because of the wanton squandering of its resources. As a result, they are tempted to turn their eyes away from this world and fix them so exclusively on the return of Christ that their involvement in the here and now is paralyzed. We do not wish to disregard or minimize the extensive contribution made by a succession of Christians who have held this view of eschatology, through more than one hundred years, to medical and educational work in many countries up to the present day. Nevertheless, some of us feel that these men and women have tended to see the task of the church as merely picking up survivors from a shipwreck in a hostile sea. We do not endorse this view either, since it denies the biblical injunctions to defend the cause of the weak, maintain the rights of the poor and oppressed (Ps. 82:3), and practice justice and love (Mic. 6:8).

3. We affirm, moreover, that, even though we may believe that our calling is only to proclaim the Gospel and not get involved in political and other actions, our very non-involvement lends tacit support to the existing order. There is no escape: either we challenge the evil structures of society or we support them.

4. There have been many occasions in the history of the church—and some exist today—where Christians, faced with persecution and oppression, have *appeared* to be disengaged from society and thus to support the status quo. We suggest, however, that even under conditions of the most severe repression, such Christians may in fact be challenging society and even be transforming it, through their lifestyle, their selfless love, their quiet joy, their inner peace, and their patient suffering (1 Pet. 2:21-25).

5. Christ's followers, therefore, are called, in one way or another, not to conform to the values of society but to transform them (Rom. 12:1-2; Eph. 5:8-14). This calling flows from our confession that God loves the world and that the earth belongs to Him. It is true that Satan *is* active in this world, even claiming it to be his (Luke 4:5-7). He is, however, a usurper, having no property rights here. All authority in heaven and on earth has been given to Christ Jesus (Matt. 28:18; Col, 1:15-20). Although His Lordship is not yet acknowledged by all (Heb. 2:8), He is the ruler of the kings of the earth (Rev. 1:5), King of kings and Lord of lords (Rev. 19:16). In faith we confess that the old order is passing away; the new order has already begun (2 Cor. 5:17; Eph. 2:7-10; Matt. 12:18; Luke 7:21-23).

II. NOT ONLY DEVELOPMENT BUT TRANSFORMATION

6. The participants at this conference have entered into the current discussions concerning development. For many Western political and business leaders development describes the process by which nations and peoples become part of the existing international economic order. For many people of the Two Thirds World it is identified with an ideologically motivated process of change, called "developmentalism." This process is intrinsically related to a mechanistic pursuit of economic growth that tends to ignore the structural context of poverty and injustice and which increases dependency and inequality.

7. Some of us still believe, however, that "development," when reinterpreted in the light of the whole message of the Bible, is a concept that should be retained by Christians. Part of the reason for this choice is that the word is so widely used. A change of term, therefore, would cause unnecessary confusion.

8. Others in our Consultation, because of difficulty in relating it to biblical categories of thought and its negative overtones, would like to replace "development" with another word. An alternative we suggest is "transformation," as it can be applied in different ways to every situation. Western nations, for example, who have generally assumed that development does not apply to them, are, nevertheless, in need of transformation in many areas. In particular, the unspoken assumption that societies operate best when individuals are most free to pursue their own self-interests needs to be challenged on the basis of the biblical teaching on stewardship (Luke 12:13-21; 16:13-15; Phil. 2:1-4). People living in groups based on community solidarity may help these kinds of societies see the poverty of their existence.

9. Moreover, the term "transformation," unlike "development," does not have a suspect past. It points to a number of changes that have to take place in many societies if poor people are to enjoy their rightful heritage in creation.

10. We are concerned, however, that both the goals and the process of transformation should be seen in the light of the Good News about Jesus, the Messiah. We commit ourselves and urge other Christian believers to reject the cultural and social forces of secularism which so often shape our idea of a good society. We believe that notions alien to God's plan for human living are often more powerful in forming our opinions about what is right for a nation than the message of Scripture itself.

11. According to the biblical view of human life, then, transformation is the change from a condition of human existence contrary to God's purposes to one in which people are able to enjoy fullness of life in harmony with God (John 10:10; Col. 3:8-15; Eph. 4:13). This transformation can only take place through the obedience of individuals and communities to the Gospel of Jesus Christ, whose power changes the lives of men and women by releasing them from the guilt, power, and consequences of sin, enabling them to respond with love toward God and toward others (Rom. 5:5), and making them "new creatures in Christ" (2 Cor. 5:17).

12. There are a number of themes in the Bible which help us focus on the way we understand transformation. The doctrine of creation speaks of the worth of every man, woman, and child, of the responsibility of human beings to look after the resources of nature (Gen. 1:26-30) and to share them equitably with their neighbors. The doctrine of the Fall highlights the innate tendency of human beings to serve their own interests, with the consequences of greed, insecurity, violence, and the lust for power. "God's judgment rightly falls upon those who do such things" (Rom. 2:2). The doctrine of redemption proclaims God's forgiveness of sins and the freedom Christ gives for a way of life dedicated to serving others by telling them about the Good News of Salvation, bringing reconciliation between enemies, and losing one's life to see justice established for all exploited people.

13. We have come to see that the goal of transformation is best described by the biblical vision of the Kingdom of God. This new way of being human in submission to the Lord of all has many facets. In particular, it means striving to bring peace among individuals, races, and nations by overcoming prejudices, fears, and preconceived ideas about others. It means sharing basic resources like food, water, the means of healing, and knowledge. It also means working for a greater participation of people in the decisions which affect their lives, making possible an equal

receiving from others and giving of themselves. Finally, it means growing up into Christ in all things as a body of people dependent upon the work of the Holy Spirit and upon each other.

III. THE STEWARDSHIP OF CREATION

14. "The earth is the Lord's and all that is in it" (Ps. 24:1); "The land is mine" (Lev. 25:23). All human beings are God's creatures. As made in His image they are His representatives, given the responsibility of caring wisely for His creation. We have to confess, however, that God's people have been slow to recognize the full implications of their responsibility. As His stewards, we do not own the earth but we manage and enhance it in anticipation of Christ's return. Too often, however, we have assumed a right to use His natural resources indiscriminately. We have frequently been indifferent, or even hostile, to those committed to the conservation of non-renewable sources of energy and minerals, of animal life in danger of extinction, and of the precarious ecological balance of many natural habitats. The earth is God's gift to all generations. An African proverb says that parents have borrowed the present from their children. Both our present life and our children's future depends upon our wise and peaceful treatment of the whole earth.

15. We have also assumed that only a small portion of our income and wealth, the "tithe," belongs to the Lord, the rest being ours to dispose of as we like. This impoverishes other people and denies our identity and role as stewards. We believe that Christians everywhere, but especially those who are enjoying in abundance "the good things of life" (Luke 16:25), must faithfully obey the command to ensure that others have their basic needs met. In this way those who are poor now will also be able to enjoy the blessing of giving to others.

16. Through salvation, Jesus lifts us out of our isolation from God and other people and establishes us within the worldwide community of the Body of Christ. Belonging to one Body involves sharing all God's gifts to us, so that there might be equality among all members (2 Cor. 8:14-15). To the extent that this standard is obeyed, dire poverty will be eliminated (Acts 2:42-47).

17. When either individuals or states claim an absolute right of ownership, that is rebellion against God. The meaning of stewardship is that the poor have equal rights to God's resources (Deut. 15:8-9). The meaning of transformation is that, as stewards of God's bountiful gifts, we do justice, striving together through prayer, example, representation, and protest to have resources redistributed and the consequences of greed limited (Acts 4:32-5:11).

18. We are perturbed by the perverse misuse of huge amounts of resources in the present arms race. While millions starve to death, resources are wasted on the research and production of increasingly sophisticated nuclear weapon systems. Moreover, the constantly escalating global trade in conventional arms accompanies the proliferation of oppressive governments which disregard people's elementary needs. As Christians we condemn these new expressions of injustice and aggression, affirming our commitment to seek peace with justice. In the light of the issues of the stewardship of creation we have discussed here, we call on the worldwide evangelical community to make the nuclear and arms trade questions a matter of prayerful concern and to place it on their agenda for study and action.

IV. CULTURE AND TRANSFORMATION

19. Culture includes world-views, beliefs, values, art forms, customs, laws, socioeconomic structures, social relationships, and material things shared by a population over time in a specific area or context.

20. Culture is God's gift to human beings. God has made people everywhere in His image. As Creator, He has made us creative. This creativity produces cultures. Furthermore, God has commissioned us to be stewards of His creation (Ps. 8; Heb. 2:5-11). Since every good gift is from above and since all wisdom and knowledge comes from Jesus Christ, whatever is good and beautiful in cultures may be seen as a gift of God (James 1:16-18). Moreover, where the Gospel has been heard and obeyed, cultures have become further ennobled and enriched.

21. However, people have sinned by rebelling against God. Therefore the cultures we produce are infected with evil. Different aspects of our culture show plainly our separation from God. Social structures and relationships, art forms and laws often reflect our violence, our sense of lostness, and our loss of coherent moral values. Scripture challenges us not to be "conformed to this world" (Rom. 12:2) insofar as it is alienated from its Creator. We need to be transformed so that cultures may display again what is "good and acceptable and perfect" (Rom. 12:2).

22. Cultures, then, bear the marks of God's common grace, demonic influences, and mechanisms of human exploitation. In our cultural creativity, God and Satan clash. The Lord used Greek culture to give us the New Testament, while at the same time He subjected that culture to the judgment of the Gospel. We too should make thankful use of cultures and yet, at the same time, examine them in the light of the Gospel to expose the evil in them (1 Cor. 9:19-23).

23. Social structures that exploit and dehumanize constitute a pervasive sin which is not confronted adequately by the church. Many churches, mission societies, and Christian relief and development agencies support the sociopolitical status quo, and by silence give their tacit support.

24. Through the application of the Scriptures, in the power of the Spirit, we seek to discern the true reality of all sociocultural situations. We need to learn critically from both functionalist and conflict approaches to human culture. The "functionalist socio-anthropology" approach emphasizes the harmonious aspects of different cultures and champions a tolerant attitude to the existing structures. This position is often adopted in the name of "scientific objectivity." By contrast, the "conflict" approach exposes the contradictory nature of social structures and makes us aware of the underlying conflicts of interests. We must remember that both approaches come under the judgment of God.

25. Given the conflicting ethical tendencies in our nature, which find expression in our cultural systems, we must be neither naively optimistic nor wrongly judgmental. We are called to be a new community that seeks to work with God in the transformation of our societies, men and women of God in society, salt of the earth and light of the world (Matt. 5:13-16). We seek to bring people and their cultures under the Lordship of Christ. In spite of our failures, we move toward that freedom and wholeness in a more just community that persons will enjoy when our Lord returns to consummate His Kingdom (Rev. 21:1-22:6).

V. SOCIAL JUSTICE AND MERCY

26. Our time together enabled us to see that poverty is not a necessary evil but often the result of social, economic, political, and religious systems marked by injustice, exploitation, and oppression. Approximately eight hundred million people in the world are destitute, and their plight is often maintained by the rich and the powerful. Evil is not only in the human heart but also in social structures. Because God is just and merciful, hating evil and loving righteousness, there is an urgent

need for Christians in the present circumstances to commit ourselves to acting in mercy and seeking justice. The mission of the church includes both the proclamation of the Gospel and its demonstration. We must therefore evangelize, respond to immediate human needs, and press for social transformation. The means we use, however, must be consistent with the end we desire.

27. As we thought of the task before us, we considered Jesus' attitude toward the power structures of His time. He was neither a Zealot nor a passive spectator of the oppression of His people. Rather, moved by compassion, He identified Himself with the poor, whom He saw as "harassed and helpless, like sheep without a shepherd" (Matt. 9:36). Through His acts of mercy, teaching, and lifestyle, He exposed the injustices in society and condemned the self-righteousness of its leaders (Matt. 23:25; Luke 6:37-42). His was a prophetic compassion and it resulted in the formation of a community which accepted the values of the Kingdom of God and stood in contrast to the Roman and Jewish establishment. We were challenged to follow Jesus' footsteps, remembering that His compassion led Him to death (John 13:12-17; Phil. 2:6-8; 1 John 3:11-18).

28. We are aware that a Christlike identification with the poor, whether at home or abroad, in the North, South, East, or West, is always costly and may lead us also to persecution and even death. Therefore, we humbly ask God to make us willing to risk our comfort, even our lives, for the sake of the Gospel, knowing that "everyone who wants to live a godly life in Christ Jesus will be persecuted" (2 Tim. 3:12).

29. Sometimes in our ministry among the poor we face a serious dilemma: to limit ourselves to acts of mercy to improve their lot, or to go beyond that and seek to rectify the injustice that makes such acts of mercy necessary. This step in turn may put at risk the freedom we need to continue our ministry. No rule of thumb can be given, but from a biblical perspective it is clear that justice and mercy belong together (Isa. 11:1-5; Ps. 113:59). We must therefore make every possible effort to combine both in our ministry and be willing to suffer the consequences. We must also remember that acts of mercy highlight the injustices of the social, economic, and political structures and relationships; whether we like it or not, they may therefore lead us into confrontation with those who hold power (Acts 4:5-22). For the same reason, we must stand together with those who suffer for the sake of justice (Heb. 13:3).

30. Our ministry of justice and healing is not limited to fellow Christians. Our love and commitment must extend to the stranger (Matt. 5:43-48). Our involvement with strangers is not only through charity, but also through economic and political action. Justice must characterize the government's laws and policies toward the poor. Our economic and political action is inseparable from evangelism.

31. Injustice in the modern world has reached global proportions. Many of us come from countries dominated by international business corporations, and some from those whose political systems are not accountable to the people. We witness to the damaging effects that these economic and political institutions are having on people, especially on the poorest of the poor. We call on our brothers and sisters in Jesus Christ to study seriously this situation and to seek ways to bring about change in favor of the oppressed. "The righteous care about justice for the poor, but the wicked have no such concern" (Prov. 29:7).

VI. THE LOCAL CHURCH AND TRANSFORMATION

32. The local church is the basic unit of Christian society. The churches in the New Testament were made up of men and women who had experienced transfor-

mation through receiving Jesus Christ as Savior, acknowledging Him as Lord, and incarnating His servant ministry by demonstrating the values of the Kingdom both personally and in community (Mark 10:35-45; 1 Pet. 2:5; 4:10). Today similar examples of transformed lives abound in churches worldwide.

33. We recognize that across the generations local churches have been the vehicle for the transmission of the Gospel of Jesus Christ, and that their primary, though not their only, role is a threefold ministry: the worship and praise of God, the proclamation in word and deed of the Gospel of the grace of God, and the nurture, instruction, and discipleship of those who have received Jesus Christ into their lives. In this way transformation takes place in the lives of Christians as individuals, families, and communities; through their words and deeds they demonstrate both the need and reality of ethical, moral, and social transformation.

34. All churches are faced at times with the choice between speaking openly against social evils and not speaking out publicly. The purpose for the particular choice should be obedience to the Lord of the church to fulfill its ministry. Wisdom will be needed so that the church will neither speak rashly and make its witness ineffective nor remain silent when to do so would deny its prophetic calling (1 Pet. 3:13-17). If we are sensitive to the Holy Spirit and are socially aware, we will always be ready to reassess our attitude toward social issues (Lk. 18:24-30).

35. Integrity, leadership, and information are essential for the transformation of attitudes and lifestyles of members of local churches. Churches are made up of people whose lives are pressured by the way their neighbors spend their money. They are often more aware of this than of the suffering and human need in their own and other countries. Often, too, they are reluctant to expose themselves to the traumas of global need and to information which would challenge their comfort. If church leadership fails to adequately stress the social dimensions of the Gospel, church members may often overlook these issues (1 Tim. 3:1-7; Heb. 13:17).

36. We should be sensitive and responsive to need within the local church. Widows, prisoners, the poor, and strangers are people who are particularly the responsibility of the local church (Gal. 6:10). We should attempt to be well informed about local human need and to seek God's will for us in meeting those needs. We should seek to minister to the poor in our local area who are not members of the church (James 1:27; Rom. 12:17).

37. Our churches must also address issues of evil and of social injustice in the local community and the wider society. Our methodology should involve study, earnest prayer, and action within the normative, ethical guidelines for Christian conduct set out in Scripture. Within these guidelines there are times, no matter the political system, when protest can be effective. Christians should carefully consider the issues and the manner in which they protest so that the identity and message of the church is neither blurred nor drowned.

38. The local church has however to be understood as being a part of the universal church. There is therefore a genuine need for help and sharing (*diakonia*) built on fellowship (*Koinonia*) between churches of different localities and contexts. In this connection we considered a model for relating churches in different areas of the world. In such "church twinnings" the relationship should be genuinely reciprocal with giving and receiving at both ends, free from paternalism of any kind (Rom. 15:1-7).

39. Such reciprocal relationships in a spirit of true mutuality are particularly needed in view of the fact that every local church always lives on the edge of compromise with its context (Rom. 12:3-18). Some churches are immersed in the

problems of materialism and racism, others in those of oppression and the option of violence. We may help each other by seeking to see the world through the eyes of our brothers and sisters.

40. With regard to the wider world community, Christian churches should identify and exchange people who are equipped through their personal characteristics, training, and Christian maturity to work across cultures in the name of Christ and of the sending church. These men and women would go as servants and stewards characterized by humility and meekness; and they would work together with members of the Body of Christ in the countries to which they go.

VII. CHRISTIAN AID AGENCIES AND TRANSFORMATION

41. In reflecting upon the Christian response to human need, we have recognized the central place of the local church as the vehicle for communicating the Gospel of Jesus Christ both in word and deed. Churches around the world have throughout history displayed active concern for the needs around them and continue to serve the needy. We call upon the aid agencies to see their role as one of facilitating the churches in the fulfillment of their mission.

42. We recognize the progress which in recent years has been made in our understanding of the Gospel and its social and political implications. We also recognize, however, the deficiencies in our witness and affirm our desire for a fuller understanding of the biblical basis for our ministry.

43. We acknowledge that the constituency of the aid agencies is generally concerned with human suffering, hunger, and need. However, we recognize that this concern is not consistently expressed with integrity. In efforts to raise funds, the plight of the poor is often exploited in order to meet donor needs and expectations. Fund-raising activities must be in accordance with the Gospel. A stewardship responsibility of agencies is to reduce significantly their overheads in order to maximize the resources for the ministry.

44. We are challenged to implement in our organizations a positive transformation demonstrating the values of Christ and His Kingdom which we wish to share with others. We must, for example, avoid competition with others involved in the same ministry and a success mentality that forgets God's special concern for the weak and "unsuccessful" (Gal. 2:10; Ps. 147:6). We should continually review our actions to ensure biblical integrity and genuine partnership with churches and other agencies. Decisions on ministry policy, including how resources are to be used, need to be made in consultation with the people to be served.

45. We need to ensure that our promotional efforts describe what we are actually doing. We accept the responsibility of educating our donors in the full implications of the way Christian transformation is experienced in the field. The Holy Spirit has led us to this ministry. In accepting the responsibility of education we recognize the process may cause some to question our approach. We will strive to educate with a sense of humility, patience, and courage.

46. In all of our programs and actions we should remember that God in His sovereignty and love is already active in the communities we seek to serve (Acts 14:17; 17:23; Rom. 2:9-15). Agencies, therefore, should give adequate priority to listening sensitively to the concerns of these communities, facilitating a two-way process in communication and local ownership of programs. The guiding principle is equitable partnership in which local people and Western agencies cooperate together. Many models for development have originated in the Two Thirds World.

Christian aid agencies should in every way encourage these local initiatives to succeed. In this way the redeemed community of the Kingdom will be able to experiment with a number of models of transformation.

47. The agencies' legitimate need for accountability to donors often results in the imposition of Western management systems on local communities. This assumes that Western planning and control systems are the only ones which can ensure accountability. Since the communities these agencies seek to serve are often part of a different culture, this imposition can restrict and inhibit the sensitive processes of social transformation. We call on development agencies to establish a dialogue with those they serve in order to permit the creation of systems of accountability with respect to both cultures. Our ministry must always reflect our mutual interdependence in the Kingdom (Rom. 14:17-18; 1 Cor. 12).

48. In focusing on the apparently conflicting requirements of our action as Christian agencies, we are conscious of our sin and compromise. In a call to repentance we include a renunciation of inconsistency and extravagance in our personal and institutional lifestyle. We ask the Spirit of truth to lead us and make us true agents of transformation (Acts 1:8).

VIII. THE COMING OF THE KINGDOM AND THE CHURCH'S MISSION

49. We affirm that the Kingdom of God is both present and future, both societal and individual, both physical and spiritual. If others have over-emphasized the present, the societal, and the physical, we ought to confess that we have tended to neglect those dimensions of the biblical message. We therefore joyfully proclaim that the Kingdom has broken into human history in the Resurrection of Christ. It grows like a mustard seed, both judging and transforming the present age.

50. Even if God's activity in history is focused on the church, it is not confined to the church. God's particular focus on the church—as on Israel in the Old Testament—has as its purpose the blessing of the nations (Gen. 12:1-3; 15; 17; Isa. 42:6). Thus the church is called to exist for the sake of its Lord and for the sake of humankind (Matt. 22:32-40).

51. The church is called to infuse the world with hope, for both this age and the next. Our hope does not flow from despair: it is not because the present is empty that we hope for a new future (Rom. 5:1-11). Rather, we hope for that future because of what God has already done and because of what He has promised yet to do. We have already been given the Holy Spirit as the guarantee of our full redemption and of the coming of the day when God will be all in all (1 Cor. 15:28). As we witness to the Gospel of present salvation and future hope, we identify with the awesome birthpangs of God's new creation (Rom. 8:22). As the community of the end time anticipating the End, we prepare for the ultimate by getting involved in the penultimate (Matt. 24:36-25:46).

52. For this reason we are challenged to commit ourselves to a truly vigorous and full-orbed mission in the world, combining explosive creativity with painstaking faithfulness in small things. Our mission and vision are to be nurtured by the whole counsel of God (2 Tim. 3:16). A repentant, revived, and vigorous church will call people to true repentance and faith and at the same time equip them to challenge the forces of evil and injustice (2 Tim. 3:17). We thus move forward, without either relegating salvation merely to an eternal future or making it synonymous with a political or social dispensation to be achieved in the here and now. The Holy Spirit empowers us to serve and proclaim Him who has been raised from the dead, seated

at the right hand of the Father, and given to the church as Head over all things in heaven and on earth (Eph. 1:10, 20-22).

53. Finally, we confess our utter dependence on God. We affirm that transformation is, in the final analysis, His work, but work in which He engages us. To this end He has given us His Spirit, the Transformer *par excellence,* to enlighten us and be our Counselor (John 16:7), to impart His many gifts to us (Rom. 12; 1 Cor. 12), to equip us to face and conquer the enemy (2 Cor. 10:3-5; Gal. 5:22-23). We are reminded that our unconfessed sins and lack of love for others grieve the Spirit (Eph. 4:30; Gal. 5:13-16). We therefore fervently pray for our sins to be pardoned, for our spirit to be renewed, and for the privilege of being enlisted in the joyous task of enabling God's Kingdom to come: the Kingdom "of . . . justice, peace, and joy in the Holy Spirit" (Rom. 14:17).

8

The Manila Manifesto

Manila, 1989

LAUSANNE COMMITTEE FOR WORLD EVANGELIZATION

From July 11-20, 1989, LCWE convened the Second International Congress of Evangelization at the International Conference Center in Manila. Lausanne II at Manila, as it was popularly called, brought together over 3,000 persons from 170 countries on the basis of the Lausanne Covenant, *adopted at the First International Congress on World Evangelization at Lausanne fifteen years earlier.*

Lausanne II was able to reflect on the work of smaller evangelical consultations held between 1977 and 1988, devoted to specific issues and themes such as gospel and culture (1978), simple life-style (1980), the COWE mini-consultations (1980), evangelism and social responsibility (1982), the work of the Holy Spirit and evangelization (Oslo, 1985), and conversion (Hong Kong, 1988). Such concerns as "modernity," "large cities," and "integrity of witness" received fresh treatment.

The results of countless study tracks were integrated into the Manila Manifesto, *"An Elaboration of the Lausanne Covenant Fifteen Years Later." The manifesto is a public declaration of evangelical convictions, intentions, and motives based on the two Lausanne II Congress themes, "Proclaim Christ until he comes," and "Calling the Whole Church To Take the Whole Gospel to the Whole World." It consists of twenty-one affirmations followed by twelve sections which were accepted at Manila as a general expression of congress concerns and commitments, and commended to delegates, churches, and Christian organizations for further study and response. The Executive Committee of LCWE has directed that the* Manila Manifesto *never be published apart from the* Lausanne Covenant, *of which it is an extension. The entire statement is reproduced below.*

INTRODUCTION*

In July 1974 the International Congress on World Evangelization was held in Lausanne, Switzerland, and issued the Lausanne Covenant. Now in July 1989 over 3,000 of us from about 170 countries have met in Manila for the same purpose, and

---

*Reprinted from *The Manila Manifesto: An Elaboration of the Lausanne Covenant Fifteen Years Later* (Pasadena, Calif.: LCWE, 1989), 3-38.

have issued the Manila Manifesto. We are grateful for the welcome we have received from our Filipino brothers and sisters.

During the 15 years which have elapsed between the two congresses some smaller consultations have been held on topics like Gospel and Culture, Evangelism and Social Responsibility, Simple Lifestyle, the Holy Spirit, and Conversion. These meetings and their reports have helped to develop the thinking of the Lausanne movement.

A 'manifesto' is defined as a public declaration of convictions, intentions and motives. The Manila Manifesto takes up the two congress themes, 'Proclaim Christ until he comes' and 'Calling the Whole Church to take the Whole Gospel to the Whole World'. Its first part is a series of 21 succinct affirmations. Its second part elaborates these in 12 sections, which are commended to churches, alongside the Lausanne Covenant, for study and action.

TWENTY-ONE AFFIRMATIONS

1. We affirm our continuing commitment to the Lausanne Covenant as the basis of our cooperation in the Lausanne movement.

2. We affirm that in the Scriptures of the Old and New Testaments God has given us an authoritative disclosure of his character and will, his redemptive acts and their meaning, and his mandate for mission.

3. We affirm that the biblical gospel is God's enduring message to our world, and we determine to defend, proclaim and embody it.

4. We affirm that human beings, though created in the image of God, are sinful and guilty, and lost without Christ, and that this truth is a necessary preliminary to the gospel.

5. We affirm that the Jesus of history and the Christ of glory are the same person, and that this Jesus Christ is absolutely unique, for he alone is God incarnate, our sin-bearer, the conqueror of death and the coming judge.

6. We affirm that on the cross Jesus Christ took our place, bore our sins and died our death; and that for this reason alone God freely forgives those who are brought to repentance and faith.

7. We affirm that other religions and ideologies are not alternative paths to God, and that human spirituality, if unredeemed by Christ, leads not to God but to judgment, for Christ is the only way.

8. We affirm that we must demonstrate God's love visibly by caring for those who are deprived of justice, dignity, food and shelter.

9. We affirm that the proclamation of God's kingdom of justice and peace demands the denunciation of all injustice and oppression, both personal and structural; we will not shrink from this prophetic witness.

10. We affirm that the Holy Spirit's witness to Christ is indispensable to evangelism, and that without his supernatural work neither new birth nor new life is possible.

11. We affirm that spiritual warfare demands spiritual weapons, and that we must both preach the word in the power of the Spirit, and pray constantly that we may enter into Christ's victory over the principalities and powers of evil.

12. We affirm that God has committed to the whole church and every member of it the task of making Christ known throughout the world; we long to see all lay and ordained persons mobilized and trained for this task.

13. We affirm that we who claim to be members of the Body of Christ must

transcend within our fellowship the barriers of race, gender and class.

14. We affirm that the gifts of the Spirit are distributed to all God's people, women and men, and that their partnership in evangelization must be welcomed for the common good.

15. We affirm that we who proclaim the gospel must exemplify it in a life of holiness and love; otherwise our testimony loses its credibility.

16. We affirm that every Christian congregation must turn itself outward to its local community in evangelistic witness and compassionate service.

17. We affirm the urgent need for churches, mission agencies and other Christian organizations to cooperate in evangelism and social action, repudiating competition and avoiding duplication.

18. We affirm our duty to study the society in which we live, in order to understand its structures, values and needs, and so develop an appropriate strategy of mission.

19. We affirm that world evangelization is urgent and that the reaching of unreached peoples is possible. So we resolve during the last decade of the twentieth century to give ourselves to these tasks with fresh determination.

20. We affirm our solidarity with those who suffer for the gospel, and will seek to prepare ourselves for the same possibility. We will also work for religious and political freedom everywhere.

21. We affirm that God is calling the whole church to take the whole gospel to the whole world. So we determine to proclaim it faithfully, urgently and sacrificially, until he comes.

A. THE WHOLE GOSPEL

The gospel is the good news of God's salvation from the powers of evil, the establishment of his eternal kingdom (Col. 2:15) and his final victory over everything which defies his purpose (1 Co. 15:24-28). In his love God purposed to do this before the world began and effected his liberating plan (Eph. 1:4; Col. 1:19) over sin, death and judgment through the death of our Lord Jesus Christ. It is Christ who makes us free (Tit. 2:14), and unites us in his redeemed fellowship.

1. OUR HUMAN PREDICAMENT

We are committed to preaching the whole (Ac. 20:27) gospel, that is, the biblical gospel in its fulness. In order to do so, we have to understand why human beings need it.

Men and women (Ge. 1:26, 27) have an intrinsic dignity and worth, because they were created in God's likeness to know, love and serve him. But now through sin (Ro. 3:9-18) every part of their humanness has been distorted (2 Ti. 3:2-4). Human beings have become self-centered, self-serving rebels, who do not love God or their neighbour as they should. In consequence, they are alienated both from their Creator and from the rest of his creation (Ge. 3:17-24), which is the basic cause of the pain, disorientation and loneliness which so many people suffer today. Sin also frequently erupts in anti-social behavior (Ro. 1:29-31), in violent exploitation of others, and in a depletion of the earth's resources of which God has made men and women his stewards (Ge. 1:26, 28; 2:15). Humanity is guilty (Ro. 1:20; 2:1; 3:19), without excuse, and on the broad road (Mt. 7:13) which leads to destruction.

Although God's image in human beings has been corrupted (Mt. 5:46; 7:11), they are still capable of loving relationships (1 Ti. 6:16), noble deeds and beautiful art. Yet even the finest human achievement is fatally flawed and cannot possibly fit anybody to enter God's presence (Ac. 17:22-31). Men and women are also spiritual beings, but spiritual practices and self-help techniques can at the most alleviate felt needs; they cannot address the solemn realities of sin, guilt and judgment. Neither human religion, nor human righteousness, nor socio-political programs can save people (Ro. 3:20). Self-salvation of every kind is impossible (Eph. 2:1-3). Left to themselves, human beings are lost forever.

So we repudiate false gospels (Gal. 1:6-9; 2 Co. 11:2-4) which deny human sin, divine judgment, the deity and incarnation of Jesus Christ (1 Jn. 2:22, 23; 4:1-3), and the necessity of the cross and the resurrection. We also reject half-gospels, which minimize sin and confuse God's grace with human self-effort (1 Co. 15:3, 4). We confess that we ourselves have sometimes trivialized the gospel. But we determine in our evangelism to remember God's radical diagnosis (Jer. 6:14; 8:11) and his equally radical remedy.

2. GOOD NEWS FOR TODAY

We rejoice that the living God did not abandon us to our lostness and despair. In his love (Eph. 2:4) he came after us in Jesus Christ (Lk. 15; 19:10) to rescue and re-make us (Ac. 8:35). So the good news focuses on the historic person of Jesus, who came proclaiming the kingdom of God (Mk. 1:14, 15) and living a life of humble service, who died for us, becoming sin and a curse (2 Co. 5:21; Ga. 3:13) in our place, and whom God vindicated by raising him from the dead (Ac. 2:23, 24). To those who repent and believe in Christ, God grants a share in the new creation (2 Co. 5:17). He gives us new life, which includes the forgiveness of our sins and the indwelling, transforming power of his Spirit (Ac. 2:38, 39). He welcomes us into his new community, which consists of people of all races, nations and cultures (Eph. 2:11-19). And he promises that one day we will enter his new world, in which evil will be abolished, nature will be redeemed, and God will reign for ever (Rev. 21:1-5: 22:1-5).

This good news must be boldly proclaimed, wherever possible (Eph. 6:19, 20; 2 Ti. 4:2), in church and public hall, on radio and television, and in the open air, because it is God's power for salvation (Ro. 1:14-16) and we are under obligation to make it known (Jer. 23:28). In our preaching we must faithfully declare the truth which God has revealed in the Bible and struggle to relate it to our own context.

We also affirm that apologetics, namely 'the defense and confirmation of the gospel' (Php. 1:7), is integral to the biblical understanding of mission and essential for effective witness in the modern world. Paul 'reasoned' (Ac. 18:4; 19:8, 9) with people out of the Scriptures, with a view to 'persuading' (2 Co. 5:11) them of the truth of the gospel. So must we. In fact, all Christians should be ready to give a reason for the hope (1 Pe. 3:15) that is in them.

We have again been confronted with Luke's emphasis that the gospel is good news for the poor (Lk. 4:18; 6:20; 7:22) and have asked ourselves what this means to the majority of the world's population who are destitute, suffering or oppressed (Dt. 15:7-11). We have been reminded that the law, the prophets and the wisdom books, and the teaching and ministry of Jesus, all stress God's concern for the materially poor and our consequent duty to defend and care for them (Am. 2:6, 7; Zec. 7:8-10; Pr. 21:13). Scripture also refers to the spiritually poor who look to God alone for mercy (Zep. 3:12). The gospel comes as good news to both. The spiritually poor, who, whatever their economic circumstances, humble themselves before God (Mt. 5:3), receive by faith the free gift of salvation (Mk. 10:15). There is no other way for anybody to enter the Kingdom of God. The materially poor and powerless find in addition a new dignity as God's children (1 Jn. 3:1), and the love of brothers and sisters (Ac. 2:44, 45; 4:32-35) who will struggle with them for their liberation from everything which demeans or oppresses them.

We repent of any neglect of God's truth in Scripture and determine both to proclaim and to defend it. We also repent where we have been indifferent to the plight of the poor, and where we have shown preference for the rich, and we determine to follow Jesus in preaching good news to all people by both word and deed.

3. THE UNIQUENESS OF JESUS CHRIST

We are called to proclaim Christ in an increasingly pluralistic world. There is a resurgence of old faiths and a rise of new ones. In the first century too there were 'many gods and many lords' (1 Co. 8:5). Yet the apostles boldly affirmed the uniqueness, indispensability and centrality of Christ. We must do the same.

Because men and women are made in God's image and see in the creation traces of its Creator (Ps. 19:1-6; Ro. 1:19, 20), the religions which have arisen do sometimes contain elements of truth and beauty (Ac. 17:28). They are not, however, alternative gospels. Because human beings are sinful, and because 'the whole world is under the control of the evil one' (1 Jn. 5:19; Ac. 10:1, 2; 11:14, 18; 15:8, 9), even religious people are in need of Christ's redemption. We, therefore, have no warrant for saying that salvation can be found outside Christ (Jn. 14:6) or apart from an explicit acceptance of his work through faith.

It is sometimes held that in virtue of God's covenant with Abraham, Jewish people do not need to acknowledge Jesus as their Messiah (Ge. 12:1-3; 17:1, 2). We affirm that they need him as much as anyone else, that it would be a form of anti-Semitism (Ro. 3:9; 10:12), as well as being disloyal to Christ, to depart from the New Testament pattern of taking the gospel to 'the Jew first . . .' (Ac. 13:46; Ro. 1:16; 2:9, 10). We therefore reject the thesis that Jews have their own covenant which renders faith in Jesus unnecessary (Ac. 13:38, 39).

What unites us is our common convictions about Jesus Christ (Jn. 1:1, 14, 18; Ro. 1:3, 4). We confess him as the eternal Son of God who became fully human while remaining fully divine, who was our substitute on the cross, bearing our sins (1 Pe. 2:24; 1 Co. 15:3) and dying our death, exchanging his righteousness (2 Co. 5:21) for our unrighteousness, who rose victorious (1 Co. 15:1-11) in a transformed body, and who will return in glory to judge the world (Mt. 25:31, 32; Ac. 17:30, 31). He alone is the incarnate Son, the Saviour, the Lord and the Judge, and he alone, with the Father and the Spirit, is worthy of the worship (Rev. 5:11-14), faith and obedience of all people. There is only one gospel because there is only one Christ, who because of his death and resurrection is himself the only way of salvation (Ac. 4:12). We therefore reject both the relativism which regards all religions and spiritualities as equally valid approaches to God, and the syncretism which tries to mix faith in Christ with other faiths.

Moreover, since God has exalted Jesus (Php. 2:9-11) to the highest place, in order that everybody should acknowledge him, this also is our desire (2 Co. 5:14). Compelled by Christ's love, we must obey Christ's Great Commission (Mt. 28:19, 20) and love his lost sheep (Jn. 10:11, 16), but we are especially motivated by 'jealousy' (2 Co. 11:2, 3) for his holy name, and we long to see him receive the honour and glory which are due to him.

In the past we have sometimes been guilty of adopting towards adherents of other faiths attitudes of ignorance, arrogance, disrespect and even hostility. We repent of this. We nevertheless are determined to bear a positive and uncompromising witness (1 Ti. 2:5-7) to the uniqueness of our Lord, in his life, death and resurrection, in all aspects of our evangelistic work including inter-faith dialogue.

4. THE GOSPEL AND SOCIAL RESPONSIBILITY

The authentic gospel must become visible in the transformed lives of men and women (1 Th. 1:6-10). As we proclaim the love of God we must be involved in loving service (1 Jn. 3:17), and as we preach the Kingdom of God we must be committed to its demands of justice and peace (Ro. 14:17).

Evangelism is primary (Ro. 10:14) because our chief concern is with the gospel, that all people may have the opportunity to accept Jesus Christ as Lord and Savior. Yet Jesus not only proclaimed the Kingdom of God, he also demonstrated its arrival by works of mercy and power (Mt. 12:28). We are called today to a similar integration of words and deeds (1 Jn. 3:18). In a spirit of humility we are to preach and teach, minister to the sick, feed the hungry, care for prisoners, help the disadvantaged and handicapped, and deliver the oppressed (Mt. 25:34-46). While we acknowledge the diversity of spiritual gifts, callings (Ac. 6:14; Ro. 12:4-8) and contexts, we also affirm that good news and good works are inseparable (Mt. 5:16).

The proclamation of God's kingdom necessarily demands the prophetic denunciation (Jer. 22:1-5; 11-17; 23:5-6) of all that is incompatible with it. Among the evils we deplore (Am. 1:1-2; 8) are destructive violence, including institutionalized violence, political corruption, all forms of exploitation of people and of the earth, the undermining of the family, abortion on demand, the drug traffic, and the abuse of human rights (Is. 59). We are also outraged by the inhuman conditions in which millions live (Job 24:1-12), who bear God's image as we do.

Our continuing commitment to social action is not a confusion of the Kingdom of God with a Christianized society. It is, rather, a recognition that the biblical gospel has inescapable social implications (Eph. 2:8-10). True mission should always be incarnational (Jn. 17:18; 20:21). It necessitates entering humbly into other people's worlds, identifying with their social reality, their sorrow and suffering, and their struggles for justice against oppressive powers (Php. 2:5-8). This cannot be done without personal sacrifices.

We repent that the narrowness of our concerns and vision has often kept us from proclaiming the lordship of Jesus Christ (Ac. 10:36) over all of life, private and public, local and global. We determine to obey his command (Mt. 6:33) to 'seek first the Kingdom of God and his righteousness'.

B. THE WHOLE CHURCH

The whole gospel has to be proclaimed by the whole church. All the people of God are called to share in the evangelistic task. Yet without the Holy Spirit of God all their endeavors will be fruitless.

5. GOD THE EVANGELIST

The Scriptures declare that God himself is the chief evangelist (2 Co. 5:20). For the Spirit of God (Jn. 15:26, 27) is the Spirit of truth, love, holiness and power, and evangelism is impossible without him (Lk. 4:18). It is he who anoints the messenger, confirms the word (1 Co. 2:4; Jn. 16:8-11), prepares the hearer, gives life to the dead, enables us (1 Co. 12:3; Ro. 8:16) to repent and believe, unites us to the Body of Christ, assures us that we are God's children (1 Co. 12:1; Ro. 8:16), leads us into Christlike character and service (Gal. 5:22, 23), and sends us out in our turn to be Christ's witnesses (Ac. 1:8). In all this the Holy Spirit's main pre-occupation is to glorify Jesus Christ by showing him to us (Jn. 16:14; Gal. 4:19) and forming him in us.

All evangelism involves spiritual warfare (Eph. 6:10-12) with the principalities and powers of evil, in which only spiritual weapons (2 Co. 10:3-5) can prevail, especially the Word and the Spirit (Eph. 6:17), with prayer. We therefore call on all Christian people to be diligent in their prayers (Eph. 6:18-20; 2 Th. 3:1) both for the renewal of the church and for the evangelization of the world.

Every true conversion (Ac. 26:17, 18) involves a power encounter, in which the superior authority of Jesus Christ is demonstrated (1 Th. 1:9, 10). There is no greater miracle than this, in which the believer is set free (Col. 1:13, 14) from the bondage of Satan and sin, fear and futility, darkness and death.

Although the miracles of Jesus (Jn. 2:11; 20:30, 31) were special, being signs of his Messiahship (Jn. 11:25; 1 Co. 15:20-28) and anticipations of his perfect kingdom when all nature will be subject to him, we have no liberty to place limits on the power of the living Creator today (Jer. 32:17). We reject both the skepticism which denies miracles and the presumption which demands them, both the timidity (2 Ti. 1:7) which shrinks from the fulness of the Spirit and the triumphalism which shrinks from the weakness (2 Co. 12:9, 10) in which Christ's power is made perfect.

We repent of all self-confident attempts (Jer. 17:5) either to evangelize in our own strength or to dictate to the Holy Spirit. We determine in future not to 'grieve' or 'quench' (Eph. 4:30; 1 Th. 5:19) the Spirit, but rather to seek to spread the good news 'with power, with the Holy Spirit and with deep conviction' (1 Th. 1:5).

6. THE HUMAN WITNESS

God the evangelist gives his people the privilege of being his 'fellow-workers' (2 Co. 6:1). For, although we cannot witness without him, he normally chooses to witness through us (Ac. 8:26-39; 14:27). He calls only some to be evangelists, missionaries or pastors (Eph. 4:11; Ac. 13:1-3), but he calls his whole church and every member of it to be his witnesses (Ac. 1:8; 8:1, 4).

The privileged task of pastors and teachers is to lead God's people (laos) into maturity (1 Co. 1:28) and to equip them for ministry (Eph. 4:11-12). Pastors are not to monopolize ministries, but rather to multiply them, by encouraging others to use their gifts and by training disciples to make disciples (Mt. 28:19; 2 Ti. 2:2). The domination of the laity by the clergy has been a great evil in the history of the church. It robs both laity and clergy of their God-intended roles (1 Th. 5:12-15), causes clergy breakdowns, weakens the church and hinders the spread of the gospel. More than that, it is fundamentally unbiblical. We therefore, who have for centuries insisted on 'the priesthood of all believers' now also insist on the ministry of all believers (1 Co. 12:4-7; Eph. 4:7).

We gratefully recognize that children and young people enrich the church's worship (Mt. 21:15, 16) and outreach by their enthusiasm and faith. We need to train them in discipleship and evangelism (1 Ti. 4:12), so that they may reach their own generation for Christ.

God created men and women as equal bearers of his image (Ge. 1:26-27), accepts them equally in Christ (Gal. 3:28) and poured out his Spirit on all flesh (Ac. 2:17-18), sons and daughters alike. In addition, because the Holy Spirit distributes his gifts (1 Pe. 4:10) to women as well as to men, they must be given opportunities to exercise their gifts. We celebrate their distinguished record in the history of missions and are convinced that God calls women to similar roles today. Even though we are not fully agreed what forms their leadership should take, we do agree about the partnership in world evangelization which God intends men and women to enjoy (Ro. 16:1-6, 12). Suitable training must therefore be made available to both (Php. 4:2, 3).

Lay witness takes place, by women and men, not only through the local church (see Section 8), but through friendships, in the home and at work. Even those who are homeless or unemployed share in the calling to be witnesses.

Our first responsibility is to witness (Mk, 5:18-20; Lk. 5:27-32) to those who are already our friends, relatives, neighbors, and colleagues. Home evangelism (Ac. 28:30, 31) is also natural, both for married and for single people. Not only should a Christian home commend God's standards of marriage, sex and family, and provide a haven of love and peace to people who are hurting, but neighbors who would not enter a church usually feel comfortable in a home (Ac. 10:24, 33; 18:7, 8; 24-26), even when the gospel is discussed.

Another context for lay witness is the workplace, for it is here that most Christians spend half their waking hours, and work (1 Co. 7:17-24) is a divine calling. Christians can commend Christ by word of mouth, by their consistent industry (Tit. 2:9, 10), honesty (Col. 4:1) and thoughtfulness, by their concern for justice in the workplace, and especially if others can see from the quality of their daily work that it is done to the glory of God (Col. 3:17, 23, 24).

We repent of our share in discouraging the ministry of the laity, especially of women and young people. We determine in the future to encourage all Christ's followers to take their place, rightfully and naturally, as his witnesses. For true evangelism comes from the overflow of a heart in love with Christ (Ac. 4:20). That is why it belongs to all his people without exception.

7. THE INTEGRITY OF THE WITNESS

Nothing commends the gospel more eloquently than a transformed life (2 Co. 6:3, 4), and nothing brings it into disrepute so much as personal inconsistency (Php. 1:27). We are charged to behave in a manner that is worthy of the gospel of Christ, and even to 'adorn' it (Tit. 2:20), enhancing its beauty by holy lives (Col. 4:5, 6). For the watching world rightly seeks evidence to substantiate the claims which Christ's disciples make for him. A strong evidence is our integrity (Pr. 11:3).

Our proclamation that Christ died to bring us to God (1 Pe. 3:18) appeals to people who are spiritually thirsty, but they will not believe us if we give no evidence of knowing the living God ourselves (1 Jn. 1:5, 6), or if our public worship lacks reality and relevance (1 Co. 14:25, 26).

Our message that Christ reconciles alienated people to each other (Eph. 2:14-18) rings true only if we are seen to love and forgive one another (Eph. 4:31-5:2), to serve others in humility (Gal. 5:13), and to reach out beyond our own community in compassionate, costly ministry to the needy (Lk. 10:29-37).

Our challenge to others to deny themselves, take up their cross and follow Christ (Mk. 8:34) will be plausible only if we ourselves have evidently died to selfish ambition, dishonesty and covetousness (Mt. 6:19-21, 31-33), and are living a life of simplicity, contentment and generosity (1 Ti. 6:6-10, 17, 18).

We deplore the failures in Christian consistency which we see in both Christians and churches: material greed (Ac. 5:1-11), professional pride and rivalry, competition in Christian service, jealousy of younger leaders, missionary paternalism, the lack of mutual accountability (Php. 1:15-17), the loss of Christian standards of sexuality (1 Co. 5:1-13), and racial, social (Jas. 2:1-4) and sexual discrimination. All this is worldliness (1 Jn. 2:15-17), allowing the prevailing culture to subvert the church instead of the church challenging and changing the culture (Mt. 5:13). We are deeply ashamed of the times when, both as individuals and in our Christian communities, we have affirmed Christ in word and denied him in deed (Mt. 7:21-23). Our inconsistency deprives our witness of credibility (1 Jn. 2:4). We acknowledge our continuing struggles and failures. But we also determine by God's grace to develop integrity in ourselves and in the church (Eph. 4:1).

8. THE LOCAL CHURCH

Every Christian congregation is a local expression of the Body of Christ (1 Co. 12:27) and has the same responsibilities. It is both 'a holy priesthood' to offer God the spiritual sacrifices of worship and 'a holy nation' to spread abroad his excellences in witness (1 Pe. 2:5, 9). The church is thus both a worshipping and a witnessing community, gathered and scattered, called and sent (Jn. 17:6, 9, 11, 18). Worship and witness are inseparable (Php. 2:14-16).

We believe that the local church bears a primary responsibility for the spread of the gospel. Scripture suggests this in the progression that 'our gospel came to you' and then 'rang out from you' (1 Th. 1:5, 8). In this way, the gospel creates the church which spreads the gospel which creates more churches in a continuous chain-reaction. Moreover, what Scripture teaches, strategy confirms. Each local church must evangelize the district in which it is situated (Ac. 19:9, 10), and has the resources to do so.

We recommend every congregation to carry out regular studies not only of its own membership and program but of its local community in all its particularity, in order to develop appropriate strategies for mission. Its members might decide to organize a visitation of their whole area, to penetrate for Christ a particular place where people assemble, to arrange a series of evangelistic meetings, lectures or concerts, to work with the poor to transform a local slum, or to plant a new church in a neighboring district or village (Col 1:3-8). At the same time, they must not forget the church's global task (Ac. 13:1-3; 14:26-28). A church which sends out missionaries must not neglect its own locality, and a church which evangelizes its neighborhood must not ignore the rest of the world.

In all this each congregation and denomination should, where possible, work with others, seeking to turn any spirit of competition into one of cooperation (Php. 1:27). Churches should also work with para-church organizations, especially in evangelism, discipling and community service, for such agencies are part of the Body of Christ, and have valuable, specialist expertise from which the church can greatly benefit.

The church is intended by God to be a sign of his kingdom (Lk. 12:32), that is, an indication of what human community looks like when it comes under his rule of righteousness and peace (Ro. 14:17). As with individuals, so with churches, the gospel has to be embodied if it is to be communicated effectively (1 Th. 1:8-10). It is through our love for one another that the invisible God reveals himself today (1 Jn. 4:12; Jn. 13:34, 35; 17:21, 23), especially when our fellowship is expressed in small groups, and when it transcends the barriers of race, rank, sex and age which divide other communities (Gal. 3:28; Col 3:11).

We deeply regret that many of our congregations are inward-looking, organized for maintenance rather than mission, or preoccupied with church-based activities at the expense of witness. We determine to turn our churches inside out, so that they may engage in continuous outreach, until the Lord adds to them daily those who are being saved (Ac. 2:47).

9. COOPERATION IN EVANGELISM

Evangelism and unity are closely related in the New Testament. Jesus prayed that his people's oneness might reflect his own oneness with the Father, in order that the world might believe in him (Jn. 17:20, 21), and Paul exhorted the Philippians to 'contend as one person for the faith of the gospel' (Php. 1:27). In contrast to this biblical vision (Php. 1:15, 17; 2:3, 4), we are ashamed of the suspicions and rivalries (Ro. 14:1-15:2), the dogmatism over non-essentials, the power-struggles and empire-building which spoil our evangelistic witness. We affirm that cooperation in evangelism is indispensable, first because it is the will of God (Php. 1:3-5), but also because the gospel of reconciliation is discredited by our disunity (Eph. 2:14-16; 4:16), and because, if the task of world evangelization is ever to be accomplished, we must engage in it together.

'Cooperation' means finding unity in diversity (Eph. 4:6, 7). It involves people of different temperaments, gifts, callings and cultures, national churches and mission agencies, all ages and both sexes working together.

We are determined to put behind us once and for all, as a hangover from the colonial past, the simplistic distinction between First World sending and Two-Thirds World receiving countries. For the great new fact of our era is the internationalization of missions. Not only are a large majority of all evangelical Christians now non-western, but the number of Two-Thirds World missionaries will soon exceed those from the West. We believe that mission teams (Ac. 20:4), which are diverse in composition but united in heart and mind, constitute a dramatic witness to the grace of God.

Our reference to the 'whole church' is not a presumptuous claim that the universal church and the evangelical community are synonymous. For we recognize that there are many churches which are not part of the evangelical movement. Evangelical attitudes to the Roman Catholic and Orthodox Churches differ widely. Some evangelicals are praying, talking, studying Scripture and working with these churches. Others are strongly opposed to any form of dialogue or cooperation with them. All evangelicals are aware that serious theological differences between us remain. Where appropriate, and so long as biblical truth is not compromised, cooperation may be possible in such areas as Bible translation, the study of contemporary theological and ethical issues, social work and political action. We wish to make it clear, however, that common evangelism demands a common commitment to the biblical gospel.

Some of us are members of churches which belong to the World Council of Churches and believe that a positive yet critical participation in its work is our Christian duty. Others among us have no link with the World Council. All of us urge the World Council of Churches to adopt a consistent biblical understanding of evangelism.

We confess our own share of responsibility for the brokenness of the Body of Christ, which is a major stumbling-block to world evangelization. We determine to go on seeking that unity in truth for which Christ prayed (Jn. 17:11, 20-23). We are persuaded that the right way forward towards closer cooperation is frank and patient dialogue on the basis of the Bible, with all who share our concerns. To this we gladly commit ourselves.

C. THE WHOLE WORLD

The whole gospel has been entrusted to the whole church, in order that it may be made known to the whole world (Mk. 16:15). It is necessary, therefore, for us to understand the world into which we are sent.

10. THE MODERN WORLD

Evangelism takes place in a context, not in a vacuum (Ac. 13:14-41; 14:14-17; 17:22-31). The balance between gospel and context must be carefully maintained. We must understand the context in order to address it, but the context must not be allowed to distort the gospel.

In this connection we have become concerned about the impact of 'modernity', which is an emerging world culture produced by industrialization with its technology and urbanization with its economic order. These factors combine to create an environment which significantly shapes the way in which we see our world. In addition, secularism has devastated faith by making God and the supernatural meaningless; urbanization has dehumanized life for many; and the mass media have contributed to the devaluation of truth and authority, by replacing word with image. In combination, these consequences of modernity pervert the message which many preach and undermine their motivation for mission.

In AD 1900 only 9% of the world's population lived in cities; in AD 2000 it is thought that more than 50% will do so. This worldwide move into the cities has been called 'the greatest migration in human history'; it constitutes a major challenge to Christian mission. On the one hand, city populations are extremely cosmopolitan, so that the nations come to our doorstep in the city. Can we develop global churches in which the gospel abolishes the barriers of ethnicity? On the other hand, many city dwellers are migrant poor who are also receptive to the gospel. Can the people of God be persuaded to re-locate into such urban poor communities, in order to serve the people and share in the transformation of the city?

Modernization brings blessings as well as dangers. By creating links of communication and commerce around the globe, it makes unprecedented openings for the gospel, crossing old frontiers and penetrating closed societies, whether traditional or totalitarian. The Christian media have a powerful influence both in sowing the seed of the gospel and in preparing the soil. The major missionary broadcasters are committed to a gospel witness by radio in every major language by the year AD 2000.

We confess that we have not struggled as we should to understand modernization. We have used its methods and techniques uncritically and so exposed ourselves to worldliness (Ro. 12:1, 2). But we determine in the future to take these challenges and opportunities seriously, to resist the secular pressures of modernity, to relate the lordship of Christ to the whole of modern culture, and thus to engage in mission in the modern world without worldliness in modern mission.

11. THE CHALLENGE OF AD 2000 AND BEYOND

The world population today is approaching 6 billion. One third of them nominally confess Christ. Of the remaining four billion half have heard of him and the other half have not. In the light of these figures, we evaluate our evangelistic task by considering four categories of people.

First, there is the potential missionary work force, the committed. In this century this category of Christian believers has grown from about 40 million in 1900 to about 500 million today, and at this moment is growing over twice as fast as any other major religious group.

Secondly, there are the uncommitted. They make a Christian profession (they have been baptized, attend church occasionally and even call themselves Christians), but the notion of a personal commitment to Christ is foreign to them. They are found in all churches throughout the world. They urgently need to be re-evangelized.

Thirdly, there are the unevangelized. These are people who have a minimal knowledge of the gospel, but have had no valid opportunity to respond to it. They are probably within reach of Christian people if only these will go to the next street, road, village or town to find them.

Fourthly, there are the unreached. These are the two billion who may never have heard of Jesus as Savior, and are not within reach of Christians of their own people. There are, in fact, some 2,000 peoples or nationalities in which there is not yet a vital, indigenous church movement. We find it helpful to think of them as belonging to smaller 'people groups' which perceive themselves as having an affinity with each other (e.g. a common culture, language, home or occupation). The most effective messengers to reach them will be those believers who already belong to their culture and know their language. Otherwise, cross-cultural messengers of the gospel will need to go, leaving behind their own culture and sacrificially identifying with the people they long to reach for Christ.

There are now about 12,000 such unreached people groups within the 2,000 larger peoples, so that the task is not impossible. Yet at present only 7% of all missionaries are engaged in this kind of outreach, while the remaining 93% are working in the already evangelized half of the world. If this imbalance is to be redressed, a strategic redeployment of personnel will be necessary.

A distressing factor that affects each of the above categories is that of inaccessibility. Many countries do not grant visas to self-styled missionaries, who have no other qualification or contribution to offer. Such areas are not absolutely inaccessible, however. For our prayers can pass through every curtain, door and barrier. And Christian radio and television, audio and video cassettes, films and literature can also reach the otherwise unreachable. So can so-called 'tent-makers' (Ac. 18:1-4; 20:34) who like Paul earn their own living. They travel in the course of their profession (e.g. business people, university lecturers, technical specialists and language teachers), and use every opportunity to speak of Jesus Christ. They do not enter a country under false pretenses, for their work genuinely takes them there; it is simply that witness is an essential component of their Christian lifestyle, wherever they may happen to be.

We are deeply ashamed that nearly two millennia have passed since the death and resurrection of Jesus, and still two-thirds of the world's population have not yet acknowledged him. On the other hand, we are amazed at the mounting evidence of God's power even in the most unlikely places of the globe.

Now the year 2000 has become for many a challenging milestone. Can we commit ourselves to evangelize the world during the last decade of this millennium? There is nothing magical about the date, yet should we not do our best to reach this goal? Christ commands us to take the gospel to all peoples (Lk. 24:45-47). The task is urgent. We are determined to obey him with joy and hope.

12. DIFFICULT SITUATIONS

Jesus plainly told his followers to expect opposition. 'If they persecuted me', he said, 'they will persecute you also' (Jn. 15:20). He even told them to rejoice over persecution (Mt. 5:12), and reminded them that the condition of fruitfulness was death (Jn. 12:24).

These predictions, that Christian suffering is inevitable and productive, have come true in every age, including our own. There have been many thousands of martyrs. Today the situation is much the same. We earnestly hope that *glasnost* and *perestroika* will lead to complete religious freedom in the Soviet Union and other Eastern bloc nations, and that Islamic and Hindu countries will become more open to the gospel. We deplore the recent brutal suppression of China's democratic movement, and we pray that it will not bring further suffering to the Christians. On the whole, however, it seems that ancient religions are becoming less tolerant, expatriates less welcome, and the world less friendly to the gospel.

In this situation we wish to make three statements to governments which are reconsidering their attitude to Christian believers.

First, Christians are loyal citizens, who seek the welfare of their nation (Jer. 29:7). They pray for its leaders and pay their taxes (1 Ti. 2:1, 2; Ro. 13:6, 7). Of course, those who have confessed Jesus as Lord cannot also call other authorities Lord, and if commanded to do so, or to do anything which God forbids, must disobey (Ac. 4:19; 5:29). But they are conscientious citizens. They also contribute to their country's well-being by the stability of their marriages and homes, their honesty in business, their hard work and their voluntary activity in the service of the handicapped and needy. Just governments have nothing to fear from Christians.

Secondly, Christians renounce unworthy methods of evangelism. Though the nature of our faith requires us to share the gospel with others, our practice is to make an open and honest statement of it (2 Co. 4:1, 2), which leaves the hearers entirely free to make up their own minds about it. We wish to be sensitive to those of other faiths, and we reject any approach that seeks to force conversion on them.

Thirdly, Christians earnestly desire freedom of religion for all people, not just freedom for Christianity. In predominantly Christian countries, Christians are at the forefront of those who demand freedom for religious minorities. In predominantly non-Christian countries, therefore, Christians are asking for themselves no more than they demand for others in similar circumstances. The freedom to 'profess, practice and propagate' religion, as defined in the Universal Declaration of Human Rights, could and should surely be a reciprocally granted right.

We greatly regret any unworthy witness of which followers of Jesus may have been guilty. We determine to give no unnecessary offence (2 Co. 6:3) in anything, lest the name of Christ be dishonored. However, the offence of the cross (1 Co. 1:18, 23; 2:2) we cannot avoid. For the sake of Christ crucified we pray that we may be ready, by his grace, to suffer (Php. 1:29) and even to die. Martyrdom is a form of witness which Christ has promised especially to honor (Rev. 2:13; 6:9-11; 20:4).

CONCLUSION: PROCLAIM CHRIST UNTIL HE COMES

'Proclaim Christ until he comes'. That has been the theme of Lausanne II. Of course we believe that Christ has come (Lk. 2:17); he came when Augustus was Emperor of Rome. But one day, as we know from his promises, he will come again (Mk. 13:26, 27) in unimaginable splendor to perfect his kingdom. We are commanded to watch and be ready (Mk. 13:32-37). Meanwhile, the gap between his two comings is to be filled with the Christian missionary enterprise. We have been told to go to the ends of the earth (Ac. 1:8) with the gospel, and we have been promised that the end of the age will come only when we have done so (Mt. 24:14). The two ends (of earth space and time) will coincide. Until then he has pledged to be with us (Mt. 28:20).

So the Christian mission is an urgent task. We do not know how long we have. We certainly have no time to waste. And in order to get on urgently with our responsibility, other qualities will be necessary, especially unity (we must evangelize together) and sacrifice (we must count and accept the cost). Our covenant at Lausanne was 'to pray, to plan and to work together for the evangelization of the whole world'. Our manifesto at Manila is that the whole church is called to take the whole gospel to the whole world, proclaiming Christ until he comes, with all necessary urgency, unity and sacrifice.

9

The Christian Gospel and the Jewish People

Willowbank, 1989

WORLD EVANGELICAL FELLOWSHIP

The Willowbank Declaration on "The Christian Gospel and the Jewish People" was unanimously adopted by a WEF consultation held at Willowbank, Bermuda, on April 29, 1989. The consultation was called to deal with the extremely sensitive issue of the relationship between Christians and Jews in the aftermath of the Holocaust. The consultation was pledged from the outset to reject every form of anti-Semitism, but it believed at the same time that an evangelical response must be made "to growing doubts and widespread confusion among Christians about the need for, and the propriety of, endeavors to share faith in Jesus Christ with Jewish people."

The Willowbank Declaration noted that the Holocaust had led some Christians to believe that Christian witness to Jews lacked credibility, while other Christians felt it was simply sufficient to support the state of Israel. It noted that many Christian bodies have quietly abandoned efforts to evangelize Jews, substituting interfaith dialogue for better understanding and cooperation in matters of civil justice and common good. The Willowbank Declaration is distinctive in affirming that the historic Christian concern "to point Jewish people to faith in Jesus Christ" remains valid.

THE CHRISTIAN GOSPEL AND THE JEWISH PEOPLE*

The Gospel is the power of God for salvation, to everyone who believes, to the Jew first and also to the Greek (Romans 1:16).

Brethren, my heart's desire and prayer to God for Israel is that they may be saved (Romans 10:1).

PREAMBLE

Every Christian must acknowledge an immense debt of gratitude to the Jewish people. The Gospel is the good news that Jesus is the Christ, the long-promised

---

*Reprinted from *International Bulletin of Missionary Research*, October 1989, 161-64.

Jewish Messiah, who by his life, death and resurrection saves from sin and all its consequences. Those who worship Jesus as their Divine Lord and Saviour have thus received God's most precious gift through the Jewish people. Therefore they have compelling reason to show love to that people in every possible way.

Concerned about humanity everywhere, we are resolved to uphold the right of Jewish people to a just and peaceful existence everywhere, both in the land of Israel and in their communities throughout the world. We repudiate past persecutions of Jews by those identified as Christians, and we pledge ourselves to resist every form of anti-Semitism. As the supreme way of demonstrating love, we seek to encourage the Jewish people, along with all other peoples, to receive God's gift of life through Jesus the Messiah, and accordingly the growing number of Jewish Christians brings us great joy.

In making this Declaration we stand in a long and revered Christian tradition, which in 1980 was highlighted by a landmark statement, "Christian Witness to the Jewish People," issued by the Lausanne Committee for World Evangelization. Now, at this Willowbank Consultation on the Gospel and the Jewish People, sponsored by the World Evangelical Fellowship and supported by the Lausanne Committee, we reaffirm our commitment to the Jewish people and our desire to share the Gospel with them.

This Declaration is made in response to growing doubts and widespread confusion among Christians about the need for, and the propriety of, endeavors to share faith in Jesus Christ with Jewish people. Several factors unite to produce the uncertain state of mind that the Declaration seeks to resolve.

The holocaust, perpetrated as it was by leaders and citizens of a supposedly Christian nation, has led to a sense in some quarters that Christian witness among Jews has been totally destroyed. Accordingly, some have shrunk back from addressing the Jewish people with the Gospel.

Some who see the creation of the state of Israel as a direct fulfillment of biblical prophecy have concluded that the Christian task at this time is to "comfort Israel" by supporting this new political entity, rather than to challenge Jews by direct evangelism.

Some church leaders have retreated from embracing the task of evangelizing Jews as a responsibility of Christian mission. Rather, a new theology is being embraced, which holds that God's covenant with Israel through Abraham establishes all Jews in God's favor for all times, and so makes faith in Jesus Christ for salvation needless so far as they are concerned.

On this basis, it is argued that dialogue with Jews in order to understand each other better, and cooperation in the quest for socio-economic shalom, is all that Christian mission requires in relation to the Jewish people. Continued attempts to do what the church has done from the first, in seeking to win Jews to Jesus as Messiah, are widely opposed and decried, by Christian as well as Jewish leaders.

Attempts to bring Jews to faith in Jesus are frequently denounced as proselytizing. This term is often used to imply dishonest and coercive modes of inducement, to appeal to unworthy motives, and in disregard of the question of truth even though it is truth that is being disseminated.

In recent years, "messianic" Jewish believers in Jesus, who as Christians celebrate and maximize their Jewish identity, have emerged as active evangelists to the Jewish community. Jewish leaders often accused them of deception on the grounds that one cannot be both a Jew and a Christian. While these criticisms may reflect Judaism's current effort to define itself as a distinct religion in opposition to Christianity, they have led to much bewilderment and some misunderstanding and mistrust.

The Declaration responds to this complex situation and seeks to set directions for the future according to the Scriptures.

I. THE DEMAND OF THE GOSPEL

Article I.1
We affirm that the redeeming love of God has been fully and finally revealed in Jesus Christ.

We deny that those without faith in Christ know the full reality of God's love and of the gift that he gives.

Article I.2
We affirm that the God-given types, prophecies and visions of salvation and shalom in the Hebrew Scriptures find their present and future fulfillment in and through Jesus Christ, the Son of God, who by incarnation became a Jew and was shown to be the Son of God and Messiah by his resurrection.

We deny that it is right to look for a Messiah who has not yet appeared in world history.

Article I.3
We affirm that Jesus Christ is the second person of the one God, who became a man, lived a perfect life, shed his blood on the cross as an atoning sacrifice for human sins, rose bodily from the dead, now reigns as Lord, and will return visibly to this earth, all to fulfill the purpose of bringing sinners to share eternally in his fellowship and glory.

We deny that those who think of Jesus Christ in lesser terms than these have faith in him in any adequate sense.

Article I.4
We affirm that all human beings are sinful by nature and practice, and stand condemned, helpless and hopeless, before God, until the grace of Christ touches their lives and brings them to God's pardon and peace.

We deny that any Jew or Gentile finds true peace with God through performing works of law.

Article I.5
We affirm that God's forgiveness of the penitent rests on the satisfaction rendered to his justice by the substitutionary sacrifice of Jesus Christ on the cross.

We deny that any person can enjoy God's favor apart from the mediation of Jesus Christ, the sin-bearer.

Article I.6
We affirm that those who turn to Jesus Christ find him to be a sufficient Saviour and Deliverer from all the evil of sin: from its guilt, shame, power, and perversity; from blind defiance of God, debasement of moral character, and the dehumanizing and destructive self-assertion that sin breeds.

We deny that the salvation found in Christ may be supplemented in any way.

Article I.7

We affirm that faith in Jesus Christ is humanity's only way to come to know the Creator as Father, according to Christ's Own Word: "I am the Way and the Truth and the Life; no one comes to the Father except through me" (John 14:6).

We deny that any non-Christian faith, as such, will mediate eternal life with God.

II. THE CHURCH OF JEWS AND GENTILES

Article II.8

We affirm that through the mediation of Jesus Christ, God has made a new covenant with Jewish and Gentile believers, pardoning their sins, writing his law on their hearts by his Spirit, so that they obey him, giving the Holy Spirit to indwell them, and bringing each one to know him by faith in a relationship of trustful gratitude for salvation.

We deny that the blessings of the New Covenant belong to any except believers in Jesus Christ.

Article II.9

We affirm that the profession of continuing Jewish identity, for which Hebrew Christians have in the past suffered at the hands of both their fellow Jews and Gentile church leaders, is consistent with the Christian Scriptures and with the nature of the church as one body in Jesus Christ in which Jews and non-Jews are united.

We deny that it is necessary for Jewish Christians to repudiate their Jewish heritage.

Article II.10

We affirm that Gentile believers, who at present constitute the great bulk of the Christian church, are included in the historically continuous community of believing people on earth which Paul pictures as God's olive tree (Rom. 11:13-24).

We deny that Christian faith is necessarily non-Jewish, and that Gentiles who believe in Christ may ignore their solidarity with believing Jews, or formulate their new identity in Christ without reference to Jewishness, or decline to receive the Hebrew Scriptures as part of their own instruction from God, or refuse to see themselves as having their roots in Jewish history.

Article II.11

We affirm that Jewish people who come to faith in Messiah have liberty before God to observe or not observe traditional Jewish customs and ceremonies that are consistent with the Christian Scriptures and do not hinder fellowship with the rest of the Body of Christ.

We deny that any inconsistency or deception is involved by Jewish Christians representing themselves as "Messianic" or "completed" or "fulfilled" Jews.

III. GOD'S PLAN FOR THE JEWISH PEOPLE

Article III.12

We affirm that Jewish people have an ongoing part in God's plan.

We deny that indifference to the future of the Jewish people on the part of Christians can ever be justified.

Article III.13

We affirm that prior to the coming of Christ it was Israel's unique privilege to enjoy a corporate covenantal relationship with God, following upon the national redemption from slavery, and involving God's gift of the law and of a theocratic culture; God's promise of blessing to faithful obedience; and God's provision of atonement for transgression. We affirm that within this covenant relationship, God's pardon and acceptance of the penitent which was linked to the offering of prescribed sacrifices rested upon the fore-ordained sacrifice of Jesus Christ.

We deny that convenantal privilege alone can ever bring salvation to impenitent unbelievers.

Article III.14

We affirm that much of Judaism, in its various forms, throughout contemporary Israel and today's Diaspora, is a development out of, rather than an authentic embodiment of, the faith, love and hope that the Hebrew Scriptures teach.

We deny that modern Judaism with its explicit negation of divine person, work, and Messiahship of Jesus Christ contains within itself true knowledge of God's salvation.

Article III.15

We affirm that the biblical hope for Jewish people centers on their being restored through faith in Christ to their proper place as branches of God's olive tree from which they are at present broken off.

We deny that the historical status of the Jews as God's people brings salvation to any Jew who does not accept the claims of Jesus Christ.

Article III.16

We affirm that the Bible promises that large numbers of Jews will turn to Christ through God's sovereign grace.

We deny that this prospect renders needless the active proclamation of the gospel to Jewish people in this and every age.

Article III.17

We affirm that anti-Semitism on the part of professed Christians has always been wicked and shameful and that the church has in the past been much to blame for tolerating and encouraging it and for condoning anti-Jewish actions on the part of individuals and governments.

We deny that these past failures, for which offending Gentile believers must ask forgiveness from both God and the Jewish community, rob Christians of the right or lessen their responsibility to share the Gospel with Jews today and for the future.

Article III.18

We affirm that it was the sins of the whole human race that sent Christ to the cross.

We deny that it is right to single out the Jewish people for putting Jesus to death.

IV. EVANGELISM AND THE JEWISH PEOPLE

Article IV.19

We affirm that sharing the Good News of Jesus Christ with lost humanity is a matter of prime obligation for Christian people, both because the Messiah commands the making of disciples and because love of neighbor requires effort to meet our neighbor's deepest need.

We deny that any other form of witness and service to others can excuse Christians from laboring to bring them to faith in Christ.

Article IV.20

We affirm that the church's obligation to share saving knowledge of Christ with the whole human race includes the evangelizing of Jewish people as a priority: "To the Jew first" (Rom. 1:16).

We deny that dialogue with Jewish people that aims at nothing more than mutual understanding constitutes fulfillment of this obligation.

Article IV.21

We affirm that the concern to point Jewish people to faith in Jesus Christ, which the Christian church has historically felt and shown, was right.

We deny that there is any truth in the widespread notion that evangelizing Jews is needless because they are already in covenant with God through Abraham and Moses and so are already saved despite their rejection of Jesus Christ as Lord and Saviour.

Article IV.22

We affirm that all endeavors to persuade others to become Christians should express love to them by respecting their dignity and integrity at every point, including parents' responsibility in the case of their children.

We deny that coercive or deceptive proselytizing, which violates dignity and integrity on both sides, can ever be justified.

Article IV.23

We affirm that it is unchristian, unloving, and discriminatory, to propose a moratorium on the evangelizing of any part of the human race, and that failure to preach the Gospel to the Jewish people would be a form of anti-Semitism, depriving this particular community of its right to hear the Gospel.

We deny that we have sufficient warrant to assume or anticipate the salvation of anyone who is not a believer in Jesus Christ.

Article IV.24

We affirm that the existence of separate churchly organizations for evangelizing Jews, as for evangelizing any other particular human group, can be justified pragmatically, as an appropriate means of fulfilling the church's mandate to take the Gospel to the whole human race.

We deny that the depth of human spiritual need varies from group to group so that Jewish people may be thought to need Christ either more or less than others.

V. JEWISH-CHRISTIAN RELATIONS

Article V.25

We affirm that dialogue with other faiths that seeks to transcend stereotypes of them based on ignorance, and to find common ground and to share common concerns, is an expression of Christian love that should be encouraged.

We deny that dialogue that explains the Christian faith without seeking to persuade the dialogue partners of its truth and claims is a sufficient expression of Christian love.

Article V.26

We affirm that for Christians and non-Christian Jews to make common cause in social witness and action, contending together for freedom of speech and religion, the value of the individual, and the moral standards of God's law is right and good.

We deny that such limited cooperation involves any compromise of the distinctive views of either community or imposes any restraint upon Christians in seeking to share the Gospel with the Jews with whom they cooperate.

Article V.27

We affirm that the Jewish quest for a homeland with secure borders and a just peace has our support.

We deny that any biblical link between the Jewish people and the land of Israel justifies actions that contradict biblical ethics and constitute oppression of people-groups or individuals.

10

Consultation on Jewish Evangelism

Zeist, Netherlands, 1991

LAUSANNE COMMITTEE ON WORLD EVANGELISM

The Fourth International LCWE Consultation on Jewish Evangelism, meeting at Zeist, the Netherlands, on August 9, 1991, adopted a brief "message" on the obligation of the "whole church to take the whole gospel to Jewish people everywhere." Attending the Zeist consultation were many Jewish Christian believers. This statement, along with the WEF Willowbank Declaration which precedes it, stands in marked contrast to statements by conciliar bodies and Roman Catholics on Christian relations with Jewish people.

BEHOLD I AM DOING A NEW THING*

As God once spoke to Israel, we hear his voice again today: "Behold, I am doing a new thing" (Isa. 43:19).

At the fourth international conference of the Lausanne Consultation on Jewish Evangelism, 150 people from five continents—including many Jewish believers in Jesus—gathered in Zeist, The Netherlands, August 5-9, 1991. In response to God's word to us, we offer the following message to the Jewish people, the churches and all those concerned with Jewish evangelism.

TO THE JEWISH PEOPLE:

We lament the resurgence of hatred against the Jewish people, against the state of Israel and we abhor every action or attitude which threatens Jewish survival.

We rejoice in God's continuing care of his covenant people. We rejoice that many have found freedom from oppression in Eastern Europe and Ethiopia, and that many have returned to the land of their fathers. We hope and pray for an end to oppression and for peace for all in the Middle East.

We implore you in this time of renewed Messianic fervour to recognise that the era of redemption has begun with Jeshua of Nazareth. He is indeed the promised divine Messiah of Israel, as well as the light to the nations, revealing God's presence and saving power to all who receive him.

"BEHOLD, I AM DOING A NEW THING," says the Lord.

---

*Reprinted from *International Bulletin of Missionary Research,* January 1992, 10-11.

TO THE CHURCHES:

We lament the teaching that the church has replaced the Jewish people in the purposes of God and we lament the widespread reluctance to share the Gospel with Jewish people. Silence has often replaced shouts of joy that Jesus came as the Jewish Messiah, the Saviour of the world and the only way of salvation.

We rejoice that the response of Jewish people to the Gospel is nonetheless gaining momentum in our time and that Messianic Jews are making a creative contribution to the life, worship and witness of the worldwide Church. We also rejoice that significant numbers of Christians are again upholding "the New Testament pattern of taking the Gospel to the Jew first . . . " (Manila Manifesto, LCWE 1989).

We implore the churches to stand with us against powers that promote anti-Semitism and to affirm the urgency of Jewish evangelism. We Jewish and Gentile believers in Jesus need to strengthen our resolve to work together, and together we call upon the whole church to take the whole Gospel to Jewish people everywhere.

"BEHOLD, I AM DOING A NEW THING," says the Lord.

Index